CRUCIBLE OF EMPIRE

CRUCIBLE OF EMPIRE

The Spanish–American War
& Its Aftermath

EDITED BY JAMES C. BRADFORD

NAVAL INSTITUTE PRESS

Annapolis, Maryland

LIBRARY OF CONGRESS CATALOGING-IN-PUBLICATION DATA
Crucible of empire : the Spanish-American War and its aftermath /
edited by James C. Bradford.
p.   cm.
Includes bibliographic references and index.
ISBN 1-55750-079-7 (alk. paper)
1. Spanish-American War, 1898. 2. United States—Territorial
expansion. I. Bradford, James C.
E715.C78 1993
973.8'91—dc20   92-46720

Printed in the United States of America on acid-free paper ∞

9 8 7 6 5 4 3 2
First printing

Frontispiece: A citizens' group from Baltimore commissioned a thirty-three-piece
silver service as a gift to Rear Adm. Winfield Scott Schley. The centerpiece reflects
Americans' sentimental attitude toward their new empire. The tallest of the four
figures, Columbia, is receiving figures that represent Cuba and Puerto Rico, while
the one representing the Philippines kneels in supplication between them. The centerpiece is 20 inches high and was designed by Charles J. Pike. *Courtesy of the Smithsonian Institution.*

For
Bob and Joann Wimbish
Mike and Susan Beal

Contents

List of Illustrations

Preface

THE EVENTS THAT LED TO THE COLLECTION OF THESE ESSAYS TOOK PLACE over a number of months. First, Joseph Dawson and Harold Langley contributed essays on William T. Sampson and Winfield Scott Schley to another book I edited, *Admirals of the New Steel Navy*. Both essays, which dealt with the Battle of Santiago and the Sampson-Schley controversy that arose from it, were a bit longer than originally planned, and grew longer when I prodded their authors to explain more fully certain statements and to respond to points made by the other. It soon became evident that the essays were growing beyond the scope of the book they were written for and beyond the theme reflected in its subtitle, *Makers of the American Naval Tradition*. Thus much interesting and useful information had to be deleted. At Dawson's suggestion a panel was presented at the annual meeting of the North American Society for Oceanic History in which he and Langley outlined the case for each of their subjects. At approximately the same time, Vernon Williams and Brian Linn presented papers at the U.S. Naval Academy's Naval History Symposium on naval officers and marines serving in the Philippines. Meanwhile, I happened to talk with David Trask about a neglected aspect of the Spanish-American War, and he told me about Ephraim Smith's excellent analysis of President McKinley's role in the settlement of the war. A discussion with William Still led me to Diane Cooper's work on George Leland Dyer. From additional discussions I learned of other historians working in the field, and this book is the result.

All of the authors responded with remarkably good humor to my requests for clarification and my suggestions for minor changes. They bore equally well the delays in preparation of the manuscript for publication. Thus it is to them that I must first acknowledge my indebtedness. Joseph Dawson and John Lenihan applied their editorial skills to the preface, as they so graciously do to most of what I write. Charles R. Haberlein, head of the photographic section of the Naval Historical Center; Harold D. Langley, Curator of Naval History at the Smithsonian; and Patty M. Maddocks, director of library and photographic services at the Naval Institute, assisted in the selection of illustrations that serve not simply as embellishments but form an integral part of the book. Jude K. Swank provided a discerning eye as she prepared the manuscript, pointing out sections requiring additional attention. Paul Wilderson provided support and patience throughout the process. The comments of the reviewers were very much appreciated, as was the meticulous work of Jonathan Lawrence, our copy editor, who did much to polish the manuscript.

My wife, Judy, and our sons, Jim and John, may not have contributed directly to this book, but their tolerance of time spent at the office and their maintenance of the "home fires" make the completion of projects such as this more enjoyable. So, too, do the friendship and support of Mike and Susan Beal and Bob and Joann Wimbish. One cannot imagine better friends, and it is in that spirit that this book is dedicated to them.

Introduction

THE SPANISH-AMERICAN WAR MARKED A TURNING POINT IN AMERICAN history. During the last half of the 1890s a sense of humanitarianism, aroused and fired by sensational journalism, led Americans to demand that their government assist the people of Cuba in securing that island's independence from Spain. Such intervention would violate one of the principles stated in the Monroe Doctrine: "With the existing Colonies or dependencies of any European power, we have not interfered, and shall not interfere." After three-quarters of a century Americans were prepared to abandon part of one of the most basic statements of American foreign policy. When diplomatic pressure alone proved ineffectual, the United States resorted to military action. The result was a people's war pressed on a reluctant administration.[1]

The United States did not enter the war to protect its citizens or their property or to expand American territory. Instead, it went to war in response to the chaos—and what was considered Spanish brutality—that accompanied the Cuban war for independence and also to maintain the principle of national self-determination. Such a reaction was unprecedented. The United States had used its navy to protect Americans and their property during times of unrest, and it had provided moral encouragement to the Latin American republics, as well as to Greece and Hungary during their wars of independence, but it had always been careful to avoid direct intervention in support of one of the belligerents. The position taken in 1898 looked forward to one of the principles of self-determination enunciated by Woodrow Wilson in his Fourteen Points two decades later.

American entry into war in 1898 differed from past practices in another way. There was no reasoned balancing of ends to be achieved with costs to be borne in the conflict, but simply an emotional response to what many Americans considered the intolerable condition of the Cuban people. The United States had never before gone to war for an abstract principle or out of a sense of moral obligation. The Quasi War with France, the Barbary Wars, and the War of 1812 resulted from challenges posed to the freedom of American sailors and commerce; the War of 1812 and the Mexican War concerned the territorial security and expansion of the United States; and the Civil War sought the continuation of the Union. The Spanish-American War was the first brought on by consideration for the lives of others, and entry into it marked the first step in what was to constitute a revolution in American foreign relations.

The war with Spain was short—less than a year long—and relatively bloodless compared to wars before and since. During the war 5,807 servicemen lost their lives, compared with 6,780 in the War of 1812, 13,271 in the Mexican War, and 25,324 in the American Revolution, the wars with the next fewest deaths. The comparison of deaths in wars is even more dramatic when stated in terms of deaths per 100,000 population. For the Spanish-American War the deaths represented 8 per 100,000 Americans; in the Vietnam War, 28; in the Korean War, 35; in the Mexican War, 62, and in the War of 1812, 83 per 100,000.[2]

The consequences of the war were as momentous as the casualties were light. Not only had the United States violated its principle of nonintervention in entering the war; even more important, it took a second step away from the tenets that had guided its development for over a century when it acquired territories in the Central and Western Pacific.

Commodore Dewey's victory at Manila Bay on 1 May 1898 led expansionists to argue that the United States needed insular bases in the Pacific to support its forces going to the Philippines. On 4 July 1898 an American expedition en route to Manila staked claim to Wake Island, and two days later Congress voted to annex Hawaii.[3] In August a protocol was signed that provided for negotiation of a peace treaty with terms providing for Cuban independence, the transfer of Puerto Rico and Guam to the United States, and American occupation of Manila until the final treaty determined the disposition of the Philippine Islands.

The acquisition of Wake Island, Hawaii, Guam, and the Philippines represented America's first significant territorial expansion outside the western hemisphere and breached America's geographical isolation by crossing one of the oceanic barriers that had previously protected the nation and its possessions. Annexation of the Philippines was particularly controversial at the time, and President William McKinley's decision to accept them has interested historians ever since, as is clearly demonstrated in the essay by Ephraim Smith included in this volume.

Acquisition of the Philippines constituted the second element in the revolution in American foreign affairs that occurred at the turn of the twentieth century and helped lay the groundwork for the third key shift in American diplomatic policy, the issuance of the Open Door Notes. During March 1898, a month before the war with Spain, American leaders had refused to join Great Britain in a joint statement affirming the right of all nations to trade and invest in China on an equal basis. This rejection mirrored American actions during the 1820s when the United States refused to join Great Britain in issuing a statement opposing Spain's attempts to regain control of its Latin American colonies or to transfer them to any other nation. In that case, the United States followed its rejection of joint action by a unilateral statement of similar principles that became known as the Monroe Doctrine. Building on the warning against "entangling alliances" contained in George Washington's Farewell Address, the Monroe Doctrine established a tradition of stating American principles unilaterally and of nonintervention in the affairs of nations outside the western hemisphere. The U.S. Navy had, to be sure, landed parties to protect American citizens and property and to punish those who attacked them, but such operations had been exercised quickly and often without orders from the U.S. government.

The Open Door Notes represented a vast change in policy and commitment. Prior to the acquisition of the Philippines, the issuance of such a policy statement would have been unthinkable, but once that step was taken it was easy to rationalize a further extension of American political involvement in Asian waters. The Open Door Notes committed the United States to the protection of equal opportunity for all nations to trade and invest in China and to the preservation of the territorial and administrative integrity of that declining empire. American citizens considered other nations' acceptance of the Open Door Notes a great diplomatic triumph and credited the United States with single-handedly saving China from being carved up into spheres of influence and colonies as had happened in Africa. Such overweening hubris presaged Americans' beliefs that they "won" both world wars of the twentieth century, rescuing the Western democracies from the autocratic emperors of Germany and Austro-Hungary and the demented militarism of the Axis powers.

The shift in America's view of the world was reciprocated by a revolution in the way world powers viewed the United States. Before the Spanish-American War, the United States was of comparatively little interest to the leaders of Europe. Although the United States had demonstrated an ability to raise and support a large army, few European military theorists believed that the United States had any intention of employing its power beyond North America. During the last half of the nineteenth century European diplomats focused their attention on the Italian and German wars of unification, the shifting alliance systems that were developing in Europe, the scramble for empire in Africa, and the division of Pacific islands into colonies and spheres of influence. British, French, Belgian, and German leaders were egged on by the Darwinian belief that only the fittest could survive the competition for limited resources.

European industrialists, especially in Great Britain and Germany, watched the economic development of the United States with ambivalence. As the nineteenth century drew to a close, the United States was becoming less a market for European manufacturers and more a competitor for world markets, but the United States rarely took the lead in commerce. In Latin America and China its traders entered markets already opened by the British, French, and others. Even Japan, the one nation "opened" to the outside world by American action, developed more extensive ties with other nations than with the United States. In seeking to modernize its military, for example, Japan turned to Great Britain to purchase ships and for assistance in operating a navy, invited the French to build a naval shipyard at Yokosuka, and sent an agent to Europe to study Germany's army.[4]

There were indications that the United States was beginning to exert itself beyond its hemisphere prior to the war with Spain, but such signs were mixed with others that seemed to indicate American policy was not changing. All these signs were overshadowed at the time by other events, making the subtle shift more evident in retrospect than it was to contemporaries.

The ambivalent attitude of the U.S. government toward overseas expansion first manifested itself in 1867. On 28 August of that year Capt. William Reynolds of the USS *Lackawanna* claimed the uninhabited Midway Islands for the United States, but less than a month later the Senate rejected a reciprocity treaty with Hawaii. In 1872 Comdr. Richard W. Meade negotiated a treaty with Samoan chieftains that gave the United States exclusive rights to establish a base at Pago Pago on the island of Tutuila, but the Senate refused to take action on the treaty. In 1875 the Senate appeared to reverse its attitude toward treaties involving the Pacific when it approved an agreement with Hawaii that provided that none of the island nation's territory could be leased or sold to a third party. In 1889 another aberration in policy occurred when the United States reluctantly accepted membership in a joint British-German-American protectorate over Samoa to preserve the independence and neutrality of the islands. American participation prevented the islands from falling under German control, but when Grover Cleveland returned to the presidency in 1893 he and his secretary of state strongly criticized American participation in what they considered an "entangling alliance."

The 1875 treaty with Hawaii brought a decade and a half of stability to the islands during which the sugar industry expanded rapidly. In 1893 foreign planters, many of them Americans, believed their interests threatened and asked U.S. minister John L. Stevens for protection. Stevens ordered 150 sailors and marines landed from the USS *Boston*. The planters' control of the Hawaiian legislature provided them with a base from which they declared the Hawaiian monarchy dissolved, established a provisional government, and dispatched agents to Washington to seek annexation into the United States. Such a treaty was quickly signed, but the Senate refused to act in the waning days of Benjamin Harrison's administration; when Grover Cleveland returned to office he withdrew the treaty. Four years later, when Japan sent a warship to the islands to protect its citizens from discrimination, the Hawaiian government again sought union with the United States. President William McKinley submitted a treaty to the Senate, but it was rejected.[5]

The United States appeared equally uninterested in acquiring territories closer to home. In 1867 it purchased Alaska from Russia, but Congress refused to approve attempts by the executive to seize further opportunities for expansion. The blockade of the South during the Civil War and the need to counter French ambitions in Mexico had convinced naval and diplomatic leaders of the need for bases in the West Indies. In January 1866 Secretary of State William Seward embarked on a cruise "for his health" to the Virgin Islands, Haiti, Santo Domingo, and Cuba. Within a year he had negotiated a treaty with Denmark to purchase St. Thomas and St. John in the Virgin Islands, the Dominican Republic asked to be annexed to the United States, Haiti offered to lease a harbor to the United States in return for the payment of Haitian debts to France, and Seward approached Sweden about purchasing St. Bartholomew's Island. Congress thwarted all these moves. On 13 January 1869 the House of Representatives rejected a resolution authorizing the formation of an American protectorate over Santo Domingo and Haiti by a vote of 126 to 36. Shortly thereafter it resolved by a vote of 93 to 43 that it was "inexpedient" for the United States to purchase any territory at that time. In March 1870 the Senate Committee on Foreign Relations recommended against the full Senate's even voting on the purchase of the Virgin Islands from Denmark and rejected a treaty to annex Santo Domingo by a vote of 28 to 28, far short of the two-thirds needed for ratification.[6]

American opposition to expansion declined sharply following Dewey's victory at Manila Bay. The perceived need for bases between California and the Philippines led Congress to pass a joint resolution annexing the Hawaiian Islands on 6 July 1898. Six months later, Comdr. E. D. Taussig of the USS *Bennington* stopped at Wake Island while en route from Hawaii to the Philippines with reinforcements and claimed it for the United States, an action quickly endorsed by the McKinley administration.[7]

When civil war broke out in Samoa in late 1898, bluejackets from the USS *Philadelphia* went ashore to guard the American consulate. On 1 April 1899 Samoans ambushed a party of British and American sailors near Apia, killing three British and four Americans, including the commander of the party, U.S. Navy Lt. Philip Van Horn Lansdale. The uprising was quickly suppressed, and by the end of the year Germany, Great Britain, and the United States agreed to a partition of Samoa that gave direct control of the easternmost islands to the United States. The Senate, which had failed to act on a treaty granting base rights a quarter of a century earlier, quickly approved the treaty and in February 1900 President McKinley placed the Samoan islands, including Tutuila with its harbor at Pago Pago, under the administration of the Navy.[8]

This revolution in foreign affairs brought by the Spanish-American War forced a total reassessment of American defense policy and led to changes as radical as those in the nation's international affairs. Prior to the acquisition of the Philippines the United States had largely limited its defense commitments to the western hemisphere. The main functions of the Army were repelling foreign invaders and defending against Indians in the West. In wartime the Navy would assist in defense of the American coast, protect American commerce, and attack the commerce of the enemy. In peacetime the Navy maintained a series of small squadrons to protect American oceanic commerce, mainly through a policy of punishment and retribution. The Spanish-American War brought the acquisition of Hawaii, Guam, and the Philippines, and opened the way for an increased American presence in China. The defense of these islands and the increased commerce in the Far East placed much greater demands on the Navy. These new responsibilities led to a massive expansion of the Navy and a commitment to build a fleet second in strength only to that of Great Britain.

When one considers the massive changes wrought by the Spanish-American War, it is surprising that the conflict has received so little attention from military historians. Several popular books and articles appeared in the wake of hostilities, and Rear Adm. French Ensor Chadwick, a veteran of the battle of Santiago, published *The Spanish-American War*, a two-volume study, in 1911. Shorter studies appeared during the next half century, but few added much to Chadwick's work, which was reprinted in 1968.[9] Most authors focused on the causes and consequences of the war and the diplomacy surrounding it; few have analyzed the operations that brought success to the United States. David Trask's *The War with Spain in 1898*, the standard account of the conflict, did not appear until 1981. Writing for *The Macmillan Wars of the United States* series imposed limitations of length on Trask and, as excellent as the book is, he could not analyze all aspects of the war.

Thus the raison d'être for this volume, in which nine authors present material that is original or little noticed in regard to the conduct of the war and the immediate postwar period. In the first essay Diane Cooper describes the activities of Lt. George Leland Dyer, U.S. Navy attaché to Spain, just prior to the outbreak of war. Little has been written about any of the Navy's attachés in Europe during this era, despite the fact that "naval attachés remained the first line of information" for the Office of Naval Intelligence (ONI) both before and during the war. The author of the standard history of the ONI sketches the activities of William Snowden Sims in France, Albert Parker Niblack and Francis Morgan Barber in Germany, and John Charles Colwell in Great Britain during this era, but makes only two brief mentions of Dyer, who was sent to Madrid as America's first naval attaché to Spain in late 1897.[10] Thus Cooper's essay addresses an important but neglected topic in American diplomatic and naval history.

David Trask's assessment of the use made by American military and naval leaders of information gained through intelligence sources during the war serves a dual purpose because it also provides an overview of operations conducted during the war. Joseph Dawson provides a more detailed examination of operations in the Caribbean and particularly of Rear Adm. William T. Sampson's blockade of the Spanish fleet in Santiago. Both Dawson and Harold Langley analyze the controversy that arose between Sampson and Commodore Winfield Scott Schley following the battle. The feud that developed between the supporters of each man poisoned relations within the officer corps for a generation and influenced how senior officers conducted themselves as late as World War II. Langley is the first person to capture the true flavor of the affair as he describes the remarkable adulation showered on Schley by his supporters.

During the Spanish-American War the United States conducted its first extensive joint operations against an enemy outside the North American

continent. Graham Cosmas describes those operations in both the Caribbean and the Pacific. Such operations, usually referred to as "amphibious operations" during that era, soon became the special function of the U.S. Marine Corps. Jack Shulimson traces the history of that service during the
decade surrounding the Spanish-American War, and describes its role in the
American victory.

Commodore Dewey's destruction of the Spanish squadron at Manila Bay
brought the United States a new empire, but its Philippine citizens were not
all pleased with trading one imperial power for another, and the American
military soon found itself engaged in its first protracted conflict against an
Asian people. When the Philippine *insurrectos* proved more difficult to defeat than the Spanish, the U.S. Army and Navy adopted harsh methods to
break the resistance. Brian Linn's analysis of the steps taken to subdue the
residents of Samar forms a virtual microcosm of the earliest of America's
"small wars," a type of conflict that would become more common during the
century ahead as U.S. forces policed the nations of the Caribbean and assisted governments of newly independent nations, such as Vietnam.

The numerous operations undertaken against the *insurrectos* required large
numbers of small naval vessels, and those gunboats and patrol craft provided
young naval officers with greater opportunities for command and independent action than had existed since at least the Civil War. Vernon Williams
analyzes career patterns in the naval officer corps of the first half of the
twentieth century to show how officers who served on the Asiatic Station,
i.e., in the Philippines and on the coast of China, experienced much more
rapid promotion than those who served in the Atlantic Ocean, Caribbean
Sea, and elsewhere.

The book closes with an essay by Ephraim Smith on William McKinley
and the decision to annex the Philippines. This is both a historiographical
study and a study in human motivation. To the continuing debate concerning McKinley Smith contributes significant new evidence from the papers
of Maj. Gen. Francis V. Greene that substantially supports the view that
McKinley was a reluctant imperialist and only gradually came to accept the
inevitability of American ownership of the entire Philippine archipelago.

As we approach the centennial of that "splendid little war," analysis continues. The essays presented here seek to call attention to and explain some
neglected and controversial aspects of that pivotal event, thereby contributing to a clearer understanding of the diplomatic and military actions that
transformed U.S. policy and America itself.

NOTES

1. The Monroe Doctrine is included in James Monroe's 2 December 1823 annual report to Congress; the quoted passage is found in James D. Richardson, *A Compilation of the Messages and Papers of the Presidents*, 20 vols. (New York, 1897–1911), 2:787. The other basic statement was included in George Washington's Farewell Address. This, the traditional view, has been challenged by Lewis L. Gould in *The Spanish-American War and President McKinley* (Lawrence, Kans., 1982), who depicts McKinley as determined to force Spanish recognition of Cuban independence and willing to take measures designed to ensure Spanish acceptance of that policy. Gould distills this view of McKinley as a strong leader in "The Man at the Helm," in *Commanders in Chief: Presidential Leadership in Modern Wars*, ed. Joseph G. Dawson III (Lawrence, Kans., 1993).

2. Comparations are for the American Revolution, War of 1812, Mexican War, Civil War, Spanish-American War, World Wars I and II, the Korean War, and the Vietnam War. Maris A. Vinovskis, "Have Social Historians Lost the Civil War? Some Preliminary Demographic Speculations," *Journal of American History* 76 (1989), 37–38.

3. Thomas A. Bailey, "The United States and Hawaii During the Spanish-American War," *American Historical Review* 36 (1931), 550–60, examines the opposition to annexation of Hawaii by many Americans, concluding that had it not been for the war, annexation would have been much delayed, if it ever took place. Robert L. Beisner, *Twelve Against Empire: The Anti-Imperialists, 1898–1900* (New York, 1968), analyzes opposition to expansion during and immediately following the Spanish-American War.

4. Hugh Borton, *Japan's Modern Century* (New York, 1955).

5. John Patterson, "The United States and Hawaiian Reciprocity, 1867–1870," *Pacific Historical Review* 7 (1938): 14–26; W. Stull Holt, *Treaties Defeated by The Senate: A Study of the Struggle Between President and Senate over the Conduct of Foreign Relations* (Baltimore, 1933), 102–6; William A. Russ, Jr., *The Hawaiian Revolution, 1893–94* (Selinsgrove, Pa., 1959); William A. Russ, Jr., *The Hawaiian Republic, 1894–98, and Its Struggle to Win Annexation* (Selinsgrove, Pa., 1961).

6. Halvdan Koht, "The Origin of Seward's Plan to Purchase the Danish West Indies," *The American Historical Review* 50 (1945): 762–67; Donald M. Dozer, "Anti-Expansionism During the Johnson Administration," *The Pacific Historical Review* 12 (1943): 253–75.

7. Thomas A. Bailey, "The United States and Hawaii During the Spanish-American War," *The American Historical Review* 36 (1931), 550–60, argues that annexation was not necessary for the prosecution of the war, but Julius W. Pratt, "The 'Large Policy' of 1898," *Mississippi Valley Historical Review* 19 (1932), 219–42, shows that American leaders believed it was.

8. George H. Ryden, *The Foreign Policy of the United States in Relation to Samoa* (New Haven, 1933).

9. Such works include Walter Millis, *The Martial Spirit: A Study of Our War with Spain* (Cambridge, 1931); and Frank Freidel, *The Splendid Little War* (Boston, 1958).

10. Jeffery M. Dowart, *The Office of Naval Intelligence: The Birth of America's First Intelligence Agency, 1865–1918* (Annapolis, 1979), 61–65.

CRUCIBLE OF EMPIRE

Diplomat and Naval Intelligence Officer: The Duties of Lt. George L. Dyer, U.S. Naval Attaché to Spain

DIANE E. COOPER

ON 28 JULY 1897 THE NEWLY APPOINTED AMERICAN MINISTER TO MADRID, Gen. Stewart Lyndon Woodford, accompanied by Lt. George Leland Dyer, the first full-time naval attaché assigned to Madrid, and Capt. Tasker Howard Bliss, military attaché, set sail for Spain to attempt to peacefully mediate a settlement between the Spanish government and the Cuban revolutionaries, thereby avoiding the dark cloud of Spanish-American hostilities hovering on the diplomatic horizon. By the time the general presented his credentials to the queen regent and officially took over the American legation on 13 September, the political and diplomatic situation had deteriorated dramatically, creating a highly volatile environment for the new American minister. Within this uncertain and constantly changing environment the Woodford Mission conducted the daily affairs of a foreign legation while striving to pressure Spain into allowing President William McKinley to mediate a Spanish-Cuban peace. Despite Woodford's efforts and optimism, circumstances forced him to ask for his passport and leave on 21 April 1898 when Spain severed diplomatic relations with the United States, plunging both nations into war.[1]

Although the ensuing war overshadowed Woodford's diplomatic work, relegating it to a few sentences or paragraphs in the annals of history, the mission's accomplishments played a major role in the development of American diplomacy at the end of the nineteenth century. Woodford's institution of the "New American Diplomacy," for example, changed the existing pattern governing the dissemination of diplomatic information to the general public.[2] Although Woodford's major responsibilities were diplomatic in nature, the two attachés assigned to assist him bore the added responsibility of assessing Spain's naval and military strength and preparations while monitoring the changing tide of Spanish public opinion.

For the most part the record of the Woodford Mission rests within the pages of the official diplomatic papers and correspondence of the United States and Spain.[3] Although these records contain President McKinley's instructions, Woodford's "Notes," and Spain's responses, they omit the daily affairs and activities that demanded the attention of Woodford and his two attachés, as well as an appraisal of the personalities and abilities of the various diplomats involved in the negotiations. This essay fills in some of those missing elements in an attempt to broaden the existing picture, rather than merely offering a general account of this diplomatic and naval venture, by selectively studying the participation of naval attaché Lt. George L. Dyer as recorded in his personal and official correspondence.

Dyer's personal correspondence during his assignment as naval attaché includes vivid descriptions of the people, culture, and countryside of Spain as well as detailed accounts of his co-workers and their activities. These letters cover two distinct periods: 28 July 1897 through 16 December 1897 and 25 March 1898 through 19 April 1898. The missing period of 17 December 1897 through 24 March 1898 coincides, unsurprisingly, with his family's three-month stay in Madrid. During this visit Dyer's eighteen-year-old daughter, Susan Hart Dyer, kept a detailed diary recording the diplomatic activities around her as well as her impressions of Spain, the diplomats, and the prospect of war. Unfortunately, little of Dyer's official correspondence still exists within the records of the Office of Naval Intelligence (ONI). Although the letters and cablegrams preserved in the National Archives record groups 38 and 45 only cover the period of 5 March 1898 through 25 April 1898, they deal almost exclusively with the strength, preparations, and movements of the Spanish fleet. Individually these sources shed new light on various aspects of the inner workings of the Woodford Mission. Together they offer a more complete understanding of the role of American diplomacy and U.S. naval intelligence in Spain preceding the outbreak of war in April 1898.

Dyer's papers are voluminous and discuss a plethora of topics, so this essay focuses on Dyer's perceptions regarding the personalities and abilities of the key American diplomats, his diplomatic and naval duties, including his assessment of both the Spanish climate of public opinion and of Spain's naval strength, and the final days of the legation. Susan Hart Dyer's views of the various participants, American and Spanish public opinion, and the legation's flight from Madrid serve to supplement or contrast her father's.

In order to verify some of Dyer's perceptions and accounts of legation activities, the personal papers of Captain Bliss and the official records of the adjutant general's office were also searched. Unfortunately, neither Bliss's personal papers nor his official reports contain any references to his activities as the U.S. military attaché in Madrid during this period.[4] Only the reports and communications received by the ONI from the naval attachés assigned to Paris, London, and Berlin offer any corroboration or additional information regarding Spain's preparations for the impending war.[5]

After nearly thirty years of naval service, including four years as head of the department of modern languages at the Naval Academy, Dyer was appointed to the post of naval attaché, which placed him "in a position to serve his country as few men in all the world ever have the fortune."[6] Dyer's personal reflections on this assignment suggest a modest, self-effacing individual who constantly questioned his own ability to measure up to the task at hand.[7] "I cannot conceive of a greater responsibility being thrust upon one . . . I wonder why it has been my lot and I pray I may be equal to all the demands."[8] Despite this seemingly unpretentious attitude, Dyer believed his abilities surpassed those of either Woodford or Bliss and considered himself a "more logical and clearer thinker [who] dominate[s] the situation."[9]

Dyer recognized his position as a unique opportunity for service, a position that increased in importance with each passing day. "I feel I am accomplishing something and that no one could have a loftier or more satisfactory post and occupation than mine. . . . Now that it has developed into such importance . . . it will be a legacy to be proud of . . . and I can feel no longer that I have not had my opportunity."[10]

Captain Bliss, "a big stout solemn looking man with a bull-dog jaw," served as Woodford's military attaché and Dyer's military counterpart.[11] After a variety of assignments, including eight years teaching French at West Point, Bliss welcomed the opportunity to serve as a member of the American legation to Madrid. Like Dyer, this post fulfilled Bliss's intellectual and professional ambitions.[12]

Although Dyer considered Bliss "an absolute opposite" from himself, he found that his colleague's intelligence, wit, good common sense, and strong character nearly made them equals. Dyer respected and valued the captain's opinions, even on the rare occasions when they differed from his own. The two men worked well together, rarely arguing, since, when disagreements arose, Bliss invariably acquiesced. Dyer noted, "We have had no collision and are not likely to as we both appreciate the fact that our strength lies in

George L. Dyer

When he went to Spain in 1897, Dyer had been a lieutenant for almost twenty years (his date of rank was 5 February 1879). He was promoted to lieutenant commander on 22 November 1898, and to commander, the rank he wears in this photograph, on 19 April 1901. Dyer served as the Naval Governor of Guam beginning 3 January 1903. He died on 2 April 1914 at his retirement home in Winter Park, Florida. *Courtesy of the George Leland Dyer Papers, East Carolina Manuscript Collection, Joyner Library, East Carolina University.*

union and both have agreed to agree on every occasion. He is a pretty strong character but I am gratified that whenever we measure this attribute . . . I prevail."[13]

Unlike Bliss, General Woodford, "a bald, blond tabby of a man who holds girls hands and brags horribly," never won Dyer's complete confidence or trust.[14] During the first few days following the legation's arrival in San Sebastian, the home of the queen regent's summer court, three incidents occurred that reaffirmed Dyer's early impressions that Woodford lacked moral stamina and was "indirect, a trimmer and time server and a sycophant to his superiors [who] yield[s] his judgment when convinced . . . for he has no fixed opinions in the face of superior mental ability."[15]

The first incident, occurring the day after the newly appointed minister arrived in San Sebastian, concerned the advisability of attending an upcoming bullfight and resulted in a major rift between General Woodford and the incumbent American minister, Hannis Taylor. Realizing this whole affair "might easily develop into a scandalous and discreditable quarrel which would be most injurious" to the legation's mission, Dyer, acting as a self-appointed intermediary, "had a plain talk" with the general and insisted he make amends.[16] Following this talk, the two ministers managed to settle their differences entirely to Taylor's satisfaction, thus avoiding any damaging repercussions.

A second major confrontation occurred the very next day, 5 September, when Woodford proposed sending a detailed letter describing the current political scene to President McKinley through the Spanish mail. Although neither Dyer nor Bliss argued with Woodford's assessment of the diplomatic situation, both strongly opposed sending the letter through the usual Spanish postal channels because they felt "nothing is inviolate in this country and letters . . . will be opened," thus giving the Spanish government and press an opportunity to obtain an idea of Woodford's views and expectations.[17] Supported by Bliss, Dyer hammered home the idea that Woodford needed to observe a strict policy of silence because any premature statements threatened to destroy the eventual impact and effectiveness of the negotiations. Dyer stressed the fact that "for months the Spanish press had been working itself into a state of frenzy over the fancied demands the new American Minister intended to make on the distracted, heart wounded, bleeding, fainting Spanish Nation and the tension was so great that any careless word that could be construed unfavorably would have set the whole pack howling like insane people."[18] As a result of Dyer's and Bliss's arguments, Woodford eventually agreed to mail the letter from France.

Two days later Woodford handed his attachés a rough draft of the first "Note" he proposed to send the Spanish government and requested their criticism, precipitating the third incident that irritated Dyer. Retiring to Dyer's room, the two attachés discussed and studied the document until well after midnight, at which time they determined not to allow Woodford to send the weak and excessively long letter. They prepared an outline of the main points they felt Woodford's letter should address and presented it to the general the next afternoon.

> Without measuring my words I told him the letter was weak and would create a bad impression, that he asked for further instructions on a point which was fully covered by what he had, that he had shown an inclination, a desire even, to shift the negotiations on to the Dept. at Wash. and merely act as an intermediary in Spain, that he had referred three times to not coveting responsibility but that it was too late now. "If you hadn't wanted the responsibility,["] I said. "Yes,["] he replied, cutting me off[, "]I shouldn't have come[.]" "That is just what I was going to say[,"] I added. Bliss sat on the other side with his face impassive and added a word now and then. The General covered his face with his hands and held them there for some time and then taking up the points I had made, seriatim, went on to argue that he agreed with us.[19]

Dyer felt that the final document, an elaboration of the attachés' list of points, offered a "manly, direct, self reliant statement" capable of pleasing the president and the American public while presenting a strong and determined front to the Spanish.[20]

These three incidents strengthened Dyer's initial impression of Woodford as an indirect and untrustworthy individual who, "when he tells us a thing we are never sure that he hasn't reserved or obscured something which would give us a clearer idea of the matter."[21] Perhaps these incidents, occurring so early in Dyer's appointment, also helped shape Dyer's perception of his duties as naval attaché, placing a stronger emphasis on his diplomatic duties than his naval responsibilities.

Dyer's orders appear to no longer exist, so it is impossible to determine whether his assignment emphasized the gathering of naval intelligence in the face of an impending war with Spain or whether his duties and responsibilities related to the intensive and vital diplomatic negotiations attempting to prevent that war. Based on the orders received by Lt. William Sowden Sims between 19 September 1896, the date he first received his appointment as naval attaché to Paris, Madrid, and St. Petersburg, and March 1897, when Sims assumed that post, a conflict over the appropriate priorities of naval attachés existed between the Navy Department and the diplomats in the field.[22] Shortly after Sims received his initial orders, Washington officially withdrew his appointment "for the present" due to a disagreement over his qualifications and diplomatic duties. Based upon his work as the intelligence officer on board the USS *Saratoga* stationed in China during the Japanese-Sino War, the Navy viewed Sims as the most qualified officer for the post and its inherent naval intelligence duties. Horace Porter, the American ambassador to France, however, supported a different naval officer whom he viewed as better suited for the diplomatic aspects of the position. Porter insisted on a naval officer qualified to assist him in "fulfilling the social duties of the embassy, which, in [his] eyes . . . was doubtless the chief function of his naval attaché," while the Navy Department urgently needed an officer capable of gathering the "best and most complete information obtainable on foreign naval progress," especially in light of a potential conflict with Spain. Despite the wording of his final orders to regard the ambassador in Paris and the ministers in St. Petersburg and Madrid "as your superior officers, and [to] comply with such instructions as they may give you," Sims's numerous naval fact-finding trips, which commenced almost immediately upon his arrival in Paris, and subsequent reports suggest all parties eventually perceived that his naval responsibilities outranked his diplomatic ones. Throughout his four-year assignment to the Paris embassy, Sims placed a high priority on gathering and transmitting foreign naval intelligence.[23]

Apparently, Dyer and Woodford saw Dyer's responsibilities in a different light. During the nine months he served as naval attaché in Madrid, it seems Dyer directed the majority of his energies to the daily diplomatic and social affairs of the American legation and to the extremely serious and sensitive correspondence and negotiations meant to avert war. While Dyer's personal correspondence tended to reflect this emphasis on his diplomatic duties over the gathering and transmission of naval intelligence, his letters also contain a number of references to confidential correspondence and assessments of the situation sent to Theodore Roosevelt, the assistant secretary of the Navy. Only Dyer's cablegrams and letters sent to Roosevelt and the Navy Department after 5 March 1897 still survive in the official records.

Dyer's diplomatic responsibilities included assisting Woodford in the preparation of official diplomatic "Notes," monitoring the Spanish newspapers and public opinion, transmitting translations of official and confidential ciphers to and from Washington, and overseeing legation protocol, especially with regard to diplomatic visits.

The preparation of Woodford's first diplomatic "Note" to the Spanish government set the standard for all future diplomatic correspondence issued by the American legation. According to Dyer, Woodford submitted a rough draft to his attachés for their criticism. Dyer and Bliss invariably tore the draft apart and reconstructed it to reflect their ideas and what they viewed as an appropriate amount of strength. Occasionally Woodford requested that each attaché prepare his own draft and submit it to a group criticism. Preparation of an official "Note" required days of discussion, writing, critiquing, and rewriting until everyone, particularly Dyer, approved of the finished product. Dyer felt he consistently ended up writing the final documents since the "result is my work in conception [and contains] all the changes we suggested in our exact language."[24] Preparing a "Note," sending a cipher, or receiving a cipher from Washington stretched their workday into long, unbroken hours of tiresome labor. On those days Dyer commonly arose "at light and did not get a moment until Eleven P.M."[25]

Woodford officially recognized the lieutenant's abilities and contributions to the mission in his 24 September 1897 letter to Secretary of the Navy John D. Long, a copy of which went to Dyer. In the letter the general characterized Dyer as "an admirable linguist, a cultivated gentleman, a trained officer," and a thoughtful and wise trusted advisor. He also portrayed Dyer's "services . . . [and] constant assistance and advice" during the long consultations and negotiations preceding the delivery of the first "Note" to the Spanish government as "simply invaluable" and stated he felt "greatly strengthened" in the future discharge of his duties due to Dyer's presence.[26]

Immediately upon their late September arrival in Madrid Dyer assumed the responsibilities of the executive officer in charge of all matters of protocol. Good intentions aside, his first diplomatic faux pas occurred before the members of the American legation had even settled into their quarters. According to Sunday's late edition of the Spanish newspaper the *Heraldo*, Prime Minister Marcelo de Azcárraga waited at his office until 5:00 P.M. that day, 26 September, for General Woodford's first visit. The article ended by noting that the American minister undoubtedly would call on Azcárraga the next day. In an attempt to lessen the seriousness of this oversight—"it did not occur to [them] that any calls would be required or expected on Sunday"—Dyer immediately telephoned George Stanton Sickles, the legation secretary, and asked him to see to the necessary arrangements.[27]

Because Dyer felt that circumstances dictated his usurping a certain amount of authority that rightfully belonged to Sickles, he took Sickles aside at the first opportunity to discuss the situation in order to avoid any difficulties or misunderstandings. He found that Sickles possessed a "remarkably sweet disposition," making him quite amenable to Dyer's requests. The only concern he expressed stemmed from the way ex-minister Taylor had excluded him in favor of the young clerk Joaquin Moreno, in whom Taylor frequently confided. Sickles demanded that Moreno be returned to his proper place if Dyer wished to avoid any future problems. With the interoffice protocol and lines of authority settled, Dyer and Sickles set about the task of ensuring that Woodford made all the proper calls in the proper order without offending anyone.

Dyer hoped to steer Woodford clear of any pitfalls by observing all the amenities of diplomatic protocol. He also strove to increase the legation's status by refusing to let more than one day elapse before returning first calls, even though such matters seemed rather trivial in light of their mission: "These matters are of singular importance and yet how insignificant when compared with the real questions which should occupy our minds and all our time."[28] While Woodford's diplomatic calls claimed priority, the calls required of Bliss and Dyer were equally important and demanded similar attention to detail and protocol. Through these diplomatic calls the two attachés managed to establish numerous contacts with the other foreign embassies and legations in Madrid, thus enabling them to form an unofficial information network.

Dyer seized every opportunity for Woodford to favorably impress the Spanish government and people. Upon learning of the queen's scheduled arrival in Madrid, Dyer and Sickles immediately set about securing permission for Woodford and his party to welcome the queen at the depot along with the Spanish governmental officials and other dignitaries. The introducer of ambassadors assured them that while Woodford's presence was not required, the Spanish government and people would consider his attendance an exquisite compliment. Anticipating a large crowd, the introducer promised to make all the necessary arrangements and see that the Americans enjoyed a good vantage point.

At 9:00 P.M. on 28 September, the legation carriage transported the diplomatic party to the train station where military troops and police officers lined the crowded streets and a regiment of cavalry guarded the entrance. The introducer of ambassadors met the Americans at the depot door and escorted them inside the row of halberdiers forming a passageway for the queen. Here the Americans joined her majesty's cabinet ministers and received every possible consideration from the Spanish as they cleared, in Dyer's opinion, a place of honor for the American contingency.

Certain that they held everyone's attention prior to the queen's arrival, Dyer carefully studied the countenances of the crowd to detect any unfavorable expressions or looks. In that moment he concluded that the Americans dominated the situation and the time had arrived when the Spanish wanted to "conciliate us . . . not because they love us, nor yet be[ca]use they are really afraid but because they [a]r[e] apprehensive . . . and have the vague notion that Uncle [S]am has more than a thousand destructive thu[nd]erbolts in reserve."[29] When the queen finally arrived, she duly noted and acknowledged Woodford's presence, increasing his solicitous and peaceful image within the realms of the Spanish court and kingdom.

Once settled into the legation's diplomatic routine, Dyer commenced his daily work, which consisted mainly of following the various political developments in Spain, Cuba, and the United States and noting their effects on the currents of public opinion. In order to fulfill his assignment as the mission's eyes and ears, Dyer tried to read the *Imparcial,* Spain's Liberal Party paper, the *Epoca,* Spain's Conservative Party paper, the *Heraldo,* Madrid's leading and most influential evening paper, the *Nacional,* the *Correspondencia de Espana,* the *Voz de Guipuizcoa,* the *Union Vazcongada,* the *Paris Temps,* and the *New York Journal* every day, and often spent the entire day studying these papers.[30] More than once Dyer noted that the Spanish newspapers attempted to create rather than reflect public opinion and, as a general rule, published negative and unflattering opinions of Woodford and his expected American ultimatums.[31]

One article published in the *Nacional* recommended "the burning of a little diplomatic wood in the Puerto del Sol as we have done before," a reference to an earlier episode concerning the burning of the German embassy's shield in an attempt to stir up public sentiment.[32] Although Dyer doubted whether the article spoke for more than a handful of radicals, he recognized the potential power this type of press possessed.

A second article compared the United States to the piratical Riff tribes in Morocco and expressed, in Dyer's opinion, the Spaniards' position and thinking in a clever and succinct manner. One of the points brought out in this article dealt with the alleged cringing attitude of the Spanish government toward the United States and its demands. Dyer noted that the newspapers constantly harped on this theme of the Spanish government's acquiescence to rather than rejection of American demands. On those infrequent occasions when the Spanish government rejected a demand, the press reported the refusal as too weak and insufficient to stem the rising tide of American interference. The article's conclusion expressed the prevalent Spanish attitude that "it would be easy eno' to whup" the United States.[33]

With each passing month newspapers reiterated this conviction and demanded that Spain increase its navy in preparation for the inevitable clash with the United States. Eventually the papers confidently declared that Spain could land 30,000 or 40,000 troops in the United States and easily rout America's "untrained militia." This boast, appearing while Dyer's family resided in Madrid, elicited the following sarcastic, jingoistic response from his teenaged daughter, Susan Hart Dyer.[34]

> When I hear such things as that I boil with rage at their crass ignorance and unmitigated conceit. I should like to ask them a few questions. 1. Where are they intending to land their troops? At New York or San Francisco? At Key West or Portland, Oregon? Portland, Maine or Galveston, Texas? 2. What will they do with their troops when they are landed? Destroy our population with one blow? March across the continent and take Salt Lake City? Or perhaps confine themselves to burning Chicago?[35]

Despite the continual efforts of the press to fire up the indignation of the Spanish people, Dyer doubted they could be easily roused. To monitor the true public sentiment in contrast to the rhetoric of the newspapers, Dyer engaged local citizens in conversation whenever possible. From the citizens of Madrid he acquired a sympathy for a proud people slowly being forced toward a war with the United States and came to view the "absolutely Quixotic attitude" of the papers as pathetic and cruel. The writers who spoke of Spanish honor and a willingness to "sacrifice the last drop of blood and the last copper" rather than appear not to resent the alleged insults and abuses heaped upon Spain by the American president remained untouched by the realities of war.[36] Their sacrifice never seemed to match that of the Spanish peasants.

Nearly every Spanish family too poor to purchase a 1,500-pesetas exemption from military service mourned the loss of a loved one in either Cuba or the Philippines. Dyer's barber, certain that fully half of the soldiers sent to Cuba had already perished, believed that the majority of the people wanted the fighting stopped no matter what the cost.[37] Dyer hoped the sick and wounded soldiers returning home and dispersing throughout the countryside would act as a leavening force for peace among the general populace. The mid-September arrival of a Spanish transport at Coruña returned over six hundred of those soldiers, the survivors of a long and perilous sea journey from Cuba during which sixty-four soldiers died. Three more died in the launch transporting them to the Spanish shore. Another fifty invalid soldiers were left in Puerto Rico to await the next transport.[38] To Dyer, this drain of men seemed a costly price for national honor.

Public opinion in Spain, as reflected by the press, tended to run against the Americans, whom the Spaniards blamed for the continuation of the Cuban rebellion. Although most of the population had grown weary of the long strain and looked forward to almost any solution, they resented American intervention and anticipated an inevitable break between the United States and Spain, believing the sooner it occurred the better.[39] The Spanish papers unitedly proclaimed "no gov't can stand a minute which will admit *in any form* the *principle* of our [American] interference in their domestic affairs."[40] Despite all the efforts and agitations of the press, Dyer continued to believe they were unable to rally the majority of the tired and indifferent Spanish people.[41]

In Dyer's opinion, the Spaniards stood at a great impasse, driven into a corner by the circumstances, "traditions, habits of thought and actions of ages [which] are a part of the constitutional fibre of this people."[42] With each passing day he grew more convinced of the impossibility of any radical change occurring in Spain without a revolution of some type. Internal affairs suffered from disorder and fierce party rivalries as the Conservatives, the Liberals, the Carlists, and the Republicans all stood ready "to spring at each other like savage dogs."[43] Across the Atlantic, American jingoes in Congress, unable to comprehend the Spanish character, impatiently awaited the opportunity to put a match to this highly flammable situation.[44]

Dyer felt destiny had placed the members of the Woodford Mission in a unique position to help this "distracted, bleeding, devoted country" pierce the "darkness and gloom which envelope[d]" its people with a "few rays of the sunshine of peace."[45] Profoundly touched by their helpless and hopeless condition, Dyer believed "a new nation [was] about to be born in the midst of Carnage and fire."[46]

Despite the pressing diplomatic duties Dyer assumed upon his arrival in Spain, he never lost sight of his duties as a naval officer. Within a few days of his arrival in Madrid, he conveyed his initial views of the "grave" situation to Roosevelt and stated that he "considered no time should be lost in making every preparation which can be done without embarrassing Woodford."[47] Circumstances, however, denied Dyer the privilege of exploiting every opportunity to gather important naval information. When the Spanish squadron arrived in Lisbon during September, presenting Dyer with a suitable occasion to review and study the Spanish navy at close range, his diplomatic responsibilities related to establishing the new minister and his staff in Spain took precedence, making it impossible for him to leave Madrid. Fortunately, the USS *San Francisco* arrived in Lisbon on 16 September, and Dyer managed to delegate the job of surveying the squadron to his friend Flag Lt. Jack Hawkes.[48]

Dyer outlined the basic procedure he and Bliss employed when gathering and transmitting naval and military intelligence to Washington in a letter he sent to Roosevelt. He obtained the majority of his information regarding the

Spanish navy through the numerous newspapers he studied and then forwarded packages of articles clipped from those papers to Comdr. Richardson Clover, the chief intelligence officer, by registered mail. With the exception of specific maps and publications requested by the War Department, Bliss "sent the exact same information" in his packets. By March 1898 Dyer was sending two packages of clippings each week with whatever verification of the more important news items he could obtain. Dyer's reliance on the news media seems in accordance with Woodford's expressed desire that his attachés remain "out of sight as much as possible so as to avoid complications" for the minister.[49] Dyer also wrote weekly letters describing the general situation and climate of opinion in Spain. Beginning in February he increased these personal assessments to twice a week due to the constant changes he perceived. By the end of March Dyer felt confident that, unless his packages had been lost or extracted from the mails, the ONI possessed a relatively complete and trustworthy account of the condition and location of the Spanish navy and the efforts of the government to ready all of its ships.

Outwardly the Spanish government assisted and encouraged Dyer's efforts to study their navy. Upon meeting Spain's minister of state, Carlos O'Donnell y Abreu, the Duke de Tetuán, Dyer reported he "was to have every facility for visiting their few ships 'de poca importancia' and that [he] would be entirely free to go anywhere [he] pleased and see everything they had," an offer he characterized as "the most unadulterated guff I have had yet."[50] Despite this official invitation, the government endeavored to suppress as much information as possible about squadron formations, vessel specifications, and movements. Dyer also noted that his identity and mission were well known in Madrid, where he was "aware of being carefully watched," a situation that increased the difficulty of securing and verifying naval information.[51]

During the early months of Dyer's appointment, when diplomatic protocol weighed heavily on his time, Washington received a considerable amount of naval intelligence from the other attachés assigned in Europe. Lieutenant Sims, assigned to Paris and St. Petersburg, compiled extensive reports on foreign navies and their capabilities, with an emphasis on armament proficiency and target practice, which helped initiate numerous changes in American naval policies. Lt. Alfred Niblack, stationed in Berlin and Rome, closely followed Spain's attempts to purchase warships and armament from Italy and Germany. In London, Lt. John C. Colwell reported on improvements in armament and ship construction. All three of these attachés participated in locating and purchasing warships for the U.S. Navy. Each attaché included assessments of the various climates of European opinion regarding the escalating hostilities between Spain and the United States. The information gathered by these officers supplemented the reports Dyer filed on the formation and movements of the Spanish fleet during March and April 1898. Following the severing of diplomatic relations between Spain and the United States, the task of securing naval intelligence from Spain fell directly to Sims and Colwell.[52]

By 16 February 1898 Dyer and the other three naval attachés had gathered and transmitted enough information to Washington for Roosevelt to compile a listing of sixty-four Spanish naval vessels in European and Cuban waters with specifications such as tons displacement, speed, armament, and age (see appendix). Roosevelt's list included the fourteen vessels destined to form Spain's first and second torpedo squadrons was well as the battleships *Pelayo*, *Vitoria*, and *Numancia*.[53] During this same time period Roosevelt wrote Secretary Long, calling his attention "to the steady way in which the Spanish force grows relatively to our own. . . . Month by month the Spanish navy has been put into a better condition to meet us." He calculated that following the loss of the USS *Maine* the Spanish seagoing armored ships numbered six to the American's seven and predicted that the odds would continue to increase in Spain's favor.[54]

In March Dyer received a cablegram from Roosevelt ordering him to keep the department fully informed of the Spanish state of affairs and to report any preparations or movements of the Spanish navy. A week later Roosevelt sent another cable directing Dyer to closely monitor the preparation and testing of the *Pelayo* and the armored cruiser *Carlos V*.[55] In compliance with Roosevelt's order to report on the preparations of the Spanish navy, Dyer telegraphed Washington on 13 March that the Spanish torpedo squadron— consisting of three destroyers, the *Furor, Plutón,* and *Terror;* three torpedo boats, the *Rayo, Azor,* and *Ariete;* and the converted cruiser, *Ciudad de Cádiz*—had left Cádiz reportedly headed for the West Indies via the Canary Islands.[56] The clippings he sent chronicled the formation of this squadron and contained references to a planned second squadron to consist of the destroyers *Osado, Audaz,* and *Proserpina*, the torpedo boats *Orion, Halcon,* and *Retamosa*, and a converted cruiser yet to be designated.[57]

On 16 March the first squadron cruised into the Canary Islands as anticipated. Three days later the Spanish government increased its national security by stopping the delivery of any information regarding the squadrons. Despite this policy, Dyer learned that Spain had belatedly assigned the armored cruiser *Colón* to the squadron detailed at the Canaries and had obtained confirmation of the squadron's scheduled departure on 23 March for Puerto Rico. He also managed to procure information regarding the preparation and deployment of the Spanish battleship *Pelayo* and the armored cruiser *Carlos V*, the two vessels about which Roosevelt had requested specific information.[58]

The *Pelayo* received a full crew and set sail on a trial cruise before the end of March, during which its trial speed averaged sixteen knots.[59] A few days after its arrival the *Pelayo* sailed for Toulon and more refitting work. Dyer reported that despite a strike on Toulon the work on both the *Pelayo* and the *Numancia* appeared to be progressing rapidly. While the *Pelayo* underwent work at Toulon the *Carlos V* received similar attention at Havre. Spain placed the highest priority upon work on both vessels, leading the populace to believe that once the *Pelayo* and the *Carlos V* joined the rest of the large ships amassing at the Cape Verde Islands the Spanish fleet would head for Cuba.[60]

By mid-April Dyer received word that the *Pelayo* had finally set sail for Cape Verde to join the torpedo squadrons and the armored cruisers *Colón*, *María Teresa*, *Oquendo*, and *Vizcaya*.[61] Based on his sources, Dyer believed that the *Colón* and the *María Teresa* both had left for Cape Verde in such a hurry that they were not properly provisioned. Despite their limited amount of food and coal, Dyer felt certain that both ships carried a full supply of ammunition.[62] On 20 April the legation sent its last transmission to Roosevelt, reporting the squadron's departure from the Cape Verde Islands, destination unknown.[63]

The *Carlos V* encountered numerous difficulties while undergoing the "installation [of equipment] for moving the guns by electricity." As of 16 April no departure estimates existed, although Dyer learned from reliable sources that the Spanish felt confident they could press the ship into emergency service on a moment's notice "working such parts as have not power applied by hand."[64] Four days later Dyer confirmed the departure of the *Carlos V* for an unknown destination.

Dyer also kept Roosevelt informed of Spain's attempts to strengthen its navy with the purchase of foreign-built vessels and armament. On 27 March 1898 he reported that the Spanish minister of the treasury was in the process of purchasing a cruiser from Italy. At the same time, negotiations between Spain and numerous foreign steamer lines continued in an attempt to secure more steamers capable of mounting guns and armament.[65] On 16 April Dyer reported on the two vessels purchased from Germany, the *Columbia* and the *Normannia*, and the British yacht *Giraldo*, which Spanish officers had taken possession of earlier in the month. Both the *Columbia* and the *Normannia* underwent reconditioning and strengthening in Germany prior to the installation of their artillery in Cádiz. Meanwhile, workers in Barcelona converted the *Giraldo* to serve as a cruiser.[66]

During April Dyer's naval intelligence reports amassed definite, verified information on twenty-one vessels refitted as cruisers. The *Mexico, Panamá, Santo Domingo, San Agustin,* and *Villaverde,* five of the fourteen transatlantic steamers converted to serve as cruisers, were refitted and armed while stationed in Cuban waters.[67]

Often Dyer's sources provided incomplete information that required an educated guess as to the destination of naval vessels or the reasons for the delays in detailing the *Pelayo* and other ships. Ciphered messages flew back and forth between Dyer, Sims, and Commodore John Adams Howell, commander in chief of the European Squadron stationed aboard his flagship, the USS *San Francisco,* anchored in Lisbon. During March Howell even sent Lt. Lloyd Horwitz Chandler to meet with Dyer and Woodford in Madrid. Although no official record or mention of this meeting seems to exist, Susan Hart Dyer did record his visit in her journal: "Lieut. Chandler came to Madrid from Lisbon incognito to confer with father. It was quite like a novel—we always passed him in the dining room and halls without so much as a look of recognition. He actually stayed two or three days in Madrid and got away without any one finding out he had been there."[68] Dyer sent daily cablegrams and letters to Washington updating and verifying the locations and condition of the Spanish vessels. As a general rule, Dyer transmitted each cable in cipher and then mailed the recipient a letter containing a second copy of the cipher.

Early in April Dyer forwarded a copy of the *Heraldo* containing an interview with Gen. José María Beránger y Ruiz de Apodaca, Spain's former minister of the marine. Beránger confidently stated that Spain had nothing to fear from an American attack on Cuba because 190 "electrical and automobile torpedoes which can work at a great distance" defended the ports of Havana, Cienfuegos, Nuevitas, and Santiago. In addition, Beránger offered two reasons for his confidence of a Spanish victory at sea. He insisted that, due to the "remarkable discipline [which] prevails on our war ships, . . . as soon as fire is opened, the crews of the American ships will commence to desert, since we all know that among them are people of all nationalities."[69]

These statements reinforced the endless articles of propaganda and official rhetoric that appeared in the press to bolster the people's confidence in the "superior bravery of the Spanish sailor, the superior discipline on board the Spanish ships and the greater fighting power of [their] Navy." The press reported that American ships carried small-powered guns that neither their officers nor crew could handle properly or efficiently. Dyer felt this belief in Spain's naval superiority accounted, in a large measure, for its growing determination to fight the United States. Many Spaniards expressed the belief that "they have nothing to lose, they could not be worse off with the war than without it . . . but that they can do incalculable damage to our commerce [and] seriously injure, if not destroy, our Navy."[70] One prominent Spaniard expressed the opinion that American naval ships lacked sufficient armament when compared to the "much more efficient" Spanish vessels that, once war was declared, would attack the American coast and inflict as much damage as possible.[71]

By March the Spanish government found itself trapped between the demands of the United States, saying "Give way or we strike," and the threats of the Carlists and dissatisfied Spaniards, saying "Give way a step and we strike."[72] The publication of the De Lome letter, in which Spain's ambassador to the United States made disparaging remarks about President McKinley, and the sinking of the USS *Maine* during February magnified those growing tensions until even the optimistic Dyer admitted that the "atmosphere is heavy and the outlook is certainly dark. . . . [W]hile I have not given up hope . . . I am less optimistic. . . . It seems as if we were rushing towards . . . the final and irrevocable rupture . . . with a fearful rapidity [and] each day draws the cord tighter."[73]

Dyer found it hard to recognize people of the United States now inflamed with a passion for war and demanding the sacrifice of so many lives to further a doubtful cause for a ungrateful people. "It is just as impossible for a Spaniard (Cuban) to love the Anglo-Saxon as for water to run up hill."[74] Americans and Spaniards alike seemed mad for war. The armistice proposal faced strong opposition from the Spanish army, which resented giving in after shedding so much blood in Cuba. In an attempt to maintain some dignity, the Spanish government refused to consider the armistice unless the Cuban insurgents proposed it. Prime Minister Práxedes Mateo Sagasta, the leader of the Liberal party, which replaced Azcárraga's Conservative ministry in October 1897, declared that Spain would make no more concessions: "The time for words [was] past the time for action [had] come."[75] The Spaniards even resisted the pope's please for a peaceful settlement to the conflict.

In an attempt to postpone the impending war with the United States, the Spanish government proclaimed an eleventh-hour armistice on Saturday, 9 April. Dyer, now convinced of the Spanish government's insincerity, believed it had granted this armistice in an attempt to avoid war and had attached some kind of string to it. With the armistice in place, Spain's and Cuba's fates once again hung in the balance of the U.S. Congress. Dyer feared the jingoists in Congress would assume Spain "dare not fight, they give way to pressure always, we have them on the run let us go to the last extreme and humiliate the Dons."[76] Despite reports of the violent demonstrations in Madrid's Puerto del Sol, Dyer felt the Spanish people exhibited little emotional reaction to the armistice. Mr. Roberts, the local druggist, believed a "mala paz [bad peace] was better than a buena guerra [good war]" and, although he considered it ridiculous and unacceptable, he felt the armistice pleased all sensible Spaniards.[77] Although Dyer refused to give up his hope for peace "until Congress puts an absolute order into a joint resolution so that the President will have no will in the matter," he went ahead and located a suitable agent in Madrid to gather and forward information to the American legation in Paris in the event he was forced to leave.[78]

One week later his hope for a peaceful outcome, based on the belief that Congress would comply with President McKinley's wishes, evaporated when he received word of the issuance of a joint congressional resolution ensuring Cuba's independence and directing the president to demand the immediate withdrawal of the Spanish flag from Cuban soil. McKinley relayed this decision to the American legation without translating it into code, thus allowing the Spanish immediate access to the contents of this final message. Rather than allow Woodford to present McKinley's ultimatum, the Spanish government informed the general that it considered all diplomatic relations between the two countries severed, rendering any further communications impossible. Upon receiving this information Woodford requested passports for himself and all members of his diplomatic party and then, late in the afternoon of 21 April 1898, officially closed the American legation in Madrid and boarded a train for Paris.

Although Woodford's exit from Madrid attracted little attention there, crowds at Valladolid and several other stops became vicious, throwing stones and protesting so loudly that the American could hear their shouting long before their train arrived at the station. Woodford firmly believed that had he delayed his departure another four hours the crowds would have become dangerous.[79]

On 23 April news that the American vessel *Nashville* had captured a Spanish steamer reached the legation members in their Paris hotel, creating a "sad, sad ending to [the] well meant efforts" of the Woodford Mission. Stopping one war by starting a worse one seemed incomprehensible to Dyer. "War is a horrible grisly thing and yet our people are mad for it! They have got it now, by Jingo!"[80]

NOTES

1. *The American-Spanish War: A History by the War Leaders* (Norwich, Conn., 1899), 10.

2. Following a breach in diplomatic security in September 1897, Woodford secured permission from Washington to grant the Spanish government the authority to publish any correspondence from the American legation in full, in part, or not at all. The major departure from existing diplomatic procedure was known as the "New American Diplomacy."

3. See *Papers Relating to the Foreign Relations of the United States, 1898* (Washington, 1901); and *Spanish Diplomatic Correspondence and Documents, 1896–1900* (Washington, 1905).

4. The letters written by Bliss to his wife during this assignment still exist; however, they are not currently part of the Library of Congress collection because the family wishes to first eliminate certain "purely personal" matters. According to the National Archives' Military Branch personnel, only a few insignificant reports from the military attaché to Madrid, Capt. Tasker H. Bliss, survive within the Army's official records and are located in Appointment, Commission, and Personal [ACP] file no. 3525. All of Bliss's remaining records and reports have been transferred from the Adjutant General's files to the ACP no. 3525 file. Apparently, the U.S. government authorized the destruction of the bulk of Bliss's work, along with that of numerous other individuals, many years ago.

5. See Record Groups [RG] 38, 45, and 80 for various entries related to these naval attachés, National Archives [NA], Washington, D.C.

6. Navy Office of Information, Biographies Branch, "Commodore George L. Dyer, U.S. Navy, Deceased," 3 June 1959; and George Leland Dyer [GLD] to Susan Hart Palmer Dyer [SHPD], 4 Sept. 1897, George Leland Dyer Papers, East Carolina Manuscript Collection, Joyner Library, East Carolina University, Greenville, North Carolina.

7. While the records contain no statement as to any special qualifications or skills that led to Dyer's appointment as naval attaché, his ability to speak and read both French and Spanish undoubtedly played a major role in the decision-making process. Prior to his appointment Dyer spent a number of years assigned to various vessels patrolling the South American and Caribbean shores.

8. GLD to SHPD, 22 Aug. and 4 Sept. 1897, Dyer Papers.

9. Ibid., 8 Sept. 1897.

10. Ibid., 12 Sept. 1897.

11. Diary of Susan Hart Dyer [SHD], 10 Feb. 1898, Dyer Papers.

12. Personal Papers of Tasker Howard Bliss, Library of Congress, Washington, D.C. Bliss ended his military career as a general and a participant in the Paris Peace Conference of 1918 at the conclusion of World War I.

13. GLD to SHPD, 8 Sept. 1897, Dyer Papers.

14. Diary SHD, 10 Feb. 1898, Dyer Papers.

15. GLD to SHPD, 10 Sept. 1897, Dyer Papers.

16. Ibid., 12 Sept. 1897.

17. Ibid., 10 Sept. 1897. For other mentions of suspected tampering with legation mail see ibid., 7 Dec. 1897.

18. Ibid., 10 Sept. 1897.

19. Ibid.

20. Ibid.

21. Ibid., 12 Sept. 1897.

22. Originally the Navy appointed Sims as naval attaché to Paris, St. Petersburg, and Madrid. Prior to his arrival in Paris, however, the Navy decided that the Madrid legation required a full-time attaché and appointed Dyer, thus relieving Sims of all duties and responsibilities connected with that post.

23. Personal Papers of William Sowden Sims, Naval Historical Foundation Collection, Library of Congress, Washington, D.C.

24. GLD to SHPD, 8 and 24 Sept. 1897, Dyer Papers.

25. Ibid., 28 Mar. 1898.

26. Stewart L. Woodford to John D. Long, 24 Sept. 1897, Dyer Papers. At the same time Woodford sent a similar letter to Gen. Russell A. Alger, Secretary of War, concerning Bliss.

27. GLD to SHPD, 27 Sept. 1897, Dyer Papers.

28. Ibid.

29. Ibid., 1 Oct. 1897.

30. Throughout his correspondence Dyer refers to newspaper clippings he sent to both the Office of Naval Intelligence and to his wife. The collection of his personal papers does not contain these clippings. The Library of Congress, however, has a large collection of Spanish newspaper clippings from the Woodford diplomatic mission to Spain, September 1897–April 1898. These volumes undoubtedly contain the clippings Dyer frequently referred to in his correspondence with Roosevelt.

31. GLD to SHPD, 29 Sept. 1897, Dyer Papers. See also letters dated 10 and 19 Sept. and 11 Dec. 1897, 31 Mar. and 11 Apr. 1898 for other references to the press and public opinion.

32. Ibid., 11 Dec. 1897.

33. Ibid., 19 Sept. 1897.

34. The term "jingo" referred to those individuals who boasted of their patriotism and favored an aggressive, threatening, warlike foreign policy. It originated during the Russo-Turkish War of 1877–78 and was applied to members of the British Conservative party who urged the government to support the Turks. The name alludes to a popular song written and sung by George M'Dermott: "We don't want to fight, but by Jingo, if we do, We've got the ships, we've got the men, We've got the money too."

35. Diary SHD, 17 Feb. 1898, Dyer Papers.

36. GLD to SHPD, 10 Dec. 1897, Dyer Papers.

37. Ibid., 4 and 19 Sept. 1897.

38. Ibid., 19 Sept. 1897.

39. Ibid., 14 Sept. 1897.

40. Ibid., 30 Sept. 1897.

41. Ibid., 8 Dec. 1897.

42. Ibid., 10 Sept. 1897.

43. Diary SHD, 30 Mar. 1897, Dyer Papers. The Carlists, adherents of the pretender Don Carlos de Bourbon (1788–1855), the second son of Charles IV of Spain, supported his recognized successor, the exiled Don Carlos, and hoped to reclaim the Spanish throne for him.

44. GLD to SHPD, 31 Aug. 1897, Dyer Papers.

45. Ibid., 18 Sept. 1897.

46. Ibid., 10 Sept. 1897.

47. Ibid., 8 and 10 Sept. 1897. In a letter dated 4 Apr. 1898, Dyer wrote to his wife, "What a pity the *Oregon* is not around. I wanted her sent six months ago." No other reference, personal or official, to this recommendation seems to exist. Assuming Dyer recommended this move during the fall of 1897, it is reasonable to believe it appeared in one of his letters to Roosevelt or the Chief Intelligence Officer [CIO], Comdr. Richardson Clover. Unfortunately, no such letter remains in Roosevelt's papers, personal or official, or in any of the official correspondence between the naval attachés and the ONI.

48. GLD to SHPD, 18 Sept. 1897, Dyer Papers.

49. GLD to Theodore Roosevelt [TR], 23 Mar. 1898, RG 38, entry 90, NA.

50. GLD to SHPD, 24 Sept. 1897, Dyer Papers.

51. GLD to CIO, 12 and 16 Apr. 1898, RG 38, entry 90, NA. See also GLD to TR, 17 Apr. 1898, RG 38, entry 100, NA.

52. See Jeffery M. Dorwart, *The Office of Naval Intelligence* (Annapolis, 1979). Also see the various letters, cablegrams, and reports filed by Sims, Niblack, and Colwell in RG 38 and 45, NA.

53. TR to Commander-in-Chief, U.S. Naval Forces, 16 Feb. 1898, RG 45, entry 20, NA.

54. TR to John D. Long, 22 Jan. and 16 Feb. 1898, in *Papers of John D. Long, 1897–1904,* ed. Gardner Weld Allen (Massachusetts Historical Society, 1939), 41, 53.

55. TR to GLD, 5 Mar. 1898, RG 38, entry 90, NA.

56. GLD to CIO, 16 Mar. 1898, ibid.

57. In a cablegram sent on 12 Apr., Dyer identified the torpedo boats in the newly organized second torpedo squadron as the *Ariete, Habana,* and *Barcelo.*

58. GLD to TR, 16 and 19 Mar. 1898, RG 38, entry 100, NA.

59. Ibid., 9 Apr. 1898, ibid.

60. GLD to CIO, 12 Apr. 1898, RG 38, entry 90, NA.

61. GLD to TR, 17 Apr. 1898, RG 38, entry 100, NA.

62. GLD to CIO, 16 Apr. 1898, RG 38, entry 90, NA.

63. Tasker H. Bliss to TR, 20 Apr. 1898, RG 38, entry 100, NA.

64. GLD to CIO, 16 Apr. 1898, RG 38, entry 90, NA.

65. GLD to TR, 27 Mar. 1898, RG 38, entry 100, NA.

66. GLD to CIO, received 12 and 16 Apr. 1898, RG 38, entry 90, NA.

67. Ibid., 16 Apr. 1898, RG 38, entry 90, NA.

68. Diary SHD, 27 Mar. 1898, Dyer Papers.

69. GLD to CIO, 16 Apr. 1898, RG 38, entry 90, NA.

70. Ibid.
71. GLD to SHPD, 29 Mar. 1898, Dyer Papers.
72. Diary SHD, 27 Mar. 1898, Dyer Papers.
73. GLD to SHPD, 26 and 29 Mar. 1898, Dyer Papers.
74. Ibid., 15 Apr. 1898.
75. Diary SHD, 20 Apr. 1898, Dyer Papers.
76. GLD to SHPD, 10 Apr. 1898, Dyer Papers.
77. Ibid., 12 Apr. 1898.
78. Ibid., 14 Apr. 1898; GLD to TR, 23 Apr. 1898, RG 38, entry 100, NA.
79. Diary SHD, 23 Apr. 1898, Dyer Papers.
80. GLD to SHPD, 17 and 19 Apr. 1898; Diary SHD, 23 Apr. 1898, Dyer Papers.

American Intelligence During the Spanish-American War

DAVID F. TRASK

IN RECENT YEARS HISTORIANS HAVE PAID INCREASING ATTENTION TO the role of intelligence in the conduct of national security affairs. The activities of British intelligence services during World War II have been publicized extensively, and the American success in breaking the Japanese codes during that conflict has also evoked considerable notice. During the Cold War years, publicity about organizations such as the U.S. Central Intelligence Agency and the Israeli Mossad has engendered a growing preoccupation with intelligence.

Government planners, decision makers, and operators of all descriptions always begin with intelligence of some sort. The variables are the quality and quantity of the information to which the users have access. Whether sound or unsound, intelligence greatly influences the behavior of national security establishments, and the historian who seeks to comprehend the evolution of national security affairs is well positioned if informed about the intelligence available to the historical actors and the use they make of it. Successful national security operations, whether diplomatic or military in nature, always require sound intelligence. Conversely, unsuccessful operations frequently stem from inadequate information about the capabilities and intentions of others.

A fully rounded description and evaluation of intelligence is an important aspect of national security history, that is, the history of how nations pursue their interests and aspirations through international political-military activity. The task is daunting—on the one hand because of the secretive nature of intelligence and on the other hand because of the preoccupation of governments with protecting the sources and methods of intelligence. Even when historians acquire considerable evidence about intelligence, it is difficult to apply the conventional tests of historical evidence. The tests that historians practice, those of *authenticity* and *credibility*, become much more onerous than usual because the clandestine nature of intelligence introduces unaccustomed complications.

Recent works on the history of national security affairs reflect expanded scholarly interest in intelligence, but much remains to be done if historians are to exploit this subject fully. Although descriptive information about discrete intelligence activity appears regularly, what is often lacking is *synthetic description* that considers the connections between specific intelligence activities and a *general evaluation* of intelligence operations.

What follows is a description and evaluation of American intelligence during the brief Spanish-American War that stresses synthesis and evaluation. Historians now have extensive, discrete analyses of intelligence during the struggle of 1898; little specific information remains undiscovered or unstudied. What often is missing in the historical literature of this brief war, even in the extensive and excellent contributions of the past generation, is a full-blown attempt to consider intelligence in general terms: What intelligence activity took place? How good was American intelligence? Did it make useful contributions to the victory? Was there a consistent pattern of inadequacy? What improvements might have been made?[1] This examination of American intelligence during the war of 1898 considers intelligence as it influenced the conduct of the struggle by the U.S. government, an approach that suggests the following topics:

1. *The effect of intelligence before the war.* How did intelligence affect prewar plans and preparations?
2. *The effect of intelligence on wartime naval operations.* How did intelligence affect three important naval developments—Commodore George Dewey's attack on Adm. Patricio Montojo's squadron at Manila, Rear Adm. William T. Sampson's blockade of Cuba to counter the operations of Adm. Pascual Cervera in the Caribbean Sea, and Spain's attempt to send Adm. Manuel de la Cámara's naval squadron to the relief of Manila?
3. *The effect of intelligence on wartime military operations.* How did intelligence influence three important land campaigns—Maj. Gen. William R. Shafter's attack on Santiago, Maj. Gen. Nelson A. Miles's invasion of Puerto Rico, and Maj. Gen. Wesley Merritt's attack on Manila?

4. *The effect of intelligence on peacemaking.* How did intelligence influence the postwar settlement?

Prewar planning for a war with Spain began in response to the Cuban insurgency that began in 1895. The U.S. Navy undertook most of this effort because it was assumed that a struggle with Spain over Cuba would be primarily a naval war and because civil authorities concerned themselves mostly with efforts to arrange a peaceful settlement through diplomatic endeavors. The outcome was a series of war plans that reflected changes in Cuba up to the climactic month of April 1898, when the nation decided for war.

Naval planning was based on three banks of information. The Navy Department drew on public information from official and private sources. Also, it routinely had access to official diplomatic and consular reports forwarded to the State Department from embassies, legations, and consulates. Finally, it had its own representatives in several foreign nations including Spain, a group of naval attachés who served in embassies and legations abroad. These attachés submitted reports to the Office of Naval Intelligence (ONI) in the Navy Department. The task of the ONI, which was founded in 1882, was to prepare papers based on the data that it collected from various official and private sources. It provided most of the intelligence that guided the naval planners. It also prepared contingency plans, as did the Naval War College located in Newport, Rhode Island. More than once, plans were drafted by special groups formed in the Navy Department, usually groups that included representatives from the ONI and the Naval War College.[2]

A succession of naval plans provided the Navy with a sound basis for action in a war with Spain. As early as 1894 Lt. Comdr. Charles J. Train produced a plan at the War College. He speculated that the Spanish navy would operate in the Caribbean Sea from its principal European base at Cádiz. The United States would blockade the coast of Cuba, seizing various shore points to serve as coaling stations. A naval engagement would take place in the Caribbean between a depleted Spanish fleet forced to depend on distant and unreliable bases and a fresh U.S. fleet operating from adjacent bases. In 1895 another Naval War College plan added detail, reflecting the start of the Cuban insurgency in February of that year. The planners assumed that the motive for war was to help Cuba gain independence. They called for naval operations in the Pacific to prevent Spain from reinforcing its fleet in the Atlantic. Spain would need forty days to reinforce Cuba, allowing the United States an opportunity to land 280,000 troops for an attack on Havana, the principal center of Spanish strength. The insurgents would deal with the Spanish garrisons in eastern Cuba. For its trouble the United States would obtain a naval base on the Isle of Pines off the south coast of Cuba.

In 1896 an officer of the ONI stationed at the Naval War College, Lt. William Wirt Kimball, produced another plan that reflected the predominance of the Navy in a possible war with Spain. It added specificity to the proposal for operations in the Pacific. The Asiatic Squadron would conduct operations against Manila, the largest port in the Philippines. This action would assure a reasonable postwar indemnity because the United States would gain revenue from the trade of the island group. Possession of Spain's principal base in the Pacific also would preclude wartime operations against American commerce in East Asian waters.

Differences of opinion between the Navy Department and the Naval War College influenced later planning. In 1896 a department plan abandoned operations in the Pacific, calling instead for the conquest of the Canary Islands in the Atlantic. This accomplishment would provide a base from which to support operations against Spain in European waters. This measure would have divided the North Atlantic Squadron, a consideration that led the president of the Naval War College, Capt. Henry C. Taylor, to criticize the idea of operations in the eastern Atlantic and to call for concentration of the fleet in the Caribbean Sea. During the summer of 1897 another planning group in the Navy Department restored the attack on Manila, not only to distract the Spanish navy but to strengthen the American bargaining position during postwar negotiations.

In April 1898, just before the American intervention, a joint Army-Navy Board drew on previous planning to formulate the final war plan. The Navy would blockade Cuba immediately, and a small Army expedition would seize a port in eastern Cuba to provide a means of supplying the insurgents. Ensuing naval operations would establish command of the sea. If these endeavors did not force a peace, the Army, given some time to prepare a large force of volunteers to augment the Regular Army, would send an expedition of fifty thousand troops to seize Havana. Meanwhile, the Asiatic Squadron would attack the Spanish squadron at Manila.[3]

In March 1898 the Navy Department created an ad hoc organization, the Naval War Board, to offer advice on naval plans and operations. During the war its membership included Adm. Montgomery Sicard, Capt. Arent S. Crowninshield, the naval historian Capt. Alfred Thayer Mahan, and Secretary of the Navy John D. Long. Mahan wanted to replace the board with a single officer who would head a centralized general staff, but his recommendation did not prevail. The Naval War Board, greatly in need of information on which to base its advice, made extensive use of wartime intelligence.[4]

Although the naval planning process was in some ways haphazard or episodic, it led to war plans that reflected a generally sound evaluation of Spain's capabilities and intentions. The Navy derived from diplomatic, consular, and attaché reporting sufficient information to develop guidance for wartime operations that emphasized American strengths and exploited Spanish weaknesses. When the war began, the Navy's North Atlantic Squadron was poised at Key West to establish a blockade of Cuba, and the Asiatic Squadron at Hong Kong was prepared to move against Manila.[5]

No such extensive planning process developed in the U.S. Army. The War Department founded a Military Information Division (MID) in 1898 that was in some ways analogous to the ONI but did not have the benefit of a senior war college to help in planning. The MID's mission was to collect information on the geography, economic resources, and armed forces of the United States and other countries. Like the ONI, it issued instructions to attachés and collated attaché reports. Its most important function was to prepare mobilization plans for the components of the land forces—the Regular Army, the militia (National Guard), and volunteers that might be recruited in time of war. In 1898 the MID had twelve officers, ten clerks, and two messengers in Washington, working with forty officers attached to the National Guard and sixteen attachés. Its budget was a mere forty thousand dollars.

The general presumption that the Navy would play the leading role in wartime operations, which proved correct, accounts for the paucity of Army operational plans compared with those of the Navy. Still, the MID proved efficient in compiling information on the Cuban situation that was most useful when diplomatic efforts failed and the United States found itself forced to seek a military decision. It followed the Cuban insurgency carefully, recognizing that Cuba was the key to the defense of the projected interoceanic canal across Central America. Like the ONI, the MID relied on diplomatic, consular, and attaché reports for its information and on whatever data it could get from travelers, business people, and other private informants. The MID did not engage in espionage because peacetime activities of this nature were then deemed unethical.

By April 1898 the Army possessed the solid base of information it needed to develop operational plans in the event of war. In particular, it had accumulated accurate data about the Spanish order of battle in Cuba and the geography of the island, although it did not have a mature mobilization plan. Cooperation with the Navy had led to provisions for Army expeditions in support of naval operations in the Caribbean Sea, although not in the Philippine Islands. The War Department intended to concentrate the Regular Army in the American southeast, from where it would depart to conduct initial operations against Cuba. It also planned to prepare a large Volunteer Army that, when ready, would join the Regulars in an attack on the main concentration of enemy troops at Havana. The Army did not make plans for operations in the Philippines. The United States contemplated only a naval attack at Manila to accomplish limited objectives; no thought of annexation had yet surfaced in Washington.[6]

Commodore George Dewey was fully conversant with the Navy Department's plans for an attack on the Spanish naval squadron based at Manila under the command of Adm. Patricio Montojo. After moving the Asiatic Squadron from Japan to Hong Kong, Dewey set about obtaining information about the operational hazards that he might encounter in Manila Bay, especially the location of Spanish batteries and mine fields. For information about the Philippines, Dewey relied principally on reports from Manila that came from the new American consul in that city, Oscar F. Williams, although he also sought information from ship crews and business people who came to Hong Kong after leaving the Philippines. Williams's reports about the fortifications of the city confirmed Dewey's assumption that they did not pose serious difficulties. Dewey received accounts of mine fields in the entrance to Manila Bay with considerable skepticism, and Williams informed him that Montojo lacked the wire needed to detonate electrical mines.

Williams left Manila on 23 April for Hong Kong. Dewey was prepared to leave his anchorage at Mirs Bay when war was declared, but he delayed his departure until Williams arrived with the latest information. The consul reported that Montojo intended to move his squadron to Subic Bay on the South China Sea, some distance north of the entrance to Manila Bay. The information was accurate. Montojo took his dilapidated ships to Subic Bay but decided to withdraw to Manila when he discovered that work on batteries supposed to have been emplaced there had not been completed.

On 30 April, stopping at Subic Bay, Dewey found out that Montojo had returned to Manila, and he steamed through the entrance of Manila Bay during the hours of darkness without encountering serious opposition. On the morning of 1 May he found the Spanish squadron anchored near Cavite, several miles south of Manila. The American squadron formed a line and moved back and forth out of range of the Spanish ships, sinking all the enemy vessels while sustaining very little damage. Dewey's intelligence had helped to gain operational success.[7]

Although his information about the defenses of Manila Bay was adequate, Dewey mishandled another intelligence problem of great political sensitiv-

Thanksgiving Dinner at Manila

Oscar F. Williams had only been in Manila a short time before the outbreak of war with Spain. Though constantly watched, he was able to obtain and send valuable information to Dewey. On 23 April Williams left Manila to join Dewey's fleet. Joining it at Mirs Bay, he briefed the officers on the latest developments in the Philippines and returned with it to Manila. This photograph of the Consul General's Thanksgiving dinner at Manila is inscribed: "Merry Christmas to Admiral Dewey from O. F. Williams, U.S. Consul, Manila, P.I., December 25, 1898." Williams appears in the left foreground and from the uniform with a single star on the shoulder strap it appears that Dewey is seated to his right. *Courtesy of the Smithsonian Institution.*

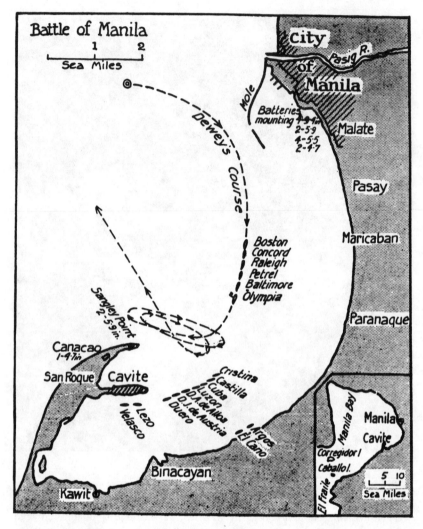

Battle of Manila Bay

Dewey's destruction of the Spanish fleet at Manila was facilitated by good intelligence, careful preparation, and an aggressive spirit. Diagram of the battle published in Herbert W. Wilson, *Battleships in Action*, 2 vols. (London, 1926). *Courtesy U.S. Naval Institute.*

ity—the nature of the Philippine insurgency against Spain and the intentions of its leader, Emilio Aguinaldo. Aguinaldo had left Luzon for Hong Kong after the failure of the first Philippine insurgency in 1896–97. In March 1898 he sailed for Europe. When he stopped at Singapore, the American consul there, E. Spencer Pratt, sought him out and then asked Dewey whether he desired Aguinaldo's presence. Dewey immediately replied affirmatively. Aguinaldo returned to Hong Kong too late to accompany Dewey to Manila, although one of his associates did so. Shortly after Dewey's victory, Aguinaldo was brought to Manila on the *McCulloch*, the American dispatch boat. Dewey encouraged him to resume leadership of the Filipino insurgency and lent him some assistance. The insurgents rapidly mobilized a formidable force that posed a serious threat to the city. Dewey made no political promises to Aguinaldo, and soon received specific instructions not to recognize him politically in any way. Although Aguinaldo later claimed that Consul Pratt and others had promised that the United States would support independence for the Philippines in return for assistance against the Spanish army, no one was ever authorized to make any such offer and it is unlikely that one was made.

Thus began the difficulties that complicated the activities of the Army expeditionary force sent to the Philippines to help Dewey capture the city of Manila. Preoccupied with his operations against Montojo and then with maintaining his squadron while awaiting the arrival of reinforcements, Dewey did not give sufficient attention to the consequences of dealing with the Filipino leader, thinking only of the help that Aguinaldo might offer and neglecting to consider the political complications that might arise.[8]

The intelligence effort associated with the Battle of Manila Bay had mixed results. It was fully sufficient to ensure operational success, but it did not consider the possible ramifications of encouraging Aguinaldo, who drew different conclusions about Dewey's actions than did the admiral. This outcome was not without precedent; field commanders have often failed to consider the political consequences of their operations, in part because of unsound political intelligence. When word of Aguinaldo's activities reached the United States, Dewey was immediately ordered to avoid political entanglements with the insurgent, but much of the damage had already been done.

Even before Dewey attacked at Manila Bay, Rear Adm. William T. Sampson blockaded Havana, the principal Cuban port, and began to close other coastal locations. This activity, following prewar plans, was intended to deprive the Spanish garrison in Cuba, numbering about 150,000 troops, of resupply and reinforcement. It was also designed to prepare the way for an attack on the main Spanish forces in Cuba located around Havana. The Army would make such an attack when it could mobilize sufficient troops, a matter of at least several months.

Meanwhile, the principal concern of the United States was to deal with a Spanish squadron of four armored cruisers and three destroyers which, under the command of Adm. Pascual Cervera, had left the Cape Verde Islands on 29 April en route to the Caribbean Sea. The Navy Department created a strong flying squadron commanded by Commodore Winfield S. Schley to maneuver against Cervera, initially basing it at Hampton Roads to counter possible enemy raids on coastal locations. The first step in countering the Spanish squadron was to locate it. The Navy Department made use of consular reporting for this purpose and dispatched several auxiliary cruisers to observe the routes available to Cervera. The *Harvard* and *St. Louis* were ordered to cruise east of the Windward Islands, and the *Yale* was posted east of Puerto Rico. These vessels could send information by cable from various ports in the Caribbean Sea.[9] Despite the American measures, Cervera managed to reach the Cuban coast. His original destination had been Puerto Rico. Sampson tried to intercept him there, taking a strong force to San Juan, which he bombarded briefly on 12 May, but Cervera had steamed to the French island of Martinique. Two of Cervera's destroyers visited Fort de France on 10 May, gaining information about Sampson's movement to Puerto Rico, and one disabled destroyer remained at Fort de France. Cervera decided to move farther west to the Dutch island of Curaçao, where he expected to find a collier to refuel his vessels. The Spanish squadron reached Curaçao on 14 May, but the expected collier had not arrived. Forced to leave the neutral Dutch port within forty-eight hours, Cervera decided to proceed northwestward to a location on the southeast coast of Cuba, Santiago. He entered that port on 19 May without encountering hostile vessels.

The auxiliary cruisers assigned to observe Cervera did not sight him. His landfalls at Martinique and Curaçao were quickly reported, but his arrival at Santiago went unobserved. The slow pace of Cervera's voyage—stemming from the poor repair of some of his vessels—and his unexpected southern route had the effect of concealing his movements, and his eventual refuge was a surprise. He had been expected at other locations—perhaps Havana, Cienfuegos, or San Juan.[10]

After Cervera's arrival in the Caribbean Sea became known in Washington, various dispositions were made to prepare for his appearance on the Cuban coast. Schley was first ordered to move to Charleston, and on 18 May he appeared at Key West. Sampson returned to Key West from Puerto Rico on the same day. The Navy Department then decided to keep Sampson at

Havana and to order Schley to blockade Cienfuegos. Auxiliary cruisers and other vessels were sent to guard three approaches to the north coast of Cuba—the passages off eastern Cuba, off Santo Domingo, and off western Cuba. Ports on the south coast of Cuba could be approached without going through any of the three guarded passages. It was deemed most unlikely that Cervera would go to Santiago because it lacked land communications to other parts of Cuba.[11]

Despite the auxiliary cruisers' failure to track down Cervera, another source of intelligence immediately reported his presence at Santiago. Before the war, an arrangement had been made to obtain reports of Spanish activity in Cuba from an agent located in the governor-general's palace in Havana. This agent, Domingo Villaverde, was a telegraph operator for an American cable company with an office in Key West, the International Ocean Telegraph Company, a subsidiary of the Western Union Telegraph Company. International Ocean owned several cable connections to Havana. When the company's manager in Key West, Martin Luther Hellings, received secret messages from Villaverde, he relayed them to a telegrapher in the White House, Benjamin F. Montgomery, who conveyed them to President McKinley. The president of Western Union, Thomas T. Eckert, was privy to these arrangements. When the war began, he transferred the Key West office to the Signal Corps. Hellings and Montgomery were later commissioned in the Signal Corps. To assure the highest degree of security, the existence of the Havana–Key West net was closely held; even Secretary of War Russell A. Alger was not informed of it.[12]

Word of Cervera's arrival at Santiago reached the White House almost immediately through the Havana–Key West connection. On 18 May Villaverde reported that Cervera was expected in Cuba soon, and on 19 May he saw messages from Cervera to Ramón Blanco, the governor-general of Cuba, reporting the Spanish squadron's landfall at Santiago. He quickly sent word to Key West and the message was then relayed to Montgomery. This information also went to Western Union headquarters in New York, from which Eckert immediately notified the War Department.[13]

The secrecy surrounding the intelligence network based in Key West contributed to a short delay in accepting its accuracy, but very soon the Navy Department and Rear Admiral Sampson decided that it was correct. Commodore Schley received orders to move eastward from Cienfuegos to Santiago. His failure to act promptly prevented the Flying Squadron from establishing a blockade at Santiago until 28 May. Cervera might have escaped, but his lack of enterprise played into the hands of the dilatory Schley. Sampson's North Atlantic Squadron arrived at Santiago on 1 June, thereby dooming

Cervera's forlorn squadron. Curiously, the Navy was unable to confirm that Cervera's ships were all at Santiago until 13 June, when Lt. Victor Blue, sent ashore to reconnoiter, reported that he had seen Cervera's four cruisers and two destroyers from a point northwest of the bay. Although the screen of vessels in the Caribbean missed Cervera and the Navy was slow in responding to the clandestine communication from Havana, the improvised intelligence system designed to track Cervera had served well enough.[14]

The early naval accomplishments of the war—Dewey's victory at Manila, Sampson's blockade of Havana, and the bottling up of Cervera at Santiago—set the stage for decisive land operations in Cuba, Puerto Rico, and the Philippines. President McKinley, who before the war had unsuccessfully concentrated on diplomatic efforts to resolve the Cuban crisis peacefully instead of through military and naval plans and preparations, now provided essential executive leadership, clarifying the war aims of the United States and preparing future operations against Spain. By early June the United States had decided that it sought, besides Cuban independence, the annexation of Puerto Rico (instead of a monetary indemnity), the annexation of an island in the Marianas to improve communications across the Pacific Ocean, and the annexation of some territory in the Philippines, yet undetermined. When Spain rejected a peace settlement on this basis, President McKinley authorized three Army expeditions of modest size to move against Spain's insular possessions, hoping that early and unrelieved pressure in several locations would induce Spain to end the war quickly. When Dewey's victory at Manila became known, McKinley ordered troops to the Philippines. Their mission was to gain control of Manila and its environs. After Cervera was blockaded at Santiago, McKinley decided to send an Army expedition to Santiago to capture that city and seize Cervera's squadron. After Santiago was secured, another expedition would attack Puerto Rico.[15]

The first order of business was to complete operations at Santiago by capturing the city and destroying Cervera's squadron. Most of the regiments of the Regular Army had been concentrated at Tampa and combined as the Fifth Army Corps under the command of Maj. Gen. William Rufus Shafter. A few volunteer units, including the First Volunteer U.S. Cavalry, known as the Rough Riders, joined the Regulars in the expedition to Santiago. Shafter was ordered to proceed quickly to Santiago, but his departure was delayed until 14 June because of confusion at the port of embarkation and faulty intelligence. On 1 June a report came from the naval attaché in Paris, Lt. William S. Sims, that some of Cervera's ships had departed for the Philippines. On 8 June, as Shafter prepared to depart from Tampa for Santiago, scouting vessels at sea reported the presence of two Spanish men-of-war in the St. Nicholas Channel north of Cuba astride Shafter's route. Sampson soon discovered that an American convoy of five ships had been mistaken for a Spanish detachment, but the expedition of seventeen thousand troops did not leave Tampa until Lt. Victor Blue of the *Suwannee,* one of Sampson's ships off Santiago, went ashore to make a visual reconnaissance and confirmed that Cervera's entire command was in the harbor.[16]

Meanwhile, the Army had made efforts to determine the military situation in eastern Cuba. Before the war began, the MID had accumulated considerable information about the terrain and the Spanish forces there. Early in April, Lt. Andrew S. Rowan was sent to the vicinity of Santiago by way of Jamaica with orders to contact the insurgents. He remained in Cuba between 23 April and 13 May, making contact with Gen. Calixto García, the commander of the Cuban insurgents in eastern Cuba, at Bayamo on 1 May. He then returned to the United States with two insurgent officers who provided valuable information. Two other men—the newspaper correspondent for the *New York Herald,* Fred O. Somerford, and Lieutenant Blue of the *Suwannee*—went to Cuba to interview the principal insurgent commander, Gen. Máximo Gómez, at Las Villas. When it became evident that Santiago would become an objective, Major General Shafter studied the unsuccessful British attempt of 1741 to take the city and also interviewed Maj. Frederick Funston of the Twentieth Kansas Infantry, who had fought with García during the earlier years of the Cuban insurgency. A careful student estimates that Shafter amassed more information about eastern Cuba than the Spanish garrison gathered in years of activity there. When Shafter arrived off Santiago, he immediately contacted García and from that time regularly received information from the insurgents, especially concerning Spanish dispositions and troop movements.[17]

After Shafter landed his army at Daiquirí and Siboney east of Santiago, he concentrated his forces around Las Guásimas and made plans to seize the city. Two considerations led him to attack before he had perfected his supply system and received reinforcements: intelligence received from the insurgents that a Spanish force of over eight thousand troops was moving from Manzanillo to reinforce the garrison at Santiago, and recognition that control of the harbor would alleviate his logistical difficulties. The decision to move swiftly precluded systematic reconnaissance of the ground between Las Guásimas and Santiago, especially the terrain and fortifications around El Caney and the San Juan heights, although the engineer officer, Lt. Col. George F. Derby, and one of the division commanders, Brig. Gen. Henry W. Lawton, developed useful information. Shafter incorrectly surmised that most of the Spanish forces were located near the entrance to the harbor at the Morro castle. Gen. Arsenio Linares, the Spanish commander, spread his forces thinly to cover all possible approaches to the city. Only about five hundred Spanish troops were positioned at El Caney, and another five hundred were on the San Juan heights. Shafter decided to move along an inland route northeast of the city instead of accepting the Navy's proposal that he advance near the shoreline protected by the guns of the naval squadron and attack the entrance to the harbor, clearing the way for a naval foray against Cervera's ships.

Shafter's plan of attack suffered from a lack of sufficient tactical intelligence; it did not provide adequate guidance for small-unit commanders. He decided to send Brigadier General Lawton's division against El Caney to eliminate a potential Spanish threat to his right flank. Then his main force, reinforced by Lawton's men moving forward along the road that connected El Caney and Santiago, would drive across the San Juan heights and seize the city.

Intelligence gaps contributed to the Fifth Army Corps' failure to capture Santiago in one bound, although the attack of 1 July gained control of the San Juan heights. The plan was compromised because Lawton did not reduce El Caney quickly. He did not reach the San Juan heights until long after the end of the battle, taking position on the right of the newly established line at noon on 2 July. The troops who attacked the San Juan heights on 1 July came under fire in congested roads and unfamiliar terrain. They were not given specific objectives, and they had trouble maneuvering into position below the heights. An observation balloon carried forward during the approach to the San Juan heights attracted enemy fire, but it also identified a previously unobserved path that allowed some units to position themselves effectively for an assault on the heights. Fortunately, the Americans eventually dislodged the few Spanish defenders and gained a commanding position from which to continue operations against the city. Instead of continuing, the disorganized and exhausted Fifth Army Corps dug in on the heights, shocked by the unexpectedly stubborn resistance of the Spanish defenders.[18]

Further gaps in tactical intelligence contributed to confusion after the battle of 1 July. The spirited enemy resistance at El Caney and the San Juan heights added to the illusion that the Spaniards possessed unsuspected numbers and strength. Shafter thought that his men had engaged twelve thousand enemy on 1 July. He and his subordinates did not realize that the Spanish garrison was in a desperate position, lacking sufficient troops, supplies, and equipment. The reinforcements expected from Manzanillo arrived at Santiago on 2 July, but they numbered only about thirty-five hundred worn-out men who placed additional strain on available resources. Shafter, who was ill during much of this period, at first considered withdrawal to positions farther from Santiago, but this suggestion was questioned in Washington.

Shafter's difficulties eased after 3 July: on that date Cervera's squadron was destroyed as it attempted to run Sampson's blockade, and soon reinforcements began to arrive from the United States, including portions of the expedition being organized to attack Puerto Rico. A determined assault, especially one supported by naval gunfire from Sampson's squadron, could easily have overrun the city, but Shafter instead decided on a siege. This cautious decision led inexorably to the Spanish capitulation of 17 July. Continuing anxiety about the difficulties of an assault on the city and about tropical disease led Shafter to settle for something less than unconditional surrender. The Spanish garrison and other troops in eastern Cuba were guaranteed passage to Spain in return for laying down their arms, an unnecessary but not unduly damaging concession. Inexperience and confusion, unavoidable consequences of haste, compromised Shafter's tactical intelligence at Santiago, but not enough to prevent ultimate victory.[19]

While the Army and the Navy concentrated their efforts on Santiago, Spain attempted to restore its position in the Philippines by sending a naval expedition eastward through the Mediterranean and the Indian Ocean. Adm. Manuel de la Cámara was given command of a squadron at Cádiz that included two armored vessels. Dewey, now promoted to admiral, did not have any ships of this nature. As early as 16 April the Navy Department ordered its attachés in Paris and London, Lts. William S. Sims and John C. Colwell, to determine the destination of the squadron at Cádiz. This task led to the creation of a spy network. Both Colwell and Sims hired secret agents to conduct espionage. Sims recruited agents to report on ship movements in the Canary Islands, Spain, and Egypt, and Colwell placed agents in England, Spain, Egypt, Belgium, and Portugal for similar purposes. This effort supplemented information gained from diplomatic and consular posts. On 26 May Sims reported that the squadron at Cádiz was destined for the Philippines, and Colwell provided the same information on 27 May. Besides establishing the attaché net, the Navy Department sent two ensigns, Henry H. Ward and William H. Buck, to England. Posing as Englishmen, they sailed from Liverpool to Gibraltar on chartered yachts with the task of observing Spanish ship movements. After reaching Gibraltar, Ward went to the Madeiras and then the Caribbean Sea, while Buck cruised in the Mediterranean. No one discovered that the two strongest Spanish vessels, the *Pelayo* and *Carlos V*, were never made fully ready for distant service.[20]

The Navy Department made several efforts to interfere with Cámara's expedition. It attempted to plant a story in Spain through one of Sims's agents to the effect that the American squadron at Santiago would move to Spanish waters after completing operations in the Caribbean Sea, hoping that this ruse de guerre would deter the departure of the Cádiz squadron. Sims was told that this story was possibly true or possibly false. On 11 June Sims was instructed to leak information through his agent in Spain that the American vessels at Santiago had been issued maps and charts of the Spanish coast, an attempt to enhance the credibility of the ruse. Also, the Navy Department dispatched two powerful monitors to the Philippine Islands to strengthen Dewey. The *Monterey* and *Monadnock* carried sufficient armament to counter the guns of Cámara's ships. Finally, the Navy Department prepared to send a strong detachment of armored ships in pursuit of Cámara, should he depart for the Philippines. On 18 June Sampson was notified that this Eastern Squadron would include three battleships—the *Oregon, Iowa,* and *Massachusetts.* As time passed the Navy Department revised the list of ships intended for the Eastern Squadron.[21]

Admiral Cámara left Cádiz on 16 June, and the United States observed his eastward progress carefully. By 5 July he had passed through the Suez Canal, but at this point he was recalled to Spain. The destruction of Cervera's squadron on 3 July left Spain exposed to an American naval attack. In any event, the catastrophe at Santiago convinced the Spanish government that it had to sue for peace. Cámara's recall canceled any threat to Dewey's position at Manila and ended all thoughts of sending the Eastern Squadron to European waters and beyond.

The extensive intelligence net set up to report on the Cádiz squadron provided timely and accurate information about its activities and eased the Navy Department's task of developing effective countermeasures. Had espionage detected the poor condition of Cámara's ships—they could not have posed a serious threat to Dewey—the Navy Department might not have worried as much as it did about the intentions and movements of the Cádiz squadron.

While the Fifth Army Corps conducted operations at Santiago, the commanding general of the Army, Maj. Gen. Nelson A. Miles, organized an expedition to invade Puerto Rico. Puerto Rico had become an American objective because it commanded the approaches to the projected isthmian canal and because its annexation would take the place of a monetary indemnity to defray the costs of the war. Miles had available a substantial amount of useful intelligence on Puerto Rico. On 15 May an Army officer, Lt. Henry H. Whitney, landed on the south coast of Puerto Rico at Ponce disguised as an

English sailor. After reconnoitering for ten days he returned to Washington, arriving there on 9 June. He brought valuable intelligence on the Spanish garrison, the topography of the island, the state of its harbors, and the political attitudes of the Puerto Ricans. Throughout this period, information also came from Philip C. Hanna, the late consul in San Juan, who communicated from a refuge in St. Thomas. Other reports came from Puerto Rican informants.

Miles was sent to Santiago to help Major General Shafter, but he left Cuba soon after the Spanish capitulation with the vanguard of his expedition to Puerto Rico. He was supposed to land at Fajardo, a point on the east coast of Puerto Rico not far from San Juan, which would have brought on an engagement with the main body of Spanish forces on the island. After leaving Cuba, however, he informed the surprised commander of his naval escort that he intended to steam to the opposite corner of the island and land at Guánica, giving as his reason the element of surprise. After getting his troops ashore at several locations on the south coast of Puerto Rico, Miles planned to strike north toward San Juan. He relied heavily on Whitney's information in shaping his operational plans, which reflected his dislike of frontal attacks and his preference for flanking and envelopment.

Miles's operations proved remarkably successful. In a campaign of less than two weeks he sent four columns northward with orders to converge on San Juan. His estimate of the situation proved accurate, and he was within striking distance of San Juan when he learned that the war had ended. During the movement north he benefited from several feats of tactical reconnaissance that uncovered unknown roads and allowed him to bypass serious obstacles. The Spanish defenders, like those at Santiago, were too few and too widely dispersed to organize a serious resistance.

Critics of Miles, among them Alfred Thayer Mahan, argued that his eccentric shift from Fajardo to Guánica created logistical difficulties and committed him to unnecessary movements over long distances and across difficult terrain. Although he gained surprise, was it proper to abandon the direct and short route to San Juan from Fajardo given the apparent weakness of the Spanish garrison? Whatever the wisdom of his plan, Miles's intelligence was sound, and he made good use of it while conducting a successful campaign.[22]

During June and July, Maj. Gen. Wesley Merritt, like Shafter and Miles a veteran of the Civil War, organized the troops assigned to the Philippine expedition and transported them to Manila Bay. Dewey's presence assured the Army of considerable intelligence regarding an attack on the city, but this information proved unnecessary. The Spanish garrison in Manila could not of-

fer serious resistance. Commodore Dewey recognized this fact and undertook negotiation of an arrangement with Manila's defenders that would
avoid armed action. The Spanish governor-general, Fermín Jáudenes, had
two concerns. First, he wanted to make an arrangement that would satisfy
his honor and that of his command, recognizing that, should he capitulate,
he would later have to face a court-martial. Second, he wanted to ensure that
the insurgents of Emilio Aguinaldo would be kept out of the city.

Dewey found a way to meet these requirements, making use of the Belgian consul in Manila, Edouard André, as a go-between in negotiations with
Jáudenes. The deal struck between Dewey and Jáudenes required that the
Americans make a token attack and that the Spanish garrison offer a token
defense before laying down its arms. It also specified that the Americans
would prevent Filipino insurgents from entering Manila proper. Major General Merritt was suspicious of this arrangement. Accordingly, he developed
operational plans that would allow his field commanders to storm the city
should Dewey's bargain with Jáudenes break down. He did not inform the
commanders of the two divisions designated to attack the city that their operations would be essentially a sham battle.

On 13 August the Americans moved against the city. After a few ex-
changes of fire the Spanish garrison displayed a white flag on the walls of the
city, and negotiations for a formal capitulation were begun. Some hitches developed, leading to unnecessary casualties, but the city was occupied without
serious fighting. The Americans fulfilled their part of the bargain and kept
the insurgents from penetrating the walled city of Manila, although they did
control some nearby suburbs.

Given the situation at Manila, tactical intelligence was of little importance, but another aspect of intelligence was of great significance—information about the capabilities and intentions of the insurgents. After Aguinaldo
resumed direct command of the insurgency in Luzon, he made rapid
progress in extending his authority. Much of his army was concentrated
around Manila, and he conducted independent operations designed to seize
the city. On 23 June he formed a civil government that took control of areas
where Spanish authority ceased to exist. The Filipino troops in the Spanish
army quickly went over to Aguinaldo. Aguinaldo rapidly conquered all Luzon except Manila and made considerable progress elsewhere in the Philippine Islands. Dewey and Merritt assumed that the insurgents could not take
Manila without American cooperation, an estimate that proved accurate.[23]

Commodore Dewey did not take Aguinaldo very seriously, in part because
of faulty advice. He relied on the former American consul in Manila, Oscar
F. Williams, the consul at Hong Kong, Rounsevelle Williams, and the Bel-

gian consul, Edouard André, for advice. These men argued that the principal objective of the insurgents was to get rid of the Spanish, and Dewey accepted this judgment. The consuls maintained that Aguinaldo would welcome—or at least tolerate—annexation to the United States. Preoccupied with his naval duties and under the illusion that the Filipinos would cooperate on future political arrangements as they had earlier on military matters, Dewey did not seek out sufficient information about the insurgents or provide thorough advice and counsel to Washington. He was content to observe his instructions, which precluded him from entering arrangements with the insurgents that might imply political recognition or acquiescence in independence. The Army commanders followed the same guidance. Both the Army and the Navy preserved acceptable relations with the insurgents while the war continued, but fundamental miscalculations of Filipino capabilities and intentions during the summer of 1898 led to extraordinary difficulties later. The McKinley administration, unaware that Aguinaldo was committed to independence, did not fully understand the state of affairs in the Philippines and did not do enough to head off future complications.[24]

The protocol signed in Washington on 12 August 1898 that ended hostilities specified the principal aspects of the postwar peace settlement except the disposition of the Philippine Islands. The Spanish government agreed to Cuban independence, the cession of Puerto Rico, and the cession of an island in the Marianas group. Only the Philippine question was left for the peace conference, which began its deliberations in Paris during September.

During the immediate postwar months, President McKinley made efforts to obtain solid facts about conditions in the Philippines, particularly about the insurgents, and he took steps to send this information to the American delegation in Paris headed by the former secretary of state William R. Day. Two high-ranking officers who had participated in the Philippine campaign, Major General Merritt and Brig. Gen. Francis V. Greene, were asked to report on conditions in the Philippine Islands. Merritt was sent to Paris, where he conveyed Dewey's views to the peace commission along with his own. Greene delivered his views in Washington. A naval officer, Comdr. Royal B. Bradford, also appeared before the peace commission. These informants added considerably to the U.S. government's knowledge of the insurgents.[25]

The issue before the president was whether to annex all, part, or none of the Philippine Islands. Advice from most of his military and naval counselors supported retention of the entire archipelago, although some, like Dewey, were circumspect. McKinley eventually decided to take all the islands, doing so without either sufficient intelligence about Aguinaldo's polit-

ical intentions or his military capabilities. The intelligence error that occurred during the summer of 1898 continued into the period of peacemaking.
Spain was forced to cede the Philippines. The U.S. Senate was asked to give
advice and consent to the peace treaty of 10 December 1898 without full information. Meanwhile, Maj. Gen. Elwell S. Otis, Merritt's successor in
command of the land forces in the Philippines, found himself often entan-
gled in and concerned about insurgent affairs, but like Dewey he did not
alert his superiors in Washington to the full dimensions of the problem. Annexation was in direct conflict with Aguinaldo's wish for independence. On
4 February 1899, just before the Senate voted on the peace treaty, hostilities
began between the American and Filipino forces around Manila. This development probably helped to decide the outcome of the vote in Washington,
which gave consent to ratification of the treaty.[26]

During the past generation, scholars who have investigated the war with
Spain have revised the prevailing historical interpretation measurably. Older
views—either that it was more a parody of war than a serious conflict or that
it was mishandled from first to last—are no longer tenable, although traces
of these interpretations still appear in textbooks.

This review of the role of intelligence during the war leads to findings that
are consistent with recent trends. Both the civilian government and the
armed services gained useful information from a considerable intelligence
effort as they developed plans and conducted operations during 1898, although certain endeavors were necessarily amateurish and some serious fail-
ures took place.

During the crisis that eventually led to war, the principal intelligence assets of the United States were diplomatic and consular reporting and the intelligence organizations of the Navy and War departments—ONI and
MID—both of which benefited from a network of attachés located in various embassies and legations overseas. There was no central collection or direction, and the United States had not yet developed a capability for espionage and covert operations. Those engaged in gathering intelligence did
not participate in policy making, but rather confined themselves to collecting
and processing information.

The exigencies of war required some improvisation to supplement existing
intelligence assets. The Navy used its attachés to organize a network of spies
in Europe that provided helpful information. Both the Navy Department
and the War Department sent agents into the field on special missions, notably to gain information from the Cuban insurgents and to track the movements of the Spanish navy. The Naval War Board made extensive use of in-

telligence in deciding on advice to be given to the McKinley administration, providing a degree of coordination. The weakest links in the intelligence network may have been those who conducted the tactical intelligence of the Army in combat situations, especially at Santiago. Like other aspects of operations in the field, tactical intelligence improved after the services overcame initial confusion and inexperience.

During the war, intelligence activity usually generated information adequate for planning and conducting field operations. Based on sound intelligence, Rear Admiral Sampson established an effective blockade of Cuba at the beginning of hostilities, and Commodore Dewey quickly defeated the Spanish squadron at Manila. Some confusion accompanied the search for Admiral Cervera's squadron as it steamed from the Cape Verde Islands to Santiago, but much of the difficulty stemmed from unsound command decisions, such as those of Commodore Schley, who dallied before finally blockading Cervera at Santiago. Intelligence collection before the land attack against Santiago on 1 July was far below par. The lack of correct information concerning the location of Spanish troops and fortifications led both to delay in reducing El Caney and to the difficulties encountered during the assault on the San Juan heights. Fortunately, the preponderance of American power at Santiago minimized the malign consequences of this intelligence failure.

By far the most important intelligence dereliction of the war was the failure to develop sound information about the capabilities and intentions of Aguinaldo and his insurgents. Commodore Dewey neglected this task during the summer of 1898, and General Otis, who took command at Manila after the end of the war, also neglected to provide Washington with sound appraisals of Aguinaldo's purposes, especially his commitment to independence for the Philippines. Accurate intelligence might have helped to head off the Philippine War of 1899–1902.

NOTES

1. This article does not attempt to add to the extant factual evidence available to historians. Its thrust is to synthesize information available in standard secondary works and to make a general evaluation of the intelligence effort. Citations are designed to guide the reader to convenient secondary summaries of the relevant information prepared by authorities who have conducted a careful examination of sources in recent years.

2. For the early years of the ONI see Jeffery M. Dorwart, *The Office of Naval Intelligence: The Birth of America's First Intelligence Agency 1865–1918* (Annapolis, 1979).

3. For prewar planning see David F. Trask, *The War with Spain in 1898* (New York, 1981), 70–85; Ronald Spector, *Admiral of the New Empire: The Life and Career of George Dewey* (Baton Rouge, 1971), 32–35.

4. Original members of the board included Capt. Albert S. Barker, Comdr. Richardson Clover, and Assistant Secretary of the Navy Theodore Roosevelt, but these men soon departed for active military duty. See Trask, *War with Spain*, 88–89; Robert Seager II, *Alfred Thayer Mahan: The Man and His Letters* (Annapolis, 1977), 369–70; Graham A. Cosmas, *An Army for Empire: The United States Army in the Spanish-American War* (Columbia, Mo., 1971), 74. For the records of the Naval War Board see U.S. Navy Dept., RG 45, NRC 371, Telegrams of the Naval War Board, 2 vols., and NRC 372, Correspondence of the Naval War Board, National Archives [NA], Washington, D.C.

5. For Adm. Alfred Thayer Mahan's postwar (1906) summary of the activities of the Naval War Board, "Narrative Account of the Naval War Board in 1898," see Robert Seager II and Doris D. Maguire, eds., *Letters and Papers of Alfred Thayer Mahan* (Annapolis, 1975), 3:627–43. For attaché reports see U.S. Navy Dept., RG 38, entry 100, "Correspondence with U.S. Naval Attachés during the Spanish-American War," NA, Washington.

6. For a summary of the Army's prewar intelligence activity and planning see Cosmas, *Army for Empire*, 30–32, 75. Cosmas concludes: "The Army, like the Navy, possessed all the essential facts about the character of the Cuban war and the forces engaged in it" (ibid., 76). See also Trask, *War with Spain*, 148–50. There is no study of the MID comparable in quality to Dorwart's work on the ONI.

7. For information about the activities of Oscar F. Williams see Charles Stuart Kennedy, *The American Consul: A History of the United States Consular Service, 1776–1914* (Westport, Conn., 1990), 198–202; G. J. A. O'Toole, *The Spanish War: An American Epic—1898* (New York, 1984), 176–78; Spector, *Admiral of the New Empire*, 45–47. For an older work of value on the events at Manila see Nathan Sargent, *Admiral Dewey and the Manila Campaign* (Washington, 1947).

8. Kennedy, *American Consul*, 202–5; Trask, *War with Spain*, 391–402; Brian Linn, *The U.S. Army and Counterinsurgency in the Philippine War, 1899–1902* (Chapel Hill, N.C., 1989), 6–7.

9. For the basic published correspondence of naval activity during the War with Spain see U.S. Navy Dept. *Annual Reports of the Navy Department for the Year 1898*, vol. 2, *Appendix to the Report of the Chief of the Bureau of Navigation* (Washington, 1898).

10. For Cervera's movements and the American efforts to observe his passage, see Trask, *War with Spain*, 111–18. For detailed information about the reports of enemy movements during the war see French Ensor Chadwick, *The Relations of the United States and Spain: The Spanish-American War*, 2 vols. (New York, 1911).

11. Trask, *War with Spain*, 119–21.

12. For a complete account of the Key West net see O'Toole, *Spanish War*, 207–9. The Florida entrepreneur Henry B. Plant also provided information on events in

Cuba. He owned a ship, the *Olivette*, which visited Havana three times a week. It was used to provide a courier connection between the consul-general at Havana, Fitzhugh Lee, and the naval headquarters at Key West.

13. Ibid., 212–14. Villaverde managed to communicate confirmation of Cervera's arrival on 20 May.

14. Blue's mission is described in Trask, *War with Spain*, 112. A long excerpt from his report is printed in Chadwick, *Spanish-American War*, 1:378–79.

15. For President McKinley's activities and the decisions to send expeditions to Santiago de Cuba, Puerto Rico, and Manila see Cosmas, *Army for Empire*, 103–5, 117–31, 176–88. See also Trask, *War with Spain*, 162–77, 339–46, 382–88. The basic collection of published documents on the activities of the Army is U.S. War Dept., *Correspondence Relating to the War with Spain and Conditions Growing Out of the Same . . . from April 15, 1898, to July 30, 1902*, 2 vols. (Washington, 1902).

16. Trask, *War with Spain*, 186–88.

17. Cosmas, *Army for Empire*, 189–90; O'Toole, *Spanish War*, 203. For Rowan's remembrance of his activities see his pamphlet *How I Carried the Message to Garcia* (San Francisco, 1922).

18. Graham Cosmas has examined the battle in his *Army for Empire*, 205–17, and in a more detailed manner in his "San Juan Hill and El Caney, 1–2 July 1898," in *America's First Battles: 1776–1965*, ed. Charles E. Heller and William A. Stofft (Lawrence, 1986), 109–48. In *Army for Empire*, 214, he wrote that Shafter had planned to seize the city in one bound, but in his later analysis he maintains that Shafter's "purpose for 1 July appears to have been to secure a favorable position for subsequent assault or siege while blocking enemy reinforcements" ("San Juan Hill and El Caney," 123). For my opposing view see *War with Spain*, 225–56. For an extended discussion of the use of the observation balloon see O'Toole, *Spanish War*, 309–11.

19. Cosmas, *Army for Empire*, 215–16, 222–23. A more detailed account of postbattle developments is in Trask, *War with Spain*, 286–319.

20. For information concerning the mission of Adm. Manuel de la Cámara, see Trask, *War with Spain*, 270–85. For the activities of the spy network see O'Toole, *Spanish War*, 227–29. Seager notes the failure to discover the disrepair of the Spanish vessels in *Alfred Thayer Mahan*, 383–84. For the missions of Ensigns Ward and Buck see Trask, *War with Spain*, 88. See also Dorwart, *Office of Naval Intelligence*, 61–65.

21. O'Toole, *Spanish War*, 228–29, 252; Trask, *War with Spain*, 143.

22. For the Puerto Rican campaign see Cosmas, *Army for Empire*, 230–36; Trask, *War with Spain*, 336–68.

23. For extensive information on the land campaign at Manila see Cosmas, *Army for Empire*, 236–42; Trask, *War with Spain*, 369–422.

24. Spector, *Admiral of the New Empire*, 84–90.

25. The Navy aborted its spy network soon after the end of the war. Sims asked the peace commission whether it wished to retain his informant, but it decided not to do so. Colwell simply informed the commission that his activities were being

stopped. A member of the commission, Whitelaw Reid, recorded this information in his diary, observing: "The Commissioners were quite satisfied [with the suspension of espionage], several of them expressing a strong dislike for this whole spy business" (H. Wayne Morgan, ed., *Making Peace with Spain: The Diary of Whitelaw Reid September-December 1898* [Austin, 1965], 42).

26. For the negotiation of the protocol of 12 Aug. 1898, the negotiation of the peace treaty of 10 Dec. 1898, and growing Filipino-American tensions from Aug. 1898 until Feb. 1899 see Trask, *War with Spain*, 423–72; Linn, *Counterinsurgency,* 8–12.

William T. Sampson and Santiago: Blockade, Victory, and Controversy

JOSEPH G. DAWSON III

WILLIAM T. SAMPSON IS ONE OF AMERICA'S UNHERALDED NAVAL HEROES. Before 1898 Sampson established a creditable record of service, fulfilling a variety of tasks and assignments, most having to do with administration or technology rather than command at sea. But in the months prior to the war with Spain Sampson found himself well positioned to receive one of the three top postings in the U.S. Navy—command of the North Atlantic Squadron. And with that assignment he had the opportunity to crown his career with combat victory at sea.

Sampson earned his opportunity at high command through diligence and through developing technological expertise. One of seven children born to Scotch-Irish working-class parents, Sampson became a model pupil in the schools of Palmyra, New York, and through merit rather than politics gained an appointment to the U.S. Naval Academy in 1857. His cadet years reflected his dedication to his studies, as Sampson excelled in the sciences and engineering, holding first place in his class during three of his four years at Annapolis and graduating first of twenty-seven cadets in 1861.[1]

During the Civil War Sampson received a variety of assignments ashore and afloat, including two years as instructor at the Naval Academy. In 1864 he was posted as executive officer in the Union monitor *Patapsco*, a part of Rear Adm. John A. B. Dahlgren's South Atlantic Blockading Squadron. On the night of 15 January 1865 *Patapsco* struck a Confederate submarine torpedo (mine) in the harbor of Charleston, South Carolina. Sampson, standing on the turret when the mine exploded, was one of the *Patapsco's* few survivors.[2]

After the Civil War Sampson occasionally served at sea, but he made his mark in the Navy through administrative or technological billets. He taught at Annapolis in the Department of Natural Philosophy, and twice occupied the position of head of the department, which later changed its name to "Physics and Chemistry." Sampson stressed that the modern naval officer "should be prepared by scientific training to adapt himself to the great and rapid changes that are liable at any moment to arise in his profession." Conducting a number of his own scientific experiments, Sampson also encouraged the scientific work of others, most notably the successes of Ens. Albert A. Michelson and his measurement of the velocity of light.[3]

With interludes at sea, Sampson further established himself in scientific and technical assignments in the 1880s. He was assistant superintendent of the Naval Observatory at Washington, D.C. (1882–1884), and joined with Adm. Stephen B. Luce in recommending the creation of the Naval War College. In 1884 Sampson became inspector of ordnance at the Torpedo Station, Newport, Rhode Island, where he and his staff applied their scientific skills to the testing of explosives, mines, and detonators. In 1885, as one of the nation's experts on coastal defenses, he served on the Endicott Board, chaired by Secretary of War William C. Endicott. This board issued a lengthy report in January 1886 concerning coastal fortifications, including an appendix by Sampson entitled "Floating Batteries."[4] Concluding his duties in the 1880s, Sampson returned to the Naval Academy as superintendent. He instituted a number of reforms and improvements, such as instigating a campaign against hazing among cadets; modernizing equipment, laboratories, and the library; and setting new rules on cadet morals and hygiene. Most significantly, however, Sampson authorized the special evaluation of cadets called the "aptitude for the service grade," a score that continues to be one of the most important that prospective officers receive while they are at the academy.[5]

Sampson's duties as superintendent ended in 1890, when he was transferred to command the protected cruiser *San Francisco*, which was under construction in California. When Sampson moved west his family went with him. He had been married to Margaret S. Aldrick of Palmyra, by whom he had four daughters. Margaret died in 1878, and in 1882 Sampson married Elizabeth S. York, with whom he had two sons. Sampson served on the *San Francisco* for less than two years before receiving new orders returning him to the East and another technological billet—inspector of ordnance at the Washington Navy Yard.[6] After about a year in this position, Sampson became chief of the Bureau of Ordnance (January 1893–May 1887). In this post at the nation's capital, Captain Sampson supervised the construction of the naval gun factory and the manufacture of gun mounts for capital ships; inspected the quality of gunpowder from private contracting firms such as E. I. DuPont de Nemours and Company; and evaluated turning systems for gun turrets and new turret designs for the Navy's ships. Sampson always maintained the highest standards and demanded the best quality steel armor that American industry could produce, rejecting substandard or second-rate armor, even that produced by the most well-known firms.[7]

By mid-1896 American political and military leaders began to pay increasing attention to the rebellion in Cuba against Spanish imperial control and, in December, Secretary of the Navy Hilary Herbert convinced a special advisory board (including Sampson) to draft naval contingency plans in case of war between the United States and Spain. The board drafted a plan, one of several such contingency plans filed in the Navy Department prior to the declaration of war. Sampson's service near Secretary Herbert and his seniority placed him in line for a prized assignment in 1897—command of the 11,000-ton battleship *Iowa*, the Navy's most modern ship.[8]

Taking his coveted assignment in the *Iowa*, Sampson, at age fifty-seven could look back on thirty-six years of service in the Navy. He appeared well and ready for his new command but, although it seems to have escaped the notice of most around him, his health was declining. Due to the lack of specific records or clinical descriptions, it is not possible to specify what malady was ruining Sampson's health, but it may have been Alzheimer's disease.[9] In the nineteenth century American military officers faced no regular medical examinations as a routine of service life; thus Sampson hid his medical problems from all but his closest family and staff members. He was not the only senior military officer who hoped to stretch his time on active service; in fact, most officers of whatever rank intended to stay on duty for as long as possible in order to receive their full paychecks. Sampson's Army counterpart in the Santiago campaign, Maj. Gen. William R. Shafter (who at age sixty-three was 6 feet tall, weighed 300 pounds, and suffered from gout and other medical troubles), was in such poor health that he should have been excluded from active field service. These facts only confirmed the need for such military reforms as routine medical examinations for officers, reconsideration of longevity in the service, and adequate retirement pay.

Due to worsening relations between the United States and Spain in 1898, President William McKinley sent the battleship *Maine* to Havana as a symbol of American interest in Cuba. On 16 February a terrific detonation shattered the *Maine* and killed more than two hundred members of the crew. No matter who or what had caused the explosion, the destruction of the *Maine* increased the likelihood of war between the United States and Spain. President McKinley wisely dispatched a court of inquiry to the scene in an effort to determine the cause of the explosion. Because of his technological expertise, Sampson was appointed president of the court, which included his close friend Capt. French E. Chadwick. On 21 March the investigators reported that the *Maine* had been destroyed by an explosion caused by an unknown external source. Although subsequent modern investigations indicated that an internal explosion—perhaps the spontaneous combustion of coal adjacent to ammunition magazines—had blown up the ship, Sampson remained convinced that the *Maine* had been "destroyed by [an] external agency."[10]

Less than a week after the *Maine* court of inquiry completed its report, Sampson became commander of the North Atlantic Squadron, the Navy's most prestigious billet. Commensurate with this posting, on 21 April Sampson was made acting rear admiral, a rank that lifted him above a dozen officers previously his senior, including the flamboyant Winfield Scott Schley, who took command of the independent Flying Squadron, designed to thwart Spanish raids on the east coast of the United States. Sampson's temporary promotion demonstrated that old seniority rankings would not necessarily dictate wartime postings. Unfortunately, Sampson lacked charisma and was noted for his aloof public demeanor; a friend once called him "statuesque and unemotional." Sampson's personality did nothing to pacify officers who had been passed over for squadron commander.[11]

Sampson saw his primary duty as the defeat of Spanish naval forces that entered North American waters. In fact, Adm. Pascual Cervera and a six-ship squadron were expected to arrive soon in the Caribbean. In the meantime, Sampson planned to assist a U.S. Army expeditionary force and prepare a blockade of ports in the Spanish-held islands. As expected, President McKinley issued orders for a blockade. Sampson's squadron steamed first to Havana, Cuba, and, leaving vessels off that port, sailed on to San Juan, Puerto Rico, and bombarded the forts there on 12 May. The venture to Puerto Rico gave the squadron operating experience, gunnery practice, and the information that Cervera was not in San Juan. The latest intelligence, received at Cap Haitien, Haiti, related that Cervera's ships had called at Curaçao and then departed on 15 May. Secretary of the Navy John D. Long ordered American forces to rendezvous at Key West, Florida. Sampson recoaled his ships there and Commodore Schley brought the Flying Squadron in on 18 May. The Americans had stationed dispatch boats to watch for Cervera, but the Spanish avoided detection and sped from Curaçao to the port of Santiago on the island's southeast shore.[12]

Schley's Flying Squadron moved out on 19 May and headed for Cienfuegos, Cuba, near the southwestern end of the island, where Cervera may have been bound. But that evening the Navy Department informed Sampson that the enemy had reached Santiago instead. During the next three days Secretary Long tried to convince Sampson of Cervera's whereabouts and wanted his admiral to order Schley to establish a blockade at Santiago. At first Sampson doubted Long's reports, and these doubts weakened his orders to Schley. For example, this message from Sampson reached Schley on 23 May: "Spanish squadron *probably* at Santiago de Cuba—4 ships and 3 torpedo boat destroyers. *If* you are satisfied that they are not at Cienfuegos, proceed with all dispatch, *but cautiously* to Santiago de Cuba, and *if* the enemy is there blockade him in port" (emphasis added). Schley himself appeared to remain unconvinced that Cervera was in Santiago, although he made no direct effort to investigate the port at Cienfuegos. Finally, on 24 May Schley learned conclusively that Cervera was not in Cienfuegos and, hampered by slow colliers and a selective interpretation of his orders, steamed cautiously toward Santiago.[13]

Schley arrived off Santiago on 26 May but shortly gave orders that aggravated Long, alarmed Sampson, and left his squadron officers perplexed. First, Schley accepted hearsay information that the Spanish ships were not at Santiago and took no action to determine Cervera's location, and second, he decided, against orders, to return to Key West. Claiming that heavy seas prevented recoaling his ships near Santiago, Schley ordered the Flying Squadron *westward*, back toward Cienfuegos. After steaming slowly for a day, Schley directed his ships to pause and for seventeen hours they idled with no orders. Capt. Robley Evans, commanding the *Iowa*, recalled: "As there had been no conference of commanding officers, we were all completely bewildered as to what this peculiar maneuvering might mean." If Schley sought calmer waters for recoaling, he could have waited off Santiago and in the meantime established the blockade, as he had been directed. Upon learning that Schley abandoned station off Santiago, Secretary Long had solid grounds for removing him from command. Removing Schley would have brought on a public outcry and probably prompted an investigation, but replacing him for cause in May would not have led to any greater controversy than exploded six weeks later between Schley and Sampson. Expecting the best from the flamboyant commodore and allowing for some degree of miscommunication, Long reacted to Schley's bewildering behavior with unmistakable orders: confirm that Cervera's squadron is in Santiago. Furthermore, Long lectured Schley on the basics: "You must surmount difficulties regarding coaling by your own ingenuity and perseverance."[14]

Not only had Long become testy with Schley, but Sampson's patience was wearing thin as well. Sampson, giving his attention to matters regarding Havana and other campaign preparations, sent a number of messages to Schley. Indicative is one dated 27 May: "You will please proceed with all possible dispatch to Santiago to blockade that port. If, on arrival there, you receive *positive* [original emphasis] information of the Spanish ships having left you will follow them in pursuit." These clear orders spelled out plainly Schley's course of action, but given the possibility of trapping Cervera in Santiago, it was time for Sampson to take charge there. Meanwhile, disputes among the Spanish officials in Santiago, who used an undersea cable to communicate with the home government, kept Cervera anchored and inactive during Schley's maneuvers.[15]

Early on the morning of 1 June the North Atlantic Squadron arrived at Santiago and the blockade became Sampson's responsibility. Assuming that he had Cervera bottled up, Sampson allowed several days to pass before a reconnaissance verified the strength of the enemy force. Sampson found Schley's blockading dispositions unsatisfactory, and consequently the admiral designed his own close blockade, "gradually shortening the radius of the [blockade's] arc of patrol from six to four miles during the day and to three at night." Relying on his technological expertise, on 8 June Sampson ordered his ships to keep a constant vigil at night using high-powered searchlights. Searchlight duty rotated through the appropriately equipped ships, which trained the big lamps on the mouth of the harbor. Furthermore, the admiral formulated precise pre-battle stations for each ship, with their bows aimed at the channel, and gave blanket orders too "close in towards [the] harbor entrance" should the Spaniards come out to offer battle. Thus by mid-June Sampson had put in place a textbook version of a blockade, one appreciated and complimented by most of his subordinates. These officers later agreed with John W. Philip, captain of the *Texas:* it was "the blockade that made the battle [of Santiago] possible."[16]

If the blockade paid off in a battle, the Spanish navy would face reorganized American forces. On 21 June Sampson's squadron was renamed the North Atlantic Fleet. The Flying Squadron ceased to exist as an independent command and Schley became the second-ranking officer in the new fleet. Additional American vessels arrived on station, giving Sampson eighteen vessels under his command—overwhelming strength in contrast to the six ships under Cervera's control plus a few auxiliaries otherwise in port. As the U.S. fleet gained strength, the excitement of the wartime footing gave way to duller routine. The Americans tried to keep alert, operated the searchlights, and sometimes left station to recoal at the captured base of

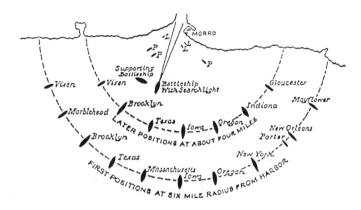

Diagram of the Blockade of Santiago Harbor

William T. Sampson carefully planned the disposition of his forces outside Santiago harbor. The blockade marked the first use of searchlights in naval warfare. This diagram is taken from William T. Sampson, "The Atlantic Fleet in The Spanish American War," *Century Illustrated Magazine* 57 (Apr. 1899), reprinted in *The United States Navy in the Spanish-American War of 1898* (1899).

Blockade of Santiago

Carlton Chapman sketched Sampson's squadron blockading Santiago Harbor. Sampson's flagship, the *New York*, is in the center with the yacht *Gloucester* to its left and the *Suwannee* to the right. Published in *Harper's Weekly* with the title "The Operations against Santiago, July 1—combined Sea and Land Attack at Aguapores." *Courtesy of the Naval Historical Center.*

Guantanamo, Cuba. Occasional distractions intruded: rumors of a second Spanish task force coming toward Cuba rang false; a dangerous attempt to sink an old American collier near the harbor entrance failed to block the channel and resulted in the capture of the collier's volunteer crew; Sampson received Gen. Calixto Garcia, one of the Cuban insurgent leaders, on the flagship, *New York;* and Secretary Long tinkered with the idea of creating an Eastern Squadron that would have siphoned away some of the ships from Sampson's fleet, but eventually dismissed the idea.[17]

Overriding these distractions came a serious challenge to Sampson's ability to conduct the campaign, one that proved to be almost greater than that of the Spanish squadron: cooperating with Maj. Gen. William Shafter, leader of the Army expeditionary force. In contrast to the American and Western Allied unified commands in twentieth-century wars (arrangements that still had their share of strains and difficulties), the Santiago campaign had no unified commander, despite the fact that the actions of the two services required close coordination. Without a unified commander for the Cuban campaign, Sampson was forced to share responsibilities with Major General Shafter, a choleric officer who possessed an outstanding record as an Indian fighter and Southwestern explorer but whose small-unit experiences, advanced age, and poor health ill-suited him for a major overseas command. Shafter may be seen as the stereotype of an Army officer whose career wilted from serving in isolated frontier forts, who seldom saw regiments gathered together for drills or training, and who appeared unconcerned about issues of strategy and military reform.[18]

Sampson and Shafter clashed virtually from the instant the campaign began. The first point of contention arose over where to put the Army ashore in Cuba. That point was solved easily enough but opened relations between the commanders on a sour note. Moreover, the initial disagreement indicated that U.S. military forces had no routine steps established for staff officers to meet together, consider common problems, and draft joint operations orders. To be fair to both parties, there were no field manuals for joint operations in 1898, and the experience gained from combined operations in the Civil War had lain dormant since 1865. In contrast to the late twentieth century, when American military doctrine said that "jointness is everything," the deficiencies of interservice coordination in 1898 emphasized the demand for reform in America's armed forces.

Another breakdown in communication and cooperation between Sampson and Shafter occurred on a more substantial matter. Shafter contended that if Cervera's squadron would not come out then Sampson's fleet must go into Santiago harbor. Of justifiable concern to the Army commander was the capability of the guns on Cervera's ships to fire on American soldiers as they marched on the city. Accordingly, Shafter concluded that his army would skirmish with the Spanish but that a naval attack through the channel should precede the Army's major assault to capture the city. How the Navy surmounted obstacles such as submarine mines in the channel and well-placed shore batteries was Sampson's concern. On the other hand, Sampson planned to operate according to Secretary Long's orders, which forbade him to place his capital ships at risk in a mined channel covered by guns on shore. In fact, standard U.S. Navy doctrine advised against direct attack of coastal fortifications with capital ships. Thus Sampson proposed to Shafter a mirror-image plan calling for the Army (with support from Cuban insurgents) to knock out the Spanish works covering the channel, after which the Navy could carefully clear the mines, allowing the battleships and cruisers to pass through undamaged. Sampson and Long naturally concurred with Alfred Thayer Mahan: "If we lost ten thousand men [soldiers], the country could replace them; if we lost a battleship, it could not be replaced." All of the senior naval leadership believed that the loss of three or four American capital ships would be a catastrophe resulting in a serious lowering of national morale. Such a loss, coming from mines and with no loss to the Spanish ships, would seem to bring the two fleets closer to equality, despite the facts that the Americans proved to be dominant in terms of gunnery, quality of ammunition, engine power, and their ships' general serviceability. With some bitterness, Shafter, supported by Secretary of War Russell Alger and most other Army officers, argued that soldiers were risking their lives not only in battle but also in disease-ridden jungles and fever-plagued trenches while Sampson and his sailors enjoyed safe duty at sea. This rift between the two commanders never healed.[19]

Meanwhile, as the Navy assisted in landing Shafter's troops at Daiquiri and Siboney (22–24 June), the governor-general of Cuba, Ramon Blanco y Erenas, received authority from Spain to take charge of all his nation's military forces on the island, including Cervera's squadron. The deplorable condition of these ships seems to have been unknown to the Americans: fouled bottoms significantly reduced the ships' speed; three of the principal Spanish ships (the armored cruisers *Cristóbal Colón*, *Vizcaya*, and *Almirante Oquendo*) either had missing or inoperable main battery guns; and some of the powder or shells stored in the Spanish magazines was overage or of poor manufacture. In short, Cervera's squadron needed to be overhauled and resupplied.[20] A perceptive officer of good judgment, Cervera reasoned that he would be in error to take out his ships and engage the Americans. But on 1 July, pressured to act by the president and his cabinet, Shafter launched a series of demonstrations against Spanish positions at San Juan heights and El Caney outside Santiago. These actions, in turn, helped to convince Governor-General Blanco that Cervera must sortie. The Spanish high command, already concerned about the vulnerability of Cervera's squadron should the city fall, may have misinterpreted the American attacks as coming from strength. Consequently, Blanco, who did not want to abjectly surrender the squadron, told Cervera to make the breakout and, with reluctance, the admiral complied.[21]

Offshore, Sampson understood that some of his vessels needed fuel and instructed the battleship *Massachusetts,* the cruisers *New Orleans* and *Newark,* and the auxiliary *Suwannee* to coal at Guantanamo on Sunday, 3 July. Allowing these ships to leave station together significantly reduced the strength of Sampson's fleet, but it still possessed a weighty advantage over Cervera's squadron.[22] In addition to fleet logistics, Sampson attended to relations with the Army, exchanging messages with Shafter. Unable to reach agreement with the general on several matters, the admiral decided to meet with Shafter again on 3 July; they had held an earlier meeting ashore on 20 June. Shafter's gout restricted him to his tent, preventing him from going to a shipboard meeting, and he had implored the admiral to come ashore once more. Indeed, Sampson had not been feeling well either. W. A. M. Goode, an Associated Press correspondent accorded a place on the American flagship, noted that Sampson "was not in very good health, and was well-nigh worn out with the tremendous strain of the past month. . . . The physical and mental strain . . . had confined him once or twice to his bed." The admiral's assistant chief of staff later remarked that "the uncertainty and anxiety of those days will never be forgotten by any one who shared them." Whatever the strain had been, on 3 July Sampson was physically capable of leaving his ship; he laced his leggings and buckled his spurs for the anticipated horseback ride to meet Shafter near Siboney. Sampson paced nervously on the bridge of the *New York.* Goode remembered Sampson saying, "If I leave, I'm sure something will happen."[23]

A few minutes before 9:00 A.M., the *New York* steamed out of its spot near the blockade arc, taking Sampson toward the rendezvous with Shafter. Capt. French E. Chadwick, Sampson's usually reliable chief of staff, had devoted the necessary time to arrange the conference with the Army, but he evidently forgot to inform Schley and other officers of Sampson's destination. There was no official transfer of command, but in Sampson's absence the role of senior American officer devolved upon Schley. Otherwise it was a routine Sunday morning: sailors began assembling for regular Sunday inspections, officers in white dress uniforms stepped along ranks of enlisted men standing at attention, and chaplains prepared for church services. Admiral Cervera knew the Americans' Sunday morning rituals and had chosen the best day to attack. By 9:25 A.M. the *New York* was almost out of signal distance. At about that time American lookouts noticed smoke in the channel and shouted the warning down to their duty officers. Then came the call: "They're coming out!" Capt. John Philip paused momentarily to note the time: 9:36. Signal flags snapped up in Robley Evans's *Iowa*: "Enemy attempting to escape." Throughout the American fleet bugle calls or electric gongs sent crewmen rushing to general quarters. Captains immediately issued a stream of orders: "Clear ship for action!" "Hoist the battle-flags!" "Lay aloft range-finders in the tops!" As his men hurried to their battle stations, Capt. John Philip of the *Texas* looked toward the harbor mouth. Decorated with streamers and flags, "the Spanish ships came out as gaily as brides to the altar."[24]

Sampson's long-standing orders to "close in towards [the] harbor entrance" automatically went into effect. In the clamor of the moment the Americans almost suffered a crippling blow: because of confusing or misconstrued orders on the bridge of the *Brooklyn* (Schley's ship), it nearly collided with the *Texas*. The ships avoided one another, with the *Brooklyn* looping away from the enemy, but soon both charged off in pursuit of Cervera, who led his ships west toward the Gulf of Mexico.[25]

Nine miles away from the opening battle, the *New York's* spotters had also seen the smoke from the funnels as the Spanish ships cleared the channel. Fearing that all his hopes of a sea victory would be dashed before his eyes, Sampson barked orders to the *New York's* helmsman to "turn back immediately." Captain Chadwick promptly directed "the chief engineer to get up all the steam possible." A few minutes later Sampson ordered a signal to his fleet: "Close in towards harbor entrance and attack vessels." The admiral's next thought was: "Oh, that we had wings!" The *New York* lurched ahead, racing to join the battle before it was over.[26]

Crucial to subsequent American debate over the battle was Cervera's decision to turn west. He rejected a melee near the channel entrance, after which his ships would scatter. Instead he ordered them to steer away from the strength of the American fleet. If one faced the channel, most of the U.S. Navy's blockaders were on the right side due to the departure of some ships to coal at Guantanamo, ships that would have been potential reinforcements for the Americans. Moreover, Cervera's turn to the west took the Spanish squadron away from Sampson himself. Had Cervera turned east he would have sent his ships toward Sampson and thus the admiral's ship would have directly participated in the battle, perhaps even allowing Sampson to play a crucial role in the defeat of the Spaniards. Instead, no American officer—not even Schley—maintained direct command of the American fleet during the fighting. Even Sampson admitted later that "in a very few moments from the first shot each [American ship] had decided what she was going to do." In other words, the American captains were unable to abide by Sampson's plan to limit the battle to a small area near the channel mouth. Meanwhile, Sampson stood by in frustration on the bridge of the *New York*. The black gang worked unstintingly to make the engines propel the ship faster, and it began "quivering fore and aft" as it picked up speed. The battle tantalized Sampson by being out of reach but within sight.[27]

Viewing the action alongside Sampson, Captain Chadwick's aide, Ens. F. H. Brumby, reported that two of the enemy ships were afire and had turned out of line and headed to the beach about six miles from the Morro, the main Spanish fort guarding the channel. Soon the Morro's guns opened up on the *New York* as it surged by doing sixteen knots, its prow curling white water in such a way as to make it appear that she had a "bone in her teeth." Chadwick asked Sampson if he wanted to reply to the Morro's guns. "No," the admiral replied, "let us get on—on after the fleet! Not one must get away!" More desperately than ever, he wanted to be in the battle. An opportunity seemed to present itself at about 10:45 when the *New York* passed close to the Spanish torpedo-boat destroyer *Furor*, which, along with its sister ship *Plutón*, already had taken numerous hits from other American ships. In fact, a crewman on the *Furor* had already waved a white flag. Captain Chadwick ordered the *New York*'s 4-inch batteries to fire at the *Furor*, needlessly sending more shells into the enemy ship, one even Chadwick admitted "was clearly done for." The *Furor* sank shortly thereafter. Having fired its only salvos of the battle, the *New York* resumed its vain chase after the other combatants.[28]

Gunfire from the *Iowa*, *Brooklyn*, and *Indiana* next took the *Infanta María Teresa* (Cervera's ship) and *Almirante Oquendo* out of action. An illustration accompanying Sampson's personal recollection of the battle calls this step "the height of the battle," but clearly shows the *New York* down the coast and well out of combat. Within a short time, however, the *New York* rushed by the two Spanish ships, by now reduced to little more than burning and smoking derelicts. The *Vizcaya* and *Cristóbal Colón* remained several miles ahead.[29]

At about 11:15 A.M., after suffering from several salvos fired by the *Texas*, *Oregon*, and *Brooklyn*, the Spanish armored cruiser *Vizcaya* ran aground near the coastal town of Aserraderos. A few minutes later (11:26) Sampson was close enough to signal the *Indiana* and *Iowa* to turn back to Santiago and reestablish the blockade: two small Spanish warships remained in the harbor and might venture out to attack the vulnerable U.S. Army transports located near Siboney. As the *New York* passed by, the *Iowa*'s sailors cheered for Sampson; the admiral asked for a casualty report, and Captain Evans replied that his ship had taken no losses. Surprised but pleased by that good news, the fleet commander then turned his attention to the last of Cervera's ships, the *Cristóbal Colón*.[30]

At about 1:20 P.M. the *Colón* surrendered, some forty-eight miles from the mouth of the Santiago channel. The *Colón* had nearly run out of coal, and shellfire from the *Oregon* and *Brooklyn* had begun ranging on her. Sampson's assistant chief of staff, S. A. Staunton, placed the *New York* "seven or eight miles astern of the *Colón* when she surrendered," but Capt. Charles Clark of the *Oregon* put the distance at "between six and seven miles." Therefore Francis Cook of the *Brooklyn* had time to board the *Colón* before the *New York* reached the scene after 2:00 P.M.[31] During the course of the battle Sampson had been near enough to witness the destruction of Cervera's squadron, but never had real control over his own ships and, except for the brief firing on the *Furor*, the *New York* did not contribute to the combat. If Sampson had completed his rendezvous with Shafter and held the conference ashore, kudos for Cervera's defeat would have belonged to Schley. Sampson's being near but not in the action on 3 July naturally complicated the awarding of credit for the victory. Schley participated in the fight, but he did not direct it. The battle of Santiago turned out to be a classic example of "a captains' fight," a pursuit-and-fire exercise in which each captain relied on his instincts and ship's capabilities.

A long-lasting controversy between Sampson and Schley (and the supporters of each) erupted as soon as the *New York* approached the *Brooklyn* on 3 July. Using signal flags, the *Brooklyn* displayed the message, "The enemy has surrendered." When the *New York* made no answering flash of congratulation, Schley signaled Sampson: "We have gained a great victory. Details will be communicated." The message was brief but not designed to raise animosities. Five minutes passed, and the *New York*'s answering signal was terse and seemed needlessly brusque: "Report your casualties." Schley probably did not know that Sampson had asked for the same information from all of his captains, but the lack of a courteous tone or friendly congratulation stung Schley. He reported one man killed and two wounded, but tried again to create a memorable exchange by sending, "This is a great day for our country." Captain Chadwick, on *New York*'s bridge with Sampson, simply acknowledged Schley's signal, declining to offer a friendly reply that might have done something to lessen the tension between the admiral and the commodore. Instead, disappointment and animosity grew. Schley hoped to take the surrender of the *Cristóbal Colón*'s captain personally; therefore he called across to Sampson: "I request the honor of the surrender of the *Cristóbal Colón.*" No response came from the *New York.* Schley had to shout his request a second time, but still got no answer. Nevertheless, Schley made ready to receive the *Colón's* officers, only to learn they had been taken to the *Resolute,* a small auxiliary.

Schley then prepared a dispatch reporting his victory to Secretary Long and intended to have it sent from the cable station at Siboney. Simultaneously, a member of Sampson's staff wrote Secretary Long a message that opened with the sentence: "The fleet under my command offers the nation as a Fourth of July present the whole of Cervera's fleet." Sampson's complete message was ungracious—it did not mention Schley—and seemed to imitate William T. Sherman's telegram to President Lincoln announcing the capture of Savannah, Georgia, in 1864. Whoever wrote the message (Chadwick was inspecting the *Colón* at the time), Sampson signed it after making only a few changes. Finally, a report indicated an unidentified ship in the vicinity. Was it Spanish? Sampson ordered Schley to take the *Brooklyn* in pursuit. The order surprised Schley; after all, the *New York* had hardly been engaged during the day, while the *Brooklyn* had participated throughout the fight. Later, Sampson's detractors questioned his logic and even his courage: Why send Schley if Sampson could go out to battle a suspected enemy? The unidentified ship turned out to be an Austrian cruiser. All of these aspects of the battle and its aftermath, together with questions about Schley's mysterious maneuvers between Cienfuegos and Santiago, combined to heighten the Sampson-Schley controversy, which intensified after the war ended.[32]

In retrospect it can be argued that the naval battle off Santiago symbolized the defeat of Spanish forces in Cuba, but in July 1898 U.S. soldiers remained in the trenches outside the city and prepared for additional combat. Major General Shafter hoped for the quick capitulation of the city, and called for the Spanish to give in. To bring about surrender, Shafter again requested that Sampson attack the enemy forts and emplacements along the channel. Again Sampson rejected Shafter's idea as too dangerous for America's most important capital ships. Adding to the impasse, each flag officer pleaded illness and refused to travel to see the other, Shafter claiming that the heat incapacitated him and Sampson probably suffering from a recurrence of his undiagnosed illness. The inability of the two senior officers to travel virtually killed the limited spirit of teamwork that had existed after the American landings at Daiquiri and Siboney in June. The general appeared to want only more action from the Navy, but because he had not exchanged liaison officers with Sampson, Shafter belligerently demanded naval action rather than work to establish a planning staff that could have considered joint options.

Unfortunately, Sampson was unable to make Shafter understand the terrible impact of losing two or three of America's modern steel warships. On the other hand, Shafter was in no mood to listen to the Navy's predictions of disaster or pleas for understanding, weighed down as he was with his own problems of poor health, logistical difficulties, disease among his soldiers, criticism from his subordinate officers (led by Theodore Roosevelt), and pressure from Washington to hold his position. If he had responded to his first impulse after the San Juan fight, Shafter would have abandoned the gains made in the assault and perhaps even withdrawn to the coast. Only Secretary of War Russell Alger's patient advice and President McKinley's rebukes kept him from retreating and thereby throwing away the Navy's victory over Cervera's squadron. Therefore, in the theater of war the impasse between the services persisted, as did Sampson's illness (after the war he specified that he "was suffering from a headache").[33]

To make matters worse, Shafter refused to permit a naval officer to be present during negotiations with the Spanish authorities. The admiral was concerned about "the surrender of shipping and the harbor," and logically expected that the Navy deserved to take control of any Spanish vessels that fell into American hands. Shafter, seconded by the commanding general of the Army, Maj. Gen. Nelson A. Miles, kept the Navy at arm's length during the talks.[34]

On 14 July officials representing Spain agreed to terms of surrender for Santiago, but Shafter neither gave the particulars to Sampson nor invited a naval officer to be present at the surrender ceremony on 16 July. Sampson belatedly ordered Captain Chadwick to rush to the ceremony, but he arrived too late to participate. These snubs further aggravated relations between the Army and the Navy. In the days to come officers of the two services bickered over which of them would man the captured vessels in the harbor. As if these disputations were not enough, Sampson and Miles fell into a protracted argument concerning naval support in the subsequent campaign against Puerto Rico.[35]

As Paul H. Carlson has argued, the blame for the lack of interservice cooperation in the Cuban campaign rests to some degree on both Shafter and Sampson.[36] President McKinley did not appoint a unified commander, so it become incumbent upon the senior officers to cooperate. Both of them declined to compromise or work closely with one another to overcome misunderstandings and rivalry. Thus their relationship, which lacked personal contact due to the ill health of both men, steadily worsened during the summer. Things were so sour between them that Shafter would not even send Sampson a personal note of congratulation after the Navy's great victory of 3 July.

Furthermore, to refuse the Navy a chair at the negotiating table was ungracious to say the least, but also clearly demonstrated Shafter's lack of strategic vision and his failure to measure up to the standards of a commander of a modern expeditionary force. It was indeed unfortunate that President McKinley had not chosen a younger, more energetic commander such as military academy graduate Wesley Merritt (who was sent instead to the Philippines).[37] Merritt's good health, West Point background, and thorough professionalism would have increased the likelihood of personal coordination with Sampson in the days before and after 3 July. Without question, the deficiencies in command arrangements confirmed the need for serious reforms in America's military forces in 1898.[38]

Sampson found his few remaining years in the Navy ruined by the controversy with Schley over command responsibility at Santiago. No doubt disappointed by being out of the fight, Sampson behaved ungraciously toward Schley after the battle. The admiral called attention to his snub of Schley by failing to offer some compliment to the commodore, while at the same time recommending promotion or awards for several other officers in the fleet. Rather than hold out an olive branch, on 10 July Sampson fed the growing rancor by telling Secretary Long that he wished to leave "any question of reward for Commodore Schley to the Department," reminding Long that Schley's questionable decisions off Cienfuegos should be taken into account. Schley's own prickly personality prompted him to claim all the credit he could and perhaps more than he deserved. Thus the behavior of both officers contributed to the Sampson-Schley controversy. Sampson wanted full credit for the victory based on his blockade plan and the notion that his fleet executed his battle plan and won the day. In his report to Long on 16 July Sampson wrote with self-congratulation: "I regard this complete and important victory over the Spanish forces as the successful finish of several weeks of arduous and close blockade, so stringent and effective during the night that the enemy was deterred from making the attempt to escape at night, and deliberately elected to make the attempt in day-light."[39]

Unfortunately for Sampson, as the controversy over credit for the victory intensified his health began to fail. He lost weight, sometimes had difficulty speaking and, according to Secretary Long, "half falters as he walks." Staying on as commander of the North Atlantic Fleet until September 1899, Sampson then took charge of the Boston Navy Yard until his health failed. He was confined to bed in the late summer of 1901.[40]

As Sampson's health declined, the controversy with Schley grew more heated. Newspapers and magazines printed letters, editorials, and articles for and against Sampson and Schley. Each side rolled out heavy artillery. Alfred

Thayer Mahan favored Sampson; George Dewey eventually supported Schley. The third volume of Edgar S. Maclay's *History of the United States Navy*, used as a textbook at the Naval Academy, condemned Schley's actions during the entire Santiago campaign. The publication of Maclay's book forced Schley to seek an official court of inquiry in an effort to settle the controversy. Sampson was too ill to testify. In December 1901, by a two-to-one vote, the court found that Schley's command in the Santiago campaign prior to 1 June 1898 "was characterized by vacillation, dilatoriness and lack of enterprise." In the battle itself, the court concluded that the *Brooklyn* changed course "to avoid getting her in dangerous proximity to the Spanish vessel," which implied that there might have been cowardice on Schley's part in maneuvering the ship. Disagreeing with the majority of the court, Dewey asserted that Schley's action displayed effectiveness and competence.[41]

Naturally dissatisfied with the court's majority report, Schley appealed his case to President Theodore Roosevelt. The president found for Sampson and wished the whole mess could be brought to an end. Echoing Secretary Long's pleas, the president wanted all officers to cease public disputes over the controversy. Only a few months later publication of Long's own book caused antagonisms to flare again.[42] In his memoirs Long sustained giving credit to Sampson and argued that Schley gave no central direction to the battle. Long's support for Sampson overshadowed his own admission that neither officer "was an essential factor in the immediate fighting." But the secretary went on to point out that Sampson would have borne blame if the Spanish had defeated the North Atlantic Fleet. Therefore, Long concluded that Sampson "should have had his country's generous and ungrudging recognition, as Dewey had it for Manila." The admiral was not there to read the secretary's conclusions. Sampson died 6 May 1902 in Washington, D.C.[43]

William T. Sampson helped personify the modernizing U.S. Navy of the late nineteenth century. His stress on scientific education, technology, and professionalism, and his reforms at the Naval Academy were all positive legacies. He conducted an excellent blockade at Santiago, but the dispute over command in the battle prevented him from becoming a national hero. Indeed, in the dregs of that controversy Sampson left a negative legacy that divided naval officers into "Sampsonites" or "Schleyites" for years to come.

NOTES

1. William T. Sampson File, Palmyra King's Daughters Free Library, Palmyra, New York; Richard S. West, *Admirals of American Empire* (Indianapolis, 1948), 24–26; Cyrus Baldwin [Principal of Palmyra Union School] to Sec. Navy Isaac

Toucey, 4 June 1857, William T. Sampson Personnel File, Naval Historical Center, Operational Archives Branch, Washington, D.C.; Carroll S. Alden and Ralph Earle, *Makers of the Naval Tradition* (New York, 1926), 273. See also "Admiral Sampson," *Scientific American* 78 (28 May 1898): 343.

2. West, *Admirals of Empire*, 54–60; *New York Times*, 20 Feb. 1899; *Official Records of the Union and Confederate Navies*, ed. Richard Rush et al., 31 vols. (Washington, 1894–1922), ser. 1, 16:176–78.

3. James R. Soley, *Historical Sketch of the U.S. Naval Academy* (Washington, 1876), 195; West, *Admirals of Empire*, 116–17; Alden and Earle, *Naval Tradition*, 274-76; "Board of Visitors Report," in *Annual Report of the Secretary of the Navy, 1878–79* (Washington, 1876), 46; *Ann. Rpt. Sec. Navy, 1877–78*, 63 [quotation]; *Army and Navy Journal* 15 (28 Aug. 1878): 739; Dorothy M. Livingston, *Master of Light: Albert A. Michelson* (Chicago, 1973), 46.

4. Robert E. Johnson, *Far China Station: The U.S. Navy in Asian Waters, 1800–1898* (Annapolis, 1979), 189, 191; Gustavus A. Weber, *The Naval Observatory: Its History, Activities, and Organization* (Baltimore, 1926), 34–39; West, *Admirals of Empire*, 120–22; Ronald H. Spector, *Professors of War: The Naval War College and the Development of the Naval Profession* (Newport, 1977), 23–24; Alden and Earle, *Naval Tradition*, 275–76; Robert Browning, *Two If By Sea: Development of American Coastal Defense Policy* (Westport, Conn., 1984), 158–64; William T. Sampson, "Floating Batteries," in *House Exec. Docs. No. 49*, 49th Cong., 1st sess., 305–13.

5. On Sampson as superintendent, see Richard S. West, "The Superintendents of the Naval Academy," *U.S. Naval Institute Proceedings* 71 (July 1945): 804–5; Park Benjamin, *The United States Naval Academy* (New York, 1900), 331–32, 338; *New York Times*, 26 Sept. 1886, 24 and 25 Aug., 17 Nov. 1887, 25 July, 18 Aug., 4 Sept. 1888; *Ann. Rpt. Sec. Navy, 1887–88*, xlii, 77, 80–81; *Ann. Rpt. Sec. Navy, 1888–89*, 25–26; *Ann. Rpt. Sec. Navy, 1889–90*, 427; *Ann Rpt. Sec. Navy, 1890–91*, 167; Sampson to parents of several cadets, all dated 13 July 1888, RG 405, Records of the U.S. Naval Academy, microcopy M-994, roll 25, National Archives [NA], Washington, D.C.; West, *Admirals of Empire*, 126–27; Jack Sweetman, *The U.S. Naval Academy, An Illustrated History* (Annapolis, 1979), 125.

6. West, *Admirals of Empire*, 55, 119–20, 127, 129, 175–77; Robert E. Johnson, *Thence Around Cape Horn: The Story of United States Naval Forces on Pacific Stations, 1818–1923* (Annapolis, 1963), 145; *Army and Navy Journal* 29 (14 and 21 May 1892): 660, 684.

7. West, *Admirals of Empire*, 178–81, 184; "Sampson's Report on Ordnance," in *Ann. Rpt. Sec. Navy, 1894–95*, 233–35, 239–40, 242, 246; William T. Sampson, "Face Hardened Armor," *U.S. Naval Institute Proceedings* 20 (1894): 818–21; Benjamin F. Cooling, *Gray Steel and Blue Water Navy: The Formative Years of America's Military Industrial Complex, 1881–1917* (Hamden, Conn., 1979), 116–18.

8. *New York Times*, 7 June 1896; Spector, *Professors of War*, 92–93; David Trask, *The War with Spain in 1898* (New York, 1981), 76–77; *Ann. Rpt. Sec. Navy, 1897*, 274.

9. Edward Beach, *The United States Navy: Two Hundred Years* (New York, 1986),

365–66. Certainly, there could have been illnesses other than Alzheimer's disease that caused Sampson's decline in health. Martin G. Netsky, M.D., has conducted extensive research into Sampson's medical history and is preparing to offer a more conclusive analysis of Sampson's illness.

10. William T. Sampson, "The Atlantic Fleet in the Spanish War," *Century* 57 (Apr. 1899): 913.

11. Trask, *War with Spain,* 121. On Sampson's personality see L. A. Coolidge, "Stories of the Fighting Leaders," *McClure's* 11 (June 1898): 181; and Alfred Thayer Mahan, *Retrospect and Prospect: Studies in International Relations, Naval and Political* (Boston, 1903), 293.

12. French E. Chadwick, *The Relations of the United States and Spain: The Spanish-American War,* 2 vols. (New York, 1911), 2:322–23; Trask, *War with Spain,* 108, 116–20; Sampson, "Atlantic Fleet," 894; Edwin A. Falk, *Fighting Bob Evans* (New York, 1931), 272–73; S. A. Staunton, "The Naval Campaign of 1898 in the West Indies," *Harper's Monthly* 98 (Jan. 1899): 178.

13. Sampson, "Atlantic Fleet," 876; Trask, *War with Spain,* 122–23; Sampson to Schley, 21 May 1898, *Ann. Rpt. Sec. Navy, 1898* 2:466; Paolo E. Coletta, *Bowman Hendry McCalla: A Fighting Sailor* (Washington, 1979): 85; John D. Long, *The New American Navy,* 2 vols. (New York, 1903), 1:276; Margaret Long, ed., *The Journal of John D. Long* (Ringe, N.H., 1956), 257; W.A.M. Goode, *With Sampson Through the War* (New York, 1899), 125.

14. Winfield S. Schley, *Forty-five Years Under the Flag* (New York, 1904), 278–81; Robley D. Evans, *A Sailor's Log: Recollections of Forty Years of Naval Life* (New York, 1901), 429; Long, *Journal of Long,* 226–27; Trask, *War with Spain,* 124–25; Long to Schley, 27 May 1898, *Ann. Rpt. Sec. Navy, 1898* 2:397.

15. Sampson to Schley, 27 May 1898, *Ann. Rpt. Sec. Navy, 1898* 2:475; Trask, *War with Spain,* 125–27, 131.

16. Staunton, "Naval Campaign," 182–83; Evans, *Sailor's Log,* 417; Sampson, "Atlantic Fleet," 889, 897, 900–991; Henry C. Taylor, "The 'Indiana' at Santiago," *Century* 58 (May 1899): 67; Sampson's orders on using searchlights (8, 11 June 1898) are in *Ann. Rpt. Sec. Navy, 1898* 2:513; Alfred Thayer Mahan, *Lessons of the War with Spain and Other Articles* (Boston, 1899), 33; Chadwick, *Spanish-American War* 1:348–49, 357, 362–63; Sampson's plans to "close and engage" are in his "Order of Battle, 2 June 1898," "Journal of William T. Sampson," Box 8A, RG 313, NA; John Philip, "The 'Texas' at Santiago," *Century* 58 (May 1899): 88. See also "The Situation at Santiago de Cuba," *Scientific American* 78 (4 June 1898): 360–61.

17. Trask, *War with Spain,* 139–40, 209, 273–75; Richard P. Hobson, *The Sinking of the "Merrimac"* (New York, 1899); Walter Russell, "Incidents of the Cuban Blockade," *Century* 56 (Sept. 1898): 655–61.

18. Paul H. Carlson, *"Pecos Bill": A Military Biography of William R. Shafter* (College Station, Tex., 1989), 172; William H. Leckie, "William R. Shafter," in *Dictionary of American Military Biography,* ed. Roger J. Spiller et al., 3 vols. (Westport, Conn., 1984), 3:978–81. On the circumstance of the Army, see for example Peter Karsten,

"Armed Progressives: The Military Reorganizes for the American Century," in *The Military in America,* ed. Peter Karsten (New York, 1980), 229–71; James L. Abrahamson, *America Arms for a New Century* (New York, 1981), 19–62; and John M. Gates, "The Alleged Isolation of U.S. Army Officers in the Late 19th Century," *Parameters* 10 (Sept. 1980): 32–45.

19. Carlson, *Shafter,* 172; Louis J. Gulliver, "Sampson and Shafter at Santiago," *U.S. Naval Institute Proceedings* 65 (June 1939): 799–800; Trask, *War with Spain,* 207; Paolo E. Coletta, *French Ensor Chadwick: Scholarly Warrior* (Lanham, Md., 1980), 87; Mahan, *Lessons of the War with Spain,* 251; Graham A. Cosmas, *An Army for Empire: The United States Army in the Spanish-American War* (Columbia, Mo., 1971), 206; Sampson to Long, 6 June 1898, *Ann. Rpt. Sec. Navy, 1898* 2:485; Russell A. Alger, *The Spanish-American War* (New York, 1901), 221–41; Graham A. Cosmas, "San Juan Hill and El Caney," in *America's First Battles, 1776–1965,* ed. Charles E. Heller and William A. Stofft (Lawrence, 1986), 121.

20. Regarding putting the Army ashore, see Sampson, "Atlantic Fleet," 904–5; and Chadwick, *Spanish-American War* 2:32–39. Regarding the Spanish ships, Assistant Chief of Staff Staunton related that "there was a lack of definite information as to the Spanish naval forces in Cuban ports." Staunton, "Naval Campaign," 176; see also 180. Robley D. Evans later talked of "the much dreaded fleet of Admiral Cervera" in "The 'Iowa' at Santiago," *Century* 58 (May 1899): 62.

21. Trask, *War with Spain,* 257–62; Cosmas, "San Juan and El Caney," 122.

22. Trask conveniently offers details of the Spanish squadron in *War with Spain,* 262.

	Cervera	*Sampson-Schley*
vessels engaged	6	10
battleships	0	4
armored cruisers	4	2
torpedo boat/destroyers	2	1
light auxiliaries	0	3
heavy guns	42	76
total displacement	23,280 tons	49,038 tons
total crew strength	2,261	2,341

23. French E. Chadwick, "The 'New York' at Santiago," *Century* 58 (May 1899): 114; W.A.M. Goode, "The Destruction of Cervera's Fleet," *McClure's* 11 (Sept. 1898): 425; Staunton, "Naval Campaign," 180; Trask, *War with Spain,* 262; Goode, *With Sampson Through the War,* 194.

24. Charles B. Davis, ed., *Adventures and Letters of Richard Harding Davis* (New York, 1917), 230; George Graham, "The Destruction of Cervera's Fleet," *McClure's* 11 (Sept. 1898): 405; Philip, "'Texas' at Santiago," 88, 90; Francis Cook, "The 'Brooklyn' at Santiago," *Century* 58 (May 1899): 96; Taylor, "'Indiana' at Santiago," 65.

25. Evans, *Sailor's Log,* 444; Schley, *Forty-five Years,* 298; Chadwick, *Spanish-*

American War 2:136; West, *Admirals of Empire*, 262–63; Philip, "'Texas' at Santiago," 90–91.

26. Sampson's personal recollections are given in Sampson, "Atlantic Fleet," 906–7. See also Chadwick, "'New York' at Santiago," 111.

27. Sampson, "Atlantic Fleet," 907; Chadwick, "'New York' at Santiago," 113; Goode, *With Sampson Through the War*, 199. For a contrasting view to the "captains' fight" thesis, see Stephen B. Luce, "The Spanish-American War," *North American Review* 194 (Oct. 1911): 616–21; Luce gives credit for the victory to Sampson.

28. Goode reported the Chadwick-Sampson conversation in Goode, *With Sampson Through the War*, 199. See also Chadwick, "'New York' at Santiago," 111–13; Chadwick's official report in *Ann. Rpt. Sec. Navy, 1898* 2:520; and official report of Lt. Harry P. Huse (executive officer of *Gloucester*), ibid., 542.

29. Sampson, "Atlantic Fleet," 907–9 (illustration on 908–9 and reproduced in West, *Admirals of Empire*, between 256–57); Evans, *Sailor's Log*, 538; Taylor, "'Indiana' at Santiago," 530–31; Cook, "'Brooklyn' at Santiago," 523; Goode, *With Sampson Through the War*, 202–3; West, *Admirals of Empire*, 260.

30. Trask, *War with Spain*, 264; Goode, *With Sampson Through the War*, 203; Cook's official report in *Ann. Rpt. Sec. Navy, 1898* 2:523; Chadwick's official report, ibid., 520; Evans, "'Iowa' at Santiago," 57; Sampson, "Atlantic Fleet," 910.

31. Trask, *War with Spain*, 264; Staunton, "Naval Campaign," 189–90; Chadwick, "'New York' at Santiago," 113; Edward W. Eberle, "The 'Oregon' at Santiago," *Century* 58 (May 1899): 110.

32. Goode, *With Sampson Through the War*, 205, 210–11; George E. Graham, *Schley and Santiago* (Chicago, 1902), 336–41, 345–48; Schley, *Forty-five Years*, 308, 310–14; Cook, "'Brooklyn' at Santiago," 99–100; Chadwick, *Spanish-American War* 2:154, 164–65; Coletta, *Chadwick*, 90–91; West, *Admirals of Empire*, 265; Chadwick's official report, *Ann. Rpt. Sec. Navy, 1898* 2:521. The original proposed "Fourth of July present" message was evidently longer, but Sampson trimmed it down. See Sampson to Long, 3 July 1898, "Journal of William T. Sampson," Box 8A, RG 313, NA.

33. Carlson, *Pecos Bill Shafter*, 180; Alger, *Spanish-American War*, 177; Shafter to Corbin, 9 July 1898, *Correspondence Relating to the War with Spain*, 2 vols. (Washington, 1902), 1:115; Lewis L. Gould, *The Spanish-American War and President McKinley* (Lawrence, 1980), 79–80, 88; Cosmas, "San Juan Hill and El Caney," 145; Trask, *War with Spain*, 302; *New York Times*, 17 Oct. 1899.

34. Trask, *War with Spain*, 304–5; Virginia W. Johnson, *The Unregimented General: A Biography of Nelson A. Miles* (Boston, 1962), 330; Sampson to Shafter, and reply, both dated 13 July 1898, in *Ann. Rpt. Sec. Navy, 1898* 2:624.

35. Trask, *War with Spain*, 316, 320, 350–52; Louis J. Gulliver, "Sampson and Shafter at Santiago," 802–4; Chadwick, *Spanish-American War* 2:249–52; *Correspondence Relating to the War* 1:297–98.

36. Carlson, *Shafter*, 187.

37. Ibid., 186.

38. Leonard D. White comments on aspects of rivalry between generals, admirals, and cabinet secretaries in *The Republican Era,* 149. A contemporary writer noted: "The great mystery of the campaign, as we have before remarked, was the failure of army and navy to cooperate actively and heartily" (*The Nation* 67 [9 Dec. 1898]: 422).

39. Sampson to Long, 10 July 1898, RG 80, entry 194/266 1/2, "Copies of Messages Received and Sent by the Naval War Board," General Records of the Department of the Navy, NA. See also Trask, *War with Spain,* 268.

40. *New York Times,* 25 Oct. and 24 Dec. 1898; 16 and 24 Feb., 16 Oct., 13 and 15 Nov. 1899; 29 Aug., 1, 3, and 24 Sept. 1901; *Army and Navy Journal* 37 (18 Nov. 1899): 273, (2 Dec. 1899): 322, (23 Dec. 1899): 399; Long, *New American Navy* 2:44–45; West, *Admirals of Empire,* 299; Long, *America of Yesterday,* 209 [quotation].

41. Robert Seager II, *Alfred Thayer Mahan: The Man and His Letters* (Annapolis, 1977), 401–2; Spector, *Admiral of New Empire,* 117–19; *Record of Proceedings of a Court of Inquiry into the Case of Rear Admiral Winfield Scott Schley, USN,* 2 vols. (Washington, 1902), 2:1829–30.

42. West, *Admirals of Empire,* 302.

43. Long, *New American Navy* 2:45–48 [quotations, 48]; *New York Times,* 7 and 10 May 1902.

Winfield S. Schley and Santiago:
A New Look at an Old Controversy

HAROLD D. LANGLEY

At the time of the United States' formal declaration of war against Spain on 25 April 1898 it was anticipated that Cuba would be the focal point of the conflict. President William McKinley had asked Congress on 11 April for the authority to use the armed forces of the United States to enforce the pacification of Cuba. In granting this request on 19 April, Congress recognized the independence of Cuba and disavowed any intention of annexing that island. The mobilization of the Army had begun on 9 March, and on 22 April Rear Adm. William T. Sampson had left Key West, Florida, to establish a blockade of Cuba. On that same day the cruiser *Nashville* fired the first shot of the war during its capture of the Spanish merchant ship *Buena Ventura* off Key West. When Congress declared war on 25 April, it made 21 April the war's effective beginning date, in part so that the capture of the ship would be legal.[1]

The possibility of a naval action against Cuba had been considered by the U.S. Navy during the administration of President Grover Cleveland. During 1894 planners at the Naval War College in Newport, Rhode Island, had discussed strategy for a war in which the United States and France were allied against Great Britain and Spain. A second group of planners considered a war involving only the United States and Spain. The group working on the larger war argued for a quick invasion of Cuba before European fleets could reach the island. The second group, anticipating the Spanish-American

War, argued that no troops should be landed in Cuba until the Spanish fleet was destroyed.

The renewal of the civil war in Cuba in 1895 prompted a new study of the possibility of war with Spain, and this plan was forwarded to the Navy Department in January 1896. Another war plan, prepared at this time by the Office of Naval Intelligence (ONI), placed the emphasis on blockading Cuba and using two American naval squadrons to attack Spain's colonies in the Caribbean. The war plans also included recommendations for the seizure of Manila in the Philippine Islands and for naval attacks on Spain itself. When the staff and students of the Naval War College studied the ONI's plan, however, they found it flawed. A blockade of Cuba would be ineffective, they argued, and none should be attempted until the Spanish fleet was defeated. The War College argued for a combined Army-Navy attack on Havana as set forth in the 1895 plan. Discussions on the merits and disadvantages of both plans continued for the remainder of the Cleveland administration.[2]

When McKinley became president in 1897, his secretary of the Navy, John D. Long, ordered a new study by a special Navy board. This group produced a plan in July 1897 that was essentially the plan of the ONI, but with a recommendation for the seizure of Matanzas as a base for future Army operations and for supplying the Cuban insurgents. Although this effort was referred to as the "official plan," it did not represent the views of the War College staff or of the McKinley administration. At the War College in 1897 the hypothetical war with Great Britain anticipated that nation attacking cities on the east coast of the United States from bases in Cuba and Bermuda. Under such circumstances, the correct response would be to keep the U.S. fleet united in order to intercept and defeat the elements of the enemy forces before they could unite. It was recognized that a threat to the American coast would lead to demands for protection of certain cities, but that it would be a mistake to yield to such pressures and divide the fleet.[3]

Between November 1897 and February 1898 Assistant Secretary of the Navy Theodore Roosevelt discussed strategy with various persons, including Lt. William W. Kimball, the author of the Naval War College's plan of 1896. Roosevelt was a strong advocate of war with Spain, and he used his position to try to hasten the work of repairing ships, buying new ones, and placing them in positions where they could be quickly deployed for raids on the Spanish mainland cities. These views were not shared by his superior, Secretary Long, or by Capt. Henry C. Taylor, the president of the Naval War College. Roosevelt and Taylor did agree, however, on the need to act quickly before Spain could send reinforcements to Cuba.[4]

After the destruction of the battleship *Maine* in Havana harbor on 15 February 1898, the war fever increased in much of the country and with it the tempo of business in the Navy Department. A month after the loss of the *Maine*, Roosevelt met with a group of senior naval officers to consider what should be done in regard to the reports of movements of Spanish vessels. They agreed that the defense of the American coast should be left to the Army. A blockade of Cuba would be imposed, and the U.S. Navy would maintain control of the waters around Cuba and Puerto Rico, but the actual conquest of Cuba would be the task of the Army. A naval blockade of the island would require all the ships the Navy could spare, but public opinion now demanded that some provision be made for the protection of the American coast. So, two days after the board met, orders were issued to establish a Flying Squadron, based at Hampton Roads, Virginia. It would consist of the battleships *Texas* and *Massachusetts*, the armored cruiser *Brooklyn*, and the protected cruisers *Columbia* and *Minneapolis*. The command of the Flying Squadron was given to Commodore Winfield Scott Schley, who took over on 28 March. The *Brooklyn* became his flagship.[5]

This action did not completely allay public anxiety, so the Northern Patrol was established under the command of Comm. John A. Howell, who was ordered to watch the coasts between Bar Harbor, Maine, and the Delaware Capes. Assisting in the work of coastal defense was the Auxiliary Naval Force, which was made up largely of naval militia. The Flying Squadron would patrol the coasts south of the Delaware Capes until it was needed in the Caribbean. A third naval force, called the North Atlantic Squadron, was based at Key West, Florida. Under the command of Capt. (later Rear Adm.) William T. Sampson, this squadron consisted of the battleships *Iowa* and *Indiana* and the armored cruiser *New York*. Sampson took command on 26 March and made the *New York* his flagship. To this force would later be added the battleship *Oregon*, which left San Francisco on 19 March on a voyage that would take it around Cape Horn. The *Oregon* was in Rio de Janeiro when Capt. Charles E. Clark, its commander, learned of the declaration of war and headed for the Caribbean.[6]

In choosing Schley for the Flying Squadron, Secretary Long was apparently trying to appease the public, and he induced McKinley to follow his recommendations. Fifteen years earlier the American people had been thrilled by the story of Schley's race against time in the Arctic to rescue the survivors of the Greely Expedition from death by cold and starvation. Surely here was a man the public could depend on to come to the rescue of any endangered city. But in giving the command to Schley, Long had to advance him over the heads of at least a dozen senior officers. Naturally this departure from established procedure did not sit well with the officers who were affected or with the chief of the Bureau of Navigation, Rear Adm. Arent S. Crowninshield. From Schley's point of view, it was a source of chagrin that Sampson, who was his junior at the Naval Academy, was promoted to rear admiral on 21 April. The next day Sampson was ordered to blockade northern Cuba, and his squadron departed from Key West on that day.[7]

In Washington a Naval War Board was established in March 1898 that included Roosevelt, Crowninshield, Rear Adm. Montgomery Sicard, who was the chairman, and Capts. Albert S. Barker and Alfred Thayer Mahan. By the time Mahan arrived home from Europe on 9 May, Roosevelt had resigned to enter the Army. Soon after this Barker was assigned to other duties, so for most of the war the board consisted of three men. The board recommended that the Navy concentrate on the outlying and poorly defended parts of the Spanish empire rather than undertake operations against Spain itself. Mahan argued that the fleet should be united for use against the naval force of Spain in the Caribbean. Land operation in Cuba could not take place until the Spanish fleet was defeated. Until that was accomplished, Mahan was opposed to risking American ships against shore-based artillery. Roosevelt held similar views in regard to shore bombardments.[8]

A different view of the proper strategy was held by Sampson and his principal officers. They wanted to bombard Havana. When this proposal was turned down, Sampson sought to limit the area to be blockaded. He wanted to concentrate on the northern coast and against the Cuban ports of Mariel, Havana, Matanzas, and Cardenas because the limited coal capacity of the blockading squadron made it impossible to begin the blockade until the colliers were in place. When Sampson was sent to the Cuban coast on 21 April, the Navy Department ordered him to include the port of Cienfuegos in the blockade because it had a rail connection with Havana. As soon as the Navy was in place on the southern coast of Cuba it would be able to escort Army transports to that island.[9]

Arriving off Havana on 22 April, Sampson extended his blockade eastward to Matanzas and Cardenas, westward to Mariel and Cabanas, and later to Cienfuegos on the southern coast. A shortage of ships made it impossible to maintain a continuous presence off the most easterly ports on the north coast. This lack of an enforcement capability made it necessary for McKinley to postpone the imposition of a blockade of the entire southern coast of Cuba and Puerto Rico until 28 June.[10]

In the course of imposing the early blockade, Sampson's flagship, the *New York*, accompanied by the double-turreted monitors *Amphitrite* and *Puritan*, shelled a Spanish battery at Matanzas on 27 April. This was the first naval action of the war. Fourteen days later, boat crews from the gunboat *Nashville* and the unprotected cruiser *Marblehead* cut two cables while under heavy fire off Cienfuegos. Unfortunately, a third cable, which gave the Spaniards a telegraphic link to their homeland by way of Jamaica, remained functional. That same day the torpedo boat *Winslow* was fired on and disabled when it attempted to enter the harbor of Cardenas. While being towed out by the revenue cutter *Hudson*, an officer and four enlisted men were killed and three others wounded. Other Spanish cables were cut in the waters off Santiago and Guantanamo, and similar small clashes between ships and land batteries took place at intervals throughout the war.[11]

Meanwhile Adm. Pascual Cervera had left Cádiz for the Cape Verde Islands on 7 April with the armored cruisers *Cristóbal Colón* and *Infanta María Teresa*. Three torpedo boat destroyers and three destroyers were waiting at the Cape Verde Islands, and two additional armored cruisers—the *Vizcaya* and *Almirante Oquendo*—arrived from Puerto Rico on 19 April. Prior to his departure from Spain, Cervera had discussed with the minister of marine, Adm. Segismundo Bermejo, what should be done in the event of war with the United States. Cervera was pessimistic and pointed out that American naval forces were three times as strong as Spain's. For that reason alone, he believed that a defensive war would have to be fought unless Spain had some allies. This and other arguments failed to dissuade the minister or the Spanish government. When Gen. Ramón Blanco y Erenas, the governor-general of Cuba, asked that a naval force be sent there, Cervera received orders to move to the Cape Verde Islands. It was a source of concern to Cervera that the squadron had been dispatched before there had been any agreement as to its role.[12]

From Cape Verde Cervera reported that during the 1,570-mile voyage from Cádiz the coal consumption of the *Cristóbal Colón* and *María Teresa* was quite large. At the usual speed of twelve (and sometimes eleven) knots, the *Colón* used 500 tons of coal and the *Teresa* about 400. Cervera reported that he needed 1,000 tons of coal to refill the bunkers of his ships. As it was, he could buy only 700 tons at Cape Verde.

On the condition of the ships themselves, Cervera noted that the *Colón* did not have its big guns installed, and only about 300 rounds of its 5.5-inch ammunition were good. Furthermore, the defective guns of the *Vizcaya* and *Oquendo* had not been changed, the *Colón*'s cartridge cases could not be recharged, and the squadron did not have a single Bustamante mine. Because the *Vizcaya* could no longer steam rapidly, it was "a boil in the body of the fleet."[13]

Cervera also reported the results of a council of war with his officers. All were aware of the fact that they were going into a war with inferior forces. They were willing to die for Spain, but felt that a defeat in the West Indies would open Spain itself to attack. The admiral himself continued to believe that a voyage to Puerto Rico would be disastrous.

These objections were considered by senior officers of the navy and by the minister of marine at a meeting held on 23 April. By this time the minister of war had received word from the governor-general of Cuba that if the people on that island became convinced that a naval squadron was not coming, an unpleasant reaction was quite possible. The senior officers and the minister of war decided that the squadron would be sent, but that Cervera would be given complete freedom of action in regard to the destination, the course, and the circumstances under which a battle might be fought or avoided. So, after he had finished coaling, filling vacancies in crews, and making what repairs he could, Cervera sailed for the West Indies on 29 April. In addition to his cruisers, Cervera's squadron now included the torpedo-boat destroyers *Furor*, *Plutón*, and *Terror*, which had joined it at Cape Verde.[14]

When the Navy Department learned that Cervera had left the Cape Verde Islands, it was assumed that he would head for Puerto Rico or eastern Cuba. Two fast auxiliary cruisers, the *Harvard* and *St. Louis*, were sent to the Windward Islands to keep watch, while a third, the *Yale*, cruised off Puerto Rico. Orders to the *Harvard* and *St. Louis* stated that if Cervera was not sighted by 10 May they were to proceed to Martinique and Guadaloupe, respectively, for new instructions. The *Yale* was to go to St. Thomas in the Virgin Islands on 13 May for the same purpose.

Upon hearing of Cervera's departure, Sampson assumed that the Spaniard's destination was Puerto Rico, and that it was possible that he might coal in Martinique. On 4 May Sampson left the blockade off Havana and headed for Puerto Rico with ten ships: the battleships *Iowa* and *Indiana*, the cruiser *New York*, the unprotected cruisers *Detroit* and *Montgomery*, the monitors *Amphitrite* and *Terror*, the torpedo boat *Porter*, the collier *Niagara*, and the armored tug *Wompatuck*. Secretary Long sent Sampson a cable that said: "Do not risk crippling your vessels against fortifications as to prevent from soon afterward successfully fighting the Spanish fleet." At the same time Long wrote a letter to Sampson in which he cautioned the admiral against operations that might weaken his squadron.

When he received Long's cable on 8 May, Sampson called his captains together for a meeting. Out of this came an agreement that they should continue to Puerto Rico. Sampson was aware of the possibility that Cervera might slip past him and threaten the blockade of Cuba, and perhaps even raid the east coast of the United States, but he thought it was most important to deny coal and supplies to the Spaniard. Having informed the Navy Department of the results of the meeting with his officers, Sampson asked that the battleships *Massachusetts* and *Texas* and three fast scouting ships be sent to him. Long responded that two of the Spanish ships that were expected to go to the West Indies were still in Spain. As for the request for reinforcements, Long said nothing about the battleships, but he did indicate that the *Harvard*, *St. Louis*, and *Yale* would be sent to St. Thomas when they had completed their cruises. The secretary also noted that Sampson should move quickly to finish his operations in Puerto Rico so that the blockade of Cuba and the base at Key West would not be endangered.

Arriving off San Juan, Puerto Rico, early on the morning of 12 May, Sampson's ships opened fire without warning. Little damage was inflicted or received, and the action ended after two hours and thirty-five minutes. This foray enabled Sampson to determine that Cervera was not in San Juan. It also gave the American crews some gunnery practice. But since the defender's guns had not been silenced nor his coal supply destroyed, Long thought that the results were not worth the risks. At the end of the bombardment Sampson stopped at Cap Haitien on the coast of Haiti. Here, on 16 May, he heard that Cervera's squadron had been seen at Curaçao two days earlier. Orders were waiting for Sampson to return to Key West. He did so, arriving there in the late afternoon of 18 May.[15]

When Cervera neared Martinique on 12 May, he received distressing news from the captain of the *Furor*, which had sailed to the French island ahead of the main fleet. Cervera learned about Sampson's attack on Puerto Rico, and that the American auxiliaries *Paris* and *New York* were watching the island. He also learned of Commodore George Dewey's victory at Manila, and that the *Terror*, which had accompanied the *Furor*, was unseaworthy and had been forced to remain in Martinique. Cervera then assembled his captains and seconds-in-command and discussed the situation that they faced. The officers were in total agreement that the squadron should go to Curaçao for the coal that was promised them. At Curaçao they found that the promised collier had not arrived, and Cervera was only able to get 600 tons on the island. Only two ships were allowed into the harbor, and their stay was limited to forty-eight hours. Meanwhile, the governor-general of Cuba had insisted to the minister of marine that a revolution would take place in Havana and on the whole island if the squadron was not sent to Cuba. He was relieved when Cervera's squadron reached Santiago on 19 May.[16]

In Washington Secretary Long was concerned that while Sampson was heading for Puerto Rico, Cervera might elude him. Accordingly, on 13 May he ordered Schley to move the Flying Squadron to Charleston, South Carolina. There it would be in a position to support the blockade or reinforce Sampson, depending on what Cervera did. No sooner was Schley in place than he was ordered to Key West to report to Sampson. He was waiting there when Sampson arrived.[17]

At their meeting Sampson indicated his belief that Cervera would head for Cienfuegos because it was the only port on the southern coast that had rail connections with Havana. Schley was ordered to Cienfuegos. To bolster Schley's squadron for the work ahead, Sampson assigned to it the battleship *Iowa*, which was then en route from Puerto Rico.

After Schley returned to his flagship, he received orders from the Navy Department to proceed to Havana. Schley notified Sampson of this development. Sampson took the view that his arrival at Key West had modified the department's orders, and that Schley should proceed to Cienfuegos as agreed.[18]

One and a half hours after leaving Key West on 18 May, Schley encountered the cruiser *Marblehead* under Comdr. Bowman H. McCalla, and exchanged signals. McCalla had just come from Cienfuegos where he had cut the cable and made contact with the Cuban insurgents there. He had arranged a signal code with the insurgents, and was now en route to Key West to load arms for them and coal for his ships. With press boats all around, he was unwilling to communicate to Schley his code arrangements with the insurgents, and he did not know that Schley was destined for Cienfuegos.

Accordingly, McCalla asked for permission to proceed to Key West with his consort, the auxiliary *Eagle*. This was granted, and the *Eagle* relayed by megaphone a message from McCalla that there was no news of Cervera. So it was that Schley was deprived of an important piece of information about the Cuban insurgents that might well have proved valuable in subsequent days.[19]

While still thirty miles from Cienfuegos, Schley and his officers heard six or seven guns fired in cadence that they interpreted as a salute. They thought it might be heralding the arrival of Cervera's force. The next day several plumes of white smoke were observed rising over the harbor, the view of which was blocked by high hills. A blockade of the harbor was instituted, and the ships of the Flying Squadron slowly steamed back and forth across the harbor.[20]

Meanwhile, a day after Schley left Key West the telegraph operator there heard from a pro-insurgent telegrapher in Havana that Cervera's squadron was in Santiago. This report was taken seriously in Washington, and Long suggested to Sampson that Schley leave one ship off Cienfuegos and take the rest of his force to Santiago. Sampson sent a copy of Long's message to Schley along with a letter of his own dated 20 May, in which the admiral expressed his doubt about the location of Cervera's force and decided to make no changes in the current dispositions. Sampson said that if Cervera had reached Santiago, his ships would have to go to either Havana or Cienfuegos to deliver the munitions of war they were reportedly carrying.[21]

Information about McCalla's arrangements with the Cuban insurgents would have been useful to Schley a few days later when three signal bonfires were sighted on the hills west of Cienfuegos. Neither Schley nor Capt. Francis A. Cook, the commander of the flagship *Brooklyn*, knew whether the signal was intended for those inside or outside the harbor. As a result, there was no communication with the insurgents.[22]

The next day the British steamer *Adula* arrived from Jamaica and asked for permission to enter the port to bring out British refugees in Cienfuegos. While conferring with the *Adula*'s officers, Schley saw a handbill from Jamaica reporting that Cervera had entered Santiago on 19 May, and that he had left the next day. If this was true, then the Spanish squadron could have reached Cienfuegos about the time that Schley and his officers heard what they thought was a salute. To be certain, Schley allowed the *Adula* to enter the port on the condition that it would come out the next morning and give him a report on whether Cervera was there. When the *Adula* came out its captain reported that Cervera had anchored at Santiago on 19 May, but had left that port on the twentieth. This information served to further convince Schley that Cervera was in Cienfuegos.[23]

At 7:30 A.M. on 23 May, the dispatch boat *Hawk* arrived with a message from Sampson. The admiral said that the report that Cervera was in Santiago was probably correct. "If you are satisfied that they [the Spaniards] are not at Cienfuegos," wrote Sampson, "proceed with all dispatch, but cautiously, to Santiago de Cuba and blockade him in port." With this came a note from Sampson saying that he thought the enclosed instructions would reach Schley by 2:00 A.M. on 23 May, and that he should be able to leave before daylight so that the Spaniards would not know what direction he took. The timing was important because Sampson anticipated that Cervera would probably make some repairs on his ships and coal them before putting to sea again. Also it was Sampson's intention to move his squadron to a position in the Bahama Channel so as to intercept Cervera in case he headed for Havana. But Schley got the message six and a half hours later than Sampson anticipated. He was also faced with an order to go to Santiago if he was satisfied that Cervera was not in Cienfuegos, but he was not convinced that he did not already have Cervera in port. Meanwhile he was busy coaling his ships.[24]

When McCalla returned from Key West in the *Marblehead* on 24 May and learned of Schley's views, he asked for permission to investigate a signal from the shore. Permission was granted, and from the Cuban insurgents McCalla learned that Cervera was not in Cienfuegos. This news was communicated to Schley, and the squadron began moving toward Santiago at 7:45 P.M. on 24 May, nearly two days later than Sampson had anticipated. Sampson had also told Long that Schley had been ordered to Santiago, but said nothing about the qualifying instructions.[25]

Since 21 May the *Yale* and *St. Louis* had been cruising off Santiago. They were joined there on 23 May by the *Harvard* and *Minneapolis*. None of these ships had discovered that Cervera's squadron was in port. On 24 May the *Harvard* left for Mole St. Nicholas in Haiti to pick up dispatches addressed to Schley.[26]

Slowed by the flooding of the *Eagle*'s forward compartments and by the breakdown of the *Merrimac*'s engine, Schley's squadron did not reach Santiago until about 6:00 P.M. on 26 May. When the *Brooklyn* anchored, the captain of the nearest ship on patrol off the port was ordered to report. This happened to be Capt. Charles Sigsbee, formerly of the ill-fated *Maine*, and now commanding the *St. Paul*. For the meeting in the *Brooklyn*, Sigsbee brought along one Eduardo Nunez, a pilot who was familiar with the harbor of Santiago. At the gangway Schley asked Sigsbee if Cervera was in the harbor, and the captain said no. During the subsequent meeting on the quarterdeck Sigsbee repeated his conclusion. Schley, who spoke fluent Spanish, began to question Nunez. The pilot expressed doubts about Cervera's ability to negotiate the channel except in smooth weather and with the assistance of tugs.

To Schley it seemed as though he had heard expert testimony that Cervera was not in Santiago. He now considered the state of his squadron—his auxiliary ships were developing mechanical problems, and the coal supply of his battleships and cruisers was becoming low. Heavy seas had made recoaling difficult. If the report that Cervera was in Santiago was a ruse, and because Sampson's force was now east of Havana looking for the enemy, it seemed wise to prepare his force for a battle or a blockade as quickly as possible. If he could not coal at sea, he would be able to do so at Key West, so at 8:30 P.M. on 26 May Schley sent a signal to his ships: "Destination Key West; via south of Cuba and the Yucatan Channel as soon as collier is ready. Speed 9 knots."[27]

The next morning Schley received via the *Harvard* Secretary Long's dispatch of 25 May. Long said that all the information in the Navy Department indicated that Cervera was in Santiago. "The department looks to you to ascertain facts, and that the enemy, if therein, does not leave without a decisive action," wrote Long. On the matter of fuel, Long asked if it was not possible to coal the *Harvard* and the squadron from the collier *Merrimac* either leeward of Cape Cruz or at Mole St. Nicholas in Haiti.[28]

Replying to Long's message on 27 May, Schley said that he regretted being unable to obey the orders of the department, but he had to go to Key West for coal. The *Harvard* had only enough coal to reach Jamaica, and the *Minneapolis* and *Yale* had a sufficient supply to make Key West. The *Merrimac* was disabled and being towed by the *Yale*. Only small vessels could coal at Gonaives or Mole St. Nicholas.[29]

Convinced that Cervera was in Santiago and that this force had to be neutralized before the invasion of Cuba could begin, Long was shocked by Schley's reply. It seemed to him that Schley was leaving his post at a critical time and that Cervera might escape. For both McKinley and Long, the receipt of Schley's message was the darkest day of the war. On 29 May Long told Schley that it was his duty to establish whether the Spanish squadron was in Santiago. All military and naval movements depended on this information. Sampson also sent messages pointing out the need for Schley to remain before Santiago. The matter was soon resolved.[30]

Schley's progress toward Key West had been determined by the speed of the *Yale*, which was towing the collier *Merrimac*. Frequent stops were necessary to secure the cable. The weather was bad. Then, on 27 May, conditions improved. Crews worked all night to load and unload coal, and when the coaling of the ships had been completed Schley announced that the squadron was returning to Santiago. It was back in place during the night of 28–29 May. On the morning of the twenty-ninth a Spanish warship could be seen inside the harbor. Schley held a conference with his commanding officers and established a blockade of the port. Later that morning Schley notified Sampson that the major vessels in Cervera's squadron had been recognized in the harbor. As for his own force, Schley said that he had an insufficient amount of coal on hand and was trying to get more. The collier and the *Vixen* were undergoing repairs. If Sampson's squadron could relieve his, then Schley could coal at Gonaives or Port au Prince.[31]

In order to ascertain the strength of the enemy, Schley transferred his flag temporarily to the *Massachusetts* and, with two other battleships, conducted a distant bombardment of the Spanish forts at the mouth of the harbor. Mindful of the department's order not to expose ships to shore-based guns, Schley kept his force at a distance. The *Iowa's* guns were fired at an extreme elevation in an effort to hit the *Colón*, but the effect was to temporarily disable the American cannon. Once he had made a reconnaissance of the harbor and probed the guns of the *Colón*, Schley returned to his flagship and to blockade duty. Sampson and his squadron arrived before Santiago early on the morning of 1 June and assumed command of the combined forces.[32]

Now that Cervera had been located, Sampson wanted to keep him where he was. The admiral worked out a plan to sink a collier across the narrow entrance of the harbor. Naval Constructor Richmond P. Hobson and a crew of volunteers were given the assignment. Hobson moved the *Merrimac* toward the harbor entrance early on the morning of 3 June. The Spanish discovered the ship and opened fire. Ten explosive devices were to be used to sink the *Merrimac* in the correct location, but the Spanish shot out the steering gear. Then only two of the explosive devices worked. As a result, the ship sank lengthwise instead of across the channel. Hobson and his crew were picked up by the Spanish and imprisoned.[33]

Sampson next established his version of a blockade. Battleships and cruisers were organized into two divisions and placed in a semicircle with steam up and bows heading toward the harbor entrance six miles away. The eastern division was organized around Sampson's flagship, the *New York*, and the western one was focused on Schley's *Brooklyn*. These fast ships were placed on the flanks so they could deal with Cervera's ships if they got past other obstacles. Inside the battleship and cruiser arc was a semicircle made up of light auxiliaries, and closer to shore torpedo boats and destroyers were deployed in another arc. During the night the battleship and cruiser arc was moved closer so that it was only four miles from the harbor entrance. But under the best of circumstances, ships tended to drift from their assigned positions at night. This raised the possibility that Cervera might be able to escape at night. To eliminate that possibility, Sampson had an imaginative solution. Beginning on 8 June, each of the battleships took turns for two hours at a time in moving to within two miles of the shore and focusing their searchlight beams up the channel. This was the first time that electric light had been used in a wartime setting.[34]

By this time there was no longer a Navy Department ban on attacking shore-based fortifications, so on 6 June Sampson began a series of bombardments of the defenses of Santiago. For the Americans this was a welcome opportunity to test their guns against real targets, but they were not able to silence the enemy batteries. The effort convinced Sampson that the fortifications did not pose a real threat, but that they would have to be taken by Army troops.[35]

In anticipation of an Army landing in Cuba, the Navy believed it was necessary to establish its own base for coaling. On 31 May Captain Sigsbee of the *St. Paul* had suggested the seizure of Guantanamo for this purpose. Presumably the Navy Board received a formal inquiry about the project, for on 3 June that body recommended that a battalion of marines, then at Key West, be sent to Santiago. Four days later the unit was placed on board the *Panther* and sent to Cuba. While en route there the *Marblehead* and two small auxiliary cruisers were taken off blockade duty and sent to Guantanamo, where they shelled shore positions and forced a Spanish gunboat to withdraw. The expedition was then joined by the battleship *Oregon*, which had just completed a 12,000-mile cruise from South America to the war zone. Marines from the *Marblehead* and *Oregon* conducted a reconnaissance of an elevated point inside the harbor and found no Spaniards. The Marine battalion unloaded its supplies and established a base camp. On the night of 11 June, the Spanish attacked the marines, who fought back, assisted by naval gunfire. The Spanish attack was repelled, but the threat to the marines was not eliminated until 14 June.[36]

Army troops had been assembled at Tampa, Florida, awaiting orders to move to Cuba. Men were loaded onto transports on 8 June, but held outside Tampa harbor until the Navy could investigate reports of Spanish warships in the Caribbean. Sampson determined that these alleged sightings were the result of misidentifications, but to reassure the Army he sent Lt. Victor Blue of the *Suwannee* ashore on a reconnaissance mission on 11 June. Dressed in uniform and wearing his sword, Blue went to the headquarters of the local commander of the Cuban insurgents. There he was furnished with a guide who took him to a spot northwest of the bay that offered a view of the whole harbor. Blue reported on 13 June that Cervera's squadron consisted of four armored vessels and two torpedo boat destroyers.[37]

Now assured that the sea lanes were safe, and under pressure from McKinley to begin the campaign, the Army landed at Daiquirí on 22 June, with naval assistance. It was the plan of Maj. Gen. William R. Shafter, the Army commander, to land as close as he could to Santiago and move overland against the city. Two days after the initial landing a second one was made at Siboney, eight miles closer to Santiago.[38]

When he heard about the American landings, Cervera wrote to a navy captain in Spain that he could not hope to get away with his squadron, but he would resist as long as possible and then destroy his ships. Subsequently, at the request of the governor-general of Cuba, Cervera was placed under that official's command. For the benefit of the governor-general Cervera listed the problems with his squadron. The heavy guns of the *Cristóbal Colón* had not been installed; the *Vizcaya* had a badly fouled bottom that reduced its speed; and two of the *Vizcaya*'s 5.5-inch guns were defective as was one in the *Almirante Oquendo*. In addition, there were only 560 reliable rounds for the Hontoria 5.5-inch guns, and the majority of the fuses were not usable. There was little in the way of coal or provisions for the squadron, and no Bustamante contact mines to block the channel. Finally, the blockading force was four times as strong as his, and any battle between the two would result in the destruction of the Spanish ships.

Compelling as these arguments were, they did not sway the governor-general, who felt that if the squadron surrendered without a fight the effect would be terrible on morale both in Spain and abroad. So, from the time he came under the jurisdiction of the governor-general, it was suggested to Cervera that he escape with his ships at night and during bad weather. On 23 June the governor-general ordered Cervera to leave at a favorable moment or when the city was about to fall to the Americans. Cervera held a council of war with his officers and there was general agreement that deteriorating conditions were forcing the departure of the squadron. Therefore, when it was no longer possible to delay what he considered to be the sacrifice of his ships and men, Cervera gave an order on the evening of 2 July for a departure the next morning.

The narrow channel would force the Spanish ships to go out one at a time and at a somewhat slow speed. They would thus be very vulnerable to the fire of the awaiting American ships. The *Infanta María Teresa* would lead the way and engage the first available American ship. The *Vizcaya*, *Cristóbal Colón*, and *Almirante Oquendo* would follow, with the destroyers *Furor* and *Plutón* behind them. It was expected that the destroyers would use their speed to escape rather than attempt to fight as the larger ships would. The Spaniards hoped that they might break through the blockade and make it to Cienfuegos or Havana.[39]

On the morning of 3 July the Spaniards observed that the blockade was weaker than usual. The battleship *Massachusetts*, the cruisers *Newark* and *New Orleans*, and the converted tender *Suwannee* had gone to Guantanamo for coal. Differences in strategic viewpoints concerning the plans for the capture of Santiago had made it necessary for Shafter and Sampson to confer that morning. The *New York* hoisted a signal to the squadron to disregard the movements of the commander in chief, and steamed east to Siboney accompanied by the armed yacht *Hist* and the torpedo boat *Ericsson*. Schley was not informed of the planned meeting, and Sampson's departure left him in command of the squadron. The ships still on blockade duty were arranged in a semicircle about eight miles wide. From east to west it included the converted yacht *Gloucester*, the battleships *Indiana*, *Oregon*, *Iowa*, and *Texas*, the armored cruiser *Brooklyn*, and the converted yacht *Vixen*.[40]

In the American ships the crews had assembled on deck for Sunday morning inspection. Lookouts in various ships saw the *Infanta María Teresa* emerging from the harbor at about 9:35 A.M. Signal 250—"The enemy is attempting to escape"—was run up on the *Iowa*. Schley had just changed into his Sunday uniform and was seated on the quarterdeck when a call was heard from the forward bridge that the Spaniards were coming out. Some weeks before this Schley had had a wooden platform about three feet high built around the conning tower of the *Brooklyn*, and he raced to it now with his field glasses in hand. From this perch he could be in close touch with Captain Cook as well as have a better field of observation. In the *Brooklyn* and in other ships men rushed to their battle stations. Watertight compartments were closed; ammunition was readied for reloading the guns; fire pumps were turned on and the decks were wet down. The instant that Schley and George E. Graham, a reporter, reached the wooden platform, the *Iowa* fired a 6-pound shot at the Spaniards, followed by a 12-pounder from the *Texas*. Schley told Cook to have the men fire deliberately and not to waste a shot.

The *Teresa* headed for the *Brooklyn*, intending to ram it. Rapid fire was directed against the *Teresa*, which abandoned the ramming plan and turned westward. This movement left a small gap between the *Teresa* and the *Vizcaya*, which was following her. The *Vizcaya* had also planned to ram the *Brooklyn*, but it now turned westward and followed the *Teresa*.[41]

The Spaniards had now broken through the battleship line, so new dispositions were necessary to carry on the chase and the fight. In the *Brooklyn* Captain Cook gave the order "Hard aport!," anticipating by a few seconds the same command from Schley. The *Brooklyn* was rapidly swung around a little more than half her tactical diameter and headed westward. At the time of the turn the *Vizcaya* was close enough to see with a naked eye its crewmen running toward the forward turret. When the turn began, the signal "Follow the flag" was hoisted on the *Brooklyn*. This signal was seen and repeated by Captain Clark in the *Oregon*. When the turn was completed, the *Brooklyn* was heading west with the two Spanish ships about a mile off its starboard quarter and another coming up rapidly astern. (It was later alleged that the *Brooklyn*'s turn endangered the oncoming *Texas* and forced it to reverse its engines to avoid a collision. This was disputed by Schley, who said that the *Brooklyn* was never nearer than five or six hundred yards to the *Texas*. At the court of inquiry in 1901 some testimony placed the *Texas* at an even greater distance.)[42]

As the fight continued the *Brooklyn* received the fire of the *Teresa* and the *Vizcaya*, as well as an occasional shot from the *Colón*, and was responding in kind. The *Vixen* was well to the westward of the *Brooklyn* and steering a parallel course. Spanish shots aimed at the *Vixen* passed over it. The *Oregon* was about two miles to the southeast of the Spanish ships and moving ahead rapidly. It was hit three times but suffered no significant damage. The *Texas* was firing its main batteries at the *Colón, Oquendo*, and *Vizcaya*. The latter ship was about 6,600 yards distant. In the *Iowa* the first shot was fired at 5,000 yards, but since then it had closed rapidly. Shots were directed at the *Teresa* from 2,500 yards, at the *Vizcaya* at 2,100, and at the *Oquendo* at 1,600. The *Indiana* directed most of its attention to the *Oquendo*.[43]

About 10:27 A.M. the *Teresa* appeared to be badly damaged. It slowed and wobbled and smoke came from its hatches and ports. Observing this, Schley turned to Cook and remarked: "We have got one. Keep the boys below informed of all the movements. They can't see and they want to know." Cook had the news passed below, where it was greeted with cheers. From that time until the end of the battle, Cook arranged to have news relayed below every few minutes. Afire fore and aft, the *Teresa* turned and headed for the shore. It was beached about six miles from Santiago harbor.[44]

The shots of the *Brooklyn* and other ships were now directed at the *Oquendo*. A short time later it was observed to be on fire and wavering. It then turned toward shore and came to rest on a beach about a half mile west of the *Teresa*.[45]

The *Vizcaya* was now off the *Brooklyn*'s starboard bow. The *Colón* was farther inshore but it was moving up rapidly on the *Brooklyn* and reserving its fire. For a time it looked as though the *Vizcaya* might outrun the pursuing *Brooklyn* and *Oregon*. Smoke was so dense at times that the effect of the American fire could not be observed. Concerned about the distances between the combatants, Schley left his platform and went down to the deck where Yeoman George Ellis was stationed at the stadimeter and calling off the ranges to the captain. Ellis told Schley that the *Brooklyn* was maintaining about the same range, but to Schley it seemed that the distance between the ships was increasing. Ellis walked toward the ship's side to verify the range. He had moved only a few feet when he was struck in the head by a Spanish shell and decapitated. Passed Assistant Surgeon Charles M. DeValin and Ensign Edward McCauley, who were standing nearby, picked up the headless body and carried it to the ship's side, evidently intending to throw it overboard. At that moment Schley glanced in their direction and called out: "No! Do not throw that body overboard! One who had fallen so gallantly deserves the honors of a Christian burial!" The two officers placed the body beside a turret and covered it.[46]

When the *Brooklyn* and *Oregon* overtook the *Vizcaya* it appeared to turn toward its antagonists. At that moment the *Vizcaya* port bow was apparently struck by a shot and there was a heavy explosion. The ship began to list to port and headed inshore. Its colors were hauled down, and it was afire fore and aft when it was beached on a reef about fifteen miles west of Santiago. In the *Brooklyn* there was some concern that the *Vizcaya* might sink before it reached the shore. Schley ordered a signal made to the *Texas* to save the crew of the Spanish ship. Informed that the signal halyards had been shot away, and that attempts to attract the attention of the *Texas* by using the Army's wigwag system of flag signals had failed, Schley remarked that Capt. John W. Philip of the *Texas* was always sensible and would act without instructions.[47]

Meanwhile the Spanish destroyers were the last to emerge from the harbor. At first the *Furor* moved toward the east, but seeing the armed yacht *Gloucester* coming from that direction, it turned and steamed westward. The *Plutón* followed it closely. The smaller batteries in the *Indiana*, *Iowa*, *Oregon*, and *Texas* opened up on the destroyers at great ranges. But it was the *Gloucester* that pounded them with its 3- and 6-pound guns. Repeatedly hit and leaking badly, the *Plutón* headed for shore. It had nearly reached the beach when a 13-inch shell from the *Indiana* struck it amidships. The forward boilers exploded and killed all but two men in the area. Many Spanish sailors jumped overboard to escape and some drowned as a result. The *Gloucester* rescued twenty-six officers and men.[48]

Attention was now directed at the *Colón*, which had worked its way closer to the shore. In the *Brooklyn* it was thought that the Spanish captain might decide to pick a spot and run his ship ashore to save his crew. While waiting for the final act, the *Brooklyn* ceased firing and the crew came up from below for a hasty lunch. Extra rounds were brought up to the batteries in case the *Colón* decided to try to escape. The *Oregon* was told to try one of its thirteen-inch guns on the enemy. It did so, and the shell landed close to the enemy's stern. Other shots were fired, and although no hits were scored, the *Colón*'s captain was apparently convinced that resistance was hopeless. He had a gun fired to the leeward as a sign of surrender, hauled down his flag, and ran his ship ashore on a bar some forty-three miles from the entrance to Santiago harbor. It was 1:15 P.M.

When the *Colón* struck its flag, a cease-fire was ordered in the *Brooklyn* and *Oregon*. The two ships then bore down on the beached Spanish vessel. Captain Cook demanded unconditional surrender. Schley signaled the *Oregon:* "Congratulations on the grand victory. Thanks for splendid assistance."[49]

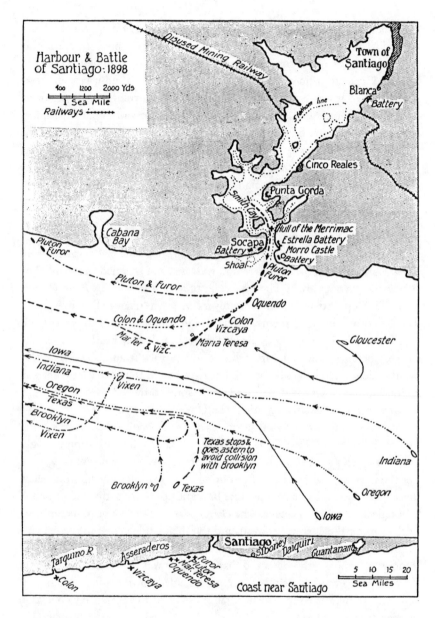

Inside the image:

Harbour & Battle of Santiago: 1898

400 1200 2000 Yds
1 Sea Mile
Railways ·····

Disused Mining Railway

Town of Santiago

Blanca Battery

Fathom line

Cinco Reales

Punta Gorda

Smith Cay

Cabana Bay

Pluton & Furor

Hull of the Merrimac
Estrella Battery
Morro Castle

Socapa Battery

Shoal

Pluton Furor

Oquendo

Colon & Oquendo

Colon
Vizcaya

Mar Ter & Viz.

Maria Teresa

Gloucester

Iowa

Indiana

Oregon

Texas

Brooklyn

Vixen

Vixen

Texas stops &
goes astern to
avoid collision
with Brooklyn

Brooklyn   Texas

Indiana

Oregon

Iowa

Santiago   Siboney   Daiquiri

Tarquino R.   Asseraderos   Guantanamo

Furor
Pluton
Mai. Teresa
Oquendo

Vizcaya

Colon

Coast near Santiago

5 10 15 20
Sea Miles

Battle of Santiago

Diagram of the battle published in Herbert W. Wilson, *Battleships in Action*, 2 vols. (London, 1926). *Courtesy U.S. Naval Institute.*

At the start of the battle Sampson was en route to Siboney when the sound of gunfire led him to run his ship around about 9:40 A.M. and head for the fighting. An hour later the *New York* fired three 4-inch shells at the *Furor*, but the rest of the battle was over by the time the admiral arrived on the scene. When the *New York* came within signal range shortly after 2 P.M., Schley sent by semaphore the news: "We have gained a great victory. Details will be communicated." This signal was acknowledged by an answering pennant. Next came an order: "Report your casualties." To this Schley was proud to reply: "Killed one. Wounded two." Apparently Sampson was surprised that the American casualties were so light. When the *New York* was still two miles away, Schley signaled: "This is a great day for our country!" The receipt of this message was also acknowledged with an answering pennant.

At 2:23 P.M. the *New York* took a position between the *Brooklyn* and the *Colón*. Captain Cook, who had been busy on the Spanish ship arranging the details for its surrender, was returning to the *Brooklyn* when he was ordered to report to the *New York*. As soon as he returned to his ship, Schley went to the *New York* to make his own report to Sampson. While Schley was in the *New York*, a report was received that a Spanish battleship had been sighted on the coast. Sampson sent the *Brooklyn* to investigate it. The vessel in question turned out to be Austrian.

During the afternoon Spanish prisoners were being picked up by American ships. When the *Brooklyn* again dropped anchor off Santiago, Capt. Robley Evans reported that Admiral Cervera and other prisoners of war were in the *Iowa*. Schley promptly made a call on Cervera at about midnight. During their talk Schley told Cervera that clothing and his personal funds would be available to him upon request. Cervera thanked Schley for his offer and said that the officers and men of the *Iowa* had already supplied the Spaniards with clothing. Cervera asked for permission to send a report on the battle to Spain. This was granted.

Before retiring Schley sent a preliminary written report to Sampson outlining the main events of the battle, and commending the captains of the *Texas, Iowa, Indiana, Oregon,* and *Brooklyn* for their "exceedingly meritorious conduct," and the commanders of the *Gloucester* and *Vixen* for "conspicuous gallantry." Sampson asked Schley to withdraw his report and suggested that some reference might be made to the *New York*, and intimated that the *Indiana* and the *Gloucester* were the closest to the *New York*. Schley did as he was requested.[50]

Meanwhile, Flag Lt. James H. Sears of the *Brooklyn* had been sent to the cable station at Siboney with a telegram to Secretary Long announcing the victory. Sears was told that if no message had been sent by Sampson, he was to transmit the one he carried. If one had already been sent, he was to bring back Schley's telegram. On the beach at Siboney Sears met Lt. Sidney A. Staunton, Sampson's aide, with a telegram from the admiral. The two officers went to the cable station together where Staunton read Sampson's telegram. Sears suggested that Sampson's message be corrected to show 1:15 P.M. as the time of the surrender of the *Colón*, instead of 2:00 P.M. as the text stated. He also suggested that the death of Yeoman Ellis be mentioned. Neither suggestion was adopted. The message in question had been drafted by an aide and had not been properly cleared by Sampson, but it bore his name. It began: "The fleet under my command offers the nation as a Fourth of July present the whole of the Spanish fleet." It then went on to give the results of the battle.[51]

This report was greeted with great enthusiasm in the Navy Department and the White House, but elsewhere in the nation its tone and content elicited criticism. Its opening sentence was reminiscent of Gen. William T. Sherman's report on the capture of Savannah during the Civil War. There was also no mention of Schley or of the other officers and ships that had won the battle. It helped to start controversy about who deserved credit for the victory and about the roles of Sampson and Schley before and after it.[52]

Convinced that an injustice had been done, some newspapers published accounts of the battle that gave all the credit to Schley. These accounts embarrassed Schley and he wrote a message to Long to that effect, adding: "Victory was secured by the force under the command Commander in Chief, North Atlantic Station, and to him all honor is due." Schley then showed the message to Sampson, who responded: "Schley this is kind and generous: I will transmit it at once."

If Schley could be gracious and open in a difficult situation, it soon became clear that Sampson was both unforgiving and indecisive. The same day he sent Schley's message to Long, he wrote separately to the secretary and for the first time complained about Schley's conduct in locating and blockading the Spanish fleet before the battle. Sampson said that in his opinion and those of his fellow officers, Schley's conduct before the battle—particularly his decision to leave Santiago to recoal—was "reprehensible." Sampson could not separate this from Schley's achievement at Santiago, so he asked the Navy Department to decide on the matter of credit for the battle and requested that Long give Schley "ample justice."[53]

This message created some problems for Long and raised almost as many questions about Sampson as Schley. If Schley's conduct was unsatisfactory, why had not Sampson reprimanded or relieved him? Also, if there were doubts about Schley's fitness, why leave him in command of the squadron?

Now that victory was won, why raise old issues and then pass the buck to the department for a decision? Could it be, as Edward L. Beach has suggested, that Sampson was suffering from Alzheimer's disease and unable to see the matter to a conclusion? Was the complaint really more the reflection of the views of Sampson's staff rather than his own? We do know that once the seed of mistrust was planted, there were those ready to nurture it. Capt. Alfred Thayer Mahan, historian, philosopher of sea power, and a member of the War Board, was both publicly and privately anti-Schley. Some of Schley's admirers believed that Rear Adm. Arent Crowninshield, the chief of the Bureau of Navigation, harbored ill feelings toward their hero. If so, Crowninshield was careful not to put anything in writing.[54]

As for Schley, his relations with Sampson had always been cordial and correct. He knew that the Navy Department was highly agitated about his movements before 1 July, but he assumed that his conduct at Santiago had made up for any deficiencies. This view seemed to be reinforced in a public way when Sampson and Schley walked arm in arm at a victory celebration in New York and were greeted by Long and other members of McKinley's cabinet. Schley himself was given a warm welcome in Washington, where he was received by the president. But a few weeks later things were quite different.[55]

Acting upon the recommendation of Secretary Long, McKinley sent to Congress a request that the promotions of Sampson and Schley to rear admiral be made permanent. This would also advance Schley by six numbers and Sampson by eight on the Navy's seniority list. Before the war, when both men had been captains, Schley was senior by one number, but when both became admirals Schley was junior by one number. Between the time this was proposed and the time it became a reality in March 1899, it was a hotly debated issue. When pro-Schley senators called upon the Navy Department for an explanation, Long naturally found it necessary to acquaint them with the contents of Sampson's critical message.

The general public also took an interest in the controversy. Alexander K. McClure, editor of the *Philadelphia Times*, wrote to President McKinley to alert him to the public perception of the situation. Claiming never to have met or to have had any direct or indirect contact with either officer, except for greeting Schley during his recent visit to Philadelphia, McClure said that "it is evident to any intelligent and dispassionate observer of existing conditions, that the administration and the navy department have become committed to an act of great injustice to the navy and the country, by the proposed promotion of Sampson over Schley." He went on to relate what he said "the intelligent and considerate public" knew, namely, that Schley had been given the command of the squadron by a signal from Sampson; that Schley's ship was nearest the Spanish when the first guns were fired and remained so until the battle ended; that after the battle Sampson sent Schley's battered ship and weary crew to investigate the report of another Spanish warship in the area; and that Sampson never congratulated Schley or others for winning the battle, but claimed credit for himself. McClure went on to compare Sampson to Gen. George B. McClellan of the Union Army during the Civil War in that each could organize a force but not use it in battle. The newspaperman said that he wrote to the president without anyone's knowledge and only to save the administration "from a blunder that would be little less than a crime." McKinley sent a copy of the letter to Secretary Long, but nothing seems to have come of it. The administration ignored this storm warning and went ahead with the advancement of Sampson over Schley that took effect on 3 March 1899.[56]

Shortly thereafter, the *New York Sun* published an editorial on the battle that quoted Lt. Cmdr. Albon C. Hodgson, the navigator of the *Brooklyn*, as saying that when Schley gave the order to turn hard aport, Hodgson questioned whether he meant starboard. Schley reportedly said no, that they were already near enough to the Spaniards. Hodgson then replied: "But we will cut down the Texas!" To this remark Schley allegedly responded: "Damn the Texas; let her look out for herself." Schley wrote to Hodgson on 6 June 1899 enclosing a copy of the editorial and asking him to "write me your denial of this oft-repeated calumny." Hodgson sent a lengthy reply in which he said: "What the Sun has printed as a part of a conversation between you and me is substantially correct, though not as to the manner in which it took place." To this Schley responded that he was not disturbed by attacks in the newspapers against himself, but that he wanted to protect Hodgson from slander. The key, to Schley, was the printing by the *Sun* of a conversation quoting each speaker directly. He therefore asked Hodgson for a short letter denying that the colloquy took place. Hodgson complied but with his letter he also enclosed another in which he wrote: "From my last letter you will gather my recollection of what occurred the day of the battle regarding the turn." In essence Hodgson was denying the accuracy of the quotations printed by the *Sun* but not that a conversation had taken place. When Schley had the letter denying the conversation published, Hodgson's veracity and honor were publicly attacked. To defend himself he asked Schley a number of times to put the denial in context and to give Hodgson permission to publish their correspondence. Schley refused in July 1899 on the grounds that the Navy Department had ordered an official investigation of the matter and that in view of this it would be improper for the admiral to publish anything on the question. Hodgson then turned to the Navy Department for justice, arguing that the scope of his denial had been misconstrued by the public. He asked the Navy Department "to take such steps as may be deemed proper to exonerate me in the eyes of the public, or give me permission to adopt such measures as may be necessary to this end." Hodgson's charges and his position on the letter of denial thus became a part of the controversy. Because no one else in the *Brooklyn* admitted hearing the alleged conversation, it became a matter of which officer's account one believed.[57]

Secretary Long was, by this point, extremely angry that the issue would not die and in November 1899 issued a circular prohibiting officers on active duty from discussing the matter in public. But debate still raged in private. Those against Schley were determined to destroy his reputation through a court of inquiry. Schley knew he had nothing to gain by keeping the controversy alive or encouraging an investigation, but he was finally forced to seek a hearing when Edgar Stanton Maclay published a history of the Navy—adopted as a text by the Naval Academy—that contained an account of the battle that libeled Schley. Capt. Robley D. Evans, who commanded the *Iowa* in the battle of Santiago, published his memoirs in 1901 under the title *A Sailor's Log*. In them he made some brief and unflattering observations about Schley's orders prior to the battle, but said nothing about Schley's conduct during the conflict itself. Credit for the victory was given to Sampson.[58]

Adm. George Dewey was ordered to convene a court of inquiry to investigate fourteen charges relating to Schley's actions from the time he was at Cienfuegos until the battle. The inquiry opened on 12 September 1901 and lasted forty days. The court took the view that Sampson's conduct was not under review, so only testimony directly concerning Schley was admitted. Schley's lawyer argued unsuccessfully that this ruling was unfair because the actions of the two officers were related. Sampson wanted to testify, but his health would not permit it. In his closing summary, Samuel C. Lemly, the Navy judge advocate, said that the court must "pass upon one of the most important questions ever considered by a naval tribunal—a question between the applicant and the morale of the service." He said that the issues at stake were more important than an individual officer. "It is for you to lay down a standard of conduct to be followed in future similar cases—a standard such as that set by our great naval commanders like John Paul Jones, Decatur, Perry, Farragut, the Porters, and others. A sense of propriety forbids my mentioning the living." That was the issue. Schley may have won his battle, but he did not project the right image of a naval officer. To uphold him now would be damaging to the morale of the Navy.[59]

Schley Court of Inquiry

The court met in Washington from 12 September to 14 December 1901. In this photographic montage Admiral of the Navy George Dewey, President of the Court, stands at the head of the table with Rear Adm. E. K. Benham on his right and Rear Adm. Francis M. Ramsey on his left. Capt. Samuel C. Lemly, Judge Advocate General of the Navy, sits between Benham and Rear Adm. Winfield Scott Schley. The civilians are attorneys. *Courtesy of the Naval Historical Center.*

SHAKE!

Schley and Dewey

The publication of this editorial cartoon by the Portland, Oregon, *Sunday Oregonian*, 15 December 1901, reflects the national interest in the Schley-Sampson controversy. *Courtesy of the Smithsonian Institution.*

After due deliberation, the court rendered its verdict. It criticized Schley for failing to act decisively between his departure from Key West to the time of the battle. As for the battle itself, he was criticized for his "loop" and for endangering the *Texas*. The court also found him guilty of an injustice to Lt. Cmdr. Albon Hodgson when he published only a portion of the correspondence that passed between the officers about the matter. In summary, the court found Schley's conduct prior to 1 June to be characterized by "vacillation, dilatoriness, and a lack of enterprise." During the battle of Santiago, however, he was self-possessed and by his own example encouraged his subordinates to fight courageously.

The president of the court, Admiral Dewey, issued a separate opinion in which he dissented from the conclusions on five points of issue prior to 1 June. As for the battle, Dewey said that Schley "was in absolute command, and is entitled to the credit due to such commanding officer for the glorious victory which resulted in the total destruction of the Spanish ships."[60] Most writers who discuss the controversy at any length end the story here. But that was not the end.

If the Navy thought that an acceptable verdict on Schley's performance had been reached or that the controversy would soon die, it was wrong. When Dewey's minority opinion was publicized it was widely hailed. Forty-two persons wrote personal letters to him to express their approval of his stand. Among them were four attorneys, one judge, and a former member of Congress. Others were ordinary citizens, businessmen, and members of patriotic or veteran groups. The Army and Navy Republican League of Los Angeles, which claimed to have one thousand active members on its rolls, adopted a resolution that praised Schley and Dewey and condemned the findings of the majority. A letter from Bernard Callahan of Brooklyn, who identified himself as a Republican who had served as an enlisted man in the Navy during the Civil War, may have been read with special interest. Callahan recalled that after the battle of Santiago, Captain Cook was entertained by the U.S. Grant Post of the Grand Army of the Republic in Brooklyn. At that time Cook reportedly told Callahan "that he gave that famous order [for the loop], to avoid being caught in a Spanish trap in that supreme moment. 'My order was approved by my gallant Commodore and the battle won by him.'" Callahan noted that this conversation took place when events were still fresh in Cook's memory and long before there was any thought of a court of inquiry.[61]

Large segments of the public soon demonstrated that they too agreed with Dewey. After the battle of Santiago, Schley had been presented with a gold medal by the citizens of Brooklyn, a gold medal set with diamonds from his home state of Maryland, and a gold and jeweled sword and belt from the people of Pennsylvania, but the court of inquiry set off a whole new round of honors and gifts. At intervals throughout the year 1902 Schley travelled to various cities to receive loving cups, silver plate and centerpieces, as well as special medals, statues, and resolutions. Honors also came from Masonic lodges. All in all it was an impressive display of public affection and support.[62]

On the other side of the issue, prominent naval officers Alfred Thayer Mahan and Stephen B. Luce supported the verdict. Mahan felt so strongly that he broke off his relationship with the popular journal *The Independent*, to which he had contributed articles, because it had sided with Schley.

Schley and his lawyers were no more ready to accept the verdict of the court than were his supporters. They promptly appealed to the Secretary of the Navy, urging that the court's findings not be approved on the grounds that the report of the facts was in conflict with the weight of the evidence. They also protested that the court had ignored the testimony of Schley and of witnesses who were favorable to him, for in so doing the court had deprived Schley of his constitutional rights. The rebuttal listed thirty-one specific instances of error. For example, in regard to the famous "loop," it disregarded the testimony of Captain Cook on how close the *Brooklyn* was to the *Texas*, and on the alleged colloquy with Lieutenant Commander Hodgson. Finally it stated that the whole proceedings on the part of the majority of the court "have been entirely irregular." Schley's rights were violated and ignored, and a grave injustice had been committed.

The judge advocate and his assistant filed their rebuttal to these objections. Not surprisingly, they found no merit in the appeal, which they said was not specific in character and contained sweeping and unsupported assertions of opinion and assertions that the findings had not been justified by the evidence. Instead they argued that it was the most "patient, exhaustive, and painstaking hearing" ever extended to any military officer. They asked that the secretary approve their findings.

Meanwhile, Sampson's attorneys petitioned the Navy to disapprove that portion of Dewey's opinion that related to Schley being in absolute command at Santiago. They argued that the question of command had not been referred to the court for its consideration. Sampson's counsel said that on three separate occasions they had appealed to the court for permission to appear and to defend the admiral's rights. Each time they were refused. In answer to one of their letters, Dewey said that the court did not consider Sampson an interested party. Yet in the minority opinion Dewey discussed matters beyond the scope of the court.[63]

It was now clear that what had begun as an inquiry to expose Schley's behavior was raising points about the actions of other officers as well. Sampson, Dewey, and Schley were all dissatisfied for various reasons. Long acted
quickly to try to bring matters to an end. He approved the findings of fact
and opinion, as well as the points made by Dewey that differed from the
views of the majority. As for Dewey's views on command and credit, Long
said the court was correct in rendering no opinion on the question. Finally,
he endorsed the recommendation that there be no further proceedings on
the subject.

While the court was still in session, Schley was retired on 9 October 1901
after forty-five years of service. The Navy Department responded to this
event with the bare minimum of courtesy. Schley had only partly won his
fight, but he did not give up. In January 1902 he sent a petition to President
Theodore Roosevelt asking for relief from the findings of the court. He
based his appeal on three grounds: first, as to who was in command at Santiago; second, whether a close and adequate blockade of Santiago had been
maintained; and third, on that portion of Dewey's dissent that covered the
passage from Key West to Cienfuegos, the blockade of that port, and the
movement from Cienfuegos to Santiago. In support of these points, Schley's
attorneys prepared three exhibits, each of which reproduced the pertinent
testimony before the court.[64]

Roosevelt reviewed Schley's appeal and the Navy Department's answer, as
well as all the official reports, the log and signal books, and the testimony.
He also called in four of the surviving captains of the five ships in the battle
besides those of Sampson and Schley. The president concluded that there
was a reasonable doubt as to whether Schley moved his squadron "with sufficient expedition from port to port." He believed that Schley's most grave error was the retrograde movement and "his disobedience of orders and mis-
statement of facts in relation thereto." But it should be remembered, said
Roosevelt, "that the majority of these actions which the Court censures occurred five weeks or more before the fight itself; and it certainly seems that if
Admiral Schley's actions were censurable he should not have been left as second in command under Admiral Sampson. His offenses were in effect con-
doned when he was not called to account for them." Roosevelt believed that
all of the appeal should be dismissed except that which related to the battle.

To Roosevelt, the questions of command and credit were really an appeal
from the action of President McKinley when he sent forward the recommendations for promotion. It was therefore a question as to whether
McKinley committed an injustice. Roosevelt concluded that neither officer
exercised any command. Sampson's claim for credit rested on his work as

commander in chief in establishing an excellent blockade, in preparing and arranging his ships, and in his standing orders in case of attack.

As for Schley, Roosevelt felt that both he and Captain Cook were entitled to credit for what the *Brooklyn* did in the fight. On the whole they did well, and the excellent record was marred only by the loop. If the *Brooklyn* had turned westward instead of eastward, it would have placed itself in a more dangerous position, but it would also have been more dangerous to the Spanish. "This kind of danger must not be too nicely weighed by those whose trade it is to dare greatly for the honor of the flag." Moreover, the danger was no greater than that facing the *Texas* or the yacht *Gloucester*. Therefore, as regards Sampson and Schley, Roosevelt concluded that McKinley had made the proper recommendations and that justice was done. There was no reason for reversing his action. In conclusion the president said: "There is no excuse whatever from either side for any further agitation of this unhappy controversy. To keep it alive would merely do damage to the Navy and to the country." So it was that Roosevelt recognized that the matter had gone well beyond the effort to humiliate Schley, and well beyond the issue of the morale of the Navy.[65]

It seems likely that neither side was happy with Roosevelt's decision. The items of concern to Sampson and his partisans, relating to Schley's conduct before the battle, and issues on which the court had spent so much time, were dismissed out of hand. When all was said and done, only the famous loop was condemned, and this did not affect the outcome of the battle.

Two and a half months after Roosevelt issued his reply, Sampson died. The fight was now carried on in print. Long's book, *The New American Navy*, published in 1903, was anti-Schley in its treatment of Santiago. In 1904 Schley published his autobiography and set forth his version of what happened in the Spanish-American War. It was Schley's contention that he was censured for what might have happened rather than for what *did* happen. In 1906 Alfred Thayer Mahan published his short history of the Naval War Board in which he again spoke about Schley's vacillation. A shorter and more popular version of Schley's life appeared serially in *Cosmopolitan* magazine in 1911 and 1912. While they were still being published, Schley died in October 1911.

Upon learning of Schley's death, Secretary of the Navy George von Lengerke Meyer issued a public statement on the loss of "a most distinguished officer" and offered the family a naval funeral, which was accepted. Admiral Dewey said that Schley "was a warm-hearted, gallant and chivalrous gentleman"; the country had lost a loyal servant and Dewey a dear friend of more than fifty years. On the day of the funeral, a brief Masonic ceremony was held at Schley's home on I Street N.W. in Washington, after which six Navy gunners from Norfolk placed the body on a caisson and accompanied it to St. John's Episcopal Church, across Lafayette Park from the White House. As the coffin was moved from the house, crowds filled the streets approaching the church and surged against the lines of police officers. Services at the church were attended by Secretary Meyer, Admiral Dewey, members of the Supreme Court, the diplomatic corps, and others from the executive branch and both houses of Congress. President William Howard Taft was in Nebraska, but his naval aide represented him. At the specific request of the president, Spanish-American War veterans who were government employees were permitted to attend the funeral, and a number of them did so. In St. John's the rector conducted services assisted by a Navy chaplain. Six retired rear admirals were designated as honorary pallbearers as well as former Justice Alexander H. Hagner of Washington and Lt. Gen. Nelson A. Miles of the Army. The procession to Arlington Cemetery was led by Rear Adm. Charles J. Badger, the commander of the second division of the Atlantic Fleet, followed by one hundred midshipmen from the Naval Academy, five companies of bluejackets, six companies of Marines from Washington and Philadelphia, and one Army artillery battery. A number of the veterans who were government employees walked to the cemetery at the end of the procession. The interment was in front of the Lee House. All in all it was an impressive ceremony.[66]

Even after the funeral Mahan and Stephen B. Luce continued their hatred. Luce went so far as to suggest to Mahan that they petition the Senate to proclaim Sampson the real victor of Santiago. Mahan saw no merit in this proposal because he believed that President Taft was pro-Schley.[67] With no other follow-up move likely, the issue slowly faded. Mahan died in 1914 and Luce and Dewey in 1917. Each man's reputation was affected by his stand on the issue of Schley. The controversy did a great deal of harm to the Navy.

As we approach the centennial of the battle of Santiago, it would be well if historians in their works could take account of the hopes and fears of the leaders of that time without losing track of the realities. Naval intelligence reports and Cervera's own memoirs, published after the war, confirm that the Spanish squadron constituted no threat to the United States. Cervera hoped to save his ships and men and to get through the war with honor. He predicted that even if Spain won a naval victory in the West Indies it would only serve to postpone an inevitable defeat because Spain had no facilities in the West Indies to repair its ships, whereas the United States had shipyards close at hand as well as plenty of money to effect repairs. None of Schley's short-comings made any difference in the battle of Santiago or the war, and these facts were known to the Navy Department long before the court of inquiry. Santiago was a victory over an inferior force. It was not much of a contest, but the Navy had to make the most of it. Whatever the degree of glory associated with the victory, Schley's enemies were determined to deny him the largest share of it. But in attempting to limit the credit given to Schley, they hurt the Navy and postponed the day when objective histories of the battle and the war could be written.

NOTES

1. Executive Session of the U.S. Senate, 25 Apr. 1898, 55th Cong., 2d sess. While doing research in the Legislative Records of the Senate on the Spanish-American War, the writer discovered that three executive sessions were still classified. Through his efforts and those of others this material was declassified in January 1969 and made available for research in the National Archives.

2. Ronald Spector, *Professors of War: The Naval War College and the Development of the Naval Profession* (Newport, 1977), 90–94.

3. Ibid., 94–98.

4. David F. Trask, *The War with Spain in 1898* (New York, 1981), 78–79. This is the most recent and complete history of the Spanish-American War.

5. Ibid., 83–87; Herbert W. Wilson, *The Downfall of Spain: Naval History of the Spanish-American War* (London, 1900), 174–77.

6. Trask, *War with Spain*, 82, 87; Richard S. West, Jr., *Admirals of American Empire* (Indianapolis, 1948), 193, 222.

7. West, *Admirals*, 108–14, 223, 193.

8. Trask, *War with Spain*, 90–91.

9. Ibid., 91.

10. Ibid., 108.

11. Ibid., 110; Wilson, *Downfall*, 181–82. Wilson says that the Americans fired 200 rounds and only killed a mule at Matanzas.

12. Trask, *War with Spain*, 64–65; Cervera to Bermejo, 8 Apr. 1898, in Rear Admiral Pascual Cervera y Topete, *The Spanish-American War: A Collection of Documents Relating to the Squadron Operation in the West Indies* (Madrid, 1899), trans. Office of Naval Intelligence and published in *War Notes No. VII* (Washington, 1899), 44 [hereafter cited as *War Notes*].

13. Cervera to Bermejo, 15, 20, 21, 22 Apr. 1898, *War Notes*, 47–48, 52, 54, 55, 57 (quotation).

14. Cervera to Bermejo, 23, 24, 29 Apr., 8 May 1898, *War Notes*, 58, 65, 68–71.

15. Trask, *War with Spain*, 114–15, 119; West, *Admirals*, 230–31. Wilson says that the Spaniards had two or three guns dismounted, several houses damaged, eight men

killed and twenty wounded. Few of the American shells exploded. See Wilson, *Downfall*, 196.

16. Cervera to Bermejo, 12, 14–15, 17, 19 May 1898, *War Notes*, 73–74, 76–78; Trask, *War with Spain*, 116–17. Cervera did not know that the auxiliary *Paris* had been renamed the *Yale*, and the *New York* was now the *Harvard*, to avoid confusing it with Sampson's flagship. See Wilson, *Downfall*, 56.

17. Trask, *War with Spain*, 120; West, *Admirals*, 232.

18. West, *Admirals*, 234, 238.

19. Ibid., 235–36.

20. Ibid., 236.

21. Ibid., 237; Trask, *War with Spain*, 122. The report of the munitions being carried was untrue.

22. West, *Admirals*, 237.

23. Ibid.; Trask, *War with Spain*, 123.

24. Trask, *War with Spain*, 122–23. The texts of documents relating to Schley's service in the war are printed in U.S. Navy Department, *Record of Proceedings of a Court of Inquiry in the Case of Rear-Admiral Winfield S. Schley, U.S. Navy*, 2 vols. (Washington, 1902) [hereafter cited as *Proceedings*]; and in Winfield S. Schley, *Forty-five Years Under the Flag* (New York, 1904).

25. Trask, *War with Spain*, 123.

26. Ibid., 124.

27. Schley, *Forty-five Years*, 277–78; Trask, *War with Spain*, 124.

28. Schley, *Forty-five Years*, 278–79. Schley later testified that he thought the dispatch of 25 May was ambiguous, and that he regarded it as a suggestion rather than an order. Also, Long was wrong about the landing places. Nunez told Schley that the areas were occupied by the Spaniards. See *Proceedings* 2:1149–50, 1473–74, 1487–88.

29. Trask, *War with Spain*, 126.

30. Schley, *Forty-five Years*, 279–80; West, *Admirals*, 249–50.

31. West, *Admirals*, 250. Schley's messages to Long and Sampson from Cienfuegos reached them after he had departed from that port.

32. Trask, *War with Spain*, 136; Schley, *Forty-five Years*, 286–87.

33. West, *Admirals*, 253–54; Trask, *War with Spain*, 137–38; Robley D. Evans, *A Sailor's Log* (New York, 1901), 439–41.

34. West, *Admirals*, 253–54; Trask, *War with Spain*, 138; Margaret Leech, *In the Days of McKinley* (New York, 1959), 222.

35. Allan R. Millett, *Semper Fidelis: The History of the United States Marine Corps* (New York, 1980), 132–33; Schley, *Forty-five Years*, 291–92.

36. Trask, *War with Spain*, 138; Schley, *Forty-five Years*, 292–93.

37. Trask, *War with Spain*, 212–13. Daiquirí is seventeen miles east of Santiago. Navy officers viewed Shafter's operation as aimed at opening the harbor of Santiago and expected the Army to advance along the beach and take El Morro, a fortification at the mouth of the harbor. McKinley and the War Department visualized a land campaign in Cuba, in which the seizure of the high ground around Santiago and the

capture of the city were early phases. For this purpose the Army moved inland. See Graham A. Cosmas, *An Army for Empire: The United States Army in the Spanish-American War* (Columbia, Mo., 1971), 206–13.

38. Trask, *War with Spain*, 214; Cervera to the Governor-General, 25 June 1898, *War Notes*, 110–11. Cervera had intended to run the blockade during a storm on 26 May, but was fearful that the *Colón* would ground itself on a rock in the harbor entrance when a pilot told him that a merchant vessel had lost a keel there earlier. See Cervera to the Minister of Marine, 27 May 1898, *War Notes*, 98.

39. Trask, *War with Spain*, 258–59. Governor-General to Cervera, 26, 28 June, 1, 2 July 1898; Cervera to Governor-General, 1 July 1898, *War Notes*, 113, 115–19.

40. Schley, *Forty-five Years*, 284–85; Wilson, *Downfall*, 297–300.

41. Schley, *Forty-five Years*, 300–301; Evans, *Sailor's Log*, 443–46.

42. Schley, *Forty-five Years*, 301–3; *Proceedings* 2:1388, 1397, 1408. Cook later testified that he gave the order, but Chief Quartermaster Nils Anderson, whose battle station was at the wheel of the *Brooklyn*, remembered Schley doing it (*Proceedings* 2:1583–84). Chief Boatswain William L. Hill testified that he heard Schley say "Port" and that the *Texas* "was fully a third of a mile from us" (*Proceedings* 2:1275). Schley says that Cook gave the order to turn, but that he would have done it in a second (*Proceedings* 2:1512). The commodore also said that he never heard of the *Texas* incident until six months after the battle. He also claimed that the *Texas* was never closer than 500 to 600 yards to the *Brooklyn* and that there was never any danger of a collision (*Proceedings* 2:1397, 1512, 1517, 1521). In its statement of facts at the end of the investigation, the Court of Inquiry in 1901 said that Cook put the helm hard aport at the same time that Schley gave the order. It also stated that the *Brooklyn* turned toward the *Texas*, and that the latter stopped and backed its engines (*Proceedings* 2:1829).

43. Schley, *Forty-five Years*, 302–3; the log of the *Vixen* is reproduced in Schley, 326–30, and is referred to hereafter as *Vixen Log*. Evans, *Sailor's Log*, 445–47. Evans initially tried to ram the *Teresa*; West, *Admirals*, 262–63.

44. Schley, *Forty-five Years*, 303–4; George E. Graham, *Schley and Santiago* (Chicago, 1902), 299–300. Graham was a war correspondent of the Associated Press and was on board the *Brooklyn* during the battle.

45. Schley, *Forty-five Years*, 304; Graham, *Schley and Santiago*, 299–300.

46. Schley, *Forty-five Years*, 305; Graham, *Schley and Santiago*, 306–14.

47. Schley, *Forty-five Years*, 304; Evans, *Sailor's Log*, 449–50.

48. Wilson, *Downfall*, 304–7; *Vixen Log*, 328.

49. Schley, *Forty-five Years*, 305–9; Graham, *Schley and Santiago*, 322–31; West, *Admirals*, 265.

50. Schley, *Forty-five Years*, 310–20; Graham, *Schley and Santiago*, 439–41.

51. Schley, *Forty-five Years*, 317; West, *Admirals*, 286–90.

52. Trask, *War with Spain*, 266–69, 299–319, 353–68.

53. West, *Admirals*, 286–91; Leech, *Days of McKinley*, 258–59; Schley, *Forty-five Years*, 335–36.

54. Edward L. Beach, *The United States Navy: 200 Years* (New York, 1986), 364–67; Robert Seager II, *Alfred Thayer Mahan: The Man and His Letters* (Annapolis, 1977), 400–403. Apparently Mr. T. A. Tompkins made a reference to Crowninshield in a letter to Long. In his reply of 23 October 1901 Long asked for specifics and said that the Navy Department would investigate any charges (Personal/Official Letterbook, No. 23, Long Papers, Massachusetts Historical Society). On 15 September 1898 Capt. Robley Evans of the *Iowa* stopped by the department and told Long about "the inefficiency of Commodore Schley when he was in command of the squadron off Santiago" (see Lawrence Shaw Mayo, ed., *America of Yesterday as Reflected in the Journal of John Davis Long* [Boston, 1923], 208).

55. West, *Admirals*, 289, 296–98; Schley, *Forty-five Years*, 340–42.

56. A. K. McClure to William McKinley, 6 December 1898. Typescript copy in the Papers of John D. Long, Massachusetts Historical Society, Boston.

57. *Court of Inquiry* 2:1716–19.

58. Ibid., 1:2–4; Edgar Stanton Maclay, *History of the Navy*, 3 vols. (New York, 1901), vol. 3, appendix 3 and p. 365; Seager, *Alfred Thayer Mahan*, 402–4; West, *Admirals*, 300–301; Evans, *Sailor's Log*, 427–59.

59. *Court of Inquiry* 2:1823.

60. Ibid., 1829–30.

61. Letters to Dewey concerning the Schley Court of Inquiry were in the custody of the Naval History Section of the Smithsonian's National Museum of American History but have since been transferred to the Manuscript Division of the Library of Congress.

62. Most of these medals and trophies are now in the Schley Collection at the Smithsonian's National Museum of American History. Accounts of most of Schley's appearances and gifts may be found in the *New York Times*.

63. Seager, *Alfred Thayer Mahan*, 405; *Court of Inquiry* 2:1923–24, 1847–1922, 1831–43.

64. Ibid., 1847–1906; Schley, *Forty-five Years*, 408–28.

65. *Court of Inquiry* 2:1923–36.

66. *New York Times*, 3, 6 Oct. 1911; *Army & Navy Journal*, 7 Oct. 1911.

67. Seager, *Alfred Thayer Mahan*, 405.

Joint Operations in the Spanish-American War

GRAHAM A. COSMAS

To AN EXTENT UNPRECEDENTED IN THE NATION'S PREVIOUS CONFLICTS, the Spanish-American War required the projection of American military power across the oceans. Although naval engagements were decisive, land forces assisted the Navy's operations and helped secure the nation's diplomatic and territorial objectives in Cuba, Puerto Rico, and the Philippines. The U.S. Army and Navy were less than fully prepared to conduct joint[1] operations, as other activities had preoccupied them during the three decades since Appomattox. Nevertheless, under strong direction from their commander in chief, President William McKinley, the Army and Navy improvised solutions to the joint operational problems they faced and, in the main, effectively carried out the national strategy.

I

The outbreak of war with Spain found both armed services in the midst of campaigns of reform and modernization driven by changing technology, the disappearance of old missions, and the ambitions of a new generation of progressively minded career officers. In both services, the objective of reform was the same: the development of forces comparable in organization, equipment, and tactics—although not in size—to those of the other major industrial powers and able to uphold, through deterrent presence or active operations, the expanding strategic and commercial interests of the United States in the late nineteenth-century world of rampant imperialism.

Change was most dramatic in the Navy. That service, under the influence of doctrines publicized (but not originated) by Capt. Alfred Thayer Mahan, scrapped during the decade before 1898 its time-honored coastal defense and commerce-raiding strategy for one of command of the sea. To carry out that strategy, the Navy replaced its aging wooden steam frigates and cumbersome monitors with a steel fleet centered around seagoing armored battleships and cruisers. Army reform was less spectacular but no less profound. As the Indian campaigns came to a close, the Army undertook a major rebuilding of the coastal defenses, viewed by Army and Navy reformers alike as the strategic shield to the sword of the Mahanian battle fleet. The Army rearmed its small standing force with bolt-action repeating rifles and new field and siege artillery, modernized its infantry tactics, and concentrated its troops at fewer, larger posts to improve living conditions and facilitate training. Through new branch schools and a rudimentary general staff college at Fort Leavenworth, the service both improved the education of its junior officers and provided an institutional base for continued reform agitation.[2]

The Army and Navy reformers of the period shared common aspirations and values, exchanged ideas, and occasionally assisted each other's efforts. They also held common assumptions about the nation's future wars. Given the absence of great land powers on the borders and the maritime and commercial character of American interests, they expected conflicts to develop over European challenges to the Monroe Doctrine, threats to American control of the Caribbean and the prospective Central American canal, and, possibly, political and economic competition in the Far East. In such wars, Army and Navy reformers agreed, the Navy would carry the burden of American offensive action, striking at the enemy's fleet, commerce, and colonies. The Army's coastal batteries would protect the fleet's bases and harbors of refuge, and Army expeditions might follow up naval successes by seizing strategic pieces of enemy territory. In 1897, Maj. Gen. John M. Schofield, who had recently retired as commanding general of the Army, summed up the prevailing view of the services' missions:

In a country having the situation of the United States, the navy is the *aggressive* arm of the national military power. Its function is to punish an enemy until he is willing to submit to the national demands. For this purpose entire freedom of action is essential; also secure depots whence supplies may be drawn and where necessary repairs may be made. . . . Hence arises one of the most important functions of the land defense: to give the aggressive arm secure bases of operation at all the great seaports where navy-yards or depots are located. It may be that in special cases military forces may be needed to act in support of naval operations, or to hold for a time important points in a foreign country; but such service must be only auxiliary, not a primary object. Foreign conquest and permanent occupation are not a part of the policy of this country.[3]

Although their leaders envisioned future maritime and amphibious conflicts, the Army and Navy did little planning or training for them before 1898. The services conducted few large-scale unilateral exercises and no joint ones. Both services lacked central planning agencies comparable to the Prussian General Staff, although the Naval War College, founded in 1884, performed some planning functions through its periodic war games and studies of hypothetical campaigns. During the various diplomatic confrontations and war scares of the Cleveland and Harrison administrations, joint planning, indeed contingency planning of any sort, appears to have been extremely informal, and little written record of it survived. Yet the planning that did occur reflected the services' emerging strategic consensus. During the Chilean crisis of 1892, for instance, General Schofield received instructions to "make an estimate of the military force which would be necessary to occupy and hold a vital point in Chilean territory until the demands of the United States were complied with," presumably after the Navy had secured control of Chile's coastal waters.[4]

For all their lack of up-to-date contingency plans, the Army and Navy possessed considerable experience in joint operations. In 1847, Army Maj. Gen. Winfield Scott and Navy Commodore David Connor cooperated in an attack on Vera Cruz that was for its time a model of effective planning and execution. Union forces in the Civil War waged extensive amphibious campaigns along the Atlantic and Gulf coasts and in the Mississippi River Valley. Army-Navy cooperation in these campaigns was not always harmonious or successful, but by the end of the war the services had mastered many of the necessary techniques, as they demonstrated in the capture of Fort Fisher in January 1865. Although neither service preserved its Civil War experiences as formal doctrine, all the senior Army and Navy commanders in the war with Spain had served in the earlier conflict. Hence, it is likely that some institutional memory of Civil War operations survived in 1898.[5]

The earlier wars had set a pattern for planning and control of joint operations. Army and Navy commanders, once assigned their mission, normally enjoyed wide latitude in executing it and cooperated as independent equals unless one had definite orders to support the other. They resolved disagreements by negotiation and compromise and, failing that, referred them back up their separate chains of command for negotiation at higher echelons and, if necessary, final resolution at the presidential and cabinet level. Such informality and divided authority were viewed with scorn by early twentieth-century reformers steeped in the gospel of efficiency and seem primitive indeed compared to the highly structured complexity of modern joint commands; yet this way of conducting affairs was typical of late nineteenth-century America, a society still governed more through informal consensus than bureaucratic hierarchy.[6]

In their command arrangements, the Americans conformed to the practice of Great Britain, the era's premier naval power and most proficient practitioner of amphibious warfare. The British, in the words of a contemporary authority, kept their naval and army commanders "independent" of one another and trusted them to "work together for the common object." In the British service, however, the navy controlled all shipping, including troop transports, whereas in the United States the Army traditionally procured and operated troopships and also at times landing craft, gunboats, and other combat and support vessels. This division of responsibility, which prevailed during the war with Spain, was to be the source of much bickering between the American services.[7]

At the level of tactics, the Navy, in order to perform its worldwide mission of protecting American lives, property, and commerce, kept up a tradition of landing operations. Naval brigades, composed of ships' marine detachments and sailors organized and armed as infantry, conducted major incursions in Korea (1871), Alexandria, Egypt (1882), and Panama (1885), and smaller contingents went ashore at innumerable places in Asia, the Pacific, and Central and South America. Although overwhelmingly preoccupied with the tactics and technology of the new armored battle fleet, Navy officers devoted some systematic thought to these operations and drew from them—and from study of similar activities of foreign services—lessons and the beginnings of a doctrine. The Navy Department in 1891 codified a decade of service thinking on the subject in its "Instructions for Infantry and Artillery" for its landing brigades. Drafted by a board that included an Army officer to advise on infantry tactics, the "Instructions," like other Navy writings on the subject, addressed such amphibious fundamentals as the loading of landing boats, formation of assault waves, command and control of the landing force, provision of fire support, and the assignment of beachmasters to organize the onshore flow of men and supplies. The Navy thus entered the Spanish-American War with at least a rudimentary doctrine for ship-to-shore operations, albeit one it had never employed in conjunction with the Army.[8]

II

During the war with Spain, President McKinley improvised an effective joint command system employing the traditional nineteenth-century institutions and administrative methods. From his White House "war room," with its situation maps and elaborate telephone and telegraph communications, he kept in close touch with the War and Navy departments and his commanders in the field. The president regularly called together his service secretaries, the senior uniformed Army and Navy officers in Washington, and representatives of the State Department and other agencies to set military strategy and overall national policy. He used these conferences to coordinate Army and Navy planning and conduct of the campaigns.[9]

Under the president's direction, Secretary of War Russell A. Alger and Secretary of the Navy John D. Long directed their services' mobilization through the War and Navy Department staff bureaus and their operations through field commanders in the Caribbean and the Pacific. Planning and coordination within the departments depended primarily on informal consultation between service secretaries, bureau chiefs, and senior line officers. To bring more system to the process, Secretary Long established a Naval War Board to advise him on strategy, and Secretary Alger used temporary boards to select mobilization campsites and for other purposes. In the weeks immediately preceding the outbreak of hostilities, Alger and Long set up a small liaison group to bring Army and Navy war plans into harmony.[10]

The joint war plan that President McKinley adopted at the outbreak of hostilities was a unilateral Navy plan with Army operations added on. Its main features came from a series of contingency plans drawn up during the previous three years by the Naval War College and various Navy Department boards. Under the plan, the fleet was to blockade Cuba, destroy as much of the Spanish navy as came within reach, and raid Manila to threaten Spain's trade with the Philippines. Meanwhile, the Army would mobilize and run guns to the Cuban insurgents. If a summer of such pressure failed to bring Spain to terms, the Army could mount an expedition against Havana in the fall during Cuba's relatively fever-free campaigning season.[11]

The plan reflected, and helped cause, significant Army-Navy differences in readiness for war. As of 19 April, when Congress, at McKinley's request, authorized armed U.S. intervention to restore peace in Cuba, the Navy was fully prepared to carry out its part of the war plan. Using funds and authority obtained soon after the blowing up of the *Maine* in February, Secretary Long and Assistant Secretary Theodore Roosevelt organized squadrons for action in the Caribbean and the Far East, procured auxiliary and supply vessels, obtained ample coal, ammunition, and stores, and doubled the Navy's personnel strength.

The Army, by contrast, anticipated only a limited need for its services at the outset and lacked legislative authority to enlarge its personnel. By the end of April, the War Department had concentrated most of the Regular Army at Tampa, Mobile, New Orleans, and Chickamauga Park as an initial force in readiness. However, a prolonged Regular–National Guard dispute over how additional wartime units should be organized dragged on in Congress until 22 April. The compromise that ended the dispute committed the War Department to raise an army, consisting largely of state-organized Volunteers, more than twice the size of the 100,000-man expeditionary force it initially had contemplated. Lacking camps, equipment, and trained staff for this multitude, the War Department struggled for the next two months to bring order out of chaos at Army bases and training camps. In the meantime, only the 25,000 Regulars of the peacetime establishment and a handful of the best trained and equipped Volunteer regiments were available for active operations.[12]

The slower pace of the Army mobilization was allowed for in the original war plan, under which the Navy was to complete its major missions largely without help from the other service. In practice, however, operations were more interdependent. Dewey's unexpectedly complete victory at Manila on 1 May created a need for immediate dispatch of an Army expedition to occupy the Philippine capital. President McKinley, in order to exploit Spain's evident naval weakness, at the same time decided to launch the Havana expedition as soon as the War Department could assemble the necessary troops, supplies, and transports. Adm. Pascual Cervera's success in slipping into the fortified harbor of Santiago with his four armored cruisers—Spain's principal naval striking force—disrupted the Havana plan. Now the Navy required Army help in accomplishing one of its own principal missions, the destruction of the enemy's fleet. Accordingly, the administration postponed the Army attack on Havana and substituted one on Santiago, with an invasion of Puerto Rico to follow.

Army-Navy differences in war readiness now became an irritant. Secretary Long continually pressed his harried colleague Alger for speed in launching the Santiago expedition at a time when the War Department was still coping with the initial difficulties of mobilizing and equipping the Volunteers. The

War Department met the immediate requirements, but only by shortchanging the big assembly camps of staff, supplies, and equipment, at eventual cost to itself in disease and scandal. At the same time, the Navy, its ships spread thin penning up Cervera, maintaining the blockade, and preparing to reinforce Dewey against a new Spanish squadron supposedly heading for the Pacific via the Suez Canal, strained to meet Army demands for convoy and assistance in landing operations.[13]

III

Once McKinley and his service secretaries determined the sequence and objectives of campaigns, they left tactical details, including those of interservice cooperation, to the field commanders. In preparation for the Santiago campaign, for example, Secretary Long on 31 May informed Rear Adm. William T. Sampson, commanding the blockading squadron, that the Army expedition was on the way and instructed him to scout landing places for it and be prepared to assist its disembarkation. Secretary Alger at the same time ordered Maj. Gen. William R. Shafter to embark his Fifth Corps, proceed under naval convoy to Santiago, land his troops at whatever point he and Sampson deemed best, and conduct operations to capture the Spanish garrison and aid the Navy in eliminating the Spanish fleet. Shafter was to "cooperate most earnestly with the naval forces in every way, agreeing beforehand upon a code of signals." Brig. Gen. Thomas M. Anderson, commanding the first Army contingent to sail from San Francisco for Manila, was told to exercise "the fullest discretion after consultation with Admiral Dewey" and maintain "hearty co-operation with the senior officer of the Navy." Anderson "must, however, be governed by events and circumstances of which we can have no knowledge. The President and Secretary of War rely upon the sound judgment of the officer in command." Such general instructions proved to be sufficient guidance for the commanders in most instances. The only exception was the Santiago campaign, for which the president failed to clarify which objective—destroying the Spanish squadron or capturing the city and its garrison—had priority, thereby ensuring a prolonged Army-Navy wrangle.[14]

In the field, Army-Navy liaison concerning campaign plans began in the first days of the war. At that time, Shafter, in charge of the assembling Army force at Tampa, sent a staff officer to Key West, the rear base for the Cuba blockade, to determine what Army expeditions the fleet could convoy and support. These discussions contributed to McKinley's decision, early in May, to push forward the attack on Havana, a plan later discarded because the troops intended for it were needed to deal with Cervera at Santiago. Shafter continued his contacts with naval commanders at Key West as he prepared to embark for Santiago, but unfortunately he had no regular communication with Rear Admiral Sampson, and hence no opportunity to concert plans with him, until the Army transports reached the Cuban coast on 20 June.[15]

In these last years before the introduction of radio, limited communications hindered both direction of operations from Washington and the concert of action between Army and Navy commanders. Messages could pass rapidly between the White House and the overseas forces over the international telegraph lines, provided operations took place sufficiently near terminals. At Santiago and Manila the Army created its own telegraph terminals by dredging up and patching into undersea cables, and it could use field telephones to connect its headquarters. Fleet commanders, however, still depended on dispatch boats or flag signals to relay messages to and from the nearest telegraph station, as well as to keep in touch with their own ships and with Army headquarters on shore. When the troops moved any distance away from the coast, as they did at Santiago, direct conferences between naval and land commanders became complex exercises in logistics. At Santiago, Sampson missed the climactic 3 July battle with Cervera's squadron because his flagship had left the blockading station to carry him on the first stage of a journey to Shafter's headquarters for a meeting aimed at resolving their operational disagreements.[16]

The degree of harmony between Army and Navy commanders varied as the result of personalities and circumstances. At Santiago, Sampson, a reserved, fastidious technician, and Shafter, a rough-and-ready Civil War Volunteer and frontier Indian fighter, managed to agree on little but the landing place of Shafter's troops. Once on shore, Shafter, preoccupied with capturing the city and its garrison, marched inland and campaigned with minimal reference to the fleet. Shafter's actions dismayed Sampson, who had expected Army assistance in breaking into the mouth of the harbor to attack Cervera's squadron, which to Sampson was the main objective of the campaign. The Navy commander's mood was not improved when Shafter, after suffering heavy casualties on 1 July in the capture of San Juan Hill and El Caney, the war's only major land engagement, demanded that the squadron support him by itself breaking through the harbor defenses. Prolonged discussions produced only a tentative Navy commitment to try to force the harbor entrance, and a plan, actually carried out, for long-range bombardment of Santiago from the sea.

All, however, ended well. Shafter's seizure of the high ground overlooking the city of Santiago prompted the Spanish squadron to run out of the bay to its destruction in the naval battle of 3 July. The Spanish garrison, hemmed in by land and sea and facing a renewed attack by a reinforced U.S. Army, surrendered two weeks later in a capitulation that included the entire eastern end of Cuba. By that time, Sampson, Shafter, and Maj. Gen. Nelson A. Miles, commanding general of the Army, who had arrived with reinforcements, had worked out a joint plan of operations calling for a Navy attempt to break into the harbor coupled with renewed Army assaults on both the city and the forts guarding the channel. Finishing the campaign on a sour note, Shafter excluded Sampson from the surrender negotiations and final ceremony, and the two commanders quarreled over ownership of some small vessels captured along with the city.[17]

The Puerto Rico campaign, launched with Army troops sent to Santiago as reinforcements but not landed there, began with an argument between Major General Miles and Rear Admiral Sampson about the size and composition of the expedition's naval escort. Sampson, preoccupied with organizing an expedition to the Mediterranean to threaten the Spanish coast and start reinforcements on their way to Dewey, sought to minimize detachments for Puerto Rico, especially because no enemy warships remained at large in the Caribbean. Eventually he met Miles's demands for more vessels and firepower than the admiral believed necessary, but not soon enough to avoid a peremptory directive from McKinley to give the Army "enough ships and strong enough," including one of the battleships, to ensure a safe landing. Following this imbroglio, the expedition went smoothly. In mid-voyage Miles prevailed on the commander of his Navy escort to switch the landing place from Cape Fajardo, on the northeastern tip of Puerto Rico near the capital city, San Juan, where most of the Spanish forces on the island were concentrated, to Ponce, on the essentially undefended southern coast. The Navy adjusted readily to this change of plan. Miles's troops, once on shore, overran Puerto Rico in a nearly bloodless campaign of rapid maneuver. Not one to share the glory, however, Miles blocked a Navy proposal to reduce San Juan by bombardment from the sea in advance of the arrival of the Army columns.[18]

At Manila, in contrast to the Caribbean campaigns, interservice harmony prevailed. Geography facilitated tactical cooperation. The Army made its approach to Manila along the bay shore, with Commodore Dewey's warships covering its flank. As the Army forces arrived at Manila in three separate contingents over a period of about a month, each detachment commander relied heavily on the Navy for local intelligence, assistance in reconnaissance, and help in disembarking troops and supplies. Once all three Army expeditions were in hand, Dewey and the Army commander, Maj.

Gen. Wesley Merritt, negotiated together for a Spanish surrender. In the semi-sham battle on 13 August that brought about the capitulation, the Navy fleet and the Army operated under a closely integrated plan aimed at providing the Spanish governor justification for hauling down his flag, establishing American occupation of the city, and keeping out the Filipino insurgent forces of Emilio Aguinaldo.[19]

When his field commanders fell out, President McKinley responded with varying degrees of forcefulness. In the case of Sampson and Shafter at Santiago, McKinley allowed his secretaries of War and Navy to argue the issue of forcing the harbor entrance in cabinet meetings and White House war councils. Refusing to make a final ruling, the president simply dispatched all available troops to reinforce Shafter, reiterated to his field commanders that they must take Santiago, and told them: "After the fullest exchange of views, you will agree upon the time and manner of attack." On the Puerto Rico escort issue, McKinley decisively took Miles's side and ordered the Navy to give the Army commander what he asked for. He also vetoed, at Miles's request, the Navy's proposed attack on San Juan.[20]

The field commanders' disagreements generated a great deal of telegraph traffic and cabinet disputation, but they had little adverse effect on American operations. Except at Santiago, Army-Navy differences were over matters of minor detail. At Santiago, Shafter, by disregarding the Navy plan for concentrating on the harbor entrance and instead driving on the city, forced Cervera out of the bay and cut off the Spanish garrison's escape route inland. He thereby contributed to a more decisive American success than the Navy's approach alone would have achieved.[21]

IV

Regardless of strategic and operational disagreements, the services in all theaters cooperated effectively at the tactical level. The Army and Navy improvised methods for transporting and convoying troops, landing them on foreign shores, and bringing the firepower of the fleet to bear in support of land operations.

As in previous wars, the Army quartermaster general procured, manned, and fitted out troop transports. He secured merchant vessels by charter or purchase and eventually borrowed some of the large armed ocean liners the Navy had earlier taken for use as scout cruisers but no longer needed after Cervera's defeat. Neither service possessed anything resembling specialized landing craft. For ship-to-shore movement of men and supplies they employed harbor tugs, lighters, small steamers, ships' boats, and whatever craft they could capture at the scene of operations. The quartermaster department's management of its civilian-crewed transports came in for much criticism, both from within the Army and from the Navy. On board these vessels, hastily converted for carrying troops, transport quartermasters, unit commanders, and civilian merchant captains frequently quarreled over the limits of their authority, which were poorly defined. On some vessels, miscalculations in provisioning caused food and water shortages; on others, ill-disciplined troops added to their own discomfort by neglecting shipboard sanitation and failing to establish organized routines for meals and exercise.[22]

Army transports steaming under Navy escort were under the orders of the senior naval officer. The largest such convoying operation, the movement of Shafter's Fifth Corps from Tampa to Santiago, involved a dozen warships, including the battleship *Indiana*, and more than thirty Army transports of varying sizes and conditions of seaworthiness. Although Major General Shafter ignored a Navy Department suggestion that he embark with his staff on the Navy flagship, the Army commander and Capt. Henry C. Taylor of the *Indiana*, senior naval officer of the convoy, stayed in constant touch through flag signals, dispatch boats, and a visit by Taylor to Shafter's transport. To ensure ready communication throughout the fleet, a Navy signal party embarked on each Army vessel. These arrangements proved sufficient to keep the columns of assorted merchantmen together, although the convoy had to travel slowly to prevent straggling and the smaller cruisers and gunboats kept busy rounding up strays. The fleet reached Santiago on 20 June well enough closed up to begin immediate landing preparations.[23]

Not all convoys went as smoothly. The commander of the *Wilmington*, which escorted some of Shafter's reinforcements later in the campaign, complained: "With the exception of the compass-course signals, . . . no attention was paid by the vessels being convoyed to other signals made, although such signals were frequently necessary." He added: "Little or no attention was paid by these transports to maintain position, and had the fleet been much larger much delay must have occurred from this source, likewise danger under ordinary war conditions."[24]

After Cervera's defeat, large convoy operations were no longer needed in the Caribbean. Naval vessels escorted the initial assault force to Puerto Rico, but the rest of that expedition embarked at various Atlantic coast ports instead of funneling through Tampa. The transports traveled individually or in small groups. After Miles shifted his landing place to Ponce, a warship kept station off the north coast of Puerto Rico to direct each incoming contingent to the new rendezvous. Much the same pattern prevailed in the Pacific, where the Manila expedition, the Eighth Army Corps, left San Francisco in three groups, the size of each determined by the availability of ships.[25]

At Santiago, Sampson and Shafter, in spite of their differences over campaign strategy, cooperated in the war's largest and most difficult landing operation. Secretary Long, at the outset of the campaign, had directed Sampson to "assist . . . landing the army to the utmost extent of your power," and Sampson did so. The two commanders met, in one of their few face-to-face conferences, on 20 June at Aserradero, a coastal town west of Santiago held by the Cuban insurgent forces of Gen. Calixto García, who had agreed to cooperate with the American attack. Sampson, Shafter, and García adopted a plan, worked out by Shafter on the voyage from Tampa, for landing the Fifth Corps at Daiquirí, a small port east of the harbor entrance, from which the Army could move either along the coast toward the forts the Navy wanted it to attack or inland toward the city, as it eventually did. The commanders arranged for diversionary maneuvers by warships and transports off several other potential landing places, for Navy support of the landing with small craft and ships' gunfire, and for Cuban troops to attack the few Spanish defenders of Daiquirí from the land side.[26]

Both commanders then drew up operational orders for the landing, scheduled for 22 June. Shafter's instructions to the Fifth Corps established the order in which his divisions were to go ashore, prescribed what supplies and equipment the troops were to carry, and provided for early disembarkation of Gatling guns, artillery, and extra ammunition if the landing met significant resistance. Shafter placed his chief quartermaster, Col. Charles F. Humphrey, in charge of the details of disembarkation. At the same time, Sampson directed the assembly off Daiquirí of most of his fleet's steam launches, cutters, and whaleboats to augment the transports' boats in landing the troops. He designated the scout cruiser *St. Louis*, an armed liner, as command ship for the operation, and her commander, Capt. Caspar Goodrich, as senior naval officer in charge. Goodrich, a former president of the Naval War College, had a background in landing operations dating back to 1882, when he had observed the British assault on Alexandria. He had participated in U.S. Navy discussions of tactics for the naval brigades.[27]

Responsibility for marshaling the transports off Daiquirí fell to Captain Taylor of the *Indiana* and his vessels of the convoy escort. On the twenty-first, after a conference with Shafter and Goodrich on board Shafter's transport, Taylor put the escort vessels to work arranging the troopships for the approach to the beach. Each transport had an identifying number painted on its side or smokestack. Using these, and a manifest of units on each vessel maintained by Shafter's headquarters, Taylor collected the ships carrying each division and arranged them in the order that the troops were to land.[28]

Americans Landing at Siboney

The Army and Navy cooperated smoothly at the start of the Santiago campaign. Maj. Gen. William R. Shafter and the Fifth Corps left Tampa under Navy escort on 14 June 1898. Arriving off Cuba's south coast, Shafter met with Rear Adm. Sampson to coordinate plans and on 22 June began landing troops at Daiquirí, the site selected by Sampson, sixteen miles east of Santiago. Shafter decided to land part of his troops at Siboney, about eight miles closer to Santiago than Daiquirí. Some of the boats from the *New York* and what appears to be native craft used by Massachusetts volunteers to land at Siboney are pictured here. All troops were ashore by 26 June. *Courtesy of the Smithsonian Institution.*

Landing operations began early on the twenty-second. Several of Sampson's smaller warships took station off Daiquirí and prepared to bombard suspected Spanish defensive positions. Other vessels, and transports carrying one of Shafter's infantry divisions, made pretended landing preparations at several points along the coast. Captain Taylor brought the Army transports into position off the actual landing site more or less in proper order to disembark troops in the sequence Shafter had directed. Meanwhile, Captain Goodrich organized the fifty-two launches and boats from the fleet and those of the transports for disembarking the soldiers. Following a method worked out for the naval brigades, Goodrich employed the steam launches to tow strings of the sailing and rowing craft. He also distributed Navy personnel among the transports' boats to ensure their proper handling.

Considering that none of the forces involved had engaged in any preliminary rehearsals (the Fifth Corps had never even conducted a corps-size maneuver on land before it embarked for Santiago), and that Daiquirí was little more than an open roadstead with a single pier, the operation went relatively well. Rough seas, wandering transports, and the difficulty of transferring heavily laden soldiers from ships to small boats—a task new to both Navy crews and Army field and company officers—delayed formation of the initial assault wave. At a little after 9:00 A.M., Captain Goodrich hoisted the prearranged signal to head for the beach, and the warships "opened a fire heavy enough to drive out the whole Spanish Army in Cuba had it been there." The landing, however, was unopposed. At about 10:00 A.M., a Navy midshipman was the first American ashore at Daiquirí. Landing operations continued for the rest of the day, hindered by the heavy surf, the reluctance of transport captains to risk their vessels close inshore, and the need to swim the horses and mules to the beach for lack of landing craft for the animals. The flow of men and material gradually accelerated as boats' crews learned their jobs and a Navy beachmaster organized the reception of incoming craft at the beach and the pier. By nightfall, about six thousand troops were on shore.

During its second day, the operation increased in efficiency and broadened in scope. Shafter, at Captain Goodrich's request, placed the masters of his transports under the Navy officer's command, an arrangement that allowed Goodrich to bring the vessels closer to shore, further speeding up disembarkation. Troops advancing overland from Daiquirí seized a second landing site at Siboney, a small port eight miles closer to Santiago, and Goodrich, at Shafter's request, transferred the principal landing operation there. Men and stores came ashore through both ports at a rate of 600 troops per hour at Siboney. Work continued around the clock as the *St. Louis* illuminated the beach with her searchlights. On 24, 25, and 26 June, the rest of Shafter's corps, 4,000 of García's Cubans (brought around from the west side of the harbor), the Fifth Corps's field guns, animals, wagons, and enough food and ammunition to start the campaign came ashore. Most of the Navy boats, and the *St. Louis*, returned to the squadron on the twenty-sixth, but throughout the rest of the campaign the Navy periodically supplemented the Army's inadequate complement of landing craft as Shafter struggled to keep a tenuous supply line functioning. The largest American amphibious operation since the landing of Scott's army at Vera Cruz thus concluded successfully, at the cost of two soldiers drowned on the first day, thirty or so horses and mules lost in swimming them ashore, a Navy cutter destroyed, and other boats damaged by surf or collisions. Unfortunately, the landing marked the high point of Army-Navy collaboration at Santiago.[29]

The Army and Navy cooperated equally well and encountered fewer difficulties in landing Major General Miles's force in Puerto Rico. As Miles had expected, the city of Ponce, and the nearby smaller port of Guánica, which the Americans occupied first, were virtually undefended. Naval vessels and their landing parties secured both ports before the Army transports arrived, capturing in the harbors more than fifty lighters used for loading sugar. Lt. Comdr. Richard Wainwright of the *Gloucester* quickly collected these to land troops and stores. Using these harbor craft, and assisted as at Santiago by the warships' steam launches, Miles put his command ashore without incident. As additional troops arrived, the Navy, at Miles's request, secured another landing point at Arroyo, east of Ponce, from which the Army could outflank Spanish roadblocks on the main highway to San Juan. Captain Goodrich of the *St. Louis*, whose vessel had brought in some of Miles's reinforcements, towed several lighters from Ponce around to Arroyo to assist the disembarkation. Goodrich's ship, and other vessels, also shelled Spanish positions in the hills to protect the landing place.[30]

The story at Manila was much the same. There, the first 2,500 Army troops to arrive went ashore at the former Spanish naval station of Cavite, south of the city, secured after the 1 May battle by sailors and marines of Dewey's squadron. Army and Navy officers jointly reconnoitered the bay shore. They selected another landing beach and campsite closer to Manila, where the other two Army contingents landed and prepared for the assault. Although conducted during the monsoon season, a time of torrential daily rains, high winds, and rough water in the bay, the disembarkation of men and stores went forward with minimal difficulty. The Army supplemented its transports' boats with Navy steam launches, captured Spanish steamers, and homemade local lighters called *cascos*, between them more than adequate landing craft for the 8,000 troops of the Eighth Corps who reached Manila before the capitulation.[31]

None of the landings in the Spanish-American War encountered significant enemy resistance; indeed, Major General Miles changed his plans for Puerto Rico in mid-voyage to avoid such an eventuality. U.S. Army and Navy officers of this period, like their counterparts elsewhere, considered an assault landing, in the face of strong enemy forces equipped with modern artillery and small arms, to be a "forlorn hope." "All the chances are against success," a Navy commentator declared in 1900, "and attempt is but courting disaster." The British debacle at Gallipoli in 1915 merely confirmed this conclusion.[32]

The record of naval gunfire support in the Spanish-American War illustrates the experience behind such pessimism. Whenever possible during the operations in Cuba, Puerto Rico, and the Philippines, the Army requested, and the Navy provided, gunfire support for engaged troops. Such action had ample precedent. In the attack on Fort Fisher during the Civil War, for example, Union warships conducted a two-day preparatory bombardment of the Confederate works, then assisted the assaulting infantry by shelling each section of the fortifications immediately ahead of the advancing columns. This was all direct fire in which the ships' gunners aimed at targets they themselves could observe. Techniques had changed little three decades later, in spite of great increases in the size, range, and power of naval guns. The Army and Navy in 1898 possessed neither doctrine, equipment, nor training for indirect fire controlled by forward observers. This meant essentially that the Navy could support land operations only when they took place close to shore and within sight of the ships.[33]

In Cuba, Navy gunners first went into action in aid of the Army on 12 May during an attempt by two companies of infantry to land near Cabanas and make contact with the insurgents. Instead of Cubans, the troops on shore encountered Spanish infantry and fell back toward the beach under heavy attack. As they did so, the Navy gunboats *Wasp, Manning,* and *Dolphin* provided covering fire. The *Wasp* alone expended eighty rounds from her 6-pounders. Under protection of the ships, the soldiers successfully reembarked.[34]

During the first day of Shafter's landing at Daiquirí, naval vessels laid down a bombardment that scattered the few Spanish troops seen near the town and destroyed many buildings and a railroad bridge. At Siboney a sharpshooting guncrew from the *Bancroft* routed a party of Spaniards trying to set up a roadblock on a hill above the village. During the 1 July engagements, two gunboats and an armored cruiser, coordinating their actions with the Army commander by flag signal, supported a diversionary attack by two Michigan Volunteer regiments along the shoreline toward Aguadores. However, their fire had little visible result beyond partially destroying a small Spanish blockhouse. The main fighting of the day, at San Juan Hill and El Caney, took place out of sight of the sea and hence beyond reach of effective naval gunfire. After the skirmish at Aguadores ended, the vessels did fire a few shells over the hills in the general direction of Santiago, but the projectiles seem to have fallen behind Shafter's lines.[35]

In Puerto Rico, the presence of warships was sufficient to drive the Spaniards from Ponce and Guánica, on the island's south coast, and several vessels fired into the hills behind Arroyo in support of the landing there. The most systematic Army use of naval gunfire support came at Manila. In the 13 August assault, Major General Merritt, following a joint plan worked out with Commodore Dewey, relied on the fire of Navy ships, which steamed along the bay shore on the Army's flank, to drive the Spanish from a stone fort and lines of trenches ahead of his troops. He specifically instructed his division and brigade commanders to advance from their own trenches only after the warships had subdued the Spanish defenders.[36]

The effectiveness of the Navy's fire in support of troops and in the fleet's several bombardments of Spanish batteries in Cuba and Puerto Rico was questionable. Ships' guns inflicted few verifiable Spanish casualties, although they did knock considerable amounts of stone and brickwork off assorted forts and blockhouses and may have driven the enemy from their positions on a few occasions. At the time, naval writers and some Army officers doubted the effectiveness of the heaviest ships' guns against batteries and field fortifications; they believed that smaller caliber pieces, able to deliver a high volume of rapid fire, were the best naval weapons against land targets. This meant that the targets must be close to shore, since the range of the smaller guns was limited.[37]

At Santiago, the Army and Navy conducted what was, for that time, an ambitious experiment in indirect fire controlled by forward observers. On 10 and 11 July, as part of an effort to increase pressure on the besieged garrison, Rear Admiral Sampson deployed several of his heavy ships off Aguadores to fire shells over the intervening hills into the city. Their fire was guided by Army officers in the trenches on San Juan Hill, who reported the fall of the projectiles by telephone to the shore and then flag signal to the ships. The vessels kept up a slow rate of fire, awaiting the Army spotters' reports between rounds. During the main period of bombardment, the ships fired only forty-six shells in the space of about two hours. For fear of hitting American troops, they directed their shots at the city itself—by then largely emptied of civilians—rather than the encircling Spanish trenches. Of the shells fired, the Army observers failed to see or hear the impact of twenty-four. Others caused visible explosions and started a few small fires.[38]

Evidencing the strained relations between Shafter and Sampson, the Army and Navy differed in their evaluations of the bombardment. Army reports generally dismissed the Navy's effort as of little effect. On the other hand, a board of three naval officers—appointed by Sampson—who made a thorough survey of the city after the surrender found that the shells had damaged or destroyed over fifty buildings and cratered several streets. However, they noted that a number of projectiles had failed to explode, some because they were of the armor-piercing type intended for use against ships rather than forts and buildings. The board also concluded that many shells had fallen in the bay or open country. Nevertheless, they suggested—with more than a trace of wishful thinking—that the bombardment "had much to do with the early surrender of the city." It seems likely that, given the slow rate of fire and the near impossibility of rapid adjustment, this method of bombardment would have contributed little to any renewed American assault on the city, had one been necessary.[39]

V

Overall, the story of joint operations in the war with Spain was one of success. In spite of a lack of prewar interservice planning, in spite of disagreements between commanders, and in spite of many operational limitations imposed by still primitive technology, notably in communications, landing craft, and gunfire direction, the Army and Navy together brought sufficient force to bear to defeat Spain. The nineteenth-century system of informal cooperation proved equal to the requirements of limited colonial warfare against a weak European power. Perhaps because of this success, continued reform agitation in both services after the Spanish-American War produced few changes in the way Americans conducted joint operations.

Immediately after the war, the Navy Department made a bid for control of the entire sea transport service, citing as justification the convoy difficulties and deficiencies in Army management on board its vessels during the war. The War Department, however, successfully defended the existing division of labor by establishing in November 1898 an Army Transport Service with permanent personnel and a set of operating regulations copied largely from those of Great Britain. The regulations, among other provisions, established procedures for controlling troops on shipboard and prescribed that, under convoy, Army transports would follow Navy direction.

At the same time, the Quartermaster's Department, by rebuilding a number of vessels purchased during the war, secured a fleet of modern, well-appointed troopships. So organized and equipped, the Army Transport Service efficiently carried thousands of soldiers to and from Cuba and the Philippines and proved more than equal to the later demands of the China Relief Expedition, the 1906 Cuban intervention, and the Vera Cruz occupation of 1914.[40]

Meanwhile, the Navy continued to develop its own landing force by reorganizing the Marine Corps to perform the mission of occupying and fortifying advance bases for the fleet. A Marine battalion had played this role in 1898 by securing Guantanamo Bay as a harbor for the squadron blockading Santiago. Following the war with Spain, the Marine Corps, at the urging of the Navy Department, gradually developed infantry and artillery regiments for an advance base force and conducted amphibious exercises with the fleet, culminating in a full-scale maneuver at Culebra in 1914. Although frequently diverted to expeditionary duty in the Caribbean, the advance base force remained in existence through World War I. During the 1920s, in anticipation of a trans-Pacific war with Japan, the Marines began thinking in terms not simply of occupation and defense of advance bases, but of their capture by amphibious assault. Out of this planning came, during the 1930s, the formation of the fleet Marine force and the development and testing of the amphibious tactics and equipment used by both the Marine Corps and the Army during World War II.[41]

Both services made major command and staff reforms following the Spanish-American War. Change was most radical in the Army, where Secretary of War Elihu Root and a cadre of progressive officers secured the establishment in 1903 of a full-fledged general staff, more or less on the Prussian pattern. Navy reformers had less success. They helped bring about the creation in 1900 of a general board with limited planning and advisory functions and the establishment in 1914 of a chief of naval operations. Unlike their Army counterparts, however, they failed in their efforts to create a true general staff for their service.[42]

In the course of these command and staff reforms, the services made one attempt to institutionalize joint planning. The secretaries of War and Navy established in July 1903 a joint board "for the purpose of conferring upon, discussing, and reaching common conclusions regarding all matters calling for the cooperation of the two services." Secretary of War Root, the joint board's principal sponsor, envisioned the board as facilitating the interservice exchange of technical information and intelligence, and as an agency for coordinating plans and preparations for coastal defense and other joint activities. "If the two forces are ever to be called upon to cooperate," he suggested a few months after the board's establishment, "the time to determine what each shall do, and the time for each to learn what the other can do, is before the emergency arises." Headed at the outset by the chief of staff of the Army and the senior admiral of the Navy, the joint board remained in existence in various forms until the eve of World War II, although its influence and activity waxed and waned depending on official interest and international circumstances. It discussed and attempted to resolve a wide range of interservice issues, including the location of America's principal Pacific naval base and the assignment of roles and missions, as well as drafting the "color" joint war plans. The joint board, nevertheless, represented evolution rather than revolution. It simply gave formal structure to the traditional system of interdepartmental consultation, with persistent disagreements still resolvable only at the presidential and cabinet level.[43]

In the years between the Spanish-American War and World War I, the joint board and the services made no fundamental changes in Army-Navy doctrine for the conduct of amphibious operations. During the early 1900s the joint board adopted regulations for overseas expeditions that largely codified the arrangements of 1898. The regulations left procurement and operation of troop transports and the planning of landing operations to the Army, while control of convoy movement and the transport of troops from ship to shore rested with the Navy. The services confined their joint exercises entirely to coastal defense. In actual expeditions, the principle of command by consultation and cooperation remained in force. Thus, in 1900, the War Department's instructions to Maj. Gen. Adna R. Chaffee, commander of the China Relief Expedition, simply enjoined him to "complete understanding and cooperation" with the U.S. Navy admiral on the scene. At Vera Cruz in 1914, Rear Adm. Frank F. Fletcher initially commanded both afloat and ashore, but he relinquished control of land operations to Brig. Gen. Frederick Funston once Army forces took over the occupation. American participation in World War I, although unprecedented in scale, produced no changes in the conduct of joint operations because each service carried out more or less independent missions. Only the necessity of mounting interwoven land, sea, and air campaigns in World War II finally compelled the United States to create genuine institutions for joint planning and command.[44]

NOTES

The views expressed in this paper are those of the author and in no way represent the views of the U.S. Army or the U.S. Army Center of Military History.

1. During the Spanish-American War era, operations involving more than one armed service were often referred to as "combined." However, throughout this essay, I have employed the current U.S. military term "joint" for operations of this nature.

2. For a convenient summary of pre–Spanish-American War military reform, see James L. Abrahamson, *America Arms for a New Century: The Making of a Great Military Power* (New York, 1981), chaps. 1–3. Army developments are summarized in Graham A. Cosmas, *An Army for Empire: The United States Army in the Spanish-American War* (Columbia, Mo., 1971), chaps. 1–2.

3. Quotation is from Lt. Gen. John M. Schofield, *Forty-Six Years in the Army* (New York, 1897), 527–28. For a general review of strategic thinking, see Cosmas, *Army for Empire*, 35–41; and Ronald Spector, *Professors of War: The Naval War College and the Development of the Naval Profession* (Newport, R.I., 1977), 81–87.

4. Quotation is from Schofield, *Forty-Six Years*, 489–90. For the development of Naval War College war games and war plans, see Spector, *Professors of War*, chap. 7.

5. Col. John F. Polk, USA, "Vera Cruz, 1847," in *Assault from the Sea: Essays on the History of Amphibious Warfare*, ed. Lt. Col. Merrill L. Bartlett (Annapolis, 1983), 74–78. The classic survey of Civil War combined operations is Rowena Reed, *Combined Operations in the Civil War* (Annapolis, 1978).

6. For command arrangements, see Polk, "Vera Cruz," 75; also Reed, *Combined Operations*, xiv–xv. For the transition in American life from localism and informality to bureaucracy and rationality, see Robert H. Wiebe, *The Search for Order, 1877–1920* (New York, 1967).

7. Brig. Gen. G. G. Aston, CB, *Letters on Amphibious Wars* (London, 1911), 143–45. Ens. Charles G. Rogers, USN, et al., "Operations of the British Navy and Transport Service during the Egyptian Campaign, 1882," *U.S. Naval Institute Proceedings* 8 (Jan. 1883): 523–625.

8. "Instructions for Infantry and Artillery, United States Navy," *U.S. Naval Institute Proceedings* 17 (1891): 569–744. Jack Shulimson, "U.S. Marines in Panama, 1885," in *Assault from the Sea*, ed. Bartlett, 107–20, discusses the Panama operation in detail. For other Navy discussion of landing operations, see the following, all in *U.S. Naval Institute Proceedings*: Lt. John C. Soley, "The Naval Brigade," 6 (1880): 271–94; Rogers et al., "Operations of the British Navy," Lt. C. T. Hutchins, "The Naval Brigade: Its Organization, Equipment, and Tactics" 13, no. 3: 303–40; "Discussion of Prize Essay, 1887," 13, no. 4: 511–46; Ens. William L. Rogers, "Notes on the Naval Brigade," 14 (1888): 57–96.

9. McKinley's system of war direction is described in David F. Trask, *The War with Spain in 1898* (New York, 1981), 169–70. See also Cosmas, *Army for Empire*, 102–3.

10. The Naval War Board is described in Trask, *War with Spain*, 88–89. Alger's administration is analyzed in Cosmas, *Army for Empire*, 139–43. For joint planning, see Memorandum, Capt. A. S. Barker, USN, and Asst. Adj. Gen. Arthur L. Wagner, USA, to the Secretary of War, 4 Apr. 1898, file no 198209, Records of the Adjutant General's Office, RG 94, National Archives, Washington, D.C. [hereafter RG 94].

11. Navy war planning is recounted in Spector, *Professors of War*, chap. 7; and Trask, *War with Spain*, 72–78, 88–91. For the Army view of the prospective conflict, see Cosmas, *Army for Empire*, 75–82.

12. Navy preparations are well summarized in Trask, *War with Spain*, 80–94. The Army's mobilization difficulties are described in Cosmas, *Army for Empire*, chaps. 3–4.

13. This account is based on Cosmas, *Army for Empire*, 117–31, 177–81; and Trask, *War with Spain*, 108–44, 162–77. For typical Navy expressions of impatience at Army slowness, see Cable, Sampson to Secretary of Navy, 7 June 1898; and Letter [Ltr], Acting Secretary of the Navy Charles H. Allen to Secretary of War, 7 June 1898, in *Annual Report of the Secretary of the Navy, 1898*, vol. 2, *Appendix to the Report of the Chief of the Bureau of Navigation*, 666–67 [hereafter *Bureau of Navigation Report*].

14. Cable, Long to Sampson, 31 May 1898, *Bureau of Navigation Report*, 480. The orders to Shafter are reproduced in Russell A. Alger, *The Spanish-American War* (New York, 1901), 63–64. Order to Anderson is quoted from War Department, *Correspondence Relating to the War with Spain and Conditions Growing out of the Same, . . . between the Adjutant General of the Army and Military Commanders in the United States, Cuba, Puerto Rico, China, and the Philippine Islands, from April 15, 1898, to July 30, 1902*, 2 vols. (Washington, 1902), 2:668–69 (hereafter *AGO Correspondence*).

15. Shafter's early contacts with the Navy are described in Ltr, Shafter to the Adj. Gen., USA, 7 May 1898; and Ltr, Lt. Col. H. W. Lawton to Adj. Gen., U.S. Forces, Tampa, 7 May 1898; both in William R. Shafter Papers, Stanford University, Stanford, California.

16. Army Signal Corps telegraph work is described in Cosmas, *Army for Empire*, 202–3. Sampson's 3 July trip, *Bureau of Navigation Report*, 506–7; and Ltr, Capt. F. E. Chadwick to Cornelia Chadwick, 4 July 1898, in Doris D. Maguire, ed., *French Ensor Chadwick: Selected Letters and Papers* (Washington, 1981), 194–95.

17. This account is based principally on Cosmas, *Army for Empire*, 205–30; and Trask, *War with Spain*, chaps. 9–11, 13–14. For Sampson's life and character, see *Dictionary of American Biography* 8:321–23. For Shafter, see Paul H. Carlson, *"Pecos Bill": A Military Biography of William R. Shafter* (College Station, Tex., 1989). Older accounts, which reproduce much of the originial documentation, are, from the Navy viewpoint, French Ensor Chadwick, *The Relations of the United States to Spain: The Spanish-American War*, 2 vols. (New York, 1911), 2:106–13, 191–210, 213–52; and from the Army side, Alger, *Spanish-American War*, 221–49. Sampson's viewpoint, with much documentation, can be followed in *Bureau of Navigation Report*, 448–51, 498, 503–4, 534–35, 609–32. Army sources are in *AGO Correspondence* 1:87–89, 91, 94, 105, 122–25, 134–36, 155–57, 164, 175.

18. Cosmas, *Army for Empire*, 230–36; Trask, *War with Spain*, chap. 15. Navy viewpoint and documents are in Chadwick, *Spanish-American War* 2:274–80; Chadwick criticizes Miles's strategy on 298–300. Alger, *Spanish-American War*, 249–55, predictably argues the Army's case. Miles's correspondence is in *AGO Correspondence* 1:276–77, 279, 281–82, 284, 286, 296.

19. Cosmas, *Army for Empire*, 236–42; Trask, *War with Spain*, chap. 18. For a contemporary view, see Lt. Carlos G. Calkins, USN, "Historical and Professional Notes on the Naval Campaign of Manila Bay in 1898," *U.S. Naval Institute Proceedings* 25 (June 1899): 299–300.

20. For McKinley's approach to the Santiago dispute, see Message [Msg], Long to Sampson, 5 July 1898, in *Bureau of Navigation Report*, 609–10. The president's rebuke to the Navy over the Puerto Rico escort is in Ltr, McKinley to Long, 20 July 1898, in Alger, *Spanish-American War*, 252–53. On the San Juan bombardment, see Trask, *War with Spain*, 361–62; and Cosmas, *Army for Empire*, 235.

21. Chadwick, who was Sampson's chief of staff at Santiago, acknowledges this point in *Spanish-American War* 2:24–25, correctly noting also that the Army and Navy approaches could and should have been combined from the start of the campaign.

22. Cosmas, *Army for Empire*, 183–87, 217–20, describes the Quartermaster Department's procurement and outfitting of troopships. For views on transport deficiencies, see Capt. William F. Birkheimer, "Transportation of Troops by Sea," *Journal of the Military Service Institution of the United States* 23 (Nov. 1898): 438–46; *Bureau of Navigation Report*, 137–41; U.S. Senate, *Report of the Commission Appointed by the President to Investigate the Conduct of the War Department in the War with Spain*, 8 vols., Senate doc. no. 221, 56th Cong., 1st sess., 1900, 1:519–20 [hereafter *War Investigating Commission*]. How it was done right is recounted in Capt. Caspar F. Goodrich, USN, "The *Saint Louis* as a Transport," *U.S. Naval Institute Proceedings* 25 (Mar. 1899): 1–9.

23. *Bureau of Navigation Report*, 663–64, 674, 676–83; John D. Miley, *In Cuba with Shafter*, 41–42.

24. *Bureau of Navigation Report*, 694–95.

25. Cosmas, *Army for Empire*, 200–201, 221–22, 230–32.

26. The landing plans are reproduced in *Bureau of Navigation Report*, 448–51; and Alger, *Spanish-American War*, 90–91. See also Miley, *With Shafter*, 55–60.

27. Shafter's order is reproduced in *Annual Report of the Major General Commanding the Army to the Secretary of War, 1898* (Washington, 1898), 150; Miley, *With Shafter*, 60. Sampson's orders are in *Bureau of Navigation Report*, 497–98; see also 487, 664. For Goodrich's background, see Maguire, *Chadwick: Selected Letters*, 284n; and Goodrich, "Saint Louis," 1.

28. *Bureau of Navigation Report*, 677–83; Miley, *With Shafter*, 46–49.

29. This account of the landing is based primarily on Captain Goodrich's report, reproduced in *Bureau of Navigation Report*, 685–88; see also 683–84, and 693. Shafter acknowledges the Navy's assistance in Cable to Adjutant General, 25 June 1898, 2:45 P.M., in *AGO Correspondence* 1:53–54. Cosmas, *Army for Empire*, 207, 209–12, summarizes the landing and Shafter's difficulties in maintaining a supply line.

30. *Bureau of Navigation Report*, 635–40, 643–44, 647, 649–50; Chadwick, *Spanish-American War* 2:296; Cosmas, *Army for Empire*, 234.

31. Cosmas, *Army for Empire*, 238–39; Calkins, "Manila Bay," 299–300; Chadwick, *Spanish-American War* 2:391–93.

32. For a representative assertion of the near impossibility of an opposed amphibious landing, see Capt. Asa Walker, USN, "Combined Maritime Operations," *U.S. Naval Institute Proceedings* 26 (Mar. 1900): 149, 153.

33. The naval gunfire at Fort Fisher is discussed in Reed, *Combined Operations*, 372–76. For the slowness of Army artillery doctrine in shifting from direct to indirect fire, see Vardell E. Nesmith, Jr., "The Quiet Paradigm Change: The Evolution of the Field Artillery Doctrine of the United States Army, 1861–1905" (Ph. D. diss., Duke University, 1977), 2–3, 256–62, 339.

34. *Bureau of Navigation Report*, 661–62.

35. Ibid., 503, 607, 615–17, 682–83, 686; Chadwick, *Spanish-American War* 2:98–100; Graham A. Cosmas, "San Juan Hill and El Caney," in *America's First Battles, 1776–1965*, ed. Charles E. Heller and William A. Stofft (Lawrence, Kan., 1986), 129.

36. *Bureau of Navigation Report*, 649–50; Chadwick, *Spanish-American War* 2:408–9; Calkins, "Manila Bay," 304–6; Cosmas, *Army for Empire*, 240–42.

37. For the Navy view, see Calkins, "Manila Bay," 302–3. For an Army view on naval gunfire, see Ltr, Matthew F. Steele to Mrs. Steele, 28 June 1898, Matthew F. Steele Papers, U.S. Army Military History Institute, Carlisle Barracks, Pennsylvania.

38. *Bureau of Navigation Report*, 611–12, 621–23; Chadwick, *Spanish-American War* 2:220–22.

39. Report, Lts. W. R. Rush and L. S. Van Duzer and Ens. L. C. Palmer, USN, to the Commander in Chief, 24 July 1898, in *Bureau of Navigation Report*, 629–30. For the Army view, see Miley, *With Shafter*, 153–54; and Alger, *Spanish-American War*, 235.

40. Navy and Army views on control of transport service are in *Army and Navy Journal* 17 and 24 Dec. 1898; *War Investigating Commission* 3:306–7, 4:952, 6:2, 418–19, 7:3, 289–90; and Walker, "Combined Operations," 154. Correspondence on creation of the Army Transport Service is in file nos. 115913, 122525, 145788, and 287644, RG 94; the last-named file contains a copy of the transport service regulations. For a summary of development of the fleet, see Erna Risch, *Quartermaster Support of the Army: A History of the Corps, 1775–1939* (Washington, 1962), 566–67.

41. Development of Navy and Marine amphibious forces and doctrine are summarized in Allan R. Millett, *Semper Fidelis: The History of the United States Marine Corps* (New York, 1980), chaps. 10, 12. See also Graham A. Cosmas and Jack Shulimson, "Continuity and Consensus: The Evolution of the Marine Advance Base Force, 1900–1922," in *Proceedings of the Citadel Conference on War and Diplomacy, 1977*, ed. David H. White and John W. Gordon (Charleston, S.C., 1979), 31–35.

42. These developments are summarized in Abrahamson, *America Arms*, 66–67, 122–23.

43. Quotations are from Elihu Root, *Five Years of the War Department* (Washington, 1904), 334–35; see also 65–66. Work of the Joint Board is summarized in Russell F. Weigley, *The American Way of War: A History of United States Military Strategy and Policy* (Bloomington, Ind., 1973), 200–201.

44. For early 1900s doctrine, see Capt. Wyatt I. Selkirk, "The Cooperation of Land and Sea Forces," *Journal of the Military Service Institution of the United States* 46 (Mar.–Apr. 1910): 317–19; for China, see Root, *Five Years*, 90–91; for Vera Cruz, see Col. James H. Alexander, USMC, "Roots of Deployment—Vera Cruz, 1914," in Bartlett, *Assault from the Sea*, 136–38.

Marines in the Spanish-American War

JACK SHULIMSON

I

THE U.S. DECLARED WAR ON SPAIN AT A TIME WHEN THE MARINE CORPS and its officers were uncertain about their role in the American defense establishment. The war, brief as it was, and its aftermath served to delineate the nature of the Marine Corps' mission in the rapidly expanding navy and in the defense of America's colonial possessions.

The publication in the *New York Journal* of the letter in which Spanish minister Dupuy de Lome referred to President McKinley as "weak and a bidder for the admiration of the crowd" and the sinking of the U.S. battleship *Maine* in Havana harbor in February 1898 galvanized American popular opinion against the Spanish. President McKinley attempted to defuse the situation by appointing a board of naval experts to determine the cause of the explosion on the American warship. Headed by Capt. William T. Sampson, the Navy court of inquiry reported on 21 March 1898 that a submarine mine, exterior to the hull, set off the forward magazines of the *Maine*. A Spanish investigating team, on the other hand, blamed an internal explosion in the forward magazines for the disaster. McKinley forwarded the Sampson board's findings to Congress without comment. Even as moderate a figure as Secretary of the Navy John D. Long, however, later observed that the sinking of the *Maine* "would inevitably lead to war, even if it were shown that Spain was innocent of her destruction."[1]

While the war fever spread through the country, the Navy Department reexamined its strategy in the event of a conflict with Spain. In March 1898

Secretary Long appointed an advisory war board consisting of Assistant Secretary Theodore Roosevelt as chairman and three naval officers, including the heads of the Bureau of Navigation and the Office of Naval Intelligence (ONI). The board had the benefit of the extensive ad hoc planning effort that had continued through both the Cleveland and McKinley administrations. Since 1895, the ONI, the War College, and the temporary strategy boards had developed several contingency plans for a war with Spain. Despite the different formulations of the various American planning documents, certain features appeared frequently: a blockade of Puerto Rico and Cuba, a possible land campaign against Havana, a blockade or assault against Manila in the Philippines, and a possible naval attack in Spanish home waters.[2]

Once the war board was formally established, it recommended to the secretary that the Navy take the offensive and not be relegated to a passive coastal defense role. Based on the consensus of the earlier war planning effort, the board suggested the close blockade of Cuba and extension of the blockade to Puerto Rico. The Navy was also to concentrate on the poorly defended outposts of Spain's insular empire, including the Philippines. As Secretary Long later explained, Spain's "undoing lay in her possessions in the East and West Indies"; there Spain was the most vulnerable and would be forced to send scarce men and ships to shore up its defenses. The board rejected any immediate operations aimed at the Spanish homeland in favor of a strategy of American sea dominance in the Caribbean and Pacific.[3]

As the naval plans took on more seriousness, the military prepared for what now appeared inevitable. Congress passed on 9 March 1898 a $50 million emergency appropriation to be shared between the War and Navy departments. The Army received $20 million, which mostly went into the coastal fortification program. War Department planners visualized only a limited mobilization. They expected the National Guard to staff the coastal defenses while the Regular Army expanded from its 28,000-man peacetime strength to form an expeditionary corps of 75,000 to 100,000 men. This corps would land in Cuba only after the Navy had established its mastery over the Spanish fleet. War Department officials failed to stock supplies for a large army because they simply "did not expect to raise one" in a war against Spain.[4]

The Navy, on the other hand, used a good portion of its approximately $30 million of the emergency appropriation to augment the fleet. It purchased cruisers in Europe, acquired several merchant auxiliary ships, and converted several private yachts into gunboats. The department concentrated the preponderance of its warships in the North Atlantic Squadron at Key West, Florida.[5]

The naval buildup also involved the Marine Corps. On 10 March 1898 Secretary Long provided Col. Charles Heywood, the Marine commandant, with guidelines on the use of the Navy's share of the emergency appropriation. The commandant was to incur expenses under the appropriation only after making an estimate of the amounts involved and receiving written approval from Secretary Long and the president. All told, the Marine Corps would eventually receive $106,529.64 under the emergency appropriation. The expenditures included the purchase of one million rounds of ammunition for the newly issued Lee rifles.[6]

Although both Secretary Long and Colonel Heywood wanted to expand the Marine Corps to meet anticipated demands, its role in any pending conflict was still vague. In a March communication to the chairman of the House Committee on Naval Affairs, Long explained the need for more marines in terms of their traditional missions. The usually authoritative *Army and Navy Journal*, nevertheless, carried a story on 12 March 1898 indicating that the Navy secretary had ordered Colonel Heywood to form two battalions ready to deploy at short notice. According to the account, "Two battalions have been made up on paper, and all the available officers of the Corps assigned to places in different companies." About the same time, the *Naval Institute Proceedings* published as one of its prize articles a piece by Lt. Comdr. Richard Wainwright. Although not specifically mentioning marines, Wainwright referred to advanced bases as the first line of defense in conjunction with the fleet. He advocated that such bases "should require such protection as is necessary to render the base safe against cruiser raids, or such light attacks as might be attempted during the temporary absence of the guarding fleet." The only obvious readily available source to establish and provide such protection for an advanced base would be the Marine Corps.[7]

The correspondence of Lt. Col. Robert Huntington, commander of the New York barracks and the most likely commanding officer of any Marine expeditionary force, reflected the uncertainties of the Marine role and the questionable readiness of its aging officer corps. Coincidentally, on the same day as the sinking of the *Maine*, Huntington wrote to Colonel Heywood expressing his concerns about the officer corps, especially in the field grade ranks and among the senior captains. Most had entered the Marine Corps during the Civil War or shortly afterward and had over thirty years of service.[8]

On 30 March 1898, when the possibility of war was much closer, Huntington speculated in a letter to his son about the mission of the Marines. He thought that Heywood planned to send him "to Key West to guard a coal pile." Huntington allowed, however, that "there is of course a possibility that we might go to Cuba. I cannot say I enjoy the prospect very much, but as my view of the war is, that it is one of humanity, I am willing to take the personal risk." Huntington proved right on both counts; he and his marines later went both to Key West and to Cuba.[9]

II

By early April the Navy had completed its initial preparations for operations against the Spanish. At Key West, the North Atlantic Squadron, now under the command of Captain Sampson, consisted of three armored battleships, several cruisers and torpedo boats, and support vessels. On 6 April 1898 Secretary Long ordered Sampson on the outbreak of hostilities to capture all Spanish warships in the West Indies and establish a blockade of Cuba. Sampson would have preferred to attack Havana but admitted "the force of . . . [Long's] reasoning that we would have no troops to occupy the city if it did surrender."[10]

Perhaps to rectify this situation, Sampson asked Secretary Long for the deployment of two battalions of marines to serve with the fleet at Key West. On 16 April Colonel Heywood received verbal orders to make the necessary arrangements. The following day, a Sunday, he met with the headquarters staff and sent out telegrams to Marine Corps commanding officers at East Coast navy yards. Planning to mount the first battalion out of New York within the week, the commandant on 18 April departed Washington to supervise the preparations personally. Back at Marine Corps headquarters, Maj. George C. Reid, the adjutant and inspector and now acting commandant, asked for and received $20,000 out of the emergency appropriation to transport and equip the expedition. By Wednesday, 20 April, the Marines had assembled 450 men from various East Coast navy yards at the New York barracks. At that point the department decided against the formation of a second battalion. Instead, the Marines increased the one battalion by 200 men. When it embarked two days later, the First Marine Battalion, under the command of Lieutenant Colonel Huntington, consisted of 631 enlisted men, twenty-one officers, and one surgeon; and it was organized into six companies, five infantry and one artillery.[11]

On Friday, 22 April, the newly purchased Navy transport, the *Panther* (formerly the *Venezuela*), docked at the Brooklyn Navy Yard. At the battalion's morning formation, Lieutenant Colonel Huntington told the men that they would embark and depart that night for Hampton Roads, Virginia. The troops greeted the news with loud cheers and song and then formed working parties to assist sailors in loading the ship. About 5:00 P.M., "the 'assembly'

Marine Detail at Charlestown Navy Yard

In early 1898 the Marine Corps issued a call to colors: "Recruits wanted for the U.S. Marine Corps; able-bodied, unmarried men, between the ages of 21 and 35 years, who are citizens of the United States, or those who have legally declared their intention to become such; must be of good habits and character and able to speak, read, and write English, and be between 5 feet 5 inches and 6 feet in height." The equipment of these recruits reflects the rapidity of enlistment. They are wearing the dress parade belt with the canteen and haversack of the Light Marching Order, but are missing the rifle, bayonet and cartridge belt which form the rest of that uniform. The standard marking for canteens was U.S.M.C., not U.S.M. as here. From the *Photographic History of the Spanish-American War* (New York, 1898). *Courtesy of the Naval Historical Center.*

was sounded and the battalion formed in line in heavy marching order, headed by the Navy Yard band." An hour later, the marines marched out of the navy yard, down Flushing Avenue, and then wheeled into the yard through the east gate. By 8:00 P.M., to the refrains of "Girl I Left Behind Me," the *Panther* set sail to join the fleet.[12]

On board the *Panther*, conditions were crowded and uncomfortable. The Navy had purchased the ship to carry a battalion of about four hundred men, not six hundred fifty. Furthermore, the troops carried on board the equipment and supplies necessary to sustain them in the field. This included mosquito netting, woolen and linen clothing, heavy and lightweight underwear, three-months' worth of provisions, wheelbarrows, push carts, pick axes, shovels, barbed-wire cutters, tents, and medical supplies. In addition, the artillery company took four 3-inch rapid fire guns. Colonel Heywood observed that the hatches for loading freight and two small ventilators in the aft section provided the only ventilation for the ship. Still, morale among the men and officers was high.[13]

The specific mission of the Marine battalion remained unclear. At the time of the unit's formation, Major Reid wrote that the Marines "are to have no connection whatever with the army, and are to report, and be at the disposal of the Commander-in-Chief of the North Atlantic Fleet." In a message to Sampson on 21 April Secretary Long referred to the Navy Department studying the possibility of "occupying the [northern Cuban] port of Matanzas by a military force large enough to hold it." He later declared that the Marine "battalion was organized especially for service in Cuba." Among the officers and men of the battalion, however, speculation abounded as to their final destination. According to Maj. Henry Clay Cochrane, a senior officer in the battalion, "Porto [*sic*] Rico is rumored," but he believed that "some port near Havana is more likely."[14]

By the time the battalion departed New York, the uncertainties and confusion of the general U.S. mobilization forced both the Army and the Navy to reconsider many of their initial assumptions. Acting on the president's message of 11 April, Congress on 19 April passed a joint resolution that recognized the independence of Cuba, demanded the withdrawal of the Spanish military forces, disclaimed any intention of the United States to annex the island, and authorized the president to use the U.S. armed forces to carry out the policy. McKinley signed the resolution the following day and sent the Spanish an ultimatum. In the meantime, after Congress rejected a War Department measure that would have increased only the Regular Army, the administration agreed with congressional leaders to support the establishment of a Volunteer Army as well as to expand the regular forces. As war approached, however, the Army, unlike the Navy, was not ready.[15]

On 20 April President McKinley held his first council of war. At the meeting, Maj. Gen. Nelson A. Miles, the commanding general of the Army, reported that the Army would not be ready for any large expeditionary campaign for at least two months. Like many other veterans of the Civil War, Miles opposed frontal assaults against well-entrenched positions. He advocated a blockade by the Navy, small raids by the Army along the Cuban coast in support of the Cuban rebels, and the seizure of Puerto Rico. The Army's position surprised Secretary Long and the other naval officers. While rejecting Sampson's initial assault plans against Havana, Secretary Long and his Navy planners had expected the Army—in conjunction with the Navy—to prepare for an offensive against the Cuban capital before the rainy season began. In fact, a joint Army-Navy board had earlier in the month proposed the landing of a small Army force at Mariel, a port town about twenty-five miles west of Havana, to establish a base of operations against the larger city. At this point, President McKinley, who had served in the Civil War as a major, overruled Long and the Navy and supported Miles's position.[16]

The conference enunciated a rather cautious military strategy in the Caribbean. McKinley approved the imposition of a blockade of Cuba, the resupply and other logistic support of Cuban insurgents, and limited U.S. land operations in Cuba. The Navy was to assume the main burden of the war. On 21 April 1898 Secretary Long promoted Captain Sampson to rear admiral and ordered him to "blockade coast of Cuba immediately from Cardenas to Bahia Honda" in the north and the southern city of Cienfuegos, "if it is considered advisable."[17]

On 22 April Sampson's squadron left Key West for Cuban waters. That same evening the *Panther*, with the First Marine Battalion embarked, pulled out of New York Harbor for Hampton Roads off Fortress Monroe. Arriving there the following evening, Lieutenant Colonel Huntington reported to Capt. Winfield Scott Schley, the commander of the Navy's Flying Squadron. Huntington received orders that the battalion would stay on board the *Panther* and await a warship that would escort the transport to Key West. Two more Marine officers, Maj. Percival C. Pope and First Lt. James E. Mahoney, joined the battalion at Fortress Monroe, bringing the number of officers to the full complement of twenty-three. Because of his seniority, Pope became second in command. Major Cochrane was assigned to the battalion staff and, in somewhat of a huff, wrote in his diary that he and Pope were unsure of their positions in the battalion.[18]

Huntington took advantage of the short interlude at Fortress Monroe to drill the troops and hold firing exercises. On the afternoons of 24 and 25 April the infantry companies practiced "volley and mass firing" while all four guns of the artillery company fired at least one round. Although morale remained high, two of the enlisted men came down with high fevers that developed into pneumonia. Another man fell off a rope ladder and was evacuated to the Army hospital ashore with a fractured limb.[19]

The men remained in good spirits when the cruiser *Montgomery* arrived to accompany the *Panther* to Key West. At 8:05 A.M. on Tuesday, 26 April, the transport steamed out of port and passed the battleships *Texas* and *Massachusetts* and the cruiser *Brooklyn* of the Flying Squadron, still at anchor. As the *Panther* went by the ships, the crews crowded the decks and "sent up cheer after cheer." The marines returned the cheers, but several of the older officers who had served in the Civil War had their reservations. Major Cochrane observed, "some of us felt anything but jolly at leaving behind the beauties of spring to be replaced by the perils of the sea and the hardships of war." On 29 April, after a three-day voyage, including a somewhat stormy passage around Cape Hatteras, the two ships arrived at Key West.[20]

On the same day, a seven-ship Spanish squadron under Adm. Pascual Cervera consisting of three cruisers, one battleship, and three destroyers set out from the Portuguese-owned Cape Verde Islands and headed west. This departure caused the Army to postpone indefinitely a planned six-thousand-man "reconnaissance in force" on the southern coast of Cuba. The Navy simply did not have enough ships both to escort the Army transports and to watch for the Spanish squadron, which could appear at any time. The departure of the Spanish squadron may also have caused the postponement of a Marine landing in Cuba. In letters to his sons and wife, Major Cochrane observed that the Marines had expected to "land in Cuba last Saturday [30 April], but now we must lie here [at Key West] for a week."[21]

III

While the U.S. fleet in the Caribbean waited for Cervera's squadron to make its appearance, the Asiatic Squadron under Commodore George Dewey had already taken the offensive. Having forewarned Dewey in late February to attack the Spanish in the Philippines in the event of hostilities, the Navy Department on 24 April 1898 informed the commodore that war had begun and that he "was to proceed . . . to the Philippines" to "commence operations at once." Acting on these orders, Dewey and his squadron slipped into Manila Bay under the cover of darkness shortly after midnight on Sunday, 1 May 1898. Although challenged by a few rounds from Spanish shore batteries on El Fraile Island near the entrance of the bay, the American naval squadron successfully eluded the Spanish defenses. Lying at anchor outside the protection of the land batteries at Manila, the older Spanish vessels were no match for Dewey's relatively modern cruisers. In the ensuing battle, which lasted a little more than seven hours, the American squadron sank or left as burning hulks all the enemy warships. At a cost of nine crewmen slightly wounded, the Americans had inflicted more than 370 casualties on the Spaniards, including 161 killed.[22]

Despite his overwhelming victory in the Philippines, Dewey's options to exploit his success were limited. As he informed Washington, "I can take city [Manila] at any time, but not sufficient men to hold." He estimated, "To retain possession and thus control Philippine Islands would require . . . [a] well-equipped force of 5,000 men." In the meantime, Marine 1st Lt. Dion Williams and a detachment of marines from the cruiser *Baltimore* occupied the Spanish naval station at Cavite, which served as a base of operations for the fleet, until reinforcements from the United States could arrive.[23]

News of Dewey's victory electrified American public opinion and reinforced the demand for a similar initiative in the Caribbean. Even before he officially heard the news from Manila, President McKinley had reversed his earlier decision to refrain from a major land campaign against Havana. In a conference on 2 May the president approved an expedition against Mariel that he had rejected at the April meeting. The vanguard of these forces were to be the troops encamped at Tampa under Maj. Gen. William Shafter, idle since the canceled "reconnaissance in force" mission. The plans for this operation went through several reiterations because there were major differences among many of the principals, including Secretary of War Russell A. Alger and Major General Miles, as well as between the Army and Navy. Although overruled by the president, Miles still opposed any major land campaign until after the rainy season. Admiral Cervera's squadron also remained a wild card. As Secretary Long informed Rear Admiral Sampson on 3 May, "No large army movement can take place for a fortnight and no small one will until after we know the whereabouts of the Spanish armored cruisers and destroyers."[24]

While the Army and Navy planners examined the feasibility of a Cuban campaign, the Marine battalion remained on board ship at Key West. On 30 April Lieutenant Colonel Huntington reported to Sampson on board the latter's flagship. The Navy commander at this time had no orders for the Marine commander, "as the plan of campaign had not yet been completed." Huntington's adjutant, 1st Lt. Herbert L. Draper, told Major Cochrane that

Sampson stated "he did not want the Marines to go away to the Army. [He] had use for them." On 3 May Sampson departed Key West with a small task force in the hopes of intercepting Cervera's squadron off Puerto Rico, leaving the Marine battalion to fend for itself.[25]

At Key West, the Marine battalion settled into a routine of drills, almost daily disputes with the Navy commander of the *Panther*, and rumormongering. Every morning the ship's small boats took the companies of the Marine battalion ashore for the drills. Although most of the officers had several years of service, the enlisted men of the battalion were largely raw recruits and required both discipline and training. Major Cochrane overheard another Marine officer describe a battalion parade as "a little Army, little Navy, and some Marine Corps." Even Huntington mentioned to his son that the men "have little idea of obeying orders" and that some were prone to stealing.[26]

On 23 May the *Panther* received orders to tow the monitor *Amphitrite*, which had been in Key West for repair, back out to the American blockading fleet. Forced to disembark in the early hours the following morning, the Marine battalion established a campsite on the beach, in effect becoming marooned at Key West without its transport.[27]

While Huntington futilely protested against his forced "grounding," his subordinate officers speculated about their mission and about their futures and the future of the Marine Corps. In typical fashion, Major Cochrane reflected much of this sentiment. Writing to his wife in early May, Cochrane observed that the Marines "are not hurrying very much to get to Cuba—unless we can have the prestige of being first. Every forward plan is suspended until the Spanish fleet is encountered." Most of his correspondence with his wife reflected the Marines' hopes for new legislation that would increase the Corps and permit promotions for the officers. Cochrane's wife noted that the war "should be an immense advantage to the Marine Corps." By late May and early June, however, Cochrane's optimism for favorable legislation had diminished: "When I think that war was declared on the 25th of April . . . , and that we embarked on the 22d, organized, equipped, and ready for duty, it annoys me that so little benefit comes from it."[28]

IV

As Huntington and his officers vented their frustrations against the Navy and against their forced inactivity at Key West, Colonel Heywood and his staff in Washington busied themselves in placing the Marine Corps on a wartime footing and lobbying for permanent legislation to benefit the Corps. They were more successful in the former activity than the latter.

At the beginning of the crisis, Heywood and his staff hoped to obtain from Congress a significant increase in personnel and a restructuring of the officer corps. The commandant was forced to settle for much less than he wanted. This was due, in part, to the legislative strategy of the McKinley administration. Congress had been considering reform of the naval officer corps for some time; the administration was supporting its own reform program, and did not want half-measures attached to the appropriation bill.[29]

On 28 March 1898 Colonel Heywood submitted a formal request for proposed legislation to Secretary Long for the restructuring of the Marine officer corps. The recommended bill contained many of the same provisions that the Corps had pushed through the years: the rank of brigadier general for the commandant, promotion for most other senior officers, an increase in the total number of officers, the temporary increase of rank for the Fleet Marine Officer, and the presidential appointment of all new staff officers in accordance with seniority in the staff and then from the list of senior Marine captains of the line. This bill contained one new wrinkle, however, in that it provided for the appointment of one-quarter of the new second lieutenants from the ranks of meritorious noncommissioned officers who passed the required examinations. Secretary Long forwarded the bill to the House Naval Affairs Committee. In its report, the committee incorporated Heywood's bill with the reform measures suggested by the Roosevelt personnel board.[30]

The incorporation of the Marine bill with the broader Navy personnel legislation, however, had its disadvantages. Because of the administration's admonition to the House Naval Affairs Committee, Congress would not consider the restructuring of the officer corps in the Naval appropriation bill. Because of the war, the Marine Corps realized through the appropriation legislation some expansion in its enlisted ranks and in the number of temporary officers. Congress authorized the inclusion of the 473 enlistments tentatively approved in March into the permanent organization and permitted the Marine Corps to recruit another 1,640 men for the emergency. The final appropriation measure, signed on 4 May 1898, contained a stipulation that allowed the president to appoint—"if an exigency may exist"—such officers to the Marine Corps as may be necessary from civilian life or from the ranks of meritorious noncommissioned officers of the Corps. These officers could serve only through the emergency and could not be appointed above the rank of captain.[31]

If Major Cochrane's reaction was typical, officers of the Marine battalion considered the measure to be grossly inadequate. Cochrane wrote to his wife in disgust that "the bill has caused great indignation among the lieutenants in our party," who probably had expected to be promoted to captain. He observed that the new second lieutenants from civilian life would all probably be the "sons of post traders." Cochrane also disapproved making officers of noncommissioned officers, writing that their temporary appointments would make them "unfit for their duties after the war." He reserved his greatest criticism, however, for what was not in the legislation. He believed that, in the same situation, the "Army would have gotten three colonels and so on with them, and thirty-six captains." All the Marines received, according to Cochrane, were some additional men and "acting second lieutenants to officer them." In agreement, Cochrane's wife replied, "I cannot see that the condition of the officers in the Corps has been improved one bit and it was such a chance to have gotten a really good organization."[32]

Colonel Heywood miscalculated in his legislative stratagem. He went along with the Navy Department policy to divorce the wartime mobilization from the permanent reform of the Navy and Marine officer corps. The commandant apparently believed that Congress would pass the Navy Department–sponsored personnel bill that would amalgamate the line and engineers. This bill now included the changes that Heywood had forwarded relating to the Marine Corps officers. Despite assurances from Heywood that the legislation was "sure to go through," many Marine officers, including Major Cochrane, remained skeptical. The skeptics proved correct. Congress was not about to touch the controversial amalgamation and "plucking" issues in the midst of the war when more pressing matters were at hand. Last-minute efforts by Heywood and his staff to separate the Marine legislation from the overall naval personnel bill failed, and there was no major wartime reformation of the Marine officer corps.[33]

Temporary officer appointments were permitted by the appropriation act, however, so the Marine officer corps did gain a wartime infusion of new blood. A jaundiced Major Cochrane provided his wife with advice for a young relative who wanted to obtain one of the new Marine commissions from civilian life. According to Cochrane, "the usual plan should be pursued." The candidate should first "make written application supported by testimonials . . . from well known men as to his character, ability, and general meritoriousness, and then to follow that up with any political, naval or social influence that he or his father or friends may have." Observing that Secretary Long was from Boston, Cochrane suggested that the young man should try to find someone from Massachusetts who could "in political parlance 'reach' him [Long]." If the candidate could not obtain someone who knew Long, "perhaps he can 'reach' Senator Lodge, Senator Hoar, or a Boston M.C. [member of Congress]." Cochrane concluded rather sardonically, "Permission to be examined once secured and the rest is easy."[34]

The system was not quite as simple as Cochrane described it. Although influence certainly helped in obtaining a commission, it was not enough to ensure one. Being from Massachusetts and knowing Secretary Long more often worked against an aspirant than for him. After recommending two young Massachusetts men for commissions, Secretary Long directed that no further appointments be made from that state. Even after receiving an endorsement of both the secretary of the Navy and the commandant of the Marine Corps, the candidates had to appear before an examining board. The Navy Department and Marine Corps were inundated with young and not-so-young applicants who wanted to go to war as Marine second lieutenants. To weed out the unfit, the board tested the applicants for physical, mental, moral, and military attributes and ranked each candidate by merit. On 21 May Colonel Heywood wrote Secretary Long that "the number of candidates already authorized to appear before the board for examination is more than sufficient to fill all the places created by the Act of May 4, 1898."[35]

By early June the examining boards had selected twenty-four men from civilian life to serve as Marine second lieutenants. Of this number, two were either the son or nephew of a member of Congress and at least seven were the sons or close relatives of military officers, while the remainder usually had some military education or experience. Although the law actually left the number of temporary commissions open-ended, Secretary Long and Colonel Heywood had decided on twenty-eight new officers for the time being. With the completion of the selection of the officers from civilian life, the remaining four officers were to come from the ranks of meritorious non-commissioned officers. Eventually the Navy Department raised the quotas so that forty-three officers served as temporary Marine second lieutenants until the end of the war. Of this total, forty were from civilian life and three were former noncommissioned officers.[36]

The selection of the new lieutenants from the enlisted ranks was somewhat different from that of the officers from civilian life. A noncommissioned officer who wanted an appointment had to submit an application through official channels to the commandant. He needed the strong endorsement of his commanding officer. Heywood would then recommend whether or not the man should be permitted to take the officer examination.[37]

Even here, however, political influence played its role. Sgt. Frank A. Kinne, hardly representative of the Marine enlisted ranks, was one of the selectees. He came from a comfortable, middle-class family. His father, G. Mason Kinne, was the assistant secretary of the Pacific coast division of a prominent international insurance company. The elder Kinne had enlisted in the Volunteers during the Civil War and risen to the rank of colonel. He was a past master of the Grand Army of the Republic and knew Secretary of War Alger. The father imposed on Alger to recommend his son for one of the second lieutenant openings. The son was a high school graduate and had received an appointment to the U.S. Military Academy at West Point but had been unable to attend because of illness. He then joined the Marine Corps and had five years of service; at the time of his application, he was an acting lieutenant on board the cruiser *New York*. Secretary Alger penned a short note to Secretary Long, describing the elder Kinne as "an old personal friend and his statements are entitled to every consideration." Sergeant Kinne received a commission.[38]

The remaining two noncommissioned officers, Sgt. Robert E. Devlin and Charles G. Andresen, were both with the deployed First Battalion before receiving their commissions. In his letter of recommendation, in which he stated that he knew each "to be a worthy and capable noncommissioned officer," Colonel Heywood asked that both men be examined at the First Battalion headquarters rather than called back to Washington. Andresen came from a much more typical enlisted background than Sergeant Kinne. Born in Norway, Andresen had immigrated to the United States as a young man and enlisted in the Marine Corps. Showing an aptitude as a soldier, he rose quickly through the ranks. At Fisher's Island in Long Island Sound, apparently during a fleet landing exercise, he served as first sergeant to Capt. Littleton W. T. Waller, who was so impressed that he highly recommended Andresen for a commission. Thanking Waller for his efforts, Andresen wrote: "Without your kindly assistance and advice it would have been impossible for me to have reached the place, where I now find myself."[39]

Although the process for selecting the new officers was subject to the vagaries of political influence, it still provided objective criteria to determine qualifications. This system rejected more than one candidate with impeccable social and personal background because of physical or mental failings. With the possible exception of the noncommissioned officers, however, most of the candidates came from middle-class or upper-middle-class families and almost all had completed high school. Given the large number of candidates seeking commissions, the examining boards had the luxury of selecting only those who showed the most promise for a military career.

The training of the new officers was quick and pragmatic. With the outbreak of the war, the Marine Corps School of Application graduated its class in April 1898 at the Washington barracks and temporarily suspended operations. The Marine Corps then used the barracks and school's facilities to indoctrinate the new officers. As Colonel Heywood observed, "The newly appointed officers were hurriedly drilled and otherwise prepared for duty as rapidly as possible, and distributed among the auxiliary cruisers, the various posts, and the First Marine Battalion."[40]

V

By June 1898, the Marine Corps battalion's days at Key West were numbered. On 18 May 1898, having eluded both Sampson's North Atlantic Squadron and Commodore William S. Schley's Flying Squadron, Admiral Cervera and his small fleet had entered the harbor of Santiago on the southern coast of Cuba. For several days the whereabouts of the Spanish fleet remained unknown to the Americans. On 27 May Commodore Schley, whose ships had just missed sighting the Spanish flotilla earlier, asked permission to abandon the quest for Cervera temporarily and return to Key West for recoaling. Following the advice of his Navy War Board, Secretary Long denied the request. The secretary observed that the Navy needed to know if Cervera was in Santiago and that Schley must surmount the difficulties of refueling. Long suggested that Schley might want to use the Guantanamo Bay area, about forty miles to the east of Santiago, for a coaling station. On 29 May, two days after first requesting relief, Schley, off Santiago, reported the enemy in port.[41]

At the same time that he had cabled Schley, apparently concerned that the latter would not be able to stay off Santiago, Secretary Long also sent a message to Sampson at Key West asking him if he could blockade Santiago and also "occupy [Guantanamo] as a coaling station." Sampson responded affirmatively and ordered Schley to maintain the blockade at all costs.[42]

On 31 May Capt. Charles D. Sigsbee, the captain of the cruiser *St. Paul*, departing Santiago with dispatches from Schley, recommended to Secretary Long that Guantanamo "be seized, and the shores garrisoned by United States troops." He believed it "a fine base for operating against Santiago." The occupation of Guantanamo also would prevent the Spanish from placing "plunging fire" on ships attempting to use the bay for recoaling. Sigsbee reported that Sampson agreed with his appraisal. According to Sampson, after "the establishment of the blockade [of Santiago], my first thought was to find a harbor which could serve as a coaling station and as a base for the operations of the fleet pending a decisive action." In any event, whether at the urging of the department or on his own initiative, the admiral ordered the reembarkation of the Marine battalion still at Key West and directed the cruiser *Marblehead* under Comdr. Bowman H. McCalla to reconnoiter Guantanamo.[43]

The Marines were more than ready to depart. The forced inactivity was causing some discord among the officers and some bad press. On 2 June Major Cochrane stated at the officers' mess that Marine Capt. George Elliott "was so loud in his clamor for war as to be disquieting." Lieutenant Colonel Huntington retorted that the *New York Herald* contained a statement that "Marines would rather eat than fight." Two days later a telegram ordering the battalion to prepare for reembarkation broke the tedium of the camp routine. By 6 June the battalion was back on board the *Panther*, except for a small guard detachment left behind and Major Pope, who was ill. The *Panther* sailed to join the fleet off Santiago the following day to "great cheering" from the crews of the ships still in port.[44]

Although their spirits were revived, the Marines still had no idea of their mission. Major Cochrane speculated that they were to reinforce Army transports in an attack on Santiago. On the morning of 10 June, when the *Panther* joined the fleet off Santiago, Sampson informed Huntington that the Marine battalion was to seize Guantanamo and hold it as a base for the fleet. Commander McCalla would serve as the overall commander of the expedition. Earlier the *Marblehead* had bombarded Spanish positions and landed a small reconnaissance detachment under the command of Marine Capt. M. D. Goodrell. Goodrell selected a campsite for the Marine battalion on a hill near an abandoned Spanish blockhouse and then returned to the ship. The *Panther* rendezvoused with the *Marblehead* on the afternoon of the tenth. McCalla sent Goodrell on board the *Panther* to brief Huntington on the situation ashore. As the Marine battalion landed, the first company formed a skirmish line and ascended the hill. According to Huntington, "we went ashore like innocents and made a peaceful camp and slept well on the tenth."[45]

Although Marine pickets heard strange noises and saw some lights during the night, there was no sign of the Spanish except for abandoned equipment, some personal belongings, and two old muzzle-loading field artillery pieces. The next morning, fearing the spread of disease, the Marines destroyed most of this material and the blockhouse. They also continued to unload their heavy equipment and move it to their campsite. Huntington and his officers were not too happy with the selection of their base camp. They were in a clearing on top of a hill, surrounded by thickets and dense underbrush, but overlooking the water. Capt. Charles McCawley, the battalion quartermaster, called the site a "faulty one" from a "military point of view." About eleven hundred yards to the front was a larger ridgeline that dominated the Marine-held hill. According to McCawley, "had the enemy been at all energetic or possessed of an ordinary amount of military knowledge they could have, in occupying this hill with sharpshooters, rendered our positions untenable."[46]

On 11 June, although not occupying the hill, Spanish troops made their presence known. At about 5:00 P.M. Spanish snipers killed two marines on an outpost. Huntington sent out a patrol, but it failed to locate the Spanish. The Marine commander, however, still felt secure. As he later wrote his son, "I do not know why I did not expect a night attack for we had a flurry in the P.M., but I did not." The enemy, however, returned on five occasions during the night. Major Cochrane, who had been directing the movement of supplies across the beach, came up to the Marine camp—now called Camp Mc-Calla in honor of the Navy commander—with reinforcements from the working parties during one of the lulls. First limiting themselves to minor probes, the Spaniards attacked in force after midnight. Cochrane called it "the beginning of 100 hours of fighting."[47]

Despite the heavy intensity of firing in the darkness, Marine casualties were relatively low. The Navy surgeon with the battalion received a mortal wound in the first major attack. About daybreak, the enemy struck in force again, killing a Marine sergeant and wounding three others. The fighting continued sporadically on the twelfth, but the Marines suffered no further casualties during the day. Cochrane wrote his wife: "We have been having no end of racket and excitement. . . . We are all worn out with the tension of fighting the scoundrels all night and all day and have another night coming on. Bullets went over my head and cannonading and fusilading all around but never close enough to hurt."[48]

With the continuing attacks on the afternoon of the twelfth, several of the Marine officers thought that the Spanish would overrun their camp if they remained. The Marines entrenched the top of the hill and moved their base camp to a lower site. Believing the enemy was bringing up more reinforcements, some of the company commanders even proposed that the battalion reembark on board the *Panther*. Major Cochrane argued forcibly against any such move, but Lieutenant Colonel Huntington remained noncommittal. Huntington reported back to Commander McCalla and referred to the possible evacuation of the battalion. Reputedly, the commander replied, "You were put there to hold that hill and you'll stay there. If you're killed I'll come and get your dead body." The matter of withdrawal soon became moot as about sixty Cuban insurrectionists, familiar with the terrain and area, reinforced the Marines.[49]

The Spaniards continued to harass the American outposts and lines through the night and next day. According to the battalion's journal, "during the night many persistent and trifling attacks were made on the camp in reply to which we used a good deal of ammunition." Major Cochrane was

Marines at Guantanamo Bay

On 28 June 1898 the *New York Herald* published a sketch by W. O. Wilson, an artist accompanying the Marines, with caption "An early morning attack on the Marines in the Trenches of Camp M'Calla." That sketch formed the basis of this lithograph published by the Werner Company of Akron, Ohio, later in 1898. The caption of the lithograph, "U.S. Navy—First Hoisting of the Stars and Stripes by the Marines on Cuban Soil—June 11th 1898," represents something of a compromise on dates. The Marines landed on 10 June and were attacked at dawn on 12 June. *Courtesy of the Naval Historical Center.*

more direct, stating there "was a vast deal of panicky, uncontrolled, and unnecessary fire." Again casualties were low, but the Marines lost their sergeant
major, Henry Good, to a sniper's bullet.[50]

At this point, Lieutenant Colonel Huntington was ready to take the offensive. The Cubans informed him that the enemy numbered some four to
five hundred troops and made their headquarters six miles to the south in the
village of Cuzco, whose well contained the only source of water for the
Spaniards. On the fourteenth, Huntington sent two companies under the
command of Captain Elliott to destroy the well. Although moving through
dense underbrush and rugged terrain and encountering stiff opposition along
the way, the Marines accomplished their mission. In the fighting they sustained three wounded and lost several men to heat prostration; their Cuban
allies lost one man and suffered several wounded. Supported by ship's batteries from below, the Marines took a heavy toll of the enemy, including the
capture of one Spanish lieutenant and seventeen enlisted men.[51]

Deprived of their water supply, the Spanish troops withdrew from the immediate environs of the Marine Corps camp. The Marines' nearest enemy
was now the Spanish garrison at the city of Guantanamo, twelve miles to the
north, which was estimated to contain three thousand to seven thousand
men. With Cuban insurrectionists in control of the countryside, the Americans had little to fear from the garrison. There soon developed an unspoken
modus vivendi. As Lieutenant Colonel Huntington observed to his son,
"The Spaniards do not trouble us and [we] only talk of troubling them."[52]

Following the action of 14 June, the Marine Corps battalion spent the rest
of its time at Guantanamo improving its fortifications and camp. The
marines also began to bask in the first publicity of their exploits. On the second day, several news correspondents, including novelist Stephen Crane, arrived at Guantanamo and began to file their dispatches. A few articles were
critical. For example, the reporter for the *New York Times* observed "that
given a free rein with repeating rifles, 500 nervous troops can waste 10,000
rounds of ammunition, killing shadows, in a single night, and not think even
then that they have done much shooting."[53]

But the *Times* article was very much the exception. More often the head-
lines spoke of "First in the Fight" and "The Gallant Marines." Crane, who
represented the *New York World*, was particularly friendly to the men of the
First Battalion. In an article entitled "The Red Badge of Courage Was His
Wig Wag Flag," Crane stated that Captain Elliott's attack on the Cuzco
well "was the first serious engagement of our troops on Cuban soil." The
novelist told about the heroics of Sgt. John Quick, who exposed himself to
enemy fire in order to signal an American ship to cease a bombardment that

threatened the Marine advance. Crane also had high praise for Huntington, referring to him as the "grey old veteran . . . and the fine old colonel" who provided the brave example to his men. Captain Elliott in his report declared that Crane accompanied him on the expedition to Cuzco and "was of material aid during the action, carrying messages to fire volleys, etc. to the different company commanders." Not lost on the public was the fact that the Marine Corps had landed and fought the Spanish while the Army, under Major General Shafter, still remained at Tampa.[54]

VI

The question of the launching of the Army expedition preoccupied the military commanders and government policymakers throughout most of May. Finally, on 26 May, the Naval War Board, the secretaries of War and the Navy, and Maj. Gen. Nelson Miles, in a meeting with President McKinley, agreed to an Army campaign against Santiago. They based their decision on the assumption that Cervera's fleet had taken refuge there.[55]

When the Navy had determined that, indeed, Cervera's entire fleet was in port, the War Department, on 31 May, ordered Maj. Gen. William Shafter to embark his troops on Army transports and steam with Navy protection to Santiago, but various problems delayed the departure of the Army for two weeks.[56] This delay hardly made for harmony in the relations between the Army and Navy off Cuba. Although Sampson and Shafter's first meeting on 20 June went well, the two leaders were soon at loggerheads. Sampson's main purpose was the destruction of Cervera's fleet, while Shafter's was the capture of the city of Santiago and its defending garrison. Each wanted the other to act first.

In order to reach an agreement, Sampson asked Shafter for a conference. On 3 July Sampson steamed westward from Santiago on board his flagship, the *New York*, to meet with Shafter at the latter's headquarters. About half an hour after setting out, Sampson, spotting smoke near the entrance of Santiago harbor, realized that Cervera had decided to try to head out and reversed course to attack the Spanish. By the time he reached the scene the battle was virtually over and the Spanish fleet destroyed.

The victory did nothing to solve the dispute between Shafter and Sampson. Although Cervera's fleet was no longer a factor, the Army had not yet taken Santiago. President McKinley directed that Shafter and Sampson meet and determine how they would cooperate to force the city to surrender. Sampson agreed to meet Shafter at Siboney, but fell ill and sent Capt. French E. Chadwick to represent him.[57]

At the conference with Shafter on 6 July, Captain Chadwick again presented Sampson's proposal that the Marines and Army capture the Socapa and Morro fortified heights to permit the Navy to clear the mines. Eventually Sampson and Shafter reached an agreement of sorts. The Navy would first shell the city of Santiago at long range with its large guns. If at the end of the bombardment the Spanish had not surrendered, Marines from the fleet, with the assistance of Cuban troops, would attack the Socapa heights. At the same time, Sampson would attempt to force the entrance with some of his smaller ships. It was unclear whether Shafter would provide troops to assist in the taking of the Morro.[58]

The commanders implemented only part of the agreement. Although on 10 and 11 July Sampson's ships fired on the city from outside the harbor entrance, the admiral and Shafter soon reverted to their original positions. Shafter still wanted Sampson to force the entrance of the harbor, but Sampson refused to do so until the ground troops had reduced the artillery batteries on the heights. At the heart of the question was the feasibility of an assault on the Morro. The Army said such an attack was not possible and the Navy said it was. For his part, Marine Maj. Robert L. Meade, who was the fleet marine officer and who would have commanded the Marine assault force on the Morro, agreed with Sampson, with some qualifications. After examining the terrain following the surrender of Santiago, he later wrote: "The most difficult part . . . would be in reaching the crest from the beach through almost impassable maniqua plants. Nothing but a narrow trail reached the crest. . . . Under such circumstances an inferior force could conduct a defense with success if properly handled but as the army in the near vicinity had successfully assaulted positions similarly defended I was certain that my assault would have been successful also, if undertaken."[59]

Events, however, overtook the dispute. With continuing Army reinforcements from the United States, including 1,500 troops under Major General Miles, Shafter squeezed the vise around the city. Finally, on 15 July, after extended negotiations and in the face of overwhelming odds, the Spanish commander of the Santiago garrison agreed to surrender.

VII

With the aborting of the campaign against the heights, the First Marine Battalion, even after the destruction of Cervera's fleet and the surrender of the city of Santiago, remained at Guantanamo Bay until the beginning of August. There had been some discussion about the battalion joining Major

General Miles and his planned expedition against Puerto Rico. The War Department, however, vetoed Marine participation.[60]

At Guantanamo, the Marines established a garrison routine. Three of the temporary lieutenants joined the battalion, together with enlisted replacements. The Marines maintained their vigil and manned their outposts, but at the same time entered into a more relaxed regimen. They nevertheless held to a high standard of health discipline, using only distilled water from the ships, burning their garbage, and changing their clothes whenever they could. One of the first battalion orders related to basic toilet habits: "Men are forbidden to ease themselves except at the latrine, and will not urinate inside the Fort or near the ramparts." On 23 July Major Cochrane observed that "our camp continues healthy, and we are trying to keep it so." In contrast to the Army, the Marines did not suffer one case of yellow fever and sustained only a 2 percent sickness rate.[61]

By the end of July, the Marine battalion was prepared to depart Guantanamo. In order to place further pressure on the Spanish in Cuba, the Naval War Board wanted to extend the naval blockade to western Cuba, where the Spanish still used ports on the southern coast that were connected by rail to Havana. The board directed that the Marine battalion seize the Isle of Pines off the southwestern coast as a "secure base for coal and against hurricanes, for the small vessels which alone could operate in the surrounding shoal water." Lieutenant Colonel Huntington at this point had some private doubts about the capability of the older officers to continue. He believed that another campaign "would clear Huntington, Harrington, Elliott, and Spicer off the roles of this battalion." Huntington stated, however, that "Cochrane . . . takes such selfish care of himself that he might last, unless somebody killed him."[62]

Fortunately for Huntington and his officers and men, they did not have to endure the hardships of further strenuous ground combat in a tropical climate. On 9 August, escorted by the cruiser *Newark*, the battalion departed Guantanamo on board the Navy transport *Resolute* for the Isle of Pines. Joined the following day by two other ships off Cape Cruz, Comdr. Caspar F. Goodrich, the captain of the *Newark* and task force commander, decided on a small digression. Acting on a suggestion from one of the ship captains, he ordered, en route to the Isle of Pines, the capture of the city of Manzanillo, west of Santiago. Although the Navy ships bombarded the city on 12 August, the news of the signing of the peace protocol calling for an armistice made the proposed landing of the Marine battalion unnecessary.[63]

Although Commander Goodrich and Lieutenant Colonel Huntington expressed disappointment about not attaining additional glory for American arms, other Marine officers were much less enthusiastic. Captain McCawley, the battalion quartermaster, later observed that the Americans badly under-estimated the size of the Spanish garrison. According to McCawley, the Spanish troops numbered nearly 4,500, not the 800 that Goodrich and his commanders had thought. Although reinforced by Cuban forces to the north of the city and by naval gunfire, the Marine battalion might have faced an almost impossible task.[64]

Upon the return of the Marine battalion from Cuba, Colonel Heywood exploited the Marine record in the war to enhance the Corps' status within the naval and military establishment. Rather than immediately dissolving the First Battalion, he kept the unit together at Portsmouth, New Hampshire, for over three weeks, ostensibly to permit the men "to rest and get the malaria" out of their system. On 10 September Colonel Heywood visited the Marine encampment and reported to Secretary Long that "the men are looking very well, none of them being sick, and there has not been a death by disease since the battalion left for Cuba." The Navy Department and the press were not slow to compare the 2 percent sickness rate of the Marine battalion with the ravages that malaria and yellow fever caused among Shafter's troops at Santiago.[65]

Finally, before disbanding in mid-September, the First Battalion paraded before the president and other dignitaries in Washington. In a heavy rain, but before a large, cheering crowd, the marines, dressed in their campaign uniforms, passed in review to the strains of "Hot Time in the Old Town Tonight" played by the Marine Corps Band. President McKinley complimented the men on their appearance and declared, "They have performed magnificent duty and to you, Colonel Heywood, I wish to personally extend my congratulations for the fine condition your men are in."[66]

Although the Marine leadership accepted with great satisfaction the public acclaim received by the Marine battalion, they still believed that the primary role of Marines in the future would be manning the secondary batteries on battleships. Even before the end of the war on 9 August 1898, Colonel Heywood sent out letters to selected ship commanders and to ship detachment Marine officers to determine the effectiveness of Marine gunnery in the sea battles of Santiago and Manila Bay. In his annual report, the commandant claimed that the secondary batteries caused the greatest damage to the Spanish ships at Santiago and that their raking fire forced the enemy to abandon their guns. He observed that a large percentage of the guns were manned by marines.[67]

The accounts by both marines and naval officers were less conclusive than Heywood professed for them. On the *Indiana*, for example, Marine Capt. Littleton W. T. Waller reported that only about a third of the Marine detachment actually manned the guns. As Capt. H. C. Taylor, the ship commander, pointed out, the Marines on the secondary battery fired about half as many as the seamen because the Marines manned the "port battery of 6-pounders, while the starboard battery was the one engaged." Another ship's commander, Capt. Robley D. Evans of the *Iowa*, agreed with Taylor: "I do not think it desirable to single out an individual division of this ship's company for special report. All the ship's company, of which the Marine Guard forms a division, have done their work in a manner creditable to themselves and their ship." Even more to the point, however, was the fact that naval gunnery during the battles of Santiago and Manila Bay was notoriously poor. American naval guns of all calibers averaged between 1 to 5 percent hits for ammunition expended.[68]

Still, neither the public nor Congress was overly concerned with the technicalities of naval gunfire. In fact, the inadequacies of the aimed firing during the two sea battles did not come out until several months later, and then appeared only in professional journals and official reports. Heywood's report containing lists of marines breveted for gallantry in action and accounts of marines in battle both on land and at sea served to satiate the nation's appetite for heroes. As the *New York Times* shrewdly noted, "This is the sort of stuff that members of Congress will read when they receive the request of [the] Colonel Commandant . . . to have an increased allowance of men and money to the Marine Corps in the next naval appropriation bill."[69]

For the Marine Corps and the nation at large, the war was over. The protocol of 12 August between the two countries ended hostilities and called for a peace treaty to be negotiated in Paris. Spain agreed to relinquish Cuba, give Puerto Rico to the United States, and permit the United States to occupy Manila until the conclusion of the formal treaty determined the fate of the Philippines. Ironically, on 13 August, the day after the protocol was signed, American forces captured Manila after token resistance by Spanish defenders. In the final Treaty of Paris, signed on 10 December 1898 and ratified in February 1899, the Spanish ceded the Philippines to the United States. Almost completely unnoticed during the war, the United States had also formally annexed the Hawaiian Islands. Thus, the immediate result of the Spanish-American War was to make the United States an imperial power in both the Caribbean and the Pacific.

The Spanish-American War also had a lasting effect on the Marine Corps. Although nearly 75 percent of Marine strength was on board ship, it was Huntington's battalion that caught the public eye and signaled portents for the future. As Colonel Heywood quickly remarked, the Marine battalion with the fleet "showed how important and useful it is to have a body of troops which can be quickly mobilized and sent on board transports, fully equipped for service ashore and afloat, to be used at the discretion of the commanding admiral." Heywood also pointedly observed that the Marine force stood "always under the direction of the senior naval officer," and thus posed no "conflict of authority" inherent in Army-Navy relations.[70]

The Spanish-American War proved to be the crucible for the Marine Corps. While not fully knowing how they would use it, naval authorities immediately ordered the establishment of a Marine battalion with its own transport. Although numbering less than a quarter of the active Marine Corps, this battalion's activities not only received public approbation but also had implications for the future relationship of the Marine Corps with the Navy. Despite a somewhat rocky start at Guantanamo, the First Marine Battalion proved itself in combat. By seizing the heights on Guantanamo, it provided a safe anchorage for Navy ships. In effect, the Marines seized and protected an advance base for the fleet blockading Santiago.

Navy strategists and planners also learned another lesson from the war. They quickly realized that Army and Navy officers may have very different and even possibly conflicting goals in a military campaign. The dispute between the Army and Navy at Santiago reflected the separate approaches of professional Army and Navy officers. For Major General Shafter and his staff, the vital objective was the capture of the Spanish garrison and the city of Santiago. On the other hand, Rear Admiral Sampson's and the Navy's aim was the destruction of Cervera's fleet. For his part, Shafter designed an overland campaign to capture the city and was unwilling to sacrifice men to take the Morro and Socapa heights overlooking the narrow channel into Santiago Bay. At the same time, Sampson refused to chance the loss of any of his ships by running the channel. Although both commanders attained their desired ends, their basic conflict remained unresolved. For the Navy, the message was that it could not depend upon the Army to secure land-based sites for naval purposes. The Navy required its own land force, and it had this in the Marine Corps.

NOTES

1. David F. Trask, *The War with Spain in 1898* (New York, 1981), xii–xiv, 35; John D. Long, *The New American Navy*, 2 vols. (New York, 1903), 1:141.

2. Trask, *War with Spain*, 72–78, 88–90; J.A.S. Grenville, "American Naval Preparations for War with Spain, 1896–98," *Journal of American Studies* (Apr. 1968): 33–47. For copies of some of the original plans see Lt. William Kimball, "War with Spain," 1 June 1896; Plan of Operations Against Spain, 17 Dec. 1896; Plans of Cam-

paign Against Spain and Japan, 30 June 1897; all in War Planning Portfolio 11, OAB, Naval Historical Division, Washington, D.C.

3. Trask, *War with Spain*, 83–90; Long, *New American Navy* 1:165–66.

4. Graham A. Cosmas, *An Army for Empire: The United States Army in the Spanish-American War* (Columbia, Mo., 1971), 87–89. See also Trask, *War with Spain*, 145–49; and Russell F. Weigley, *History of the U.S. Army* (New York, 1967), 299.

5. Trask, *War with Spain*, 82–88; Margaret Leech, *In the Days of McKinley* (New York, 1959), 195–96.

6. Secretary of the Navy [SecNav] letters [ltrs] to Commandant of the Marine Corps [CMC], 10 Mar., 6 and 11 Apr. 1898, Letters Received, "N," RG 127; CMC ltrs to SecNav, 13 and 15 Mar., 6 and 9 Apr. 1898, Letters Sent to the Secretary of the Navy [LSSN] 7:187, 194–95, 245–46, 252, RG 127, National Archives [NA], Washington, D.C.; CMC, *Annual Report, 1898*, 6.

7. SecNav ltr to CMC and copy of ltr to C. A. Boutelle, 10 Mar. 1898, Letters Received, "N," RG 127, NA; *Army and Navy Journal* (12 Mar. 1898): 515; Lt. Comdr. Richard Wainwright, "Our Naval Power," *United States Naval Institute Proceedings* (Mar. 1898): 39–87, 48.

8. Lt. Col. R. W. Huntington ltr to CMC, 15 Feb. 1898, Letters Received, "N," RG 127, NA.

9. Huntington ltr to Bobby, 30 Mar. 1898, Col. R. W. Huntington Papers, Marine Corps Historical Center [MCHC], Washington, D.C.

10. Long ltr to CinC, U.S. Naval Force, NA, 6 Apr. 1898, and Sampson ltr to Sec-Nav, 9 Apr. 1898, reprinted in *Appendix to the Report of the Chief of the Bureau of Navigation*, 171–73.

11. CMC ltrs to SecNav, 18 and 23 Apr. 1898, LSSN 7:250–52, 266, RG 127; Acting CMC ltr to SecNav, 19 Apr. 1898, Letters Received, "N," RG 127; entries for 17–22 Apr. 1898, and Battalion Orders 1–3, 19–20 Apr. 1898, in Journal of the Marine Battalion under Lt. Col. Robert W. Huntington, Apr.–Sept. 1898, RG 127, NA [hereafter Journal of the Marine Battalion]; CMC, *Annual Report, 1898*, 7, 10; Charles L. McCawley, "The Marines at Guantanamo," n.d., MS, 2–4, Maj. Gen. Charles L. McCawley Papers, MCHC; "Marine Battalion at Guantanamo," reprinted in *Appendix to the Report of the Chief of the Bureau of Navigation*, 440–41. Graham A. Cosmas observed that the "Marine mobilization coincides in time with the order for concentration of most of the Regular Army at Chickamauga Park, New Orleans, Mobile, and Tampa, which went out on 15 April [1898]" (Cosmas, comments on author's draft chapter, Mar. 1990).

12. "Marines to Start Tonight," clipping from *Brooklyn Eagle*, 22 Apr. 1898, General Clipping File, Maj. Henry Clay Cochrane Papers, MCHC; *New York Times*, 23 Apr. 1898, 4; McCawley, "Marines at Guantanamo," 2–4; "Marine Battalion at Guantanamo," 440–41; CMC, *Annual Report, 1898*, 6.

13. "Marine Battalion at Guantanamo," 440–41; CMC ltr to SecNav, 23 Apr. 1898, LSSN 7:250–52, RG 127, NARA; Cochrane ltr to Betsy, 22 Apr. 1898, Cochrane Papers.

14. Maj. George C. Reid ltr to Pendleton, 12 Apr. 1898, in Maj. Gen. Joseph H. Pendleton Papers, MCHC; Long message to Sampson, 21 Apr. 1898, reprinted in *Appendix to the Report of the Chief of the Bureau of Navigation*, 174–75; Cochrane ltr to Betsy, 23 Apr. 1898, Cochrane Papers; Long, *New American Navy* 2:5.

15. Trask, *War with Spain*, 54, 150–52; Cosmas, *Army for Empire*, 93–102.

16. Leech, *Days of McKinley*, 198–99; Trask, *War with Spain*, 153–54; Cosmas, *Army for Empire*, 102–7; Long, *New American Navy* 2:9.

17. Trask, *War with Spain*, 108, 153–54; Cosmas, *Army for Empire*, 107; Long ltr to Sampson, 21 Apr. 1898, reprinted in *Appendix to the Report of the Chief of the Bureau of Navigation*, 174.

18. Entries for 23–26 Apr. 1898 in Journal of the Marine Battalion; entries for 23–28 Apr. 1898, diary, Cochrane Papers; Lt. Col. R. W. Huntington report to CMC, 30 Apr. 1898, Letters Received, Historical Section, RG 127, NA; McCawley, "Marines at Guantanamo," 8–10; CMC, *Annual Report, 1898*, 6.

19. Entires for 23–26 Apr. 1898 in Journal of the Marine Battalion; entries for 23–28 Apr. 1898, diary, Cochrane Papers, MCHC; Lt. Col. R. W. Huntington report to CMC, 30 Apr. 1898. Modifications continued to be made on the Lee rifles. See Chief, Bureau of Ordnance ltr to CMC, 22 July 1898, Letters Received, "N," RG 127, NA.

20. Entries for 26–29 Apr. 1898 in Journal of the Marine Battalion; Cochrane ltr to Betsy, 26 Apr. 1898, folder 51, Cochrane Papers; McCawley, "Marines at Guantanamo," 8.

21. Trask, *War with Spain*, 162–63; Cosmas, *Army for Empire*, 111–12; Leech, *Days of McKinley*, 198–99; Cochrane ltr to Betsy and boys, 4 May 1898, Cochrane Papers.

22. Long ltr to Dewey, 24 Apr. 1898, and Dewey report to SecNav, 4 May 1898, reprinted in *Appendix to the Report of the Chief of the Bureau of Navigation*, 67, 69–72.

23. Dewey to Long, 4 and 13 May 1898, reprinted in *Appendix to the Report of the Chief of the Bureau of Navigation*, 68, 97–98; Trask, *War with Spain*, 105; Bernard C. Nalty, *The United States Marines in the War with Spain*, rev. ed. (Washington, 1967), 6.

24. Cosmas, *Army for Empire*, 121–30; Leech, *Days of McKinley*, 214–16; Trask, *War with Spain*, 163–67; Long ltr to Sampson, 3 May 1898, reprinted in *Appendix to the Report of the Chief of the Bureau of Navigation*, 366. Cosmas observed it was his understanding that "McKinley had unofficial reports of Dewey's victory at the time he began to revise strategy on 2 May" (Cosmas comments to the author, Mar. 1990).

25. Entry for 30 Apr. 1898 in Journal of the Marine Battalion; McCawley, "Marines at Guantanamo," 10; entry for 3 May 1898, diary, Cochrane Papers; Trask, *War with Spain*, 114.

26. Entries for 1–24 May 1898 in Journal of the Marine Battalion; entry for 31 May 1898, diary, Cochrane Papers, MCHC; Huntington ltr to Bobby, 27 May 1898, Huntington Papers, MCHC.

27. Huntington ltrs to CMC, 25 May and 3 Nov. 1899, McCawley ltr to CMC, 8 Jan. 1900, and Commodore George C. Remey endorsement to CMC, 25 May 1898,

Letters Received, Historical Section, RG 127, NA; Huntington ltr to Bobby, 27 May 1898, Huntington Papers.

28. For examples of this correspondence, see Cochrane ltrs to Betsy, 6, 9, 12, 28 May and 1 June 1898, and Betsy ltrs to Cochrane, 24 and 25 Apr. 1898, folder 51, Cochrane Papers.

29. *New York Times*, 25 March 1898, 3.

30. CMC ltr to SecNav, 28 Mar. 1898 with enclosures, LSSN 7:210–77, RG 127, NA; U.S. Congress, House, *Reorganization of Naval Personnel, HR 10403, with Accompanying Report*, HR 1375, 55th Cong., 2d sess., 1898, 12–13.

31. U.S. Congress, Senate, 55th Cong., 2d sess., 29 Apr. 1898, *Congressional Record* 31:4422; CMC, *Annual Report, 1898*, 11.

32. For the Cochrane correspondence, see Cochrane ltrs to Betsy, 6, 9, 12–13 May 1898, and Betsy ltr to Cochrane, 12 May 1898, folder 51, Cochrane Papers.

33. U.S. Congress, House, 55th Cong., 2d sess., 19 May 1898, *Congressional Record* 31:5058–59; CMC, *Annual Report, 1898*, 16–17; SecNav, *Annual Report, 1898*, 54–57; Cochrane ltrs to Betsy, 12 and 28 May 1898, folder 51, and entry, diary, 4 June 1898, Cochrane Papers.

34. Cochrane ltr to Betsy, 1 June 1898, folder 51, Cochrane Papers.

35. CMC ltr to SecNav, 5, 9, 13–18, 20–21, 25 May and 6 June 1898, LSSN 7:305, 308–14, 329–45, 353, 370–74; Asst. SecNav ltr to CMC, 3–4 May 1898, Letters Received, "N," RG 127, NA.

36. Asst. SecNav ltr to CMC, 3–4 May 1898, Letters Received, "N," RG 127, NA; CMC, *Annual Report, 1898*, 11. The records do not indicate why a fourth NCO was not commissioned. Sergeant Henry Goode, the sergeant major of the Marine battalion under Huntington, was nominated. One can surmise that his untimely death at Guantanamo prevented his appointment and that the war ended before another choice could be made.

37. CMC ltr to SecNav, 18 June 1898, LSSN 7:415, RG 127, NA.

38. C. Mason Kinne ltr to Secretary of War, Gen. R. A. Alger, and attached ltrs and endorsements, 24 June 1898, Letters Received, Historical Section, RG 127, NA.

39. CMC ltr to SecNav, 6 June 1898, LSSN 7:372–74, RG 127, NA; Lt. Charles G. Andresen ltr to Waller, 5 May 1899, L.W.T. Waller Papers, 1896–1902, MCHC.

40. Capt. F. H. Harrington, School of Application ltr to CMC, 18 Apr. 1898, Letters Received, Historical Section, RG 127, NA; CMC, *Annual Report, 1898*, 11, 15. See also Hans Schmidt, *Maverick Marine, General Smedley D. Butler and the Contradictions of American Military History* (Lexington, Ky., 1987), 7.

41. Exchange of messages between Long and Schley, 27–29 May 1898, reprinted in *Appendix to the Report of the Chief of the Bureau of Navigation*, 397–400.

42. Exchange of messages, 28–30 May 1898, reprinted in ibid., 398–400.

43. Sigsbee ltr to SecNav, 31 May 1898, reprinted in ibid., 412–14; Rear Adm. William T. Sampson, "The Atlantic Fleet in the Spanish War," *Century Magazine*, n.d., 886–913, 903, in Printed Material Folder, H. C. Taylor Papers, Library of Congress [LC], Washington, D.C.

44. Entries for 1–7 June 1898, in Journal of the Marine Battalion; entries for 1–7 June 1898, diary, Cochrane Papers, MCHC.

45. Entry for 4 June 1898, diary, Cochrane Papers; McCalla ltr to Sampson, 19 July 1898, reprinted in Maj. Richard S. Collum, *History of the United States Marine Corps* (New York, 1903), 348–49; McCawley, "Marines at Guantanamo," 9; Nalty, *The United States Marines in the War with Spain*, 9; Huntington ltr to Bobby, 19 June 1898, Huntington Papers.

46. McCawley, "Marines at Guantanamo," 15–17.

47. Ibid.; entries for 11–12 June 1898 in Journal of the Marine Battalion; Huntington ltr to Bobby, 19 June 1898, Huntington Papers; entries for 11–12 June 1898, diary, Cochrane Papers.

48. Entries for 11–12 June 1898, diary; and Cochrane ltr to Betsy, 12 June 1898, folder 51, both in Cochrane Papers.

49. Entries for 11–12 June 1898 in Journal of the Marine Battalion. The discussion about the proposal evacuation is contained in Cochrane's diary (entries for 11–12 June, 25 Aug. 1898, and in flysheet in back of diary for 1898, Cochane Papers) referring to interviews with several other witnesses. He also mentions the incident in a letter to his wife (Cochrane ltr to Betsy, 14 June 1898, folder 51, Cochrane Papers). Cochrane was not a witness to McCalla's refusal and gives conflicting accounts. In a separate report Commander McCalla only stated: "The mistake of locating the camp between the main position and the outpost was corrected . . . at my suggestion" (McCalla ltr to Sampson, 19 July 1898, reprinted in Collum, *History of the United States Marine Corps*, 348–49).

50. Entries for 12–13 June 1898, Journal of the Marine Battalion; entry for 13 June 1898, diary, Cochrane Papers.

51. Entries for 14 and 19 June 1898, Journal of the Marine Battalion.

52. Huntington ltr to Bobby, 4 July 1898, Huntington Papers.

53. Journal of the Marine Battalion; McCawley, "Marines at Guantanamo," 28, 31–40; entries for 13–15 June 1898, diary, Cochrane Papers; *New York Times*, 17 June 1898.

54. Clippings "First to Fight" and "The Gallant Marines," n.d., n.p., General Clipping File, Cochrane Papers; R. W. Stallman and E. R. Hagemann, eds., *The War Despatches of Stephen Crane* (New York, 1964), 140–54, 171–72, 267–74; Capt. G. F. Elliott ltr to Huntington, 18 June 1898, reprinted in CMC, *Annual Report, 1898*, 29.

55. Trask, *War with Spain*, 172–73; Cosmas, *Army for Empire*, 179–80.

56. Long ltr to Schley, 27 May 1898, reprinted in *Appendix to the Report of the Chief of the Bureau of Navigation*, 397; Long message to Sampson, 31 May 1898, quoted in Sampson, Report of Operations of North Atlantic Fleet, 3 Aug. 1898, reprinted in ibid., 480.

57. Trask, *War with Spain*, 291–93; Rear Adm. W. T. Sampson, Report of Operations of Blockading Squadron off Santiago, 15 July 1898, reprinted in *Appendix to the Report of the Chief of the Bureau of Navigation*, 609–10; SecNav, *Annual Report, 1898*, 14.

58. "Minutes of a conversation between Captain Chadwick of the Navy, representing Admiral Sampson, and General Shafter," 6 July 1898, reproduced in Sampson, Report of Operations, 15 July 1898, 610. Chadwick in his history, however, states that Shafter had agreed to attack the Morro (French Ensor Chadwick, *The Relations of the United States and Spain, The Spanish American War*, 2 vols. [New York, 1911, reissued in 1968], 2:208). Trask agrees with Chadwick that Shafter agreed to attack the Morro, "although for unexplained reasons this aspect of the plan was not made explicit in the minutes of the meeting" (Trask, *War with Spain*, 293). Cosmas comments that from "3 July on, Shafter was engaged in his own negotiations with the Spanish commander, General Toral, looking to the surrender of the garrison. I'm not sure how thoroughly, or even whether, he kept Sampson filled in on this" (Cosmas comments to author, Mar. 1990).

59. Lt. Col. Robert L. Meade ltr to Maj. Charles L. McCawley, 18 Mar. 1899, McCawley Papers.

60. Entries for 17–21 July 1898, diary, Cochrane Papers; Trask, *War with Spain*, 350, 353.

61. First Marine Battalion Order no. 3, 21 June 1898, Journal of the Marine Battalion; McCawley, "Marines at Guantanamo," 45–48; Cochrane ltr to Betsy, 23 June 1898, Cochrane Papers.

62. A. T. Mahan, "The War on the Sea and Its Lessons," *McClures*, n.d., 527–34, 532, in Printed Material Folder, Taylor Papers; Huntington ltr to Bobby, 29 July 1898, Huntington Papers.

63. G. F. Goodrich ltr to CinC North Atlantic Fleet, 13 Aug. 1898, reprinted in *Appendix to the Report of the Chief of the Bureau of Navigation*, 301–3.

64. Ibid.; McCawley, "Marines at Guantanamo," 43–45.

65. Cochrane ltr to Betsy, 22 Aug. 1898, Cochrane Papers; Chief, Bureau of Navigation ltr to CMC, 8 Aug. 1898, Letters Received, Historical Section, and CMC ltr to SecNav, 10 Sept. 1898, LSSN 7:567–68, RG 127, NA; Ira Nelson Hollis, "The Navy in the War with Spain," *Atlantic* (Nov. 1898): 605–16, Printed Matter Folder, Taylor Papers, LC; *Army and Navy Journal*, 17 Sept. 1898, 68. Malaria and yellow fever played havoc with the U.S. Army's Fifth Corps before Santiago. On 27 July 1898, more than 4,000 soldiers in the corps were in the hospital and a few days later the death rate reached fifteen per day (Cosmas, *Army for Empire*, 251–52). Although Marine Corps sanitary practices in part accounted for their low sickness rate, the Marines were fortunate that the Guantanamo sector remained dry and bred few of the mosquitos that spread the yellow fever and malaria among the Army troops.

66. *Army and Navy Journal*, 24 Sept. 1898, 95.

67. CMC, *Annual Report, 1898*, 14; Army and Navy Journal, 27 Aug. 1898, 1,088.

68. Capt. Littleton W. T. Waller ltr to Colonel Commandant, USMC, 1 Sept. 1898, in CMC, *Annual Report, 1898*, 44–45; H. C. Taylor ltr to SecNav, 18 Sept. 1898, Correspondence Folder, July–Sept. 1898, Taylor Papers, LC; Capt. R. D. Evans ltr to Lt. Col. R. L. Meade, 31 Aug. 1898, Letters Received, Historical Section, RG 127, NA; Lt. John Ellicott, USN, *Effect of the Gun Fire of the United States Vessels in the*

Battle of Manila Bay (1 May 1898), Office of Naval Intelligence, War Note No. 5, Information from Abroad (Washington, 1899).

69. CMC, *Annual Report, 1898;* "Record of the Marines," *New York Times,* 23 Oct. 1898, 13.

70. CMC to SecNav, 12 Dec. 1898, LSSN 7:84–85, RG 127, NA.

The Struggle for Samar

BRIAN M. LINN

The STRUGGLE FOR SAMAR WAS PROBABLY THE MOST VICIOUS, AND CERTAINLY the most controversial, campaign of the Philippine War of 1899–1902. Although the campaign has provoked an extensive literature, just why the fighting on this isolated and strategically unimportant island should have escalated to the level seen in the Balangiga Massacre and the American efforts to turn the island into a "howling wilderness" remains a puzzle nearly a century later. Doctrinaire explanations that emphasize such factors as the inhabitants' savagery, the inherent brutality of imperialism, American racism, or the frustration of fighting an Asian guerrilla war are less than satisfactory.

The Samareños were not a particularly violent people, and many were indifferent toward, if not actually friendly to, the American occupiers. Some soldiers and marines did indeed behave in an appallingly callous manner, but many of their comrades sought to protect and aid Filipino civilians. Samar's terrain was formidable, its native guerrillas were resourceful, and the U.S. military forces committed to its pacification were insufficient, but the Americans met and mastered potentially greater obstacles elsewhere in the Philippines. One factor that has largely been ignored so far is the failure of the U.S. Army and Navy to cooperate in joint operations. On no other island did the Americans make as sustained an effort to harness their military and naval forces toward the suppression of indigenous resistance, and on no other island were the consequences of miscommunication and conflicting service missions as serious.[1]

Certainly the island of Samar would seem to offer a casebook study for joint Army-Navy operations. The island's geography made some form of combined service policy a necessity for any occupying power. The 5,200 square miles of this "dark and bloody island" are divided into a narrow coast region and a rugged series of mountains and river valleys that cover most of the interior. In 1900 that interior was still a virtual terra incognita of swamps, volcanic peaks, tropical forests, and boulder-strewn rivers. The rugged terrain and harsh climate made communications difficult and forced most of Samar's 200,000 inhabitants to live in small villages or barrios along the river valleys and coast. There they eked out a precarious existence growing *abaca* (Manila hemp), rice, and yams, and supplementing their meager diet with fish. Land communications—even along the coast—consisted of little more than hunting paths, often obscured by razor-sharp grasses and replete with leeches and other parasites.

The island posed an equally formidable challenge to naval forces. Although boats could steam up many of the rivers for several miles, floods, sandbars, tree limbs, and shifting channels made river navigation a constant gamble. The island's surrounding seas were largely uncharted; moreover, they were filled with reefs, shoals, and erratic tides which, when combined with the twice-yearly monsoons and frequent typhoons, made ocean travel a continual challenge. To add further to the U.S. Navy's problems, Samar was separated from the neighboring island of Leyte to the southwest only by the narrow San Juanico Strait, for some eighteen miles little wider than a river. The island's geography, terrain, and climate made joint operations between land and waterborne forces a necessity, but also contributed to the island's being viewed as hell on earth by many of the sailors and soldiers stationed there.

The Army and Navy officers who served on Samar not only had virtually no theoretical background in joint operations but were assigned different, and occasionally contradictory, missions. Although the Civil War had witnessed a number of successful collective efforts, Army-Navy relations in the Spanish-American War were too often characterized by personal squabbles and irresponsible parochialism. During the Philippine War, neither the organizational structure nor the assigned duties of either service allowed much chance of sustained interservice coordination. Charged not only with defeating the anticolonial guerrillas, the *insurrectos*, but also with fulfilling President McKinley's orders to win over the Filipino populace to American imperial rule, the Army, as John Morgan Gates has noted, pacified the islands with a schoolbook in one hand and a Krag rifle in the other. The Navy's mission consisted largely of blockading the archipelago's waters and preventing

Pack Train on Samar

The rugged terrain and lack of roads made Navy logistical support vital on Samar. When operating in the interior American troops had to be supplied by carabao pack trains. *Courtesy U.S. Army Military History Institute.*

insurrecto smuggling, duties carried out chiefly by gunboats and steam launches. The administrative structure of both services prevented clear communications and the uniform direction of policy. Army command was centered in the Division of the Philippines, headquartered in Manila, but individual military units were scattered in over four hundred garrisons throughout the archipelago, often isolated from Manila's directives both by poor communications and by geography. Navy organization was even more diffuse: not until 1903 would there be a permanent Philippine Squadron Commander, and in the meantime the senior authority was the flag officer of the Asiatic Station, whose attention was also directed toward potential Great Power conflict in Asia. As a result, both in Manila and the boondocks, an officer could enjoy the most cordial relations with his colleagues from other services, but nowhere could he find an organization designated to oversee combined operations nor a command structure that could facilitate interservice contacts.[2]

Given this lack of central direction, it is not surprising that joint operations in the Philippine War were extemporaneous affairs for specific tasks, most commonly the capture of an important village or an attack on a suspected enemy stronghold. Such improvised tactics proved sufficient in 1899 and early 1900 during the fighting in northern Luzon and in the relatively bloodless operations in the southern Philippines. Nor did the shift in Filipino resistance from conventional to guerrilla warfare in 1900 substantially affect the off-the-cuff approach to joint operations. While the Army pacified the countryside, the Navy's gunboats and launches carried troops to isolated coastal villages, provided firepower for river expeditions, and brought supplies and reinforcements for long-range raids. These affairs were usually the result of impromptu meetings between officers in which procedures, transport, logistics, and fire support were hammered out. A spectacular example of the potential flexibility and speed offered by this informal improvisation was the capture of Emilio Aguinaldo in March 1901, the result of close personal cooperation between the Army officer who commanded the expedition and the Navy officer who transported it. Because American forces were usually so successful, the few instances of interservice conflict, such as those during the Legaspi and Iloilo landings, were overlooked or quietly tabled by superior officers without any attempt at resolution. However, the campaign on Samar would demonstrate the limits of this task-oriented approach and bring to the surface much of the potential friction underlying joint operations.[3]

The American presence was first felt in Samar shortly after the outbreak of the Philippine War on 4 February 1899. In an effort to isolate the main insurgent forces on Luzon, the Army commander in the Philippines, Maj. Gen. Elwell S. Otis, requested that the Navy blockade the interisland transport of money, men, and supplies. Although the Navy had few gunboats available for the Visayas, it stationed one off the northern coast. According to Samar's insurgent commander, Brig. Gen. Vicente Lukban, the blockade prevented him from either returning to Luzon or asserting his authority over Leyte. Moreover, because much of Samar's coastal population was dependent on imported food, the blockade contributed to a severe shortage: in July Lukban claimed he was subsisting on sweet potatoes in the morning, boiled rice for lunch, and rice soup in the afternoon. Further indication of the blockade's effectiveness is Lukban's early realization that "war is not solely sustained by balls [bullets] but also and principally by food," and his efforts to mobilize the population to grow more crops.[4]

Samar might well have been left to the Navy indefinitely and bypassed completely by American ground forces had it not been for the island's importance as a producer of Manila hemp. By late 1899 this product, essential to the cordage industry, was in such short supply that Secretary of War Elihu Root ordered Otis to take steps to open up those Philippine ports engaged in the *abaca* trade. Otis dispatched Brig. Gen. William Kobbé with a provisional brigade, assisted by the *Nashville* and *Helena*, and on 26–27 January 1900 the Forty-third Infantry, U.S. Volunteers, occupied the two major ports of Calbayog and Catbalogan. Apparently believing that Lukban had been decisively defeated, Kobbé left Samar in the hands of Maj. Henry T. Allen and a reinforced battalion of the Forty-third. Allen set about confidently to restore order, win over the population, and reestablish the vital hemp trade.[5]

The American landings inflicted substantial casualties on Lukban's forces, but the mountains and jungles of Samar offered ready sanctuary to Lukban, who retreated fifteen miles up the Gandara River and established a new headquarters at the village of Mataguinao. Despite their lack of firearms, the insurgents combined effective guerrilla tactics with a thorough knowledge of Samar's terrain. They specialized in mantraps, ranging from bamboo stakes and spring-driven spears to baskets filled with logs and rocks, effectively preventing soldiers from surprise marches or night operations and forcing even large patrols to move cautiously through the mountains and jungles. Occasionally they would use Samar's dense foliage to ambush small detachments, attacking the soldiers with native machetes, or bolos. In order to prevent any Filipino collaboration with the occupiers, the insurgents resorted to terrorism, attacking or burning towns and villages garrisoned by the Americans and forcing much of the population into the mountainous interior. Filipinos suspected of giving aid to the soldiers were kidnapped, tortured, mutilated, and killed.[6]

In the face of this resistance, Major Allen became convinced that until the guerrillas were defeated he could neither protect the population nor secure a necessary supply of hemp. Although he had fewer than five hundred soldiers he embarked on a campaign far more ambitious than Kobbé had envisioned, launching expeditions into the interior, posting small detachments in scattered villages, and using his troops to bring in the hemp crop. Kobbé had taken most of the Navy's ships with him, so the Forty-third's officers often had to borrow the vessels of friendly hemp merchants in order to patrol along the coast and river valleys. Despite their impressive marching and fighting abilities, Allen's numbers were too small for all these tasks; moreover, by deploying his forces throughout northern Samar he made himself vulnerable to guerrilla counterattacks. Under local commanders, Samar's *insurrectos* burned villages, harassed American patrols, and attacked isolated garrisons. The resurgent guerrilla movement—especially the vicious battle at Catubig in April in which fifteen soldiers were killed—prompted extensive criticism from both Otis and Kobbé that Allen had overextended himself. In May, Maj. Gen. Arthur MacArthur visited the island and decided that the Army should go on the defensive, holding on to Calbayog and Catbalogan but avoiding further attempts to control the interior. Over Allen's protests, MacArthur withdrew the Forty-third to Leyte and replaced it with a weak battalion of the Twenty-ninth Infantry, U.S. Volunteers. By July the first American attempt to conquer Samar had ended in failure.[7]

Although the Americans had failed to pacify the island, the operations in 1900 had demonstrated the potential of joint operations. Maj. John C. Gilmore praised the "moral effect" of the *Pampanga*'s covering fire, which on several occasions drove away the numerous guerrilla snipers who had plagued his soldiers.[8] Ensign Yates of the same gunboat led an amphibious force of sailors, soldiers, and native police against the fortified town of Santa Margarita and captured it. On occasion sailors mounted automatic rifles on shallow draft steamers or boats and accompanied military expeditions into the interior. In July the *Pampanga* and *Panay* shelled insurgent positions and then sent out armed boats to support an unsuccessful attempt to capture these entrenchments. The Navy also assisted Army operations against the guerrillas' food supply and turned over confiscated livestock to the soldiers to supplement the monotonous Army rations.[9]

Despite these successes, a variety of factors prevented joint operations from achieving more than temporary gains in 1900. The close proximity of Samar to other islands, especially Leyte, forced the Navy to devote most of its efforts to cutting off seaborne commerce. Nevertheless, Army officers complained that resistance on Samar was due to outsiders, especially Taga-logs, who received weapons and reinforcements from their compatriots on Luzon. Further problems were created by the ambiguity over the administra-tive authority for Samar and its surrounding waters. In the first six months of 1900, the Army forces on Samar were successively part of Brig. Gen. William Kobbé's Provisional Brigade, the Office of the Military Governor of Albay and Catanduanes, the Visayan Military District, the Department of the Visayas, and finally of the Department of Southern Luzon. To compli-cate matters further, Samar and Leyte were combined and separated several times, often while each island was being given a new district infrastructure. The Army's many reorganizations were made without consideration for the Navy's continued placement of the islands in its Fourth Patrol Area, which encompassed the Visayas and part of Mindanao but excluded Luzon. For both services, Samar marked a frontier—the farthest extreme of organiza-tional and operational borders. Given this administrative confusion, it was largely left up to individual Army and Navy officers to develop and imple-ment joint operations and policies, with the resulting risk of conflict with the rules established by other post commanders and gunboat captains.[10]

The most important source of friction, however, was almost inherent in the divided missions of the Army and Navy in the Philippine War. Until 20 May 1900, blockading ships operated under strict rules to intercept any vessel that flew the Filipino flag, carried contraband (which could be inter-preted as including food and hemp), or attempted to enter or leave a re-stricted port. This conflicted with the mission of the Forty-third, which was not only to suppress insurrection but to serve as an agent of "benevolent as-similation" and to revive the hemp trade. In order to achieve those goals, Kobbé's headquarters on 19 February 1900 removed most of the licensing re-quirements on hemp boats. But these orders had no validity over the Navy's gunboats, which continued to follow their own instructions and blockade the surrounding waters, impede coastal trade, confiscate or destroy hemp and rice, and refuse to honor the permits issued by garrison officers on Samar or Leyte. When Leyte was transferred to the Department of the Visayas, and Samar to the Department of Southern Luzon, the situation became even more strained. On Leyte, the Forty-third's commander, Col. Arthur Murray, was a strong believer in benevolent assimilation and wanted to demonstrate the benefits of American rule by encouraging Leyte's commerce. Following Kobbé's directives, Murray and his subordinate, Allen, made great strides in reviving the trade of hemp from Samar for rice from Leyte. However, in July 1900 Samar fell under the authority of Col. E. E. Hardin, who wanted to prevent all Samar-Leyte trade and demanded that the Navy step up its inter-diction efforts. When the gunboats *Pampanga* and *Panay* revoked his trade licenses and confiscated hemp and rice, Murray threatened to drive them away from the Leyte coast. The controversy eventually reached all the way back to Manila, where MacArthur sided with the Navy and ordered a strict blockade. Frederick Sawyer, who commanded the *Panay*, later pointed out that the dispute did not reflect interservice rivalry but an intraservice differ-ence over counterinsurgency policy between two Army officers. Although petty, the controversy was a strong indicator of a fundamental problem: U.S. joint service operations in the Philippines had no administrative parameters, no coherent policy, and no clear command.[11]

Between the withdrawal of the Forty-third in July and the island's transfer back to Brig. Gen. Robert P. Hughes's Department of the Visayas in May 1901, Samar remained a military backwater. With the exception of an abortive campaign in December 1900 and January 1901, when the Army made an effort to destroy Lukban's sanctuaries, U.S. soldiers remained largely confined to Calbayog and Catbalogan. Unable to garrison most towns or protect the population, American patrols became more punitive and destroyed housing, food, and hemp. The occasional support lent by pa-trolling gunboats allowed for the extension of such operations. Typical was an expedition of two officers and twenty-four soldiers of the Twenty-ninth Infantry who boarded the *Panay* on 2 February 1901 to investigate the abduc-tion of three Filipinos who had aided the Americans at Pandang. Upon their arrival they found the village deserted except for one old man who confirmed the abduction and reported the townspeople had fled with the guerrillas into the mountains. Frustrated and convinced that "every indication pointed to a perfect sympathy with the insurgents on the part of the inhabitants," the Americans burned Pandang and returned empty-handed.[12] With the Army's forces so weak, it was perhaps inevitable that combined operations during this period should be restricted to sporadic and retaliatory missions that did little beyond demonstrating that the Americans' capacity to inflict damage on the civilian population was equal to that of the guerrillas.

The decision to grant civil government to Leyte in May 1901 rendered the continued turbulence on Samar intolerable; accordingly, Brigadier General Hughes was given personal control over operations on Samar. A brief visit soon convinced him that "the present stations know nothing beyond gunshot range of their stations, except what is learned through uncertain sources," and that the war would continue as long as Samar's guerrillas could obtain supplies from the interior and from Leyte.[13] On 13 June 1901 he extended the naval blockade to all of the island's ports and instructed garrison officers stationed in coastal towns to seize all civilian boats except those necessary for fishing. He built supply camps in the major river valleys, especially Lukban's former headquarters at Mataguinao, and ordered commanders in garrison towns to send patrols to congregate on these interior camps, in the process sweeping the interior, destroying crops, and flushing the guerrillas. To further prevent smuggling from Leyte; he garrisoned a battalion of the Ninth Infantry in the heretofore peaceful southern towns of Balangiga, Lanang, Santa Rita, and Basey where, as he later noted, Lukban "had little control, and there was no organization and armed enemy to contend against."[14] Hughes's attempt to use gunboats to support his operations up the Gandara River was delayed when the *Mindoro* ran aground on a sandbar, but the Navy extended its patrols to protect the new coastal garrisons. With the coast thus protected and the interior more accessible, Hughes's forces could finally undertake sustained operations. One company under Capt. Henry Jackson not only marched completely across the island but on 13 August badly wounded Lukban and captured his family and most of his papers. By September Hughes believed the campaign was virtually over and, claiming that the "enemy has been in hiding for two months, and are liable to stay so," he departed for Cebu.[15]

Hughes may have been convinced of the success of his policies by the very real evidence of its effects on the civilian population. When American soldiers burned out crops and *abaca* in the interior, the Samareños soon lost all means of supporting themselves. Their plight was exacerbated by Hughes's encouragement of special protected areas or "colonies" where civilians would be segregated from the guerrillas.[16] Too often this population resettlement meant that several thousand people were confined within areas devastated by two years of warfare. Calbayog, which had been almost deserted in May, grew to five thousand inhabitants by June; in another area along the Gandara River the population went from six thousand to twenty thousand in three months. The Army's destruction of crops and the Navy's blocking of coastal trade and fishing caused widespread deprivation. Typical was the southern town of Guiuan, where by July the situation was so bad that the post commander, Maj. John J. O'Connell, predicted mass starvation unless he could obtain rice. As protests from the garrisons mounted, Hughes moderated his orders about food destruction, urged that carabao be spared, and established conditions under which food could be imported from Leyte. By September such informal relief efforts proved clearly inadequate and, faced with the specter of widespread famine, Hughes authorized post commanders to appoint one Filipino representative to purchase rice for each of the occupied towns. How this arrangement would complicate the Navy's task does not seem to have been considered.[17]

Ironically, although the population suffered terribly, the Americans' destruction of crops may have further increased the ferocity and desperation of the resistance. Forced out of their mountain retreats and cut off from their normal sources of supply, the guerrillas soon found that Hughes had spread his forces too thin and that garrisons and expeditions were often undermanned and vulnerable. Even the long-occupied port of Calbayog was attacked on 29 July, although the arrival of the *Princeton* and her heavy batteries quickly discouraged the insurgents. In September and October the guerrillas launched sporadic but effective raids, mauling American supply trains, besieging towns, and ambushing isolated patrols. By far the worst of these incidents was that of 28 September, when townspeople and guerrillas virtually annihilated Company C, Ninth U.S. Infantry, at Balangiga. Fortunately, the gunboats already on station were able to prevent other towns from sharing Balangiga's fate. The *Arayat*, for example, alerted Army garrisons of the massacre and drove off *insurrectos* who were sniping at the soldiers occupying Pambujan and Guiuan.[18]

The Balangiga Massacre catapulted Samar into the full attention of the Army high command. In the following month, Maj. Gen. Adna R. Chaffee, commander of the Division of the Philippines, expanded the American forces on Samar to twelve battalions of regular infantry and seven companies of Philippine Scouts, roughly four thousand men. Not to be outdone, Rear Adm. Frederick Rodgers reinforced the blockading flotilla with virtually all of his smaller ships. In addition, Rodgers offered the Army the temporary loan of a three-hundred-man Marine battalion under Maj. Littleton W. T. Waller. Rodgers's generosity stretched his resources in other areas; in December he complained that the Samar-Leyte theater had "got nearly all our force afloat."[19]

The concentration of military and naval forces in the Samar theater was not accompanied by a similar focus on the problem of coordinating joint operations. Not only was there no headquarters or overall command, but there were almost no facilities—beyond personal contact—to allow officers to plan operations or even to exchange information. Although the Navy had located most of its available forces off the island, it did not even designate a special commander, so each gunboat captain was virtually autonomous. The Marines, after their arrival in October, fell into an organizational limbo that Waller exploited by claiming to be the commander of an independent subdistrict. Yet the confusion in the maritime services paled beside that created by the Army. Brig. Gen. Jacob H. Smith arrived in early October believing he would soon command the Sixth Separate Brigade, comprising all military forces on Samar and Leyte. But Chaffee had also promised Hughes the overall direction of the campaign. Hughes, who interpreted Smith's appointment as a sign of Chaffee's displeasure, proceeded to interfere in tactical deployments and challenge Smith's authority and judgment. To complicate matters further, Leyte, ostensibly the other half of the Sixth Brigade's responsibility, had already been placed under a civil government suspicious of any attempts by the military to restrict the island's trade or interfere with the rights of its citizens. Given this balkanization and its potential for administrative chaos, the likelihood of any coordination whatsoever would seem remote.

Nevertheless, Smith, a strong advocate of joint service cooperation, made a number of necessary adjustments. He was convinced that resistance on Samar would continue as long as the guerrillas could live on food grown in the interior or brought from Leyte; so his primary objective was to separate the guerrillas from the civilian population that supplied them. To this end he decided on an intensified naval blockade, military occupation of interior towns, and sweeps of the countryside in battalion strength. His first official declaration of policy, on 21 October, urged "both army and navy officers . . . to take all possible precautions to stop illicit trade in rice, hemp, and other contraband of war."[20] To assist the naval blockade, Smith required all boat owners to obtain passes and to paint their boats red; he limited civilians at each garrisoned town to six fishing vessels and restricted those to nearby waters; and he gave officers freedom to destroy or confiscate any vessel that violated those orders. In the next few months successive directives closed the ports of Leyte, circumscribed the hemp and rice trade, limited the numbers of passes garrison commanders could issue, and required that native boats always be guarded by one or more soldiers. To aid cooperation and further reduce the possibility of mistakes, Smith insisted that Army coastal patrols at sea identify themselves to gunboats and that gunboats give preliminary signals before opening fire. Both gunboats and soldiers were authorized to demolish any village suspected of signaling American positions to the *insurrectos*. To demonstrate his policies in action, in November Smith coordinated an Army sweep of northern Samar with increased naval gunboat patrols of the San Juanico Strait and northern coast, thereby preventing the guerrillas from fleeing by water.[21]

Smith's efforts to secure joint service cooperation appeared to reap immediate rewards. By his own estimates, between 10 October and 31 December 1901, soldiers and sailors killed or captured 759 *insurrectos* and 587 carabao, and destroyed 10,036 *cavanes* of rice, 1,662 houses, and 226 boats. The Army and Navy sent gunboats and launches farther up Samar's rivers than ever before; in November Lt. Walter G. Penfield reported that the Gandara River was filled with Navy boats assisting Army operations. Capt. Hugh D. Wise, commander of the launch *Rafaelito*, drove away snipers hiding along the high banks of Samar's rivers by building a seven-foot turret with a Gatling gun on top of his bridge. Waller's Marines also obtained vital naval support for their patrols of the Basey-Balangiga area and in their successful assault on a guerrilla camp several miles up the Sojoton River. Yet another instance of cooperation was the support given by the Navy gunboats to Maj. Edwin F. Glenn's investigations of the *insurrecto* logistical system. With the assistance of the *Villalobos* and *Frolic*, Glenn landed at several towns on Samar and Leyte, interrogating suspects and raiding suspected guerrilla storehouses. Comdr. William Swift sought "to obtain the assignment to posts of [Army] officers with whom we could cooperate heartily and with good prospects of success."[22]

Smith's directives also appeared to establish good social relations between the services. Both Army and Navy officers cooperated for mutual benefit, as when a Navy captain leaked to Glenn the rumor that Smith was planning to withdraw some of the blockading ships. Glenn immediately wrote Smith's adjutant that such a course would be "absolutely fatal" and Smith never issued the orders.[23] In a similar vein, Swift requested post commanders to keep tidal charts and make maps of bays and rivers. In January he reported to Rear Admiral Rodgers that he knew the Army officers on the Gandara River "quite well. I can meet them and discuss these questions with them with about the same freedom as if they were in the naval service."[24] Rodgers himself noted the "cordial relations which now exist between the Army and Navy," and in turn praised the work of sailors and marines. One of the rare instances of interservice brawling occurred when the war was virtually over and sailors on liberty became "drunk, noisy, boisterous and insubordinate, using vile language, cursing and reviling the Officer of the Day, who was endeavoring to suppress the disorder they created."[25]

Although it appeared efficient, the American combined service effort suffered from an intrinsic weakness at its very center. Smith had spent almost thirty years as a company officer, and he soon reverted to leading small patrols into the countryside without letting his staff know of his whereabouts. Preferring to command by example, he neglected to either coordinate or delegate, with the result that his subordinates could not obtain consistent advice or directions. Despite his ostensible determination to eliminate all sources of the guerrillas' food supply, Smith vitiated his restrictions with a number of exemptions under which post commanders could import food or allow their post's inhabitants to fish outside the area outlined in his general orders. He also failed to clarify the command structure, with the result that post commanders continued to exercise the dispensation granted them by Hughes to allow civilians to transport food. Navy officers, who believed that all passes were bound by the narrow restrictions established under Smith's early directives, soon complained: "It was impossible for the officers who issued the passes to exercise any supervision over them and consequently the pass became a most convenient cloak under which to pursue contraband traffic."[26] On 14 January Rear Admiral Rodgers summed up the Navy's frustration in a blast at Smith's lax direction: "It may safely be said that if the military operations on shore were conducted by the Army with the same unflagging zeal, energy and unity of purpose that characterized the movements afloat, that the termination of hostilities on Samar would be a matter of weeks instead of months."[27]

Rodgers's criticism was not only unfair but ignored the problems faced by ground forces on the island. In contrast to their Navy compatriots, who seldom witnessed the effects of the blockade at first hand, soldiers on Samar were literally face to face with the starvation, disease, and suffering brought about by the food deprivation policy. With their towns filled with hungry Filipinos, many of them only too eager to cooperate, post commanders were caught in an intolerable dilemma. For many of them, humanitarian concern for their charges and a sense of professionalism overrode Smith's directions to let the population suffer. Lt. Col. Charles Robe's repeated demands that he be allowed to import food to Calbayog so irritated Smith that he eventually relieved him. In a similar instance, Lt. Campbell King argued that the population of Guiuan had irrevocably committed themselves to the American cause and that the Army had consequent obligation to feed them. In the face of these demands, Smith allowed post officers special permission to bring in food, but he failed to notify Navy captains of these exceptions. Not surprisingly, gunboats disregarded the special passes and continued to sink or confiscate boats, leading post officers to accuse the Navy of destroying any hope of winning over the population. There were also several complaints about gunboats turning their considerable firepower on the wrong targets. When the *Arayat* shelled a pro-American rally of over one thousand Filipinos, Lt. Harry H. Tebbetts bitterly noted, "the effect was to cause the utmost confusion and alarm among the natives along this part of the coast, to whom but that very day I had guaranteed all the protection that the U.S. could afford."[28]

By January 1902, despite enormous military and naval resources, an impartial observer might have concluded that the situation on Samar had degenerated. Warfare was endemic in the countryside, with soldiers, guerrillas, rebels, bandits, and refugees all making violent passage through the interior. Agrarian brigands, or *ladrones*, preyed on civilians and often committed atrocities that were blamed on the guerrillas. The Americans found that they now faced resistance from the *Diosdios* sect—religious rebels who followed their own apocalyptic vision of a heaven on earth. On 24 December a *Diosdios* band forced a combined Filipino-American patrol to "run a veritable gauntlet of bolomen," killing seven Americans and wounding six others in a few seconds of frantic hand-to-hand combat. The patrol's commander concluded his report with the ominous disclaimer: "Who [the attackers] were and where they came from can not be ascertained."[29] Another officer reported on the growing anarchy near Laguan: "The entire area appears to be in a state of brigandage or at least lawlessness in addition to its hostility toward American rule. I desire to report further that I found the people of Mercedes badly frightened, and it appeared that this state of affairs had existed some little time. They state that at night everybody collected for protection in the Municipal Building and I found this building to be a curious arsenal of bolos, cane spears, and piles of rocks prepared to resist an attack."[30] In some cases, Americans encouraged this social conflict. After one joint American-Filipino operation in which residents of one town attacked guerrilla supporters in another, Navy Lt. William R. Shoemaker noted with some satisfaction, "It is said a feud had been inaugurated between the people of Guiuan and Salcedo that will last a hundred years."[31]

Even more disturbing was increasing evidence of a breakdown of morality and discipline among the American armed forces. Smith harangued his officers with intemperate and vindictive orders, at various times stating that he wanted the interior of the island made a "howling wilderness," that no prisoners should be taken, that all males over ten years of age be considered hostile, that the population of Leyte was uniformly disloyal and responsible for the attack on Balangiga, and that the sooner everyone died the sooner there would be peace. The general's erratic behavior and his failure to achieve decisive results also attracted criticism from powerful civilian leaders. Henry T. Allen, former military commander of Samar and newly appointed head of the Philippine Constabulary, bluntly asserted that Smith was "loco"; and Gov. Luke Wright complained: "General Jakey Smith is in reality accomplishing very little . . . in the direction of pacifying the island. The fact is, it was a mistake to put him in charge in the first instance. Whilst he is undoubtedly a combatative [*sic*] man, he is wholly lacking in tact, judgement and administrative capacity and from all I hear—and I hear a good deal—makes more trouble than he allays."[32]

Unfortunately, some officers proved all too willing to follow Smith's inhumane directives. While delirious with fever, Waller ordered the summary execution of eleven Filipino porters, an event Chaffee termed "one of the most regrettable incidents in the annals of the military service of the United States."[33] In an attempt to head off an incipient rebellion, Capt. William Wallace shot seven prisoners at Borongonan on 4 December 1901. Equally reprehensible were the actions of Major Glenn, who between October 1901 and January 1902 kidnapped civilians from both Leyte and Samar, tortured suspects—including three priests—and conspired in the murder of at least ten Filipinos. Glenn's conduct not only demonstrated a "reckless disregard for human life" but contributed greatly to the growing impasse between the Army and the civil government.[34] As noted earlier, many officers disregarded Smith's directives and did their best to protect the population and prevent troop misconduct. However, the actions of Waller, Smith, Glenn, and others made it possible for anti-imperialists to accuse U.S. military personnel in general of cruel and inhumane conduct.[35]

By January 1902 there was a growing conviction that the American campaign had stalled. Naval operations came to a virtual halt in January when the monsoon made Samar's seas and rivers even more dangerous. A joint operation up the Quinanpundan River had to be abandoned when the escorting gunboat could not make it over a newly formed sandbar and the soldiers encountered washed-out trails, floods, ten days of continuous rain, and the ubiquitous guerrilla mantraps. The very success of some officers in pacifying their immediate areas hampered Army efforts; Capt. Mark L. Hersey complained, "Most of our men seem to have reached the limit of their endurance for long hikes. There being no enemy in the immediate vicinity, all hikes are long now [between] 10 to 15 days."[36] In addition, Smith's orders to make a "howling wilderness" of the interior had become so much a reality that troops had to take virtually all their food with them. Grim evidence of the famine in Samar's countryside was furnished by Major Waller's disastrous attempt to lead his battalion in a march across the southern tip of the island between 28 December 1901 and 19 January 1902. Although they did not encounter a single *insurrecto*, eleven marines either were abandoned or died of starvation and fatigue before the Army could rescue them. Finally, after three months of intensive operations, the Army had reached the limit of its resources. American field commanders needed to rest their soldiers and bring up supplies before launching a new assault on the interior. Unfortunately, Smith and his staff were distracted at the very moment that the administrative and logistical skills necessary to supervise this regrouping were most needed.

In January the growing storm between Brigadier General Smith and the civil government of Leyte finally broke. Sixth Brigade headquarters had constantly encroached on Leyte's civil government by closing ports, attempting to place all civil officials under military authority, and interfering in the island's commercial trade. Smith claimed in justification that the island was "a seething cauldron of discontent, and ere long the inhabitants of it will have to undergo the same heroic treatment which is being applied to Samar."[37] No less provocative were the actions of the Sixth Brigade's intelligence chief, Major Glenn, who routinely kidnapped Leyte's citizens and transported them to Catbalogan for interrogation and, frequently, physical abuse. Moreover, Glenn's naval escort confiscated boats along the Leyte coast and towed them back to Samar, refusing to release them despite Gov. James H. Grant's appeals. By January the activities of Smith and his subordinates had raised a storm of protest from Grant, from Leyte's inhabitants, from numerous merchants, and from the Philippine Commission headed by William H. Taft in Manila. Mindful that his predecessor had been relieved because of his inability to accept the commission's authority, Chaffee hurried to Samar to resolve the impasse. Privately concluding that "General Smith has worked very hard on Samar, but I cannot say that he worked with good judgement," Chaffee pressured Smith to modify his policies, accept civil government authority, and adopt pacification techniques that distinguished between friends and enemies.[38] Chaffee also took steps to restore discipline, beginning the procedures that would ultimately result in the courts-martial of several Army and Marine officers.

Chaffee's reforms were a definite improvement, but they were never fully implemented because by the time he departed on 28 January 1902 the monsoon had abated and the Americans were very close to victory. The guerrillas, whose success had always owed more to the weakness of the occupying forces than to their own military strength or popular support, were now desperate. With the interior devastated, with the Americans controlling the rivers and coasts, with the population segregated in concentration camps, and with the naval blockade still firm, the *insurrectos'* traditional sources of food had disappeared. They were now dispersed into scattered bands of ragged fugitives who spent more time searching for food than fighting the Americans. On 18 February a daring raid by Lt. Alphonse Strebler of the Philippine Scouts captured Vicente Lukban. The guerrilla leader was sick, malnourished, and disgusted with the war. Although Lukban's chief subordi-

Meeting at Balangiga

In the foreground, left to right, Rear Adm. Frederick Rodgers, Commander of the Asiatic Squadron; Brig. Gen. Jacob H. Smith, Army commander on Samar; and Maj. Littleton W. T. Waller (in pith helmet), Marine commander on the island, at Balangiga in 1901. It was probably at this meeting that Smith gave Waller his orders to lay waste to anything that might be of value to the *insurrectos. Courtesy U.S. Army Military History Institute.*

nate, Gen. Claro Guevarra, immediately assumed command and declared he would continue to fight, Lukban advised him to surrender. Failing to revitalize the resistance and aware that more and more of his guerrillas were surrendering, Guevarra opened negotiations with Brigadier General Smith on 18 March, and a week later Naval Cadet J. H. Comfort took Smith and a small party up the Gandara River to discuss terms.[39] After prolonged negotiations, on 27 April Smith's successor, Brig. Gen. Frederick D. Grant, accepted the surrender of Samar's guerrillas; on 16 June military rule on Samar was formally concluded and civil government begun. The longest and most brutal pacification campaign in the Philippine War had ended.[40]

The cost of the American victory was high. The destruction of crops, boats, and houses, the deportation of civilians to the coast, and the interdiction of outside food supplies by the naval blockade had come close to creating a true "howling wilderness" of Samar. Anti-imperialist journalists and editors seized upon the revelation of the atrocities by Waller, Glenn, and Smith, and denounced American involvement in the Philippines. Even the pacification of the island was illusory, for by 1904 a full-fledged revolt had broken out that would require another two years of campaigning by the U.S. Army and the Philippine Constabulary. Interestingly enough, many former *insurrecto* officers collaborated enthusiastically in the American campaigns against bandits and sectarians.

In many respects, the Samar campaign marks the nadir of American involvement in the Philippines. For most of their history the American armed forces had operated separately, and the arbitrary and amorphous nature of the command structure of both services in the Philippines was an invitation to chaos. Indeed, their very orders put them at cross-purposes: in addition to defeating the guerrillas, the Army's central function was to conciliate the population; the Navy's was to maintain a blockade that must inevitably punish civilians and guerrillas alike. On Samar, geography, personal inclination, and poor administration prevented the exchange of information that might have resolved differences and permitted fuller cooperation. The spasmodic nature of the overall campaign, the savagery of the resistance, and the physical challenges of the terrain increased the frustration of the troops and their successive commanders. The resulting harshness of the American response was yet a further source of division. The success of the American joint operations on Samar must be measured against these problems and judged accordingly.

In the years following the pacification of Samar, neither service showed interest in resolving the administrative and operational problems demonstrated by the campaign. In the Army's later operations against Moros, bandits, and religious sectarians the Navy's gunboats established blockades, transported troops, provided additional firepower, and served as floating supply depots for American ground forces. Yet while these cooperative efforts were often successful, they remained largely improvised arrangements. Soldiers and sailors in the area of operations developed joint methods and practices that were sufficient to defeat the poorly armed opponents the Americans faced, but they seldom sought to pass on the lessons they learned to their colleagues.[41] At the senior command levels, there was little effort to establish even the rudiments of joint administration. In fact, service rivalry and obstructionism was the rule rather than the exception among senior officers. Despite what were often the most cordial personal relations, military and naval officers indulged in a long and bitter feud over whether America's fortified naval base should be in Subic Bay or Manila Bay. The refusal of either service to cooperate in joint maneuvers and the continuing debate over which service would provide an expeditionary force for Asian intervention further poisoned relations. Over a quarter of a century after the end of the Samar campaign, the Army's senior commander in the Philippines confided that in planning for the defense of the archipelago he did not take into consideration the operations of the Navy because he did not believe that either service would honor its peacetime agreements. This confession was not only an indictment of the lack of joint cooperation between the services in the Pacific, but proved an all-too-accurate prediction of the interservice confusion and mutual recriminations that would accompany the American defeat in the Philippines during World War II.[42]

NOTES

Research for this article was made possible by a grant from the U.S. Marine Corps Historical Center and by a National Endowment for the Humanities Summer Stipend. Some of the ideas in this article first appeared in "The Howling Wilderness," *Naval History* 4 (Fall 1990): 10–15.

1. For the Philippine War, see John Morgan Gates, *Schoolbooks and Krags: The United States Army in the Philippines, 1898–1902* (Westport, Conn., 1973); Brian McAllister Linn, *The U.S. Army and Counterinsurgency in the Philippine War, 1899–1902* (Chapel Hill, N.C., 1989). For a sample of the writings on the Samar campaign, see Donald Chaput, "Atrocities and War Crimes: The Cases of Major Waller and General Smith," *Leyte-Samar Studies* 12 (1978): 64–77; E. M. Holt, "Resistance on Samar: General Vicente Lukban and the Revolutionary War, 1899–1902," *Kabar Seberang Sulating Maphilindo* 10 (Dec. 1982): 1–14; Joseph Schott, *The Ordeal of Samar* (Indianapolis, 1964); Paul Melshen, "He Served on Samar," *U.S. Naval Institute Proceedings* 105 (Nov. 1979): 43–48; Stanley Karnow, *In Our Image: America's Em-*

pire in the Philippines (New York, 1989), 189–94; Stuart Creighton Miller, *"Benevolent Assimilation": The American Conquest of the Philippines, 1898–1903* (New Haven, 1982), 200–204, 219–39.

2. Linn, *U.S. Army and Counterinsurgency*, 20–27; Vernon L. Williams, "The U.S. Navy in the Philippine Insurrection and Subsequent Native Unrest, 1898–1906" (Ph.D. diss., Texas A&M University, 1985), 66–72; Frederick Sawyer, *Sons of Gunboats* (Annapolis, 1941), 52; William R. Braisted, *The United States Navy in the Pacific, 1897–1909* (Austin, 1958), 81; Barbara B. Tomblin, "The United States Navy and the Philippine Insurrection," *American Neptune* (July 1975): 183–96.

3. Williams, "U.S. Navy," 55, 137–48.

4. Brig. Gen. Vicente Lukban to Local President of Zumarraga and Inhabitants of the Same, 9 June 1900, exhibit 18, General Courts-Martial [GCM] 34401, Edwin F. Glenn, Records of the Office of the Judge Advocate General, RG 153, Washington National Records Center, Suitland, Md.; Vicente Lukban to Antonio Luna, 8 July 1899, cited in John R. M. Taylor, *History of the Philippine Insurrection Against the United States, 1899–1903* (unpublished galley proof, 1906, microcopy 254, NA), exhibit 1321, pp. 58–59 HK; Holt, "Resistance on Samar," 4.

5. Maj. Henry T. Allen to Adjutant General [AdjGen], Provisional Brigade, 10 Feb. 1900, 43d Inf., 3d Btln., Letters Sent [LtrS], Records of the Adjutant General's Office, RG 94, ser. 117 [hereafter cited as RG 94/series], National Archives [NA], Washington, D.C.; Maj. Henry T. Allen to AdjGen, 1stDist, Dept. of Visayas [DeptVis], 20 Apr. 1900, Henry T. Allen Papers, box 32, Library of Congress [LC], Washington, D.C.; Maj. John C. Gilmore to AdjGen, Division of the Philippines [DivPhil], 12 May 1900, RG 94/117, 43d Inf., 2d Btln., LtrS. For the "hemp crisis," see Norman G. Owen, "Winding Down the War in Albay, 1900–1903," *Pacific Historical Review* 48 (Nov. 1979): 575–78.

6. Maj. Henry L. Hawthorne to Brig. Gen. Luther R. Hare, 27 Dec. 1900, *Annual Report of the War Department* [*Rept. of War Dept.*], 1901, 1:6:480; Maj. Narcisco Abuke to Anon., 7 Oct. 1900, Philippine Insurgent Records, NA microfilm pub. 254, select doc. 846.1; Brig. Gen. Robert P. Hughes to Chief of Staff and AdjGen, DivPhil, Records of U.S. Army Overseas Operations and Commands, 1898–1942, RG 395, entry 2483 [hereafter cited as RG 395/entry], box 28, NA; Brig. Gen. Robert P. Hughes to Chief of Staff and AdjGen, DivPhil, 16 June 1901, RG 395/2550, box 1; Taylor, *History of the Philippine Insurrection*, 82–83 HS; Rear Adm. Frank Wildes to Comdr in Chief, U.S. Naval forces on Asiatic Station [USNFAS], 6 May 1902, Naval Records Collection of the Office of Naval Records and Library, RG 45, NA microcopy 625, area file 10, roll 391 [hereafter cited as RG 45/roll no.]; Lt. Edgar S. Macklin to AdjGen, Sixth Separate Brigade [6thSepBrig], 15 Jan. 1902, RG 395/3815, LtrS 155. For *insurrecto* atrocities, see RG 153, GCM 34401; Lt. Ward Dabney to Adj., 25 Oct. 1901, RG 395/2574, box 2; Maj. John C. Gilmore to Adj., 3 Apr. 1900, RG 94/117, 43d Inf., 2d Btln., LtrS. American testimony on guerrilla atrocities must be treated with suspicion, as some of the most vocal denunciations of insurgent misconduct were by officers themselves guilty of war crimes.

7. *Rept. of War Dept.*, 1900, 1:4:398; Maj. Henry T. Allen to AdjGen, 31 Mar. 1900, Allen Papers, box 32; Maj. Henry T. Allen to AdjGen, 1stDist, DeptVis, 30 Mar. and 30 Apr. 1900, Allen Papers, box 32; Brig. Gen. Robert P. Hughes Testimony, Senate Committee on the Philippines, *Affairs in the Philippine Islands*, 57th Cong., 1st sess., Sen. doc. 331, p. 545; William A. Kobbé, "Diary of Field Service in the Philippines," William A. Kobbé Papers, U.S. Army Military History Institute, Carlisle Barracks, Pa.; James A. LeRoy, *The Americans in the Philippines*, 2 vols. (Boston, 1915), 2:188–89.

8. Maj. John C. Gilmore to AdjGen, 1stDist, DeptVis, 24 June 1900, RG 94/117, 43d Inf., 2d Btln., LtrS.

9. Maj. John C. Gilmore to Adj., Sub-Dist. of Samar, 13 Apr. 1900, RG 94/117, 43d Inf., 2d Btln., LtrS; Maj. Henry to Allen to AdjGen, Visayan Military Dist., 15 Apr. 1900, Allen Papers, box 32; Maj. Henry L. Hawthorne to Commanding Officer [CO], 4thDist, Dept. of Southern Luzon, 30 July 1900, and endorsement by Capt. Cleveland Williams, 9 Aug. 1900, RG 395/3503, box 1, Letters Received [LtrR] 31; Williams, "U.S. Navy," 200–204; Lt. Delbert R. Jones to Adj. 26 May 1900, RG 94/117, 43d Inf., Co. G, LtrS 10; Maj. John C. Gilmore to Capt. Frederic R. Payne, 29 June 1900, RG 94/117, 43d Inf., 2d Btln., LtrS; Maj. Henry L. Hawthorne to Brig. Gen. Luther R. Hare, 8 Dec. 1900, *Rept. of War Dept.*, 1901, 1:6:471–73.

10. Maj. John C. Gilmore to AdjGen, DivPhil, 12 May 1900, RG 94/117, 43d Inf., 2d Btln., LtrS; Capt. Robert H. Noble, memorandum, 18 July 1901, RG 395/2550, box 1.

11. Office of Military Governor of Albay and Catanduanes, field order no. 1, 19 Feb. 1900, Allen Papers, box 32; Col. Arthur Murray to AdjGen, DeptVis, 2 Apr. 1900, rept. no. 4, Allen Papers, box 32; Col. E. E. Hardin to CO, 1stDist, DeptVis, 6 Aug. 1900, RG 94/117, 29th Inf., LtrS; Col. E. E. Hardin to Headquarters [HQ], 4thDist, Dept. of Southern Luzon, 7 Aug. 1900, RG 94/117, 29th Inf., LtrS; Sawyer, *Sons of Gunboats*, 56; Williams, "U.S. Navy," 118–19.

12. Capt. Owen T. Kenan to PostAdj. Catbalogan, 28 Feb. 1901, RG 395/3450, box 1, LtrR 177; Lt. R. O. Patterson to Adj. 3 Jan. 1901, RG 395/3450, box 1, LtrR 49; Lt. L. S. Carson to Adj. 5 Jan. 1901, RG 395/3450, box 1, LtrR 16; Lt. J. N. Kineborough to Adj. 3 Feb. 1901, RG 395/3503, box 1, LtrR 70.

13. Brig. Gen. Robert P. Hughes to Chief of Staff and AdjGen, 14 May 1901, RG 395/2483, box 28.

14. Senate, *Affairs*, 540, also 553–54; Brig. Gen Robert P. Hughes to Capt. Robert H. Noble, 13 June 1901, RG 395/2552; Capt. Robert H. Noble, memorandum; Capt. A. B. Buffington to Capt. Leslie F. Cornish, 14 June 1901, RG 395/3447; Fred R. Brown, *History of the Ninth U.S. Infantry, 1799–1908* (Chicago, 1909), 555–65.

15. Brig. Gen. Robert P. Hughes to AdjGen, DivPhil, 11 Sept. 1901, *Rept. of War Dept.*, 1902, 1:9:623; Brig. Gen. Robert P. Hughes to Chief of Staff and AdjGen, 3 June 1901, RG 395/2550, box 1; Comdr. J. R. Selfridge to Chief of the Bureau of Navigation, 9 Oct. 1901, RG 45/390. Typical of the food deprivation operations were those of the Army garrison at Laguan, which in one month destroyed 145 houses,

5,025 bushels of rice, and 5 carabao; see "Report of Operations for the Garrison of Laguan, Samar, P.I., for the month of June 1901," RG 395/2483, box 34.

16. Lt. Arthur L. Conger to CO, Borongan, 23 July 1901, RG 395/2550, box 1; Brig. Gen. Robert P. Hughes to AdjGen, 1 June 1901, RG 395/2552; Brig. Gen. Robert P. Hughes to CO, Laguan, 8 July 1901, RG 395/2550, box 1; Capt. Robert Noble to CO, Guiuan, 31 Aug. 1901, RG 395/3817, LtrR 257; testimony of Capt. Waldo E. Ayer, RG 153, GCM 30739, Jacob H. Smith; Senate, *Affairs*, 554–69.

17. Maj. John J. O'Connell to AdjGen, July 1901 RG 395/3815, LtrS 75; Capt. Robert H. Noble to "My dear O'Connell," 5 Aug. 1901, RG 395/3818, LtrR 235; Maj. John H. O'Connell to CO, Tacloban, 22 July 1901, RG 395/2574, box 1; Brig. Gen. Robert P. Hughes to Capt. Francis E. Lacey, 24 July 1901, RG 395/2550, box 1; Capt. Robert H. Noble to Lt. McCue, 27 July 1901, RG 395/2550, box 1; Capt. Robert H. Noble to CO, Catbalogan, 9 Sept. 1901, RG 395/2551; Adj to Lt. John B. Schoeffel, 10 Sept. 1901, RG 395/3447, LtrS 145; Capt. Robert H. Noble to all COs, 10 Sept. 1901, RG 395/2503, box 1, LtrR 310; *Affairs in the Philippine Islands*, 554–69.

18. Maj. Gen. Adna R. Chaffee to Maj. Gen. Henry C. Corbin, 25 Oct. 1901, Henry C. Corbin Papers, box 1, LC; Eugenio Daza y Salazar, "Some Documents on the Philippine-American War in Samar," *Leyte-Samar Studies* 17 (1983): 165–87; Richard Arens, "The Early Pulahan Movement in Samar," *Leyte-Samar Studies* 11 (1977): 59–65; Holt, "Resistance on Samar," 9–10; Comdr. J. R. Selfridge to Chief of the Bureau of Navigation, 9 Oct. 1901, RG 45/390; Lt. W. R. Shoemaker to Senior Squadron Commander [SenSquadCmdr], 5 Nov. 1901, RG 45/390.

19. Rear Adm. Frederick Rodgers to Maj. Littleton W. T. Waller, 16 Dec. 1901, Littleton W. T. Waller Papers, box 1, U.S. Marine Corps Historical Center, Washington, D.C. For U.S. Army manpower see HQ, DeptVis, General Order 66, 1 Nov. 1901, RG 395/2505.

20. HQ in the Field, 1stDist, DeptVis, field orders no. 1, 21 Oct. 1901, *Rept. of War Dept.*, 1902, 1:9:206.

21. HQ, 6thSepBrig, circ. no. 7, 27 Dec. 1901, *Rept. of War Dept.*, 1902, 1:9:211; Capt. A. B. Buffington to CO, Calbiga, 10 Oct. 1901, RG 395/3447, LtrS 183; Lt. George H. Shields to COs on Gandara River, 1 Nov. 1901, RG 395/2496, LtrS 5; complete texts of most of Smith's orders can be found in *Rept. of War Dept.*, 1902, 1:9:206–15; Rear Adm. Frederick Rodgers to Cmdr in Chief, USNFAS, 29 Oct. 1901, RG 45/390; Lt. George H. Shields to Cmdr. J. K. Cogswell, 16 Nov. 1901, RG 395/2571, box 2, LtrS 29; Lt. T. J. McConnell to AdjGen, 21 Nov. 1901, RG 395/2574, box 1; Capt. Henry L. Jackson to AdjGen, 6thSepBrig, 30 Nov. 1901, RG 395/2574, box 1; *Manila American*, 10 Dec. 1901.

22. Cmdr. William Swift to SenSquadCmdr, USNFAS, 8 Jan. 1902, RG 45/391; Lt. Campbell King to AdjGen, 6thSepBrig, 12 Nov. 1901, RG 395/2815, LtrS 122; Lt. Dana T. Merrill to AdjGen, 6thSepBrig, 14 Nov. 1901, RG 395/2574, box 1; Lt. W. R. Shoemaker to Cmdr in Chief, USNFAS, 30 Nov. 1901, RG 45/390; Cmdr. J. K. Cogswell to Brig. Gen. Jacob H. Smith, 9 Jan. 1902, RG 395/2571, box 4, LtrR 169;

Maj. [Constant?] Williams to AdjGen, 6thSepBrig, 18 Feb. 1902, RG 395/2573, box 1, LtrS 21; *Rept. of War Dept.*, 1902, 1:9:432–33, 436–41; Maj. Edwin F. Glenn to Lt. Cmdr. J. T. Helm, 18 Oct. 1901, RG 45/390, Ens. C. H. Fischer to Senior Officer Present, 31 Oct. 1901, *Rept. of War. Dept.*, 1902, 1:9:435–36; Capt. Hugh D. Wise to Capt. George Montgomery, 26 Feb. 1902, RG 395/2571, box 4, LtrR 2663; Lt. Walter G. Penfield to Chief Engineering Officer, 30 Nov. 1901, RG 395/2571, box 1, LtrR 885; testimony of Lt. John H. A. Day, RG 153, GCM 10196, Lt. John H. A. Day, 80–82; Lt. Cmdr. J. M. Helm to Cmdr. William Swift, 6 Jan. 1902, RG 395/2571, box 2, LtrR 43; *Manila Times*, 31 Jan. 1902.

23. Maj. Edwin F. Glenn to AdjGen, 6thSepBrig, 11 Nov. 1901, RG 395/2573, box 2, LtrS 25.

24. Cmdr. William Swift to SenSquadCmdr, USNFAS, 8 Jan. 1902, RG 45/391; Cmdr. William Swift to AdjGen, 6thSepBrig, 21 Dec. 1901, RG 395/2571, box 1, LtrR 1150.

25. Maj. Frank deL. Carrington to CO, U.S. Naval Force, 6 Mar. 1902, RG 395/3447, LtrS 98; quote "most cordial" from Rear Adm. Frederick Rodgers to Brig. Gen. Jacob H. Smith, 27 Oct. 1901, RG 395/3454; Brig. Gen. Jacob H. Smith to Rear Adm. Frederick Rodgers, 4 Nov. 1901, RG 395/3451.

26. Cmdr. William Swift to SenSquadCmdr, USNFAS, 8 Jan. 1902, RG 45/391; Lt. Cmdr. J. M. Helm to Cmdr. William Swift, 6 Jan. 1902, RG 395/2571, box 2, LtrR 43; HQ, 6thSepBrig, special orders 12 and 21, 16 and 26 Nov. 1902, RG 395/2576; HQ, 6thSepBrig, to CO, Guiuan, 22 Nov. 1901, RG 395/2571, box 1, LtrR 300; David L. Fritz, "Before the 'Howling Wilderness': The Military Career of Jacob Hurd Smith," *Military Affairs* 43 (Dec. 1979): 185–90.

27. Rear Adm. Frederick Rodgers to Cmdr in Chief, USNFAS, 14 Jan. 1902, RG 45/391.

28. Lt. Harry H. Tebbetts to Adj., Mao, 21 Sept. 1901, RG 395/2483, box 47; Lt. George H. Shields to CO, Calbayog, 17 Oct. 1901, RG 395/2595, LtrS 18; Lt. Col. Charles Robe to Capt. Waldo E. Ayer, 21 Nov. 1901, RG 395/3454, box 1; Capt. Waldo E. Ayer to Lt. Col. Charles Robe, 21 and 22 Nov. 1901, RG 395/2573, box 1; Lt. Campbell King to AdjGen, 6thSepBrig, 19 Nov. and 3 Dec. 1901, RG 395/3815, LtrS 128 and 137; Maj. Frank deL. Carrington to CO, USS *Frolic*, 18 Dec. 1901, RG 395/3447, LtrS 250; Gov. James H. Grant to Capt. Waldo E. Ayer, 2 Jan. 1901, RG 395/2571, box 3, LtrR 31.

29. Capt. Francis H. Schoeffel to Adj., 24 Dec. 1901, *Rept. of War Dept.*, 1902, 1:9:456–57; Maj. Frank Carrington to AdjGen, 6thSepBrig, 26 Feb. 1902, RG 395/2573, box 1, LtrS 45; Capt. Henry L. Jackson to AdjGen, DeptVis, 8 Oct. 1901, RG 395/2483, box 47; Lt. N. V. Ellis to AdjGen, 6thSepBrig, 27 Feb. 1902, RG 395/3815, LtrS 163; Taylor, *History*, 85HS.

30. Lt. Campbell King to Adj., Laguan, 27 Aug. 1902, RG 395/2483, box 34; Lt. Col. Charles A. Dempsey to Anon., 21 Mar. 1901, RG 395/3817, LtrR 76.

31. Lt. W. R. Shoemaker to Cmdr in Chief, USNFAS, 30 Nov. 1901, RG 45/390.

32. Luke E. Wright to William H. Taft, 13 Jan. 1902, William H. Taft Papers, ser.

3, roll 34, LC. The reference to "loco" is found in Henry T. Allen to Brig. Gen. J. Franklin Bell, 26 Mar. 1902, Allen Papers, box 7; Henry T. Allen to William H. Taft, 16 and 24 Jan. and 7 Feb. 1902, Allen Papers, box 7; Arthur W. Ferguson to William H. Taft, 1 Feb. 1902, Taft Papers, ser. 3, roll 35.

33. HQ, DivPhil, General Orders 93, 7 May 1902, RG 395/2070.

34. Maj. Gen. George W. Davis, 16 Feb. 1903, RG 153, GCM 34401. See also, RG 153, GCM 30757, Lt. Norman E. Cook; RG 153, GCM 30756, Lt. Julien E. Gaujot; RG 153, GCM 10196; Maj. Gen. Henry C. Corbin to Commanding General, Div-Phil, 24 Mar. 1902, RG 95/AGO 425353; Lt. Gen. Nelson Miles to Secretary of War, 19 Feb. 1903, RG 94/AGO 389439; Maj. Charles H. Watts to AdjGen, DivPhil, 1 Apr. 1902, RG 94/AGO 482616; Richard E. Welch, Jr., *Response to Imperialism: The United States and the Philippine-American War, 1899–1902* (Chapel Hill, N.C., 1979), 138–41; John Schumacher, *Revolutionary Clergy: The Filipino Clergy and the National-ist Movement, 1850–1903* (Manila, 1981), 144–46.

35. HQ of the Army, General Orders 80, 16 July 1902, file 3490–27, Records of the Bureau of Insular Affairs, RG 350, NA. For evidence that many soldiers refused to sanction atrocities, see Capt. William M. Swaine testimony, RG 153, GCM 34401; Elihu Root to Theodore Roosevelt, 12 June 1902, RG 153, GCM 30739; "Investiga-tion regarding the character of the recent War on the Island of Samar, P.I., conducted by Colonel Francis Moore, 11th U.S. Cavalry, (Special Investigator), in obedience to instructions contained in letter of Adjutant General, Division of the Philippines, dated June 20th 1902," RG 94/AGO 411745.

36. Capt. Mark L. Hersey to AdjGen, 6thSepBrig, 1 Feb. 1902, RG 395/2853, LtrS 27; Comdr. J. K. Cogswell to Brig. Gen. Jacob H. Smith, 9 Jan. 1902, RG 395/2571, box 4, LtrR 169; Lt. Edgar A. Macklin to AdjGen, 6thSepBrig, 13 Jan. 1902, RG 395/2399, LtrRF35.

37. Brig. Gen. Jacob H. Smith, "Campaign in Samar and Leyte," *Manila Critic*, 1 Feb. 1902.

38. Maj. Gen. Adna R. Chaffee to Maj. Gen Henry C. Corbin, 17 Mar. 1902, Corbin Papers, box 1; *Rept. of War Dept.*, 1902, 1:9:216-25; James H. Grant to Capt. Waldo E. Ayer, 2 Jan. 1902, RG 395/2571, box 3, LtrR 31; H. N. Cole to Henry T. Allen, 10 Jan. 1902, Taft Papers, ser. 3, box 34; Maj. Gen. Adna R. Chaffee to Theodore Roosevelt, 25 Feb. 1902, Theodore Roosevelt Papers, LC, ser. 1, roll 25; Maj. Gen. Henry C. Corbin to Commanding General, DivPhil, 24 Mar. 1902, RG 94/AGO 425353; Maj. Edwin V. Glenn to Col. J. P. Sanger, May 1902, RG 94/AGO 425323.

39. Lt. Harry H. Tebbetts to Adj., 23 Jan. 1902, RG 395/3378, LtrS 1; Lt. N. V. El-lis to AdjGen, 6thSepBrig, 27 Feb. 1902, RG 395/3815, LtrS 163; Lt. L. W. Jordan to AdjGen, Laguan, 22 Mar. 1902, RG 395/2574, box 1; Naval Cadet J. H. Comfort to Cmdr in Chief, USNFAS, 27 Mar. 1902, RG 45/391; Eugene F. Ganley, "Mountain Chase," *Military Affairs* 24 (Winter 1960): 203–10.

40. Reports of Operations in the Sixth Separate Brigade, *Rept. of War Dept.*, 1902, 1:9:416–74.

41. *Army and Navy Journal*, 3 Dec. 1904 and 29 July 1905; Capt. Harold P. Howard to Adj, 30 Jan. 1905, Harold P. Howard Papers, RG 39, MacArthur Memorial Archives, Norfolk, Va.

42. Maj. Gen. Johnson Hagood to Gen. William Lassiter, 30 May 1928, Johnson Hagood Papers, RG 11, box 186, file 5, South Carolina Historical Society, Charleston, S.C.; Braisted, *United States Navy*, 216–23; Louis Morton, "War Plan Orange," *World Politics* 11 (Jan. 1959): 225–50; Roy K. Flint, "The United States Army on the Pacific Frontier, 1899–1939," in *The American Military in the Far East*, ed. Joe C. Dixon (Washington, 1980), 139–59.

Naval Service in the
Age of Empire

VERNON L. WILLIAMS

THE SPANISH-AMERICAN WAR WAS THE CULMINATION OF YEARS OF EXPANsionist pressures at work in the United States. Although expansion produced tremendous changes for American society, no change was greater than for the U.S. Navy. Indeed, one of the major driving forces behind the imperialism of the 1890s was Alfred Thayer Mahan's desire to produce a navy worthy of a major power. Only with such a navy, Mahan reasoned, could the United States hope to achieve a more significant place among the community of nations. Thus, the Navy became both a cause for and the product of American foreign policy. In the years that followed the war, increasing demands were placed on the Navy to support the power long sought by the United States. Later world wars demanded much of the Navy's leadership, and the Navy, in turn, relied heavily on combat-tested officers who had received valuable training and experience early in their careers. This essay will test the hypothesis that the Spanish-American War and subsequent naval opportunities in the Pacific empire made the Asiatic Station *the* station of opportunity for young officers and provided a training ground for naval officers who rose to flag-level commands in World War II. Further, changes in the Navy during this time placed new demands on young naval cadets and ensigns, in part because the type of operations conducted in the Philippines and China involved numerous small craft that they were assigned to command. Service on the Asiatic Station thus presented junior officers with dramatic opportunities for independence of action, command of vessels, other career-building levels of responsibility, and rapid advancement (by nineteenth-century standards). Officers with such experience had a distinct advantage over those who did not receive such opportunities.

Adm. James O. Richardson, reflecting on the significance of an officer's early career, was convinced it played a major role in how far one would go: "Young officers may logically ask whether there is any real relationship between the early years of an officer's career in the Navy and the attainments or accomplishments of his mature years. I am one of those who think that there is such a direct and logical relationship, and that the earlier a young officer, even as a midshipman, gives all that he has to the full performance of his duty, the higher the later return on his investment."[1] Adm. Yates Stirling reached essentially the same conclusion: "When I look back upon my service in the Philippines, I recognize it to have been the most beneficial, if not the most exciting, episode of my younger career."[2]

What impact did these opportunities and the changes taking place in the Navy have on the careers of naval officers? Do patterns emerge that demonstrate specific areas of opportunity (e.g., assignments for command, assignments producing initiative and creativity, or advancement advantages), and are these patterns supported in the career outcomes statistics? During the war, did Cuban or Philippine operations provide special opportunities for significant numbers of younger officers to influence the future officer corps? What role did postwar duties in the Philippine War and the Boxer Rebellion in China play in contributing career-enhancing assignments? Answers to these questions will clarify the fundamental changes occurring in the Navy and show how those changes produced an officer corps equipped to deal with the demands placed on it in the twentieth century.[3]

The data shows clearly that the influence of Asiatic service—particularly the Philippines—on the career of a naval officer was substantial and that such service was significant in the professional development of not only many young aspiring Navy and Marine officers but also of older, more experienced officers. This is especially true for the immediate postwar period. Although short-lived, the aberrant demands for ships in China and the Philippines produced a dramatic need for large numbers of small vessels and officers to serve in the inland waterways of America's new Pacific empire. No such advantage appeared outside the Asiatic Station. War service in the Cuban theater of operations brought little opportunity (such as command) for younger officers other than the combat experience frontline service provided. With the surrender of the Spanish, a South Atlantic assignment ceased to be as significant as an Asiatic assignment in producing career-enhancing training and experience for the junior officer. It is true that Cuban

Montgomery M. Taylor

Taylor entered the Naval Academy in 1886, was commissioned an ensign in 1894, and promoted to lieutenant, junior grade, on 3 March 1899. Only three months later he was promoted to lieutenant (2 June 1899), and after another five months was given command of the gunboat *Pampanga*, on whose deck he is pictured above. Compare his career with that of George L. Dyer, who entered the Navy twenty years before him. Dyer served in the rank equivalent to lieutenant, junior grade, for six years (1873–1879), while Taylor served 3 months. Dyer was a lieutenant for nineteen years, Taylor for six. Taylor took command of a ship shortly after becoming a lieutenant, but Dyer served as a lieutenant for almost twenty years before he obtained a command. Dyer's first command, the converted yacht *Yankton*, was little larger than Taylor's *Pampanga*. Dyer was later promoted to commander and captain and given a tombstone promotion to commodore on the same day he retired from the Navy. His most important command was as naval governor of Guam. Taylor rose much higher, ending his career as a full admiral commanding the Asiatic Squadron from 1930 to 1933. His career demonstrates the impact the Spanish-American War could have on an officer's career. *Courtesy of the Naval Historical Center.*

service provided some rapid advancement and the attention of higher authorities, but most of the officers thus rewarded were senior officers with limited future service—certainly not those who would command during World War II.

Wartime service in the Philippines proceeded along different lines. In the initial stages, following the Battle of Manila Bay and while Dewey was waiting for ground troops to arrive, a blockade provided numerous assignments for junior officers. Many of these assignments included gunboat duty in which naval cadets and ensigns received command and other responsible positions historically not available to officers of that rank.[4] As the summer progressed and land operations began, naval assignments increased proportionately. Thus career-rewarding opportunities began before the end of hostilities in Spanish-held Philippines, before the onset of hostilities with Filipino nationalists, and before the Boxer Rebellion in China.[5]

The increase in the number of officers assigned to the Asiatic Station during the nine years after the Battle of Manila Bay reflected both greater American interest in the Far East and an expansion of the role the Navy was to play in national affairs. The growth of the Navy is apparent when one looks at the increases in shipbuilding and the development of naval activities throughout the world since 1890, but certainly nowhere is that growth more apparent than in Asiatic waters, especially in the Philippines, where the numbers of officers and the duties of those officers expanded well beyond any pre-1890 expectation.

Personnel Breakdown

After the war with Spain, the United States began to assert its will and power in East Asia, beginning with the subjugation of the Filipinos. At the same time, it maneuvered for a voice in Asian affairs equal to those of the great powers present in China. The number of naval officers sent to the Asiatic Station was an indicator of the American commitment to military and political power in that region. Assignments to other important stations, such as the North Atlantic and South Atlantic, did not compare in spite of the preoccupation with Germany and perceived threats to American interests in the western hemisphere.[6]

Analysis of personnel sent to the Asiatic and Atlantic stations during the nine years after 1898 will focus on line officers—the group of officers from whom selection for higher command, namely flag rank, eventually would be drawn.[7] Line officers included admirals, commodores,[8] captains, commanders, lieutenant commanders, lieutenants, lieutenants (jg), ensigns, naval cadets, and midshipmen.[9] Only those officers serving in Asiatic or Atlantic waters were included in the survey.[10] The percentages of line grades assigned to these three stations varied during the nine years. The key element in officer assignments was not the number of officers selected for that location but the percentage of Navy-wide totals assigned to the station, indicating trends in those assignments. These trends reflect not only increased or decreased significance of the station at a particular time, but often indicate other important forces at work at a specific time or place, such as China during the Boxer Rebellion in 1900.

The first group includes the assignments of captains, commanders, and lieutenant commanders to the Asiatic and Atlantic stations. Although there was some fluctuation in the totals of this group, the total number assigned to the Asiatic remained relatively low (see Figure 1). These officers commanded the major combat ships, and their assignment to a theater was dependent on the number of larger ships in a particular station. Most of the Navy's senior officers (below flag), like most of its largest ships, were assigned to the Atlantic (see Figure 2). With few exceptions, cruisers were the largest ships in the Asiatic Station, so most higher ranking officers assigned to the Asiatic held administrative positions ashore.[11] Even the cruiser commands, in prewar days held by senior officers, were assigned to officers below the rank of captain. However, in almost all cases, 80 to 95 percent of the Navy's captains, commanders, and lieutenant commanders were serving in non-Asiatic waters. The very nature of operations in the Philippines and in other Asiatic waters ensured that junior officers would be more important to the Navy in that region and thus play a more active role in operations. Officers below the rank of lieutenant commander were needed to command and crew the ever-expanding fleet of small gunboats and ships scraped together by the Navy in the Far East.

Assignments for the four lowest officer ranks indicate clearly that officers in the lower grades had a higher probability of Asiatic service. At the peak on 1 July 1901, 67 percent of all ensigns in the Navy were serving in ships on the Asiatic Station (see Figures 3 and 4). The percentages for naval cadets and midshipmen were remarkably high for the entire period. In all cases, Asiatic assignment dominated the statistics. Even in the later years, as the Philippine War began to subside, the Asiatic Station employed a high percentage of the Navy's junior officers. Only by 1906 did the percentage in the upper two ranks in the junior category, lieutenants and lieutenants (jg), decline to very low levels. These patterns had profound implications for the Navy in the next several decades: the younger officers were gaining valuable experience that junior officers of the pre-1890s Navy did not receive.

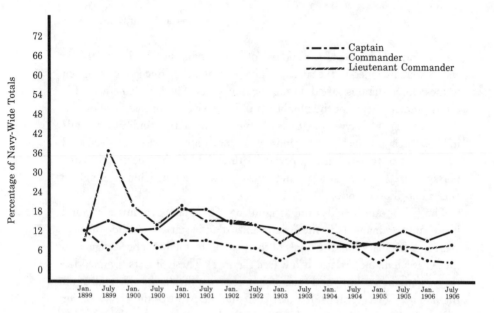

Figure 1 Trends in Officer Assignments to the Asiatic Station
Captain, Commander, Lieutenant Commander 1899–1906

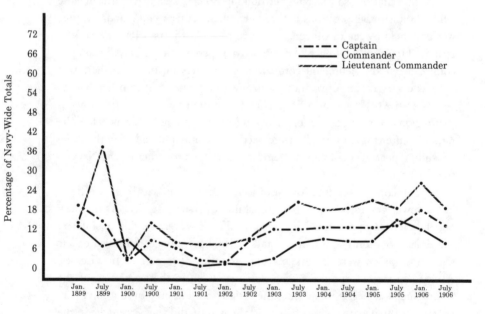

Figure 2 Trends in Officer Assignments to the Atlantic Stations
Captain, Commander, Lieutenant Commander 1899–1906

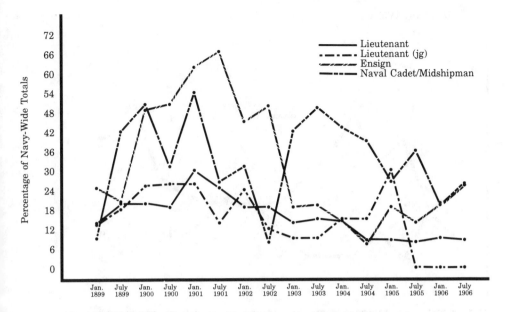

Figure 3 Trends in Officer Assignments to the Asiatic Station
Lieutenant, Lieutenant (jg), Ensign, Naval Cadet, Midshipman 1899–1906

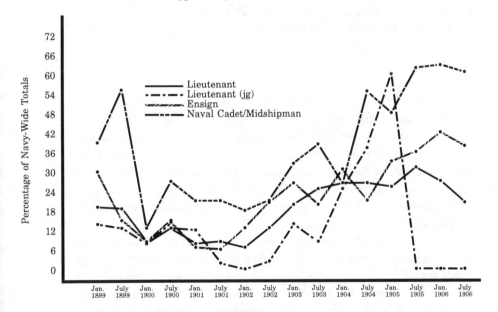

Figure 4 Trends in Officer Assignments to the Atlantic Stations
Lieutenant, Lieutenant (jg), Ensign, Naval Cadet, Midshipman 1899–1906

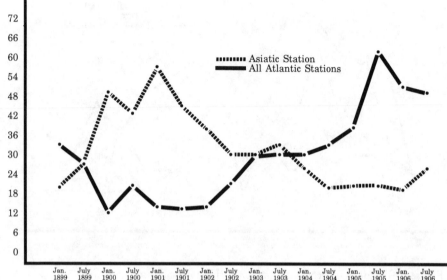

Figure 5 Ensign/Naval Cadet–Midshipman Composite
Asiatic Station vs. All Atlantic Stations 1899–1906

In his history of naval administration, Charles Oscar Paullin states that during the nineteenth century, officers suffered from slow promotions that condemned them to spend "the best years of their lives in subordinate stations, occupied often with trifling and routine tasks.[12] Junior officers at the turn of the century had no such experience; there was in fact a shortage of naval officers. President Roosevelt said that in 1902 the Navy had fewer than half the number of officers necessary to fill the complements of the ships in the fleet and those under construction.

To meet this increased demand, the course of study at the Naval Academy was shortened.[13] The class of 1902 graduated early, and a majority of the cadets found their way to the Asiatic Station. Richardson recalled that "forty-one of the fifty-nine members of my class [1902] saw duty on the Asiatic Station during their first year after graduation," bringing the total of naval cadets on the Asiatic to the highest number assigned there up to that time.[14]

Such a shortage of officers meant that relatively inexperienced officers were often assigned to gunboats and other small ships whose size dictated a small crew commanded by junior officers. As a consequence, the large numbers of the lowest grades present in the Asiatic region, together with the new opportunity for command or increased responsibility, developed a window of opportunity for career-line officers (see Figure 5), and these were the ones who were young enough to serve through World War II.

Neither assignment category of nonline or warrant officers was present in the Asiatic in large numbers at any time during this period. The majority of these officers were in the Atlantic and other non-Asiatic areas where larger ships and shore stations existed. With regard to Asiatic service, the highest point was 1901, when 25 percent of all warrant officers in the Navy were in Asiatic waters. These figures are influenced by the shift of engineers from nonline to line officer status during this period. Clearly, the trend of assignments moved toward the now expanded line, leaving the majority of nonline and warrant assignments for stations other than the Asiatic.

An even higher percentage of Marine officers were stationed in Asiatic waters. By 1 January 1900 almost half of all the Marine officers in the service were assigned to the Asiatic Station. Unlike their naval counterparts, Marine officers enjoyed a window of opportunity in the Philippines and in China for the short term. Later, these opportunities would move from the Asiatic to locales such as Cuba, Haiti, Santo Domingo, Vera Cruz, and other Caribbean scenes where the Marines were assigned career-advancing tasks shoring up gunboat diplomacy in the western hemisphere. Asiatic service after 1902 remained a steady 20 to 25 percent for Marine Corps officer personnel. For the Marines, the Spanish-American War and the early years of Asian service would be but the beginning of a more worldwide experience, more traditional in scope than that of the Navy.

Command Trends

Command is essential to the development of an officer. Due to the unique demands placed on naval resources on the Asiatic, many officers were given opportunities to assume positions of command. Still other officers served in positions where assignments provided areas of responsibility not typical in prewar times as they assumed berths as second- or third-in-command. The service records of officers assigned to the Asiatic, Atlantic, North Atlantic, and South Atlantic stations[15] from July 1898 until 1906 were surveyed to determine which officers received command assignments, second-in-command assignments, or third-ranking positions in an assignment location.[16] The objective was to see where command or responsibility opportunity was concentrated and how often that experience was gained by junior officers. Specifically, did service in any particular station provide more career-enhancing opportunities than in other stations?

By 1898 stagnant conditions had left many of the older officers in grades that brought no promise of command. With the naval expansion after the Spanish-American War, scores of these older junior officers advanced quite rapidly, even though they had little experience to equip them for higher command. A survey of assignments indicates that this situation changed radically in the decade after 1900. Junior officers with little service received opportunities to command or were thrust into other areas of high responsibility—opportunities that would groom them for higher commands in the future.

Positions were divided into four assignment categories, each according to the kind of ship the officer served upon: major combat ships, gunboats over five hundred tons, gunboats under five hundred tons, and support ships. In each case, the rank of the commanding officer, the executive officer, and the third-ranking officer was recorded, providing an indication of who received commands and the quantity of commands and other leadership positions available in each category. Not surprisingly, most of the commands in the major combat ship category (battleships, cruisers, and monitors) went to captains and commanders. In spite of this practice, three commands went to lieutenant commanders, probably an indication more of the shortage of officers than of any long-term trend. The number of commands available on major combat ships was relatively small at any time, including the periods when the United States sent additional large ships to the Far East to meet the Boxer Rebellion in China.

The relative absence of captains on the Asiatic Station was due primarily to the assignment of most of the larger combat ships to Atlantic waters. Captains traditionally commanded those ships, and as Roosevelt's new naval construction began to come off the ways, there were new demands for captains, most of whom were assigned to the Atlantic fleet.

After 1903 three of the major combat ships on the Asiatic Station were used as flagships, each with a rear admiral on board. It is possible that, with the increasing demands for captains in the Atlantic fleet, the Navy assigned the ships on the Asiatic Station to commanders because a flag officer would also be on board. Beginning in 1903, commanders rather than captains commanded the majority of the large ships on the Asiatic Station. Although the numbers are small, a trend toward entrusting major ships to less senior officers is apparent.

In the larger gunboats there was an increase in the number of commands available and in the number of mid-level officers receiving these positions. Although lieutenants served in only four of the command positions, other positions of responsibility on board the gunboats went to junior officers who were within the top three ranking officers on board.

Perhaps the most important command category was the gunboats under five hundred tons. These vessels offered many of the naval cadets, midshipmen, and ensigns their first taste of responsibility, and many young officers aggressively sought assignments to them. Chester Nimitz wrote his grandfather from Cavite in the Philippines, "I told you about trying to get one of the gunboats down here. Well, the powers that be have assured that I will have command of the U.S. gunboat *Panay*." The fact that the *Panay* was small (less than one hundred feet long) failed to dim his enthusiasm. He reasoned, "I can practice piloting and navigation and so forth as well on a small ship, and besides it should teach me a certain amount of self-reliance and confidence.[17]

Frederick Sawyer, referring to his receipt of orders to command the *Panay* in 1900, observed that "this was an unexpected windfall as the duty was much sought after by junior officers." Sawyer lightheartedly rationalized that more senior officers passed up opportunities to command gunboats "due to greater experience and better judgement" and that the junior officers' "good fortune simply demonstrated the triumph of enthusiasm over experience."[18]

The fact that the gunboats usually operated alone—often without direct supervision by a senior squadron commander—forced the novice officer and any other more junior officers aboard to make independent decisions and presented an opportunity to gain self-confidence. It was perhaps the independent nature of the assignment that appealed to many of the younger officers. Writing about their early commands, many of these officers remark on the "roving commissions" they expected to have. Ens. William Leahy wrote in his diary in May 1901 that "the *Mariveles* will be island duty but it will be independent duty with my own command and I consider a most desirable assignment."[19] Lt. Henry Wiley remembered his first command on the Yangtze in China: "We maintained a gunboat patrol on the Yangt[ze] River, and commands of the gunboats were very desirable berths." He too had "a roving commission" that stretched "from Kiukiang in Kiang-si Province to the westward as far as I could go on the Yangt[ze] or its tributaries."[20] Nimitz, full of anticipation, wrote his grandfather that the *Panay* "will be ready in about two weeks from now, and she will cruise in the southern islands of the Philippine group." He emphasized how large an area his new command was to cover, saying "these little boats get roving commissions—that is, they can visit any ports they choose."[21]

Sawyer described his patrol area in the Visayas as "hundreds of smaller islands and [it] extended north to Luzon at the straits of San Bernardino and

USS *Urdaneta*

Built for Spain at the Cavite Arsenal in 1882–83, this iron-hulled gunboat was typical of the vessels captured during the Spanish-American War and put into service by the Navy. On 17 September 1899 it ran aground in the Orani River near Manila and was attacked by *insurrectos*, who killed its commanding officer, Naval Cadet Welborn C. Wood, and several crew members before taking it captive. Recovered by the United States, it was recommissioned at Cavite on 12 May 1900 and served as a guard ship at Olongapo, Subic, and Cavite, and surveyed several potential sites for a naval base. It is shown here in 1901 at the Olongapo Navy Yard at Subic Bay, when it was commanded by Cadet John E. Lewis. *Courtesy LCDR John E. Lewis and the Naval Historical Center.*

was generally considered the most desirable of the four stations." He added that "we were all delighted when our further orders came to proceed to the latter station." Isolation probably was the key to the desirability of the assignment. Sawyer explained that gunboat captains acted under general instructions and "were usually very much their own masters and their movements were seldom interfered with."[22]

Not all officers realized the value of their early opportunities. In 1902 Midshipman James O. Richardson, impatient with the old gunboat *Quiros*, requested transfer to a battleship. He complained that he "was not learning anything about the material or the technical side of the navy." His commander disagreed with him, saying, "Young man, there is nothing in the navy more important than the enlisted man, and you can learn more about how to handle him on a small ship than you can on the larger ships in the navy."[23] Richardson, looking back at the incident, agreed with the assessment, saying that the "subject of handling enlisted men is the most difficult and most important thing for a young officer to learn." He concluded that service on small ships "is best for the rounded development of a young officer."[24]

Ens. William Moffett's early tour of duty in Manila as captain of the port—although not a command on board ship—is illustrative of the kind of responsibility available for an ensign. Commodore Dewey was quite taken with the young Moffett and gave him the command of salvage operations in Manila harbor, directing him to remove the Spanish wrecks creating a hazard to navigation in the harbor. Historian Edward Arpee observed that this was a major task, for "continued operations on land and sea were impossible to pursue efficiently until the hulks . . . had been completely cleared." It took Moffett only a "few days" to clear the wrecks, bringing more notice to himself from Dewey.[25]

Purchase of the ex-Spanish gunboats and other small ships captured during the war with Spain dramatically increased the number of command opportunities in the Philippines (more than in any other geographical location).[26] Lieutenants were traditionally the most junior officers entrusted with commands of small ships, but the shortage of junior officers opened opportunities to officers below that rank. On the Asiatic Station lieutenants (jg), ensigns, and naval cadets commanded almost one-half of the smaller gunboats.[27]

The high number of commands going to naval cadets, ensigns, and lieutenants (jg) provided a large number of additional positions of responsibility, such as executive officer, to officers more junior than their commanders, which meant that other ensigns and naval cadets had numerous opportunities to have leadership roles aboard ship and to command shore parties, patrols, and other expeditions ashore.[28] Midshipman James Richardson served as executive officer of the *Quiros* (an ex-Spanish gunboat rated at 350 tons), where the only officers on board were one lieutenant and two midshipmen: "From an operational point of view, the duty was fine for a young officer, for there was a spirit of adventure about and things happened." As executive officer, Richardson was responsible for forty enlisted men.[29] Lt. Bradley Fiske received orders to the gunboat *Yorktown*, where he became the executive officer, responsible for "the entire routine of the ship: cleanliness, instruction, liberty, and leave," as the ship steamed for months in the islands to enforce American policy and obtain Filipino acceptance of that occupation.[30]

Other officers were not so happy with the responsibility that came their way. In July 1901 Ensign Leahy transferred from command of the *Mariveles* to the *Glacier*, a transport vessel. Leahy wrote that, as third-in-command, he was assigned duty "as Chief Engineer, which is not altogether to my liking." He complained that the ship's machinery was in a state of disrepair due to "neglect and it is not pleasing to be responsible for the performance of a neglected department on board ship."[31] While not pleasant duty for a young ensign, the assignment produced lessons that Leahy never forgot.

Even supply ships furnished some of the younger officers with opportunities for command. Most of these ships were large transports, steamers, refrigerator ships, distilling ships, and colliers, but some were small support boats like station tugs that were put under the command of ensigns and, occasionally, boatswains. Adding these commands to the already large list of commands from other categories on the Asiatic, the command experience of the naval officer corps during this period cut across rank lines and provided the most extensive opportunity for command or responsibility anywhere in the Navy.

Figures 6, 7, and 8 illustrate trends present in all assignments for naval cadets, midshipmen, and ensigns holding a position of command, second-in-command, or third-ranking officer. Two observations can be made regarding these three categories of assignments: First, the Asiatic Station dominated in all three—a 61 to 2 advantage in command assignments, a 115 to 17 advantage in executive officer billets, and a 72 to 40 advantage in third-ranking opportunities. Second, the opportunities for responsibility on the Asiatic Station occurred during the window of opportunity discussed earlier. It is evident that this window began to close as the Philippine War was brought under control, as the Boxer Rebellion in China was dispatched, and as civil government began to assume a greater share of responsibility for the Philippines.

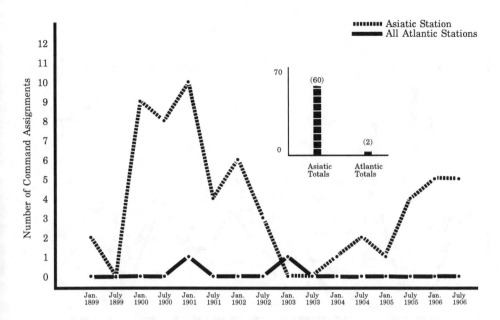

Figure 6 Command Trends Ensign/Naval Cadet–Midshipman Composite Asiatic Station vs. All Atlantic Stations 1899–1906

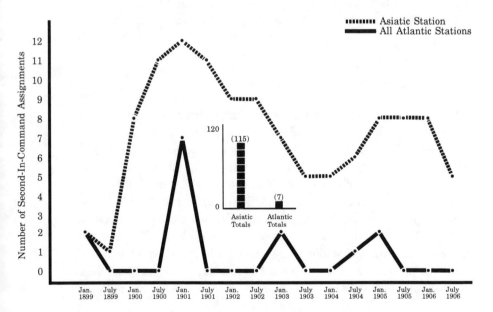

Figure 7 Second-In-Command Trends Ensign/Naval Cadet–Midshipman Composite Asiatic Station vs. All Atlantic Stations 1899–1906

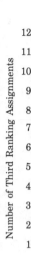
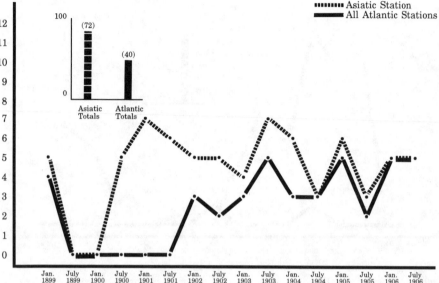

Figure 8   Third-In-Command Trends Ensign/Naval Cadet–Midshipman
Composite Asiatic Station vs. All Atlantic Stations 1899–1906

Impact on Flag Rank

Analysis of officers serving on the major stations has thus far stressed the opportunities available to naval officers to serve in position of command or responsibility. It remains to examine the effect early service had on an officer's subsequent career. To make such an assessment, four questions have been addressed: First, did any particular station or geographical location influence an officer's chances of achieving flag rank? Second, did early command assignment or responsibility opportunities indicate future success in the Navy? Third, was there any correlation between the level of flag rank and service on any particular station or geographical location? And finally, did class standing influence achievement of higher flag levels, and was there any relationship between location and responsibility assignments and class standing?

For the purposes of this survey, flag rank is defined as any rank above captain in the Navy and colonel in the Marine Corps. To be considered a flag officer, an individual had to have served on active duty at least one day at flag-level rank. Thus, officers who received "tombstone" promotions to flag rank at the time of their retirement from the service were not included. Officers who held permanent ranks below flag but served in positions in temporary flag grades were included.

Additionally, the survey included all the flag officers of the Navy and the Marine Corps who had been in service during the period 1 May 1898 to 31 December 1906 and thus had the opportunity for service during the immediate postwar period. The officer must also have received his first flag rank after 1 May 1898. The element of opportunity was the critical factor in determining inclusion in the test group. In this study, 389 flag officers fall within the definition used (see Figure 9). Of the total, 245 served on the Asiatic Station, 253 did not, and 145 served on both stations. These figures include all service without regard to command, second-in-command, or third-ranking assignments. It is clear that general service on either station reflected little difference for the officer corps. The dramatic difference came for officers who received commands and other authority positions.

The 100 officers with service only in the Far East were subdivided by the highest flag rank achieved and whether they held command, second-in-command, or third-ranking assignments. Table 1 shows that 96 percent of all officers assigned only to the Asiatic Station held command, second-in-command, or third-ranking opportunities at some time during their tenure on the station. In contrast, only 62 percent of all officers receiving assignments on the Atlantic Stations (without any Asiatic duty) served in a command or responsibility berth. Many of these assignments were lieutenant commander and above. No distinction was made concerning what kind of assignment or how many different assignments were held during the nine-year period. To qualify, an officer had to hold such an assignment only once. Clearly, the statistics indicate that Asiatic service had a positive effect on an officer's chances to rise in rank within the Navy. Taking into account the large numbers of junior officer command/responsibility positions present on the Asiatic in comparison to the lack of similar service on the Atlantic (see Figures 6–8), the percentages in Table 1 confirm junior officers' perceptions that service on the Asiatic—particularly duty with the gunboats—represented opportunity not available in such quantity elsewhere in the Navy.

In looking further at Asiatic and Atlantic assignments and controlling for service in both areas, only fifty officers (about 35 percent) received responsibility assignments in both geographical areas. Taking into account the flag officers who received authority positions in both the Asiatic and the Atlantic, and weighting the Atlantic assignments for weak junior officer opportunity, it must be concluded that the Asiatic provided some measure of influence upon those careers. This is especially true when it is seen that Asiatic

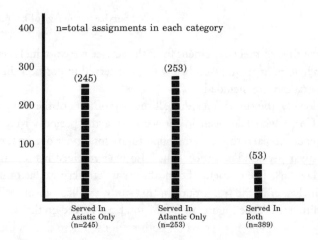

Figure 9 Service Patterns All Assignments Included 1898–1906

Table 1 Flag Success Location and Responsibility Factors 1898–1906

	(n=100) Asiatic Only	(n=108) Atlantic Only	(n=145) Both
1-2 Stars	74	53	48
3 Stars	6	1	1
4 Stars	15	13	1
5 Stars	1	0	0
Totals	96 (96%)	67 (62%)	50 (35%)

n=total responsibility assignments

Table 2 Flag Rank by Class Standing U.S. Naval Academy 1898–1906

	Quartile			
	1st	2nd	3rd	4th
1-2 Stars	56	61	73	109
3 Stars	4	8	7	12
4 Stars	8	12	17	17
5 Stars	0	2	0	2
Totals	68	83	97	140

Number of Missing Observations: 1

Number of Observations: 388

assignments were unique in kind and quantity and represented opportunities rarely found elsewhere. Whether examining general service assignments or responsibility opportunities, the record indicates that those serving in the Asiatic had a marked advantage over those who did not.

The evidence suggests the need for the addition of more service years in the study—perhaps extending from 1898 until 1920. It is true that the window of opportunity was a brief one for officers serving on the Asiatic, but the region offered continued, albeit reduced, opportunities. The same can be said for other stations, such as the Atlantic commands. If the period of the study were extended, would the data in Table 1 remain weighted in favor of Asiatic service, or would it begin to equalize with other regions with the post-1900 expansion of the New Navy and the opportunities brought with the growing American power in the world?

One final factor requires examination: the role played by the Naval Academy cannot be overemphasized when looking for patterns or factors of prejudice in naval careers. If one looks at class rank at the academy and the highest flag levels reached by each of the officers in the flag study, it is apparent that class standing played no role in the attainment of rank, at least not in the traditional sense in which higher standing might indicate the increased probability of success in a future career. According to Table 2, the lower the class standing the more likely an officer would make flag. The fourth quartile provided 36 percent of the flag officers in the study. The bottom half of all classes produced 61 percent of all flag officers, meaning that there were many in the upper half who did not make flag.

If higher class standing did not improve an officer's chances for advancement, did early opportunities for responsibility combined with class standing have any effect? Studies demonstrate that there was little significance attached to service experience when tied to class standing. For example, Asiatic-only service with authority positions never exceeded 35 percent, and none of the data presented any discernible pattern suggesting an association or relationship with class standing. Although an officer's service seems to indicate some impact on future career outcomes, class standing, even when broken down by service experience, was not a factor in determining success as a flag officer.

Conclusion

Service in the Navy was transformed with the Spanish-American War. Long before Commodore Dewey sailed into Manila Bay, the Old Navy faded from view and the United States was committed to a New Navy capable of enforcing expansionist ideas abroad. As national policy moved in this direction, change in the officer corps was inevitable. The young, inexperienced Naval Academy graduates of Theodore Roosevelt's time recognized that the world had changed. Men like Nimitz, Leahy, Fiske, and Richardson recognized that fate had placed them in an enviable position, and they were quick to take advantage of it. Whether one was a naval cadet or captain, command of a ship brought recognition, satisfaction, and resolution of aspiration. Long denied to most naval officers, command or the promise of command became a possibility for every officer in the turn-of-the-century Navy. The optimism of the times was justified as officers looked to a future with no limits, no boundaries beyond which they and their nation could not go.

The officer statistics are helpful in determining the importance of service on the Asiatic, not only to the young junior officers but also to many of the older officers with long times in grade. The acquisition of the Philippines, the Philippine War, and the increased importance of the Asiatic Station played a significant role in the development of the Navy in the early years of the twentieth century. It was a time when the United States was the most powerful industrial power in the world but could not yet determine political and military events. The turn of the century was a growing time for naval officers, for the Navy, and for the United States.

NOTES

1. James O. Richardson, *On the Treadmill to Pearl Harbor* (Annapolis, 1973), 65.

2. Yates Stirling, *Sea Duty: The Memoirs of a Fighting Admiral* (New York, 1939), 89.

3. Naval Officer Service Data Base, History Department, Abilene Christian University, Abilene, Texas. This database is organized as two separate but related databases. The first includes all naval warrant and commissioned (Navy and Marine Corps) assignments to the Asiatic, Atlantic, and Caribbean theaters, 1898–1906. The second database includes only those officers who reached flag rank while on active duty and not before 1898. SPSS Statistical software was used for summary and comparative statistics. All figures are compiled from information in this database.

4. Although war service was similar in Cuba and the Philippines, there were some dramatic differences in the experiences of junior officers. The geography of the Philippines—particularly the thousands of miles of inland and coastal waterways—produced demands on naval assets well beyond what the Navy needed in Cuba. In meeting the demands in the Philippines, younger officers found themselves alone, many times in command of a ship, attempting to exert American foreign policy in an isolated and alien territory far from the councils of more senior officers and often with only the sketchiest guidelines for performance of their duties. Those who per-

formed well under these circumstances proved that they could be trusted to execute good seamanship, exercise wise judgment, and provide expertise.

5. For more details relating to the blockade and other naval operations in the Philippines, see Vernon L. Williams, "The U.S. Navy in the Philippine Insurrection and Subsequent Native Unrest, 1898–1906" (Ph.D. diss., Texas A&M University, 1985).

6. For a discussion of the Navy's concern with the threat from Germany and the resulting large ship assignments, see Williams, "U.S. Navy." In terms of Navy-wide ship deployments, the Atlantic enjoyed more major combat ships, but more men—especially younger officers—were present in the Asiatic.

7. The naval service database surveys four categories or officer groupings: line, nonline, warrant, and Marine officers. Only one group of officers appears in more than one category: engineer officers in the Navy had traditionally not been line officers, but in 1899 they were amalgamated with officers of the line. Thus part of the rise in line officer assignments must be attributed to the inclusion of engineer officers into the line category. In 1898 and January 1899, engineers are in the nonline category. After January 1899, all engineers are listed as line officers.

8. The grade of commodore was replaced by the rank of rear admiral in two levels in March 1899. The rank of commodore was not revived until World War II. See Clark G. Reynolds, *Famous American Admirals* (New York, 1978), vi.

9. In 1902 the grade of naval cadet was changed to that of midshipman. Both titles referred to the graduate of the Naval Academy who had not been commissioned an ensign. These titles or ranks were equivalent.

10. During the years covering this study, the Atlantic Station was sometimes divided into South and North Atlantic Stations. At other times it was a combined Atlantic fleet. For the purposes of this study, the divisions were maintained in order to separate wartime assignments before 1900.

11. Shore assignments are not included in Figures 1–6.

12. Charles Oscar Paullin, *Paullin's History of Naval Administration, 1775–1911* (Annapolis, 1968), 457. This volume is a collection of Paullin's articles on naval administration that appeared in *Proceedings* of the U.S. Naval Institute from 1905 to 1914.

13. Henry C. Taylor, "Annual Report of the Chief of the Bureau of Navigation," in William H. Moody, *Annual Report of the Secretary of the Navy, 1902* (Washington, D.C., 1902), 21.

14. Richardson, *On the Treadmill*, 68.

15. Asiatic assignments were compared with all Atlantic assignments. The resulting observations indicate if service on the Asiatic was unique in producing opportunities for junior officers or if Atlantic assignments produced similar advantages for the emerging naval professional. Because Atlantic service was divided several ways during the period studied, all Atlantic assignments were grouped together to compare with the Asiatic. In all cases, only assignments to ships of each station were included; shore and special assignments were not included.

16. Officers in the three highest ranking positions in every assignment were surveyed to identify those officers who were in positions of authority. Hereafter, the use of the phrase "authority positions" will apply to all three groups of command assignments surveyed: command, second-in-command, and third-ranking officer.

17. E. B. Potter, *Nimitz* (Annapolis, 1976), 69–70.

18. Frederick Sawyer, *Sons of Gunboats* (Annapolis, 1946), 194.

19. William Leahy, Diary, Leahy Papers, State Historical Society of Wisconsin, 101.

20. Henry A. Wiley, *An Admiral from Texas* (Garden City, 1934), 110–11.

21. Potter, *Nimitz*, 69.

22. Sawyer, *Sons of Gunboats*, 16, 23–25.

23. Richardson, *On the Treadmill*, 72–73.

24. Ibid., 73.

25. Edward Arpee, *From Frigates to Flat-Tops: The Story of the Life and Achievements of Rear Admiral William Adger Moffett, U.S.N., "The Father of Naval Aviation," October 31, 1869–April 4, 1933* (Lake Forest, 1953).

26. Williams, "U.S. Navy," 82–84.

27. Out of a total of 156 available commands of small vessels on the Asiatic from 1898 to 1906, officers below the rank of lieutenant held seventy-two. See Vernon L. Williams, "CTABS1" ("Cross Tabulation 1," SPSS [Statistical Package for the Social Sciences], is available from the author), 25.

28. For examples of command and other operational duties of Philippine-based naval officers, see chaps. 4–6 in Williams, "U.S. Navy."

29. Richardson, *On the Treadmill*, 69.

30. Paolo Coletta, *Admiral Bradley A. Fiske and the American Navy* (Lawrence, Kans., 1979), 60–61.

31. Leahy, Diary, 103.

William McKinley's Enduring Legacy: The Historiographical Debate on the Taking of the Philippine Islands

EPHRAIM K. SMITH

THE CONTROVERSY OVER WILLIAM MCKINLEY'S DECISION TO ACQUIRE THE
Philippines in 1898 has endured among historians of American foreign policy for nine decades. Numerous scholars, largely utilizing the same information, have offered a plethora of interpretations. Historical scholarship has
too often reworked familiar facts and issues. No consensus has developed on
whether McKinley was a reluctant or enthusiastic expansionist, on the degree to which he led public opinion, or on the relative importance of other
factors that may have influenced his final decision. Historians in the past
thirty years have largely rehabilitated McKinley's reputation. The pattern of
the evidence, old and new, suggests that the burden of proof rests with those
who have portrayed McKinley as a clever or confident imperialist.[1]

The Enigmatic McKinley

The paucity of information on McKinley's personal opinions on the
Philippines and on other matters of importance has troubled historians.
Margaret Leech concluded in 1959 that "the inner minds of few public men
have been so well concealed." McKinley seldom wrote a private letter; he let
visitors do much of the talking; and at times he "obscured his views by a fog
of phraseology, conventional or oracular." In 1961 Ernest R. May found that
there was "practically nothing" in McKinley's own hand in his papers in the
Library of Congress, and that the "enigma of McKinley's personality makes

it exceedingly hard to plumb the motives beneath his policies." The president's modus operandi may have been in part responsible for the lack of such materials. In an important biography of McKinley in 1963, H. Wayne Morgan noted that the president's "reliance on manipulation and conciliation required unwritten understandings and personal agreements that kept him from history's limelight, for he could not advertise his methods without destroying them." As Morgan added two years later, the president "had no taste for the written word."[2]

Following the publication of these pioneering studies, there was some improvement in the availability of manuscript materials. In the late 1960s and early 1970s the Library of Congress received significant additions to the papers of George B. Cortelyou, who had served McKinley first as assistant secretary and then as secretary. These new accessions included Cortelyou's shorthand diary and McKinley's handwritten drafts of important instructions to the American peace commissioners in Paris. If these documents suggest that McKinley was firmly in command within his own administration, there remained the challenge of interpretation. Lewis L. Gould, in a 1980 study of the McKinley presidency, conceded that reconstructing McKinley's thought process is "very difficult," requiring "the accumulation of small clues, some inference, and a close knowledge of his working habits." One year later, David F. Trask, having presented a detailed analysis of territorial expansion, candidly added that because "McKinley held his decision so close, revealing his inner thoughts to no one, it is impossible to completely rule out other interpretations of his course." In 1982 Stuart Creighton Miller noted that McKinley played "his cards so close to his chest that his real intentions continue to baffle historians to this day."[3]

The First Revelations

Scholarly disagreement over the acquisition of the Philippines cannot be attributed to a lack of information on the administration's official position. The State Department published the bulk of the diplomatic correspondence in 1901. That record and subsequent memoirs and biographies suggest incremental decision making, progressing from the retention of a coaling station to the entire archipelago.[4] The administration's instructions to Commodore George Dewey to attack the Spanish squadron in the Philippines also became quickly available. In his annual report for 1898, for example, Secretary of the Navy John D. Long reproduced the text of the cable of 24 April 1898, ordering Dewey to proceed to the Philippines and to commence "operations at once, particularly against the Spanish fleet." The following year, Henry

Cabot Lodge, in his history of the Spanish-American War, credited the assistant secretary of the Navy, Theodore Roosevelt, with an earlier order of 25 February 1898 instructing Dewey to prepare for offensive operations in the Philippines.[5]

Scholars also benefited from an early insider's view of how McKinley had reached his decision on the disposition of the islands. Charles Emory Smith, a former postmaster general in the McKinley administration, discussed that question in the 11 October 1902 issue of the *Saturday Evening Post*. After McKinley had instructed the peace commissioners in September not to accept less than Luzon, the next six weeks, according to Smith, were "a time of investigation, reflection and discussion." As more information came in from the peace commissioners and military advisers, "the greater appeared the difficulties of division and the more imperative the reasons for limiting the choice to the whole of the archipelago or none." In the end, the president reached "with great reluctance" the conclusion that Spain must cede the entire archipelago. He had been "not insensible to the increased national prestige and commercial advantages" and the augmented prestige accruing to his administration, but the president "saw the perplexities and responsibilities on the other side, and had there been no other question he would have relinquished the gain if he could have saved the entanglements." Although McKinley knew that public sentiment favored expansion, "he led public sentiment quite as much as public sentiment led him," and the "popular manifestations" on his western speaking tour in October "were in response to the keynotes he struck." Public opinion alone, Smith argued, would not have forced McKinley's decision had he not also felt a strong sense of duty. Having reached his decision, the president "was firm and unfaltering" even when the peace commissioners in Paris feared a break in the negotiations.[6]

For over eighty years, scholars have also had access to the president's ex post facto remarks on the Philippines. In each of these interviews, McKinley stated that he had initially been opposed to the retention of the Philippines but finally concluded he had no feasible alternative but to acquire all of the islands. Although McKinley discussed this question with Jacob Schurman, president of Cornell University, in late 1898 or early 1899,[7] and with Henry S. Pritchett, superintendent of the Coast and Geodetic Survey, in May 1899,[8] his most well-known statement was allegedly made to a delegation of Methodist visitors at the White House on 21 November 1899. According to an article published by Gen. James F. Rusling in the 22 January 1903 issue of the *Christian Advocate*, McKinley stated that the "truth is I didn't want the Philippines, and when they came to us, as a gift from the gods, I did not know what to do with them." He had sent Dewey's squadron to Manila to

President William McKinley and the War Cabinet

McKinley sits at the left with his cabinet clockwise around the table: Secretary of the Treasury Lyman J. Gage, Attorney General John W. Griggs, Secretary of the Navy John D. Long, Secretary of Agriculture James Wilson, Secretary of the Interior C. N. Bliss, Postmaster General Charles Emory Smith, Secretary of War Russell A. Alger, and Secretary of State William R. Day. *Photograph from Alden March, The History and Conquest of the Philippines and Our Other Island Possessions (William E. Scull, 1899).*

capture or destroy the Spanish fleet, and the islands "had dropped into our laps." First considering the retention of only Manila or Luzon, McKinley had walked the floors of the White House and prayed for divine guidance. Finally "one night late it came to me," McKinley explained, that it would be "cowardly and dishonorable" to return the Philippines to Spain, that it would be "bad business and discreditable" to turn them over to "our commercial rivals," and that the Filipinos "were unfit for self-government." Accordingly, there was nothing left to do but "to take them all, and to educate the Filipinos, and uplift and civilize and Christianize them, and by God's grace do the very best we could by them, as our fellow-men for whom Christ also died."[9]

Charles S. Olcott's two-volume biography of McKinley in 1916 provided even more significant information. Apparently chagrined to discover that the president "did not commit to paper his plans and purposes, nor his inmost thoughts and aspirations," Olcott nevertheless introduced previously unpublished material secured from some of McKinley's closest associates. He quoted, for example, a note in McKinley's own hand: "While we are conducting war and until its conclusion we must keep all we get; when the war is over we must keep what we want."[10] Olcott also published the president's letter to William Day, chairman of the American peace delegation, soliciting the commissioners' views on the Philippines. Having just returned from a speaking tour of midwestern states, McKinley added in this letter of 25 October that there "is a very general feeling that the United States, whatever it might prefer as to the Philippines, is in a situation where it cannot let go."[11]

Olcott also excerpted the diaries of George Cortelyou. He quoted, for example, an entry Cortelyou had made in June 1898 that the president "is the strong man of the Cabinet, the dominating force; but with it all are such gentleness and graciousness in dealing with men that some of his greatest victories have been won apparently without any struggle." Olcott also quoted Cortelyou's claim a month later that McKinley had "worked incessantly" on the American response to the Spanish peace overture, and that the final changes "were largely his own and his guiding hand will be seen at every point in the negotiations." Olcott used this same source to reveal that the final armistice terms were identical with those the president had jotted down on a slip of paper before he began his deliberations with the cabinet. Unfortunately, the Cortelyou diary held few entries for the fall of 1898, so it revealed little of the president's handling of the peace negotiations and his final decision on the Philippines. Olcott largely relied on the official diplomatic record and previously unpublished personal correspondence for his conclusion that "the President kept in close touch, by cable, with all the proceedings, was consulted on every point of difference, and gave his answers with invariable firmness and decision."[12]

Early Interpretations

Making uneven use of these and other available materials, early historians did not hesitate to evaluate the conduct of diplomacy during the McKinley administration. Although modern scholars might find some of the specific arguments familiar, there are some important differences. As a recent study has revealed, most scholarship before 1920 approved of the Spanish-American War and, albeit more reluctantly, the acquisition of the Philippines. Whatever apologetic tone might have crept into some accounts on the latter question, many historians of the period concluded that the emergence of the United States as a world or imperial power had been one of the salutary effects of the war and its aftermath.[13]

Most scholarship stressed the significance of the Battle of Manila Bay and reflected a widespread belief in the initial innocence of American intentions toward the Philippines.[14] Most scholars regarded the orders to Dewey as military in nature.[15] If it was reassuring to know that the islands had not come to the United States as the result of an expansionist plot, most historians admitted that a variety of motivations influenced the final decision. Much emphasis was given to a sense of responsibility for the future welfare of the Filipinos. Some historians also recounted Dewey's problems with Adm. Otto Von Diederichs, the commander of a German squadron that had arrived in Manila Bay after the American victory. American retention of the islands had apparently prevented the archipelago from becoming a future source of possible international conflicts. Yet there was some recognition that American intentions were not completely altruistic. Carl R. Fish, for example, concluded that public opinion "received direction from two forces particularly powerful at the White House—the influence of capital seeking new fields for exploitation, and the enthusiasm of the missionary element filled with the idea of the good we could do there." According to John H. Latané, the president had been profoundly influenced by the European partitioning of China and saw the Philippines as a possible foothold in the Orient. The "larger business and commercial interests" shared this interest. Because the religious community also perceived missionary opportunities in the islands, popular opinion soon "overwhelmingly" favored keeping the entire archipelago.[16]

Scholars also disagreed on McKinley's role. In some studies, he barely comes into focus.[17] Latané, however, argued that the president, and not

Dewey, Congress, the peace commissioners, or the public, had been responsible for the acquisition of the islands. Challenging the prevailing consensus about the inevitability of events after the Battle of Manila Bay, Latané contended that McKinley "had it in his power to bring about an entirely different result." Using Cavite as a base, the American squadron could have remained in Manila Bay "without the aid of a single regiment from the United States." Because the arrival of these reinforcements caused friction with the Filipinos, the "parting of the ways" occurred when McKinley sent the first military expedition from San Francisco. Making extensive use of the diplomatic correspondence published in 1901, Latané ascertained that the president had not made up his mind by September on how much of the archipelago to retain. By late October differences of opinion had also developed among the American peace commissioners on the Philippine question. In spite of warnings that a rupture of the negotiation might result, the president insisted that Spain cede all of the islands.[18]

Whatever the sophistication of Latané's insights in 1907, his work was largely superseded nine years later by Olcott's detailed biography of McKinley. The "same iron will that had resisted a premature beginning of the war," Olcott wrote in typical hagiographical style, "was now devoted to its prosecution with sharpness and decision." However, as evidenced by Olcott's reproduction at length of the president's explanation to the Methodists, McKinley had not anticipated the implications of his orders to Dewey. Olcott thus noted that although McKinley "felt a natural revulsion against the acquisition of a vast unknown territory," the president recognized that "the people would never be satisfied" if the Philippines remained with Spain. Finding his cabinet divided on the Philippines in July, McKinley had decided to postpone that question until the peace conference. He affably scuttled a proposal from his secretary of state to keep only a coaling station. Whatever his initial reluctance in the summer, the president's speeches in October were partly an attempt to educate the American people on their new responsibilities. The president had also displayed commendable firmness during the peace negotiations in Paris. McKinley, Olcott concluded, had been "the first of our Presidents to respond to the call of a broad philanthropy towards other less fortunate peoples."[19]

Disillusionment with McKinley and the Imperial Adventure

While generations of scholars mined the new documentation that Olcott had introduced, the next two decades saw a substantial revision of his assessment of McKinley's decision on the Philippines. Increasingly, historians described the acquisition of the Philippines as a grievous error. Some historians, unlike those of an earlier, more chauvinistic age, were less confident about the benefits of extending American institutions abroad. Scholars were also influenced by a growing disillusionment with World War I and the Treaty of Versailles. As Jerald A. Combs has noted, historians compared previous conflicts with World War I and "found them to be products of similar factors—not idealism or national survival but blundering and rapacity." Diplomatic historians thus "generally berated the Spanish-American War as one of brutal aggression and the acquisition of the Philippines as a serious mistake."[20]

James Ford Rhodes's history of the McKinley and Roosevelt administrations (1922) is an early example of this revisionism. As Joseph A. Fry has noted, Rhodes popularized the image of a cowardly McKinley who had been forced into a needless war,[21] but his treatment of the Philippine question was more complex. Relying on the earlier works by Chadwick and Olcott, Rhodes felt that McKinley had driven a hard bargain in negotiating the protocol with Spain. Moreover, the enthusiastic crowds on the president's western tour had "only confirmed what he had already determined." It was also clear to Rhodes, after reading the official diplomatic correspondence, "that the decision of the main points rested with the President, who used the communications from the Commissioners as materials on which to base his own judgment." Yet, while Rhodes found the president's explanation to the Methodist delegation to have been sincere and honorable, McKinley "had no right to commit his country to a dangerous course . . . on account of a religious sentiment." Since the president's popularity had been greatly increased by a victorious war, he should have persuaded the country to return the islands to Spain.[22]

Although most subsequent studies also viewed the keeping of the Philippines as unfortunate, few followed Rhodes's lead and accorded McKinley an influential role. It became conventional to assume that the president had little to do with the real decision. Some members of the emerging progressive school of historians, for example, suggested that McKinley had been a tool of economic interests. Acutely aware of the problems associated with the rise of industrial America, this new generation of scholars, as Richard Hofstadter has noted, were "disposed to think more directly about the economic issues of society, and to look again at the past to see if economic forces had not been somewhat neglected." Harold U. Faulkner, for example, argued in 1924 that growing American productivity and $1,210,291,913 of exports in 1898 had made "the matter of foreign markets important." Financial imperialism,

Faulkner concluded, "provided the great cause" of the conflict with Spain, who "had come to her senses and was prepared to make any concessions before hostilities commenced, but war was nevertheless declared."[23]

Three years later, the socialists Scott Nearing and Joseph Freeman also accepted economic determinism in *Dollar Diplomacy: A Study in American Imperialism*. Citing Roosevelt's orders to Dewey, Nearing and Freeman added that the "meaning of this secret order and of America's interest in the Philippines did not become clear" until the signing of the peace treaty. Their analysis of the published diplomatic and military correspondence "revealed that the Philippines were acquired to meet the demands of expanding industry and commerce." Dewey had received instructions to report on the resources of the archipelago, and earlier in the year the New York Chamber of Commerce had petitioned McKinley to protect their interests in the Chinese empire. "This demand of American business for better facilities for trading with China, including an Open Door policy," Nearing and Freeman argued, "led McKinley to include in his instructions to the peace delegation" the statement that the United States could not be indifferent to commercial opportunity in the Philippines.[24]

Other considerations may have influenced the scholarly diminution of McKinley's role in the taking of the Philippines. This new approach may have been a response to the emerging negative consensus about the president's lack of courage in failing to avoid war with Spain. It may also have reflected the impression, cultivated by McKinley in his ex post facto statements in 1899, that he had been captured by events. Indeed, in the early 1920s additional information suggested that the president had been less than discerning about the Philippines. According to a recollection published by H. H. Kohlsaat in 1923, McKinley confessed in 1898 that he had to consult a globe upon hearing of Dewey's victory because "I could not have told where those darned islands were within 2,000 miles!"[25]

Theodore Roosevelt on Center Stage

Other revelations hardly enhanced the president's image. Certain items in a two-volume collection of the correspondence of Henry Cabot Lodge and Theodore Roosevelt, published in 1925, suggested that McKinley might have been a victim of an expansionist cabal to seize the Philippines. As early as September 1897, Roosevelt, having presented his views on war plans to McKinley during a carriage ride, wrote Lodge shortly afterward that the American Asiatic Squadron should blockade and take Manila in the event of war with Spain. More significantly, Lodge had written Roosevelt on 24 May 1898 "in confidence but in absolute certainty, that the administration is grasping the whole policy at last." Noting that troops and naval vessels would be sent to the Philippines and that Puerto Rico had not been forgotten, Lodge added that it appeared as though the McKinley administration "is now fully committed to the large policy that we both desire." In contrast to the views of Lodge and Roosevelt, the president was vacillating on the Philippines. By mid-July, Lodge wrote that the president "is worrying over the Philippines—he wants to hold them evidently but is a little timid about it."[26]

It now appeared that Theodore Roosevelt had been more familiar than the president with the geography of the Orient. To be sure, historians had not been totally ignorant about the assistant secretary's role in 1898.[27] Yet few scholars seemed to have sensed that this might have been anything more than normal military precautions or evidence of Roosevelt's jingoism. The few earlier critics of the Spanish-American War who wrote before World War I seem to have accepted Lodge's assertion in 1899 that "no one had dreamed that the war meant the entrance of the United States into the Orient." Tyler Dennett, in his pioneering study of American diplomacy in East Asia (1922), wrote that the intent of the February orders to Dewey "appears plainly to have been to remove the menace of the Spanish fleet rather than to acquire Manila." By the mid-1920s, Nearing and Freeman had thus taken a minority position in implying that Roosevelt's orders had an imperialist context.[28]

Other historians, using the newly published Lodge-Roosevelt correspondence, went beyond insinuation. Charles Beard, an economic determinist and leading progressive historian, quickly perceived the implications of this material. In *The Rise of American Civilization* (1927), he and Mary R. Beard quoted the correspondence to demonstrate that "a number of active politicians had early perceived the wider implications of a war with Spain." To assume that the State and Navy departments had been "unconscious of the economic and strategic utility of the Philippines, especially in view of American operations in the Pacific for a century past," the Beards wrote, "is to imagine that they were lacking in the sophistication commonly displayed by the Anglo-Saxon peoples on such occasions." Yet this same correspondence left the authors uncertain about McKinley's role. "Just what was going on in the bottom of McKinley's mind is not entirely plain," they wrote.[29]

Emphasizing the influence of public opinion rather than an economic interpretation, Walter Millis had similar difficulty with McKinley in his popular *The Martial Spirit* (1931). Rather than McKinley, it had been Roosevelt (whose picture adorned the frontispiece) who had committed the United States to a new policy in the Orient. Aware that collecting Asiatic territories was fashionable and that the Philippines might be valuable, the assistant secretary had used the Spanish Asiatic squadron as a pretext to seize the islands. Lodge and Roosevelt, the "two conspirators," had engineered Dewey's appointment and later "concocted" the instructions of 25 February. "Thus were we committed," Millis wrote, "by a lesser official at the Navy Department, to a course of action which was never contemplated by the American people and which was to have the most far-reaching and most dubious results." Millis, however, was not as successful in delineating McKinley's role. The president, he noted, had done nothing to discourage Roosevelt. When the latter had discussed in September 1897 the need for an attack on Manila, the president had listened "in his pleasantly enigmatic way, and apparently said nothing." Whether McKinley fully appreciated the significance of his final orders to Dewey in April, Millis wrote, "one can only guess." Though he found the president's intentions obscure, Millis could not shake his suspicions. Impressed by the "striking promptitude" of the president's decision to send troops before reliable word had arrived of Dewey's victory, Millis wrote that it was difficult "to conclude that our annexation of the Philippines was a wholly accidental proceeding."[30]

McKinley as Victim of Large Policy

Other historians of the period were more decisive about whether McKinley had been a participant or a victim in an expansionist plot. In 1932, Julius W. Pratt, for example, published a seminal article arguing that Roosevelt and Lodge were the architects of a large policy that brought the Philippines and other territories within the American orbit, and that McKinley and his secretary of state had been "genuinely surprised by the new responsibilities which the war thrust upon them." Four years later, in a detailed study challenging earlier interpretations that the business community favored war with Spain, Pratt noted that Roosevelt's preparations laid "an Asiatic empire at the feet of the United States." Uncertain whether Roosevelt was attempting to conquer an empire or merely waging effective war, Pratt nevertheless concluded that McKinley, after the Battle of Manila Bay, "was now clay in the hands of the little group of men who knew all too well what use to make of the war."[31]

With the deepening cynicism and isolationism of much opinion in the 1930s, Pratt's large policy thesis quickly became the consensus on McKinley and the Philippines. In the first edition of his monumental textbook in 1936, Samuel Flagg Bemis wrote, for example, that McKinley had been "seduced" by the advocates of a large policy who desired the Philippines "as a valorous young swain yearns for the immediate object of his feelings, knowing only the passion of the present and seeing only the more appealing allurements of the hour." "Looking back on those years of adolescent irresponsibility," Bemis concluded, the taking of the Philippines had been "a great national aberration." Two years later, A. Whitney Griswold wrote that a "small rather self-conscious, politically effective group of expansionists," under the "cover of a war to liberate Cuba and complete the American hegemony of the Caribbean," had "schemed the annexation of colonies in the China Sea." The longstanding appeal of this interpretation is evident in Howard Beale's assessment in 1956 that Roosevelt's actions as assistant secretary of the Navy ensured "our grabbing the Philippines without a decision to do so by either Congress or the President, or least of all the people."[32]

The Role of Public Opinion

If Walter Millis had been uncertain about the president's part in the events associated with the Battle of Manila Bay, his assessment of McKinley was devastating. As a young congressman from Ohio, McKinley had made "the first of his many successful applications of the ear to the ground" and "became a protectionist." In discussing how popular clamor had forced an apparently needless war with Spain, Millis noted that a courageous statesman might have avoided the conflict with Spain, adding that McKinley "in his successor's famous phrase, had 'no more backbone than a chocolate eclair.'" Likewise, the president, attempting to reconcile the acquisition of an empire with his own stricture against forcible annexation, once again "applied his ear to the ground."[33]

Although Tyler Dennett had argued in 1933 that behind McKinley's "mask of amiability" there "was self-discipline and decision of character," most historians were not willing to challenge the popular interpretation that the president lacked a firm backbone. For the next three decades, many studies emphasized the role of public opinion. In his important 1936 study, for example, Julius Pratt emphasized the role of key Social Darwinian intellectuals who helped create a climate for expansionism in the 1890s. The conversion of the business community after the Battle of Manila Bay and the support of many religious spokespersons for imperialism increased the pressure on McKinley. More recent interpretations that stressed a "psychic crisis," Manifest Destiny and Mission, the impact of a foreign policy elite, or political expediency are also associated with the role of public opinion in shaping McKinley's decision.[34]

Cold War "Realists" Critical of a Policy of Drift

Already seen by most historians as the patsy of the large policy expansionists and/or subservient to public opinion, McKinley's reputation further suffered in the 1950s at the hands of the emerging "realist" school of historians and political theorists. As Jerald A. Combs has noted, American involvement in World War II discredited "the idea that a peaceful national demeanor, neutrality, and the oceanic moat surrounding the United States could shelter America from the clash of great powers abroad." With much more at stake in a nuclear world, scholars of the realist persuasion usually castigated utopian crusades and called for a more prudent foreign policy based on national self-interest. Not surprisingly, the realists expanded on the stereotype of McKinley, beset by hysterical public opinion, stumbling into an unnecessary war with Spain.[35]

The realists were equally critical of the expansionists and McKinley's inability to anticipate the consequences of this war. In 1951, for example, Hans Morgenthau criticized McKinley for having led the nation "beyond the confines of the Western Hemisphere, ignorant of the bearing of this step upon the national interest, and guided by moral principles completely divorced from the national interest." In the same year, George F. Kennan wrote that McKinley, in later defending Dewey's actions, "showed a very poor understanding of what was really involved and professed to believe a number of strategic premises that simply were not true." The sending of military forces to the Philippines appeared to have been determined primarily by a "very able quiet intrigue by a few strategically [placed] persons in Washington," which, had it not been for the war hysteria following Dewey's victory, might have ended "in the rigors of a severe and extremely unpleasant congressional investigation." According to Robert Osgood, even Alfred T. Mahan and Theodore Roosevelt were motivated by "an aggressive national egoism and a romantic attachment to national power rather than by any fear for national security." No one in Washington was aware of the imperial implications of Dewey's mission, Louis J. Halle argued in 1960, and McKinley, trying "to catch up" with the march of events, was at "a loss to know what we should do with the Philippines." There "never was a decision to attach the Philippines to us," Halle concluded, "until it was found that they virtually were attached already."[36]

The New Left Contribution

Several studies by New Left historians soon challenged the realist view of McKinley. Rejecting the scholarly preoccupation with hysterical public opinion and the "great aberration" of 1898, these historians, increasingly disillusioned by Cold War policies, emphasized the economic origins of American imperialism. The Philippines, these scholars argued, were acquired as part of an effort to provide an outlet for industrial or agricultural surpluses. Thomas McCormick, for example, argued that "Hawaii, Wake, Guam, and the Philippines were not taken principally for their own economic worth, or for their fulfillment of the Manifest Destiny credo, or for their venting of the 'psychic crisis.'" Instead, they were obtained "largely in an eclectic effort to construct a system of coaling, cable, and naval stations into an integrated trade route which could facilitate realization of America's one overriding ambition in the Pacific—the penetration and, ultimately, the domination of the fabled China market."[37]

Such so-called New Left interpretations have been challenged by other historians. Robert L. Beisner, however, has warned that it is "highly misleading to think in terms of a unified American business community, backed by a determined government, striving unremittingly to break into the markets of Asia and Latin America." "The behavior of American officials and businessmen," Beisner added, "does not support the carefully measured, symmetrical case put forward by LaFeber, Williams, McCormick et al." Also, Paul Varg has argued that the fabled China market was more myth than reality, and David M. Pletcher has recently suggested that some historians have failed "to give sufficient attention to the profound gap between rhetoric and results in late-nineteenth-century economic expansionism."[38]

At times, the debate can be downright contentious. In a stimulating article on "American Imperialism: The 'Worst Chapter' in Almost Any Book," James A. Field argued that the influence and consistency of the alleged expansionist intellectuals of the 1890s had been exaggerated, that American missionary societies were more concerned with India than China, and that American shipping, cable, and naval interests were more oriented to the Atlantic and Europe than to the Pacific. Field also suggested that new technology and the lack of a dependable source of coal created a situation in which Dewey "not only had to destroy a fleet but also had to capture a harbor." The new acquisitions in the western Pacific, Field concluded, "were in one sense the product of the new technological developments; in another, they can be seen as historical 'accidents.'" In response, Walter LaFeber argued that "the question is not how many battleships or cables were in the Pacific before

1898, but why McKinley and his advisers were able to move so rapidly into the Pacific after Dewey's victory at Manila Bay." If the decade of the 1890s, LaFeber added, "is the 'worst chapter' in American diplomatic historiography, and I do not believe it is, the fault does not belong to those who have replaced 'aberration' and 'accident' with more useful, coherent, and defensible approaches to understanding the decade." Beisner, suggesting that Field's assault on the influence of Social Darwinists was "persuasive" but does not "take us anywhere new," argued that "America's preoccupation with Hawaii, China, the Philippines, and Korea, despite the nation's traditional and still-intact Atlantic orientation, graphically demonstrates the strength of the 'new paradigm' in American diplomacy that arose in the 1890s." The evidence "remains convincing," Beisner added, "that American statesmen at the end of the nineteenth century believed profoundly that the international stakes in Asia were high."[39]

McKinley's Role Rehabilitated

If their emphasis on economic factors has been challenged, New Left scholars rehabilitated McKinley's role. McKinley and other national leaders, William Appleman Williams wrote in 1962, considered America's problems "in an inclusive, systematized way that emphasized economics." It was a mistake, Williams added, to view McKinley and his advisers as "largely passive servants." By June 1898 the McKinley administration was "very pointedly and vigorously dealing with the issue of overseas economic expansion without waiting for a debate about imperialism, or for various Englishmen to offer suggestions as the proper strategy." Over the next decade, other studies, including the influential works of Walter LaFeber and Thomas McCormick, Jr., augmented the thesis that a competent McKinley had consciously and deliberately advanced the fashioning of a new empire in Asia based on markets and the open door.[40]

If Ernest R. May's impressive multinational study in 1961 on the emergence of the United States as a world power reinforced the traditional image of McKinley as motivated by political expediency and lacking in courage,[41] other scholars reemphasized the president's role. In contrast to the realists, who portrayed McKinley as an ineffectual bumbler, and the New Left historians, who perceived the president as consciously advancing American economic interests, these scholars took a more eclectic middle-ground position.[42] According to a 1957 doctoral dissertation by John Layser Offner, for example, McKinley, in spite of a critical lapse of leadership in March, pursued a consistent Cuban policy and delayed war with Spain. Two years later,

Margaret Leech, also critical of McKinley's excessive cautiousness and indecision in the face of war, nevertheless published a sympathetic biography revealing the more human and occasionally determined side of the president. Paolo E. Coletta, in an article published in 1961, argued that McKinley firmly controlled policy during the peace negotiations in Paris. In two major revisionist studies in 1963 and 1965, H. Wayne Morgan argued that McKinley was a shrewd handler of men and strongly defended his conduct of diplomacy in 1898. John A. S. Grenville and George Berkeley Young, in a 1965 volume on the relationship of politics, strategy, and diplomacy, also rejected the traditional assessment of McKinley. Two years later, Paul S. Holbo demonstrated how McKinley, anxious to maintain his control over foreign policy, effectively marshaled his forces in 1898 to defeat the Turpie-Foraker amendment recognizing Cuban independence.[43]

William Wirt Kimball and Naval War Plans

McKinley's reputation was also indirectly rehabilitated by scholars questioning the importance of a large policy conspiracy. The experiences of World War II and the emergence of the United States as the leader of the "free world" offered new perspectives. As Hugh De Santis has noted, "the growing coordination of military strategy and diplomacy" since 1945 undermined the large policy thesis. Drawing on previously unexploited records in his important study of the U.S. Navy in the Pacific (1958), William Braisted noted that the Navy Department, long before Roosevelt's tenure as assistant secretary, had prepared a contingency plan calling for the temporary occupation of Manila. The following year, Margaret Leech wrote that Roosevelt's communication to Dewey late in February "was at once repetitive and premature, and had no actual bearing on subsequent events." Independently of Leech, Louis Halle also concluded that Roosevelt apparently "had no thought" of acquiring the Philippines in making the arrangements for the assault on the Spanish squadron at Manila.[44]

The most comprehensive assault on the large policy thesis, however, came a few years later. In 1966, John A. S. Grenville and George Berkeley Young argued that naval preparations in 1898 and McKinley's approval of a 24 April cable authorizing offensive operations in the Philippines and the other preparations in early 1898 were in accordance with a plan developed by officers in the Navy Department and the Naval War College. The final draft of this plan envisioned that the temporary retention of Manila would deny Spain needed revenue, provide a base of operations, and force an early peace and indemnity. Roosevelt and Lodge had played no part in the formulation of this plan. "One conclusion appears to be inescapable," Grenville and Young wrote. "But for the existence of a war plan that bears the signature of Lieutenant William Wirt Kimball, the United States would not have extended her sovereignty over the Philippine Islands."[45]

Although Grenville's discovery of additional war plans led him to reemphasize in 1968 the importance of naval strategists, not all Filipino or American historians accepted this conclusion. The "arrival of the Americans in the Philippines," Oscar Alfonso wrote of Roosevelt in 1970, "if it was any one man's making, was his doing." Although aware of Kimball's preparation of war plans, Alfonso nevertheless concluded that Roosevelt, who had already developed a "rationale for a colonial-imperial program," was largely "instrumental in bringing America's might to Philippine shores" and, after the Battle of Manila Bay, was "anxious not to let the opportunity slip by" of taking the islands from Spain. Ronald Spector, in a more direct attack on Grenville's position, cautioned in 1971 that the variety of war plans "suggests that there were more differences of opinion among American naval officers regarding American strategy and foreign policy than has generally been supposed." "To assign to them full responsibility for the American acquisition of the Philippines," Spector added, "is as short-sighted as to attribute it to the intrigues of Theodore Roosevelt and Henry Cabot Lodge."[46]

Even so, there are more recent exceptions to the trend to deemphasize the role of Roosevelt and the large policy advocates. In a history of the Philippines, Renato Constantino wrote in 1975 that "American expansionists in strategic government positions" whipped up enough public indignation against Spain in 1898 "to maneuver the United States into declaring war." "While American capitalists were primarily interested in protecting the millions they had invested in Cuban industry," Constantino added in a reference to the 25 February orders to Dewey, "expansionists like Theodore Roosevelt . . . had bigger plans." Nine years later, G. J. A. O'Toole, in a popular study written with an engaging style and an interpretation reminiscent of Walter Millis, also placed the assistant secretary center stage. In a somewhat ambivalent blend of older and newer interpretations, Roosevelt, portrayed by O'Toole as on intimate terms with the expansionists, implemented the naval war plans (and also increased his own chances for future military glory) by sending the famous orders to Dewey. In contrast, Richard H. Collin argued in 1985 that the final revised plan was "almost identical to Kimball's original" and that it "was William W. Kimball, rather than Theodore Roosevelt or William Randolph Hearst, who masterminded the war of 1898 with Spain."[47]

McKinley as Conspirator: Recent Scholarship on Events Before the Battle of Manila Bay

If the role of large policy expansionists has been exaggerated, and if one also has to be careful about assigning too much influence to naval planners, just how does William McKinley fit into the pattern of events surrounding the Battle of Manila Bay? Scholars are aware that McKinley approved the final orders to Dewey, and that he authorized, within a few days after the Battle of Manila Bay, the sending of reinforcements to the islands. Indeed, according to the memoirs of McKinley's secretary of war, Russell A. Alger, "the determination to send an army of occupation to the Philippines was reached before Dewey's victory occurred." In one of the most provocative articles on the subject, Timothy G. McDonald suggested in 1966 that "McKinley may have gone to war with Spain over Cuba in order to get the Philippines," and that he had delayed war until Dewey's squadron received vital ammunition rushed from Hawaii. Robert L. Beisner, however, wrote in 1975 that the McDonald article was "an example of the kind of pulp-magazine history that should have been published in *Imaginary Tales*" and "ingeniously argued but totally unconvincing and innocent of documentation."[48]

Although few historians, as Lewis Gould wrote in 1980, "contend that the president had decided before May to take the Philippines for the United States," there has been much speculation. Ernest R. May, whose 1961 study depicted a cowardly McKinley capitulating to public opinion, nevertheless acknowledged that there "is a faint possibility that from the very outset of the war the President nurtured in his mind the hope of taking from Spain some part of her Pacific empire." Two years later, Thomas J. McCormick argued that the McKinley administration had wanted from "the very beginning" of the war a commercial and military foothold in the Philippines, and that Roosevelt's earlier preparations had fallen "within the main lines of the 'larger policies' of the administration" of which the assistant secretary had been largely ignorant. Likewise, Walter LaFeber noted in 1963 that the "result of the Battle of Manila Bay can hardly be termed a lucky accident." The "threat of war with Spain in Cuba, combined with the dangerous threat to the open door in Asia, had constrained the administration to make thorough preparations for offensive operations in the Pacific." Although eschewing economic determinism, H. Wayne Morgan wrote in 1965 that McKinley had been "hardly ignorant" of the Battle of Manila Bay or its consequences. The "suspicion lingers," Morgan wrote, "that he knew the train of events Dewey's arrival in Manila Bay would set in motion"; no one "in politics as long as he could have thought otherwise."[49]

Historians writing more recently have also differed on McKinley's role and attitudes *before* the Battle of Manila Bay. In 1971 Graham A. Cosmas was inclined to accept McKinley's later explanation that the consequences of sending Dewey to Manila Bay were unanticipated before 1 May 1898. A year later, however, Daniel B. Schirmer argued that the McKinley administration "reached the decision to seize and hold the Philippines in the winter of 1897-98, after Dewey left Washington for the scene of action." In contrast, David F. Trask wrote in 1981 that in sending Dewey to Manila the McKinley administration "had in mind no other purpose than the relatively limited desire to exert pressure on Spain at a weakly defended colonial outpost," and that prior to 1 May "no thought had been given to army operations in the Philippines." Similarly, Richard E. Welch, Jr., has written in a recent study that Dewey's presence in Manila Bay "was not part of any grand scheme to promote the economic or strategic interests of America in the Far East," but "was primarily the result of a war plan . . . to hurt the enemy wherever he is vulnerable."[50]

McKinley as a Reluctant or Purposeful Expansionist: Recent Scholarship on Events After Manila Bay

Disagreement also persists about McKinley's actions and intentions after the victory of 1 May. Historians are not in agreement whether McKinley was a reluctant or enthusiastic expansionist. Margaret Leech, for example, portrayed the president as a hesitant expansionist in an influential 1959 study. Although McKinley had acted as a "neutral moderator" with "a certain parliamentary adroitness" during the cabinet discussions on the peace protocol, his personal doubts had "disfigured the clarity of his confidential instructions" to the peace commissioners in September. Considerably influenced by the report of Gen. Francis V. Greene, who had just returned from Manila, McKinley reached a decision before undertaking a speaking tour of the midwest in October. During that tour, McKinley told his audiences "that he believed the United States could not give up the Philippines, and asked them if they agreed that the acquisition was a moral obligation." In 1961 Ernest May depicted the president as even more subservient to public opinion than did Leech. McKinley, May wrote, had held his "foggy middle ground" in August, had written largely "delphic" instructions to the peace commissioners in September, and postponed a decision until late October. Whatever his wishes, the "sole concern of the President was with the mood and whim of public opinion." Having "found his answer" during the October tour, the president remembered "the crisis that brought on the war" and "wanted only to hear the people's wishes and obey."[51]

Other historians have seen a more purposeful McKinley. Paolo E. Coletta, a biographer of William Jennings Bryan and the author of several studies on the diplomacy of the period, argued in 1961 that the stereotypical image of McKinley as weak and indecisive "does not fit his handling of the peace negotiations and the acquisition of the Philippines." Instead of having attempted to convince the American people that it would not be right to take the Philippines, McKinley had "added to and led the expansionist clamor."[52] A few years later, H. Wayne Morgan, a biographer of McKinley, argued in another study that the territorial acquisitions of 1898 were "part of a conscious program of extending American power into the arena of international politics and trade, and not by accident or default." From the beginning, McKinley had been inclined to retain all of the Philippines. Whatever he may have implied in his comments to others, "he knew that postponement would develop and focus public opinion in support of his decision to retain the islands." Aware of the possible consequences when he ordered the attack on the Philippines, McKinley sent reinforcements and acted during the negotiations "as only an expansionist could." Biding his time, testing public opinion, and maneuvering support for his position, McKinley in the end "adroitly appeared to 'capitulate' and accept the islands just as he had 'capitulated' to the demand to free Cuba." The president, Morgan concluded, "found the prospects of American expansion satisfying."[53]

Coletta and Morgan were not alone in this assessment. In 1966, John A. S. Grenville and George Berkeley Young concluded that the president had patiently waited for growing public support for "his own firm policy" and subsequently "made it appear that he had only gradually and reluctantly been driven to the conclusion that his duty to God, national honor, the Filipinos, and the Cubans demanded that the United States assume the burden of governing the Spanish colonies." Thomas J. McCormick, in a 1963 article and 1967 monograph written from a New Left revisionist perspective, also detected little hesitancy in the McKinley administrations' efforts to obtain a foothold in the Philippines. Apprehensive over threats to the China market and desirous of securing a military base, the administration had rushed troops to Manila with "almost unseemly haste." If there was any indecision, it was only on how much of the Philippines to retain. In acquiring the Philippines and other new possessions in 1898, the president had practiced "pragmatic expansionism."[54]

These pioneering studies in the 1950s and 1960s set the tone for much of the subsequent discussion. Some historians have, for example, differentiated between the initial predilection for a coaling station and the final decision to take all the islands. In a masterful synthesis, Charles S. Campbell argued in

1966 that the fait accompli presented by Dewey's victory, in the context of American naval interest in the Far East and the seemingly ominous threats to the open door in China, foreshadowed the retention of at least a base. The sending of reinforcements, which the president approved routinely "without consideration of long-range consequences," made such a decision "virtually certain." Ultimately, the popular appetite for colonies and military opinion on the difficulty of defending Manila or Luzon alone led McKinley to conclude there was no alternative save annexation of the entire archipelago. The enthusiastic responses of his October audiences only confirmed but did not "inspire" this decision.[55]

Even the latest scholarship is not in agreement. In 1981 David F. Trask's exhaustively researched *The War with Spain*, a major revision of the traditional thesis that the Army had performed poorly, partially reflected the earlier interpretations of Ernest May and Margaret Leech in his discussion of the Philippine question, but like most recent historians he is much more impressed with McKinley's leadership. The president, Trask argued, "emerges as a serious strategist who effectively related the use of force to the achievement of larger political goals." Having striven "mightily to avoid the break with Spain," Trask noted that McKinley "was most reluctant to support annexation of the Philippine Islands." Prewar military planning had not contemplated "major territorial acquisitions"; military pressure on the Philippines was part of a "soundly conceived" strategic design to force an early peace settlement rather than to acquire an empire in the Pacific. When McKinley detected no consensus on the islands by late July as he undertook negotiations leading to the end of the war, he decided to postpone a decision and "manipulated the Cabinet throughout the discussions to achieve a predetermined outcome." His views "remained fluid" until he ascertained in October that the people favored annexation. He then turned to the task of supporting this view. McKinley had thus become an expansionist against his better judgment only after he sensed a groundswell of opinion that he felt compelled to honor. "In deciding the question," Trask concluded much as had May earlier, "the President had not governed events; events had governed him. Remembering the hysteria early in 1898 after the sinking of the *Maine*, he feared to contest the popular mood." McKinley's position, Trask suggested in an interesting insight, was similar to that of his secretary of the Navy, John D. Long, who, faced with a seemingly unavoidable situation, reluctantly acquiesced in the acquisition of the Philippines but "never became an enthusiast."[56]

Trask was not the only recent historian to portray McKinley as a cautious expansionist. In 1982 Stuart Creighton Miller also disagreed with those who were "convinced that McKinley was an imperialist all along." Writing that "limited evidence" on the president's position suggested "that not until August did he decide to keep all of Luzon, and in October the entire archipelago," Miller concluded that the president's "cautious path to his decision that fall indicates his reluctance to retain the Philippines." Richard E. Welch, taking a position closer to that of Morgan, Coletta, and Grenville, argued in 1979 that the president's decision was "reached only gradually" after "a careful assessment of personal, political, and national advantages." There "was no grand design, but there was calculation." Having decided by early October to acquire all the islands, McKinley "sought to foster public acceptance for colonial expansion." Neither "an indecisive man nor a far-sighted man," McKinley left himself "an escape hatch by assuming a posture of indecision" and "waited for annexationist sentiment to gain increasing support, and he did not wait in vain."[57]

In 1980 Lewis L. Gould made a much more forceful case for McKinley as an expansionist in his influential revisionist study portraying him as "the first modern President." Just as Trask had been influenced by May, Gould's discussion of McKinley's role on the Philippines reflects in part the earlier work of H. Wayne Morgan and Paolo E. Coletta. Although apparently disagreeing with Morgan's argument that McKinley must have known the consequences of sending Dewey to Manila, Gould does argue that the president's conduct "from May 2 onward indicates that he had never given serious consideration to relinquishing the archipelago." With the only real question being how much of the Philippines to retain, Gould found McKinley becoming "something of an imperial tutor to the American people." After the signing of the peace protocol in August, the president "continued his policy of public indecision about the future of the islands while simultaneously shaping events aimed at full American control." McKinley's addresses during the October tour were "masterful examples of how an adroit leader can set the terms of a public discussion in his own favor." "From Dewey's victory onward," Gould concluded, "he guided events so that American annexation became logical and, to politicians and the people, inevitable."[58]

Robert C. Hilderbrand came to somewhat similar conclusions in 1981 independently of Gould's work. In a study of executive management of public opinion, Hilderbrand found that the McKinley administration "marked the beginning of self-conscious presidential management of public attitudes in foreign affairs." Both before and after the start of the Spanish-American War, the president had worked behind the scenes to influence public opinion. Having decided to keep the Philippines during the summer, McKinley "allowed the American commitment to deepen in the Philippines, strengthening the position of the annexationists but refusing to take part in public or private debates of the question." "Making good use of his talent for dissimulation," Hilderbrand wrote, "McKinley guided the public from one position to the next, moving always closer to full retention of the islands." Waiting only for the most appropriate moment to reveal his position, McKinley deliberately gave the impression during the first half of his October tour that he was "being influenced by the public's response to his remarks." If McKinley was gauging public reaction, Hilderbrand concluded, "he did so more to test his own success than to determine the course he should follow."[59]

Gould and Hilderbrand were not the only scholars to give McKinley a high rating. In 1982 a political scientist, John S. Latcham, reevaluated, as had Gould, the common assumption that McKinley was merely an average president. Utilizing James David Barber's typology of presidential character and the psychoanalytical theories of Karen Horney, Latcham concluded that McKinley had "not only an active character trait, but one that was *distinctly* so." The president's "active-positive character, expansive world view, and remarkably successful and flexible political styles," Latcham argued, "combine to give *this* president the strength of personality to lead the nation in a period of deep crisis."[60]

In a 1987 study of the impact of ideology on American policy, Michael Hunt took a revisionist position on McKinley as a strong leader. Instead of being an aberration or watershed, the 1890s, Hunt argued, were simply "the last stage in the rise to hegemony of the notion of the dynamic republic." McKinley had "warmly embraced" an assertive foreign policy based on a premise previously accepted by Hamilton, Jefferson, and Polk, that "greatness abroad would glorify liberty at home." The president's foreign policy revealed "not a master plan but rather a consistent devotion to those ends that publicists had already linked to national greatness—commercial prosperity, territorial expansion, and military security." Americans also viewed other peoples, Hunt noted in this study of cultural values, on the basis of a "racial hierarchy." In the case of the Philippines, this racial superiority "carried obligations that could be ignored only at the cost of throwing doubt on that superiority itself."[61]

More Rehabilitation: McKinley as Negotiator

Recent scholarly assessments of the peace negotiations have enhanced McKinley's reputation. Although he may have seen McKinley as bowing to public opinion in his final decision on the Philippines, David F. Trask was impressed with McKinley's resolute skill as a negotiator. During the discussions leading to the signing of a peace protocol in August, Trask noted, McKinley "largely controlled discussion of peace terms within his Administration." Later, during the negotiations in Paris, the president "refused to bend, as firm in peace negotiations as in wartime councils." Three years later, John Offner, in a detailed assessment of the negotiations in July and August, also found that "McKinley clearly dominated the peace talks as the nation's chief negotiator and policymaker." Believing that McKinley may not have had firm designs on securing all of the Philippines in August because he would then have been more likely to delay "signing the protocol until the Army had captured Manila," Offner portrayed McKinley as a determined and skillful negotiator. Having previously been careful to avoid initiating talks, the president had subsequently been inflexible "on almost all points" in negotiations with Jules Cambon, the French ambassador in Washington. At a critical point, McKinley had also played a "key role" in preventing the talks from rupturing over Spanish insistence that the Cortes be consulted. McKinley, Offner concluded, "apparently accomplished more in enlisting Cambon's aid than Cambon did in altering McKinley's policies." In 1992 Offner further rehabilitated McKinley's reputation in *An Unwanted War*, a multi-archival study of the Spanish-American War from an international perspective.[62]

Even a Machiavellian McKinley

Some historians have even transformed McKinley into a president who would have outmaneuvered Machiavelli. Walter Karp's tightly crafted *The Politics of War*, published in 1979, is perhaps the most polemical of such interpretations. Drawing on carefully selected information from the pivotal studies of the 1950s and 1960s, Karp portrayed the president as the "master of the fait accompli, the patient contriver of circumstances which, as he would ruefully announce, gave him no choice but to do exactly what he privately wanted." The key to McKinley's "grand design" for "national unity and cohesion" was to transform the United States into a world power. Without anyone realizing it, McKinley had engineered American involvement in the war with Spain, and then emerged as the masterful architect of a large policy of expansionism. "To conquer and rule the Philippines as an American colony was William McKinley's principal war aim," Karp argued, and "to press home all its fateful consequences was to be his principal postwar intent." Having encouraged Roosevelt's preparations for an assault on the Philippines, McKinley quickly ordered an expeditionary force to the Philippines after Dewey's victory. The president then pushed through the annexation of Hawaii, and saw to it that the American flag was raised on Puerto Rico.

Feigning reluctance, McKinley, with references to duty and destiny, helped orchestrate a campaign to weaken the traditional aversion to a colonial empire. In the meantime, he selected an expansionist-minded peace commission. And even though there was "no popular mandate" in October for acquiring all the Philippines, McKinley informed the head of his delegation that public opinion "made any other alternative impossible." "With matchless guile and unshakable aplomb," Karp concluded, "President McKinley had carried America across a great divide."[63]

Karp's portrayal of a scheming and seemingly omniscient McKinley has found both defenders and detractors. In a popular history entitled *Sitting in Darkness: Americans in the Philippines* (1984), David Haward Bain acknowledged his indebtedness "to Walter Karp, who showed me the light." Bain thus portrayed McKinley as "a mandarin who let others do his maneuvering for him, seeming only reluctantly to acquiesce" when in reality he was "seldom surprised by the rush of events because he was only very rarely not in control of them." Whatever he may have said privately, McKinley had "resolutely set about instituting a policy of expansionism." In a recent review essay, Lewis Gould criticized Bain's use of sources and questioned an interpretation that, like those of Walter Karp and some New Left revisionist historians, portrayed McKinley "as a sort of imperialistic evil genius." Gould was equally critical of G. J. A. O'Toole's *The Spanish-American War*, written in the tradition that portrays McKinley as having "a chocolate eclair for a backbone." In contrast to these two interpretations, Gould posited his alternative that McKinley "was the first modern president with a varied record of success and failure." Whichever interpretation of McKinley prevailed, Gould added in a statement which seems to sum up the prevailing moderate consensus, "everyone should concede" that McKinley "made policy between 1897 and 1901, not Theodore Roosevelt, and that it is wrong to view his administration as if he was not in charge."[64]

Yet some historians are still troubled by the extent to which McKinley was in charge of events. In a detailed synthesis in 1988 of the foreign policy of the McKinley administration, John Dobson portrayed the president as a reticent expansionist. Acknowledging that McKinley was "the arbiter of his administration's foreign policy" and was capable at times of "intensive leadership," Dobson nevertheless found McKinley's policy on the Philippines to be characterized by "irresolution." Neither "a risk taker nor an ideologue," McKinley was simply an "astute politician" working "toward a solution that would satisfy the largest number of people." McKinley's practice of operating without a long-range plan and reacting to immediate crises by seeking the least disruptive solution, could, as in the Philippines, lead "to unanticipated and quite dangerous consequences." In an even more critical assessment of McKinley, Stanley Karnow argued in a 1989 study of Philippine-American relations that a "cabal of willful men," the champions of expansion in 1898, had manipulated the president, "whose sincerity and virtuous innocence were exceeded only by his ignorance and almost paralytic indecisiveness." Because McKinley had neither policy goals or decisiveness, he was unable to lead and was "fated to follow." Undergoing a gradual conversion of the Philippines, McKinley ultimately "drifted toward complete annexation of the islands."[65]

Scholars and the Evidence

In attempting to reconstruct McKinley's thoughts about the Philippines, historians have only a few statements by the president of his personal views. These private comments, much like the administration's official position, display caution, indecision, and even misgivings on the Philippines. In June 1898, as we have seen earlier, Senator Lodge found the president being "a little timid" about taking the Philippines. A month later, the president informed William M. Laffin that he had doubts about retaining more than Luzon but that apart from having the United States "act with great magnanimity and show European governments that a lofty spirit guides us," he favored "the general principle of holding on to what we get." On 5 September, McKinley, having told Frederick Holls that "his mind was as yet a blank, so far as a decision upon the point of keeping or giving them back, was concerned," and left the impression that he "evidently inclines very strongly to the view that we had better give them back under proper guaranties for good government on the part of Spain." Sensitive to popular complaints about the condition of the American forces in Cuba, Puerto Rico, and the Philippines, McKinley informed Holls that he did not think "public opinion will sanction an indefinite continuation of this state of affairs in possessions so far away as the Phillipines [sic] and said that to give up the Phillipines now would mean a great storm of criticism this winter but that to retain them would be to mean permanent criticism thereafter." Believing that Spain would abandon the other islands if the United States took just Luzon, McKinley was also "very much inclined at the present time to allow Germany to have either one of the Philippines or one of the Ladrones, if it can be done without offending the other powers, especially England and Russia."[66]

Faced with the task of drafting instructions for the peace commissioners, McKinley in mid-September had the Philippines very much on his mind. On 14 September McKinley asked Pierre Smith whether "it would not be just as well to keep only one Island in the Philippines, provided trade with the other Islands remained free and unrestricted, as for the United States to take all the Islands." Whitelaw Reid, riding in a carriage with the president the same day, found that the president "seemed timid about the Philippines and oppressed with the idea that our volunteers were all tired of the service and eager to get home." The next day, McKinley informed a delegation from the National Civil-Service Reform League Federation that he hoped they came "prepared to tell him just how much of the conquered territory should be retained, and just how much should be left within the control of Spain." McKinley, however, did inquire whether they felt "the possession of Manila would facilitate the expansion of our trade in the Orient," and "nodded a good deal" when he received an affirmative response. Apparently still having reservations about retaining the entire archipelago, the president, in meeting with the American peace commissioners in mid-September, again expressed apprehension that territorial expansion would become less attractive "when the difficulties, expense and loss of life which it entailed, became more manifest."[67]

This evidence seems to create difficulties for those historians who see McKinley as a forceful expansionist. Some of these historians directly confront the evidence. H. Wayne Morgan, referring to Whitelaw Reid's diary reference on the president's timidity on the Philippines, has written that "McKinley's remarks reported here ought not be taken too literally. . . . Drawing opinions from other men was a favorite weapon of his, and he was not likely to reveal to Reid at this time any final convictions or secrets." Lewis L. Gould has taken a similar but more carefully qualified position. Referring to the president's comments in May and June to Lodge and Laffin, Gould argued that McKinley's "qualms are less telling than his actions" and that the president "was careful to keep his options open and his purposes obscure." Even in his comments to visitors in September, Gould noted, "McKinley maintained his noncommittal posture on the fate of the Philippines." The opposition of the anti-imperialists, Gould added, would build as "McKinley's purposes became clearer."[68] Although not all historians have been quite as conscientious in introducing and attempting to reconcile potentially contrary evidence, those who have portrayed a more purposeful McKinley have, like Gould and Morgan, stressed the president's direction of events rather than his rhetoric. Lacking more forceful expansionist statements from McKinley, New Left historians, emphasizing the opinions of business people and the reports of military officials such as Gen. Francis V. Greene and Comdr. R. B. Bradford, have placed the Philippine question in the broader context of the open door in Asia.[69]

A Case Study: McKinley's Statement to the Methodist Delegation

Historians have given a variety of readings to McKinley's ex post facto statements on the Philippines, particularly his famous interview with Gen. James F. Rusling and the Methodist delegation in 1899. Rhodes, following Olcott's lead, concluded McKinley had "told exactly the truth as he saw it." However, Millis, having ascertained that public opinion was uppermost in McKinley's mind, found it curious that in "vouchsafing to the President this remarkable and curiously well-reasoned revelation, Providence completely overlooked the patent wisdom of vouchsafing a similar one to General Aguinaldo." Leech suggested that an emotionally wrought president "had found on his knees the argument that reconciled him to a course he had described as 'criminal aggression,'" but most scholars, like Millis earlier, have been skeptical. Although Beard in 1927 quoted the president's comments, McKinley's statements about divine guidance received little or no attention, for example, in the major works of the New Left historians. More traditional scholars like Morgan concluded that McKinley's comments to his Methodist visitors were "a classic outline of his alternatives," although he had "prefaced them with a disingenuous explanation of how the islands came to the United States." Garel A. Grunder and William E. Livezey noted the lack of references to prior planning, the threatened China market, the interests of other nations in the islands, the influence of public and editorial opinion, and any references to political advantage. Similarly, Coletta suggested that in disclaiming any personal choice McKinley "had used the old trick of shifting responsibility to vague collectives, by talking about fate, destiny, good intentions, and problems too complex for the human mind to master.[70]

In 1975 Robert Ferrell raised additional questions by noting that General Rusling had also penned a somewhat similar account that recalled Lincoln confessing to having received divine assurance just before the Battle of Gettysburg. As Lewis Gould noted in 1980, there was "the possibility that Rusling improved on McKinley's words with a device that had served him once before." In addition, Gould, having discovered that McKinley had made similar statements to other visitors in November 1899, suggested that the president "was leaking information to friends and critics in order to offset attacks on the Philippine policy." In this context, Gould concluded, the president's remarks to the Methodist delegation "have at best a modest value as a description of his thoughts a year before they were made; their famed religious context is very questionable." Two years later, however, Stuart Creighton Miller, commenting on McKinley's references to a divine authority in statements on the Philippines, argued that McKinley "was a devout

man living in an age of religious revivalism and renewed evangelical missionary efforts throughout much of the world, so his actions and perceptions
were likely to have been sincere."[71]

More Recent Evidence

Although Rusling's recollection has long been available, a document has
recently been introduced that may influence scholars. On 19 November 1898
McKinley informed Chandler P. Anderson and Thomas Jefferson Coolidge
in a White House interview that he had sent Dewey to the Philippines "to
capture or destroy" the Spanish fleet "to protect our commerce and embar-
rass them at home," but that Manila had become "a question from which we
could not escape." After Dewey's victory, the president added, Manila Bay
was the safest and only available harbor. While that factor alone made the
question of abandonment "hardly an open one," McKinley added that the
naval victory and the ensuing American occupation had contributed to an
early end of the war. He also referred to the American pride in keeping the
islands "under temporary control, at least," and mentioned the necessity of
"protecting the natives in so far as they need protection." After "most careful
and conscientious and profound consideration," McKinley had been "unable
to arrive at any other conclusion than that we must keep *all* the islands."
They could not be returned to Spain, and if they were given to another European power "we should have a war on our hands in fifteen minutes." Duty
and destiny required the United States to undertake its own responsibilities,
McKinley added, and "the people should not be alarmed or anxious about
their ability to fulfill their obligations." Nonetheless, McKinley complained
of the added responsibilities and the burden of such decisions and predicted
"for myself and for the people nothing but anxiety for the next two years."[72]

The Anderson memorandum, McKinley's earliest and most detailed surviving explanation in private conversation of his decision on the Philippines,
will undoubtedly engender conflicting interpretations. Those scholars who
see McKinley as a subtle expansionist or clever mandarin may well note that
the president's comments, like later ones, were vague. In view of the impending struggle over ratification, these historians would be justified in in-
quiring whether McKinley's comment about the inevitable force of events
was only a clever political ploy. Having earlier stated in one of his October
1898 speeches that "duty determines destiny," had not McKinley ignored the
fact, as one historian has noted, that the president had "prescribed the nature
of that duty"?[73] Were his allusions in November to Dewey, destiny, and duty
merely more of the same?

Taken more or less at face value, the Anderson memorandum offers additional insight into McKinley's decision-making process. Moreover, although it is possible to perceive the president as an imperialist tutor in his statement that the American people must not be alarmed about accepting their duty and destiny, the bulk of the memorandum appears to substantiate the outlook of those historians who have portrayed McKinley as a reluctant or hesitant expansionist. Comparing the obvious similarities between the Anderson memorandum and the president's subsequent private and public statements, it appears that McKinley's repeated statements may have been a sincere reflection of the dilemma in which he found himself and that some historians may "have attributed too much deviousness" to his position on the Philippines.[74]

The religious references found in the presidents' later statements to Rusling and Pritchett are missing in the Anderson account, and McKinley also apparently chose not to emphasize the economic advantages of retaining all of the archipelago. This latter omission might indicate that the attraction of the China market may have been more influential in the earlier determination to retain a coaling station or Luzon rather than the final decision to keep the entire archipelago. During the interview with Anderson and Coolidge, McKinley had also spoken of how the proximity of the various islands had prevented, among other factors, a decision to keep one island. This reference to the interdependence of the islands seems to reflect the testimony and advice of American military advisers in Washington and Paris.[75]

New Evidence

Scholars have not yet fully exploited the available materials on the role of Maj. Gen. Francis V. Greene, U.S.V., who met with the president in late September and early October 1898. Ever since the publication of the official correspondence, historians have known that the president had found Greene, who had just returned from the Philippines, to be well informed. The president had quickly forwarded Greene's report to the American peace commissioners in Paris. Although historians have turned to this report in their efforts to reconstruct the president's decision, they seem to have ignored Greene's personal papers in the New York Public Library. This collection reveals that Greene visited the White House five times between 27 September and 1 October 1898. During the first session, which lasted for three hours, Greene handed the president a document (now found in the Cortelyou Papers) arguing that returning the Philippines to Spain would lead to civil war, that handing them over to the Filipinos would result in anarchy, that giving them to Germany or Japan would be cowardly, and that the establishment of a joint protectorate would be impractical. The only solution was to take the entire archipelago. Having read this list of options in silence, McKinley, according to a later address prepared by Greene for the New York City Republican Club in 1915, turned "with that kindly smile which was so characteristic of him" and replied: "General Greene, that is very advanced doctrine. I am not prepared for that. Do you know the instructions that I have given to the Commissioners in Paris?" When Greene replied in the negative, McKinley added that "I have instructed the Commissioners to take the City and Bay of Manila and such additional portions of the Island of Luzon as they think necessary for naval purposes, and to return the rest of the Islands to Spain."[76]

Notwithstanding this information, General Greene, in this and two other lengthy interviews with the president on 28 and 30 September, continued to offer an opposing point of view. According to his later recollection, Greene informed McKinley that retaining only a portion of Luzon and returning the rest of the islands to Spain would be "a terrible mistake, would destroy the results of the war with Spain, would injure his own reputation as the Leader [sic] in this brief but highly successful war, and would certainly involve us in war with some powerful nation which desired the possession of the Philippines in order to establish itself in the Orient." "I utterly failed," Greene later wrote in 1915, "to shake his previous opinion or to induce him in any way to modify his opinions." At the end of their third session, however, the president, noting that he was soon to leave on a speaking tour, smiled at Greene and added: "Perhaps when I come back I may think differently from what I now think."[77]

This important document, portions of which are published in this essay for the first time, should be treated with caution. Although based in part on cryptic references in his 1898 diary, Greene prepared this address almost seventeen years after the original interviews. Greene's reconstruction of his own position is corroborated by documents in the Cortelyou Papers, but he may have erred in attempting to recall in 1915 the president's exact words in 1898. Although the peace commissioners had been instructed on 16 September not to accept less than the cession of Luzon, the official published correspondence contains no subsequent order to return the remainder of the archipelago to Spain. If Greene had garbled the president's actual wording, he certainly would not have misunderstood McKinley's stated position. As the first high-ranking American military official to return to Washington from the fighting in the Philippines, Greene was rushed to the White House. Over the next three days, he spent between seven and eight hours with the president on questions relating to the Philippines. This was no brief conversation or interview. Although it is possible to argue that McKinley was merely "testing the waters" and concealing his real opinion from Greene, the evidence strongly suggests that he was opposed to retaining all of the Philippines. By late September and early October, McKinley, obviously interested in gauging public opinion during his upcoming tour, was not yet willing to move beyond the retention of Luzon. However, he may have been more influenced by these sessions than Greene later realized. There are strong similarities between Greene's presentation of the options on the Philippines and McKinley's statement a year later to the Methodist delegation.

Conclusion

Future documentary discoveries may well alter the interpretations of McKinley's decision to acquire the islands. The introduction of new materials has influenced McKinley historiography over the years. The publication in 1925 of the Roosevelt-Lodge correspondence, for example, helped persuade many scholars that an expansionist cabal unknown to the president had pursued a large policy which led to the unfortunate annexation of the Philippines. Some three decades later, scholars, introducing previously unpublished war plans, challenged the large policy thesis and indirectly contributed to the rehabilitation of McKinley's reputation. The newer accessions to the Cortelyou Papers may also provide more insights into the workings of the McKinley administration.

There is a striking consistency in the pattern of the available evidence on McKinley's decision on the Philippines. Superficially, it indicates that McKinley, initially favoring keeping only a coaling station, had, after considerable contemplation and some hesitation, moved gradually to support the retention of first Luzon and then the entire archipelago. Yet, scholars, drawing upon basically the same resources available for over half a century, have presented diametrically opposing interpretations. As with most major historical controversies, scholarly interpretation has been influenced by the impact of contemporary events, as Jerald Combs and other historians have noted.

This scholarship, sometimes stimulating and full of productive insights and sometimes a tedious reworking of the same old story, also appears to have been influenced as much by intuitive assessments of McKinley as by the historical record. The studies portraying McKinley as some kind of super Machiavelli are a case in point. Although there does seem to be a consensus that McKinley was an able president who, particularly after the Battle of Manila Bay, dominated decisions on the islands, these scholars have carried revisionism beyond the existing evidence. Weaving a tale of conspiracy and intrigue on McKinley's part, these studies seem to ignore the president's innately conservative and cautious personality. According to this approach, McKinley never had a moment's doubt or miscalculated as he faced one of the most momentous decisions of his career. Such accounts, while stimulating, have as much value as the earlier canard that McKinley had "no more backbone than a chocolate eclair."

Other scholars, whose more moderate interpretations are usually marked by meticulous research, have also resorted to a measure of intuitive judgment. Facing a scarcity of McKinley materials, they have portrayed McKinley as a more manipulative or forceful expansionist, have placed the Philippine issue in the context of the open door, or have viewed the administration's actions from an annexationist perspective. Some advocates of this approach have virtually ignored the president's own explanations of his actions. Scholars who perceive a more cautious or reluctant president have the advantage of the official correspondence and McKinley's later explanations. Even these historians, however, have had to decide whether this record should be taken at face value. Many have found it difficult to accept, for example, the veracity of the president's comments to the Methodist delegation.

Whether because of the emotional connotations of the decision to acquire colonies, the nature of the president's method of operation, or other reasons that may not be altogether clear, the elusive McKinley seems to have been a special burden for historians for nine decades. The historical records, however, may not be quite as slender as some historians have assumed. The publication of the Anderson memorandum and the new evidence from the Greene Papers presented in this essay seem to strengthen the position of those who have seen McKinley as a reluctant expansionist. If they had not done so before, historians should at least now acknowledge that the president's several explanations of his decision were remarkably similar in tone and content.

In view of the nature of historical inquiry, the debate will obviously continue. Perhaps the best we can hope for is that those advocates of McKinley as a subtle or masterful imperialist will consider whether McKinley might really have been indecisive and not consistently the artful machinator. Historians of the contrary persuasion, in spite of the prevailing evidence, might also consider whether McKinley, in his *apologia pro sua vita* as a hesitant and reluctant expansionist, might indeed have been the consummate actor. If nothing else, such doubts only enhance one's respect and maybe even a grudging affection for a president who, unwittingly or not, has provided so many scholars with a sustained challenge.

NOTES

1. This essay, which concentrates on McKinley's role, has a much more narrow focus than most existing studies of the period. Unlike most historiographical efforts, however, it discusses the introduction of significant evidence over the years. I am indebted to several fine historiographical and bibliographical studies on McKinley, the Spanish-American War, and the imperial age. Joseph A. Fry, for example, has published an excellent historiographical essay suggesting that McKinley's role in the coming of the Spanish-American War has been greatly rehabilitated ("William McKinley and the Coming of the Spanish-American War: A Study of the Besmirching and Redemption of an Historical Image," *Diplomatic History* 3 [Winter 1979]: 77–97); while his essay is the starting point for anyone interested in McKinley, Fry only indirectly touches on the decision to acquire the Philippines. For the latest bibliographical comments on that topic, see Robert L. Beisner's thoughtful *From the Old Diplomacy to the New, 1865–1900*, 2d ed. (Arlington Heights, Ill., 1986), 120–41, 161–64, 175–81; the updated bibliography in Lewis L. Gould, *The Spanish-American War and President McKinley*, new print (Lawrence, Kans., 1986), 151–60; and the detailed notes in David F. Trask, *The War with Spain in 1898* (New York, 1981), 514–16, 520–24, 590–623. Hugh De Santis provides an excellent discussion of the debate over American imperialism in the late nineteenth century, with excellent bibliographical footnotes, in "The Imperialist Impulse and American Innocence, 1865–1900," in *American Foreign Relations: A Historiographical Review*, ed. Gerald K. Haines and J. Samuel Walker (Westport, Conn., 1981), 65–90. Jerald A. Combs has provided a valuable assessment of how traumatic generational events have influenced changing interpretations of the Spanish-American War and imperialism in *American Diplomatic History: Two Centuries of Changing Interpretations* (Berkeley, Los Angeles, London, 1983), 73–97, 182–96, 269–77, 367–73. I would like to express my appreciation to David F. Trask and Lewis L. Gould for having read and criticized earlier drafts of this paper, although I am of course solely responsible for any errors of fact or interpretation.

2. Margaret Leech, *In the Days of McKinley* (New York, 1959), 36; Ernest R. May, *Imperial Democracy: The Emergence of America as a Great Power* (New York, 1961), 112–14; H. Wayne Morgan, *William McKinley and His America* (Syracuse, 1963), 528; H. Wayne Morgan, *America's Road to Empire: The War with Spain and Overseas Expansion* (New York, 1965), 18.

3. Lewis L. Gould, *The Presidency of William McKinley* (Lawrence, Kans., 1980), 6; Trask, *War with Spain*, 450–56, 615–16; Stuart Creighton Miller, *"Benevolent Assimilation": The American Conquest of the Philippines, 1899–1903* (New Haven and London, 1982), 16.

4. On 3 June 1898, for example, Secretary of State William Day, in response to a possible peace overture, informed the American ambassador in London that Spain could retain the Philippines except for "a port and necessary appurtenances." Eleven days later, Day added that the Filipino insurgents "have become [an] important fac-

tor in the situation and must have just consideration in any terms of settlement";
therefore it was "most difficult without fuller knowledge to determine as to disposition of Philippine Islands." Two months later, the peace protocol signed with Spain
simply stipulated that the United States would occupy the city, bay, and harbor of
Manila pending the negotiation of the final treaty. In mid-September, McKinley instructed the American peace commission not to accept less than the cession of Luzon, and in late October to demand the entire archipelago (Day to John Hay, 3 June
1898, in Tyler Dennett, *John Hay, From Poetry to Politics* [New York, 1933], 190–91;
U.S. State Department, *Papers Relating to the Foreign Relations of the United States,
with the Annual Message of the President: Transmitted to Congress, December 5, 1898*
(Washington, 1901), 819–903, 935–38). French Ensor Chadwick drew upon this official correspondence for his treatment of the negotiations in *The Relations of the United
States and Spain: The Spanish-American War* (New York, 1911), 2:427–73.

5. The instructions of 24 Apr. are in *Annual Report of the Navy Department for the
Year 1898: Report of the Secretary* (Washington, 1898), 6. Lodge was only able to provide a summary of these instructions in his *The War with Spain* (New York and London, 1899), 48. John D. Long, in a 1903 history of the Navy's contribution during the
war, reproduced a portion of the text instructing Dewey, in the event of war, "to see
that the Spanish squadron does not leave the Asiatic coast, and then offensive operations in the Philippine Islands" (*The New American Navy* [New York, 1903],
1:179–82).

6. Charles Emory Smith, "McKinley in the Cabinet Room," *Saturday Evening
Post* 2 (11 Oct. 1902): 6–7. See also "Address of Hon. William R. Day," *Hamiltonian*
(Feb. 1902): 3–5; and John D. Long, "The Personal Characteristics of President
McKinley," *Century Illustrated Monthly Magazine* (Nov. 1901): 146.

7. Schurman, whom McKinley appointed to the commission to be sent to the
Philippines, recalled his interview with the president in a 4 Nov. 1899 article in *Out-
look*. When Schurman had said he was opposed to the taking of the archipelago,
McKinley replied "that in general neither the people nor the Government of the
United States had desired to take the Philippines, but were compelled to do so to
prevent serious international complications" (President Schurman on the Philippine
Situation: The Immediate Duty of the United States," *Outlook* 63 [4 Nov. 1899]: 534).
Just over two years later, in an address before the Reform Club of Boston on 20 Jan.
1902, Schurman directly quoted McKinley as having said that "I didn't want the
Philippine Islands, either; and in the protocol to the treaty I left myself free not to
take them; but—in the end there was no alternative" (Jacob Gould Schurman,
Philippine Affairs: A Retrospect and Outlook, an Address [New York, 1902], 1–3).

8. While visiting at the White House on 2 May 1899, Pritchett recalled ten years
later, he had found the president in a reflective mood about the war and the taking of
the Philippines. After lighting up a cigar, McKinley told Pritchett that what "he had
done he had considered with great care; that he had not only thought over them but
prayed over them; and that he could only hope that the outcome would be justified."
Having initially opposed the keeping of any portion of the islands, McKinley added

that "the difficulties of the alternative had gradually influenced him." He thus desired first only a coaling station, then Manila Bay, then Luzon, "and, finally, he had come to the decision that the occupancy of the entire island group was, under the circumstances, the wisest course for his Government to pursue." From the nature of the president's references, Pritchett assumed that his decision had been profoundly influenced by public opinion and a belief that "our government of the Philippines would be a sort of a national missionary effort, which would result in great good to the people of these islands and exert a most salutary effect on our own politics" (Henry S. Pritchett, "Some Recollections of President McKinley and the Cuban Intervention," *North American Review* 189 [Mar. 1909]: 397–403).

9. James F. Rusling, "Interview with President McKinley," *Christian Advocate* (New York), 78 (22 Jan. 1903): 137–38.

10. Charles S. Olcott, *The Life of William McKinley* (Boston and New York, 1916), 1:vii–xii, 2:165.

11. "The interdependency of the several islands," McKinley added, "their close relations with Luzon, the very grave problem of what will become of the part we do not take, are receiving the thoughtful consideration of the people, and it is my judgment that the well-considered opinion of the majority would be that duty requires we should take the archipelago" (McKinley to Day, 25 Oct. 1898, in Olcott, *William McKinley* 2:107–8).

12. Olcott, *William McKinley* 2:55–56, 62–67, 93–128.

13. Combs, *American Diplomatic History*, 73–92.

14. For an explanation similar to that made by McKinley to the Methodist delegation (except lacking the religious overtones), see Willis Fletcher Johnson, *America's Foreign Relations* (London, 1916), 260–70.

15. John Holladay Latané reproduced these orders in his 1907 study as evidence of efficient naval preparations for war (*America as a World Power, 1897–1907* [New York and London, 1907], 29–30). Another historian, Archibald Gary Coolidge, wrote in 1908 that "seldom has an event of the kind been less due to foresight or premeditation" than the acquisition of the Philippines. Some Americans may have "dreamed dreams about the Pacific" and "naval officers have had visions of coaling stations in all sorts of places," Coolidge argued, "but it is safe to say" that when Dewey was finally ordered to Manila, "President McKinley and his cabinet had no thought of getting possession of the three thousand odd islands which have since come into American hands" (*The United States as a World Power* [New York, 1908], 148–49).

16. Johnson, *America's Foreign Relations*, 261–62; Coolidge, *United States*, 148–52; Carl Russell Fish, *American Diplomacy* (New York, 1919), 421; Latané, *America as a World Power*, 38, 72–73.

17. Albert Bushnell Hart did not even list McKinley in his index in *The Foundations of American Foreign Policy* (New York, 1901). Johnson argued in 1903 that Whitelaw Reid, one of the peace commissioners, had played the crucial role in the decision to retain the entire archipelago (Willis Fletcher Johnson, *A Century of Expansion* [New York and London, 1903], 284–85).

18. Latané, *America as a World Power*, 71–73, 78–79. Like many later studies, Latané quoted a dispatch of 26 Oct. from Hay to the American peace commission found in *Foreign Relations, 1898*, 935–36. Richard N. Leopold argued in 1963 that this cable, while printed in the 1901 official correspondence, was never transmitted to Paris, and that the American delegation received its instructions in a different draft forwarded two days later ("The *Foreign Relations* Series: A Centennial Estimate," *Mississippi Valley Historical Review* 49 [Mar. 1963]: 598–99).

19. Olcott, *William McKinley* 2:38, 57–75, 93–128, 190–91, 349–50.

20. Combs, *American Diplomatic History*, 114–15, 153, 182.

21. Having conducted "faultless" diplomacy up to 31 Mar., Rhodes wrote, McKinley then "abandoned his policy and went over to the war party"; he had "not the nerve and power to resist the pressure for war." Had only a more confident and determined man like Mark Hanna been president, Rhodes added, "there would have been no war with Spain" (James Ford Rhodes, *The McKinley and Roosevelt Administrations, 1897–1909* [New York, 1927], 57–64). For an assessment of the impact of Rhodes's study on McKinley's reputation, see Fry, "William McKinley," 77–78.

22. Rhodes, *McKinley and Roosevelt Administrations*, 97–109. According to Combs, Rhodes's earlier friendship with John Hay may have moderated his criticism of the war and its aftermath. Combs also argues that Rhodes was not a cultural relativist but a conservative isolationist (*American Diplomatic History*, 182–85).

23. Richard Hofstadter, *The Progressive Historians: Turner, Beard, Parrington* (New York, 1968), 42–43; Charles Crowe, "The Emergence of Progressive History," *Journal of the History of Ideas* 27 (Jan.–Mar. 1966): 109–15; Harold Underwood Faulkner, *American Economic History* (New York and London, 1924), 621–25.

24. Scott Nearing and Joseph Freeman, *Dollar Diplomacy: A Study in American Imperialism* (New York, 1925), 252–55.

25. H. H. Kohlsaat, *From McKinley to Harding: Personal Recollections of Our Presidents* (New York, 1923), 68.

26. Apparently attempting to reassure Roosevelt, who had earlier written that there must be no peace until Puerto Rico and the Philippines had been secured, Lodge added in July that the taking of Guam indicated that something would be retained in the Philippines. A month later on 15 Aug., Lodge wrote that the administration "seems to be hesitating about the Philippines, but I hope they will at least keep Manila, which is the great prize, and the thing which will give us the Eastern trade" (Henry Cabot Lodge, ed., *Selections from the Correspondence of Theodore Roosevelt and Henry Cabot Lodge, 1884–1918* [New York and London, 1925], 1:278–79, 299–302, 309, 323–24, 329–30, 337).

27. In 1899 Lodge had credited Roosevelt with the cable of 25 Feb. instructing Dewey to prepare for offensive operations in the Philippines. Roosevelt, in his autobiography in 1913, mentioned that Lodge had stopped by his office just as this cable was being drafted. Roosevelt's autobiography also revealed, as did Dewey's memoirs, that the assistant secretary had advised the commodore to seek out political influence to secure the command of the Asiatic squadron (Lodge, *War with Spain*, 48;

Theodore Roosevelt, *Theodore Roosevelt: An Autobiography* [New York, 1913], 210–14; George Dewey, *Autobiography of George Dewey* [New York, 1913], 167–69).

28. Lodge, *War with Spain*, 227; for the possible impact of Lodge's statement, see Combs, *American Diplomatic History*, 80; Tyler Dennett, *Americans in Eastern Asia* (New York, 1922), 616, 631–32.

29. Charles A. Beard and Mary R. Beard, *The Rise of American Civilization* (New York, 1927), 2:372–75.

30. Walter Millis, *The Martial Spirit: A Study of Our War with Spain* (Cambridge, 1931), 78–82, 85–87, 111–12, 173–75.

31. Julius W. Pratt, "The 'Large Policy' of 1898," *Mississippi Valley Historical Review* 19 (Sept. 1932): 219–42; Julius W. Pratt, *Expansionists of 1898: The Acquisition of Hawaii and the Spanish Islands* (Baltimore, 1936), 22, 221–22, 326–27.

32. Samuel Flagg Bemis, *A Diplomatic History of the United States* (New York, 1936), 467–75; A. Whitney Griswold, *The Far Eastern Policy of the United States* (New Haven and London, 1938), 10–16, 31, 34–35; Howard Beale, *Theodore Roosevelt and the Rise of America to World Power* (Baltimore, 1956), 70. Although both Bemis and Griswold were uncertain as to the extent of the assistant secretary's imperial aspirations before the Battle of Manila Bay, this dimension was largely ignored by Henry F. Pringle, whose 1931 biography emphasized Roosevelt's lust for a "military-spiritual adventure." This "adolescent" desire to be a soldier also seemingly influenced Roosevelt's plea to Lodge in May opposing peace negotiations until Puerto Rico and the Philippines had been taken. "The details, presumably," Pringle noted, "would prolong the war" (*Theodore Roosevelt: A Biography* [New York, 1931], 175–81, 187).

33. Millis, *Martial Spirit*, 6–7, 114, 175, 371–84.

34. Dennett, *John Hay*, 177–78, 208–9; Pratt, *Expansionists of 1898*, 1–33, 230–360; Richard Hofstadter, "Cuba, the Philippines, and Manifest Destiny," in *The Paranoid Style in American Politics and Other Essays* (New York, 1965), 145–87; Frederick Merk, *Manifest Destiny and Mission in American History: A Reinterpretation* (New York, 1963), 231–57; Ernest R. May, *American Imperialism: A Speculative Essay* (New York, 1968), 16–43, 192–230. The influence of Hofstadter's "psychic crisis" interpretation can be seen in Robert Dallek's argument in 1983 that the "reasons for going to war, the way in which the country fought, and the decision to take colonies at the close of the fighting had more to do with relieving internal strains than with serving American interests abroad" (*The American Style of Foreign Policy: Cultural Politics and Foreign Affairs* [New York, 1983], xi–xx, 4–31). The strongest recent statements about the role of public opinion can be found in May, *Imperial Democracy*, 255; and Trask, *War with Spain*, 452–54. See also Richard E. Welch, Jr.'s conclusion that "McKinley was a politician, and the most important influence was his calculation that annexation promised the greatest political gain and offered the fewest political dangers" (*Response to Imperialism: The United States and the Philippine-American War, 1899–1902* [Chapel Hill, N.C., 1979], 10). An opposing point of view stressing McKinley's strong sense of duty can be found in Morgan, *William McKinley*, 412.

35. Combs, *American Diplomatic History*, 197–99; De Santis, "Imperialist Impulse," 68–69; Fry, "William McKinley," 82–83.

36. Hans J. Morgenthau, *In Defense of the National Interest: A Critical Examination of American Foreign Policy* (New York, 1951), 23; George F. Kennan, *American Diplomacy 1900–1950* (Chicago, 1951), 17–18. Osgood wrote that "there was much in the imperialist and expansionist rationale, especially in its martial code of virility and honor, which had no logical relation to a realistic view of world politics" (Robert Endicott Osgood, *Ideals and Self-Interest in America's Foreign Relations* [Chicago, 1953], 28, 46–47). Unlike some of the realists, Halle conceded that "it would have been virtually impossible for the McKinley administration to have avoided the acquisition of the Philippines" (Louis J. Halle, *American Foreign Policy: Theory and Reality* [London, 1960], 179, 184–89).

37. Thomas McCormick, Jr., "Insular Imperialism and the Open Door: The China Market and the Spanish-American War," *Pacific Historical Review* 32 (May 1963): 155. The impact of the New Left historians on McKinley historiography is discussed in De Santis, "Imperialist Impulse," 70–72; Combs, *American Diplomatic History*, 278–80; and more generally in Irwin Unger, "The 'New Left' and American History: Some Recent Trends in United States Historiography," *American Historical Review* 72 (July 1967): 1237–63.

38. Beisner, *From the Old Diplomacy to the New*, 1st ed. (New York, 1975), 22–23; Paul A. Varg, *The Making of a Myth: The United States and China, 1897–1912* (East Lansing, Mich., 1969), 36–53; David M. Pletcher, "Rhetoric and Results: A Pragmatic View of American Economic Expansionism, 1865–98," *Diplomatic History* 5 (Spring 1981): 93–105. See also Marilyn Blatt Young, "American Expansionism, 1870–1900: The Far East," in *Towards a New Past: Dissenting Essays in American History*, ed. Barton J. Bernstein (New York, 1968), 176–201. "It would be inconceivable," Young wrote four years later, "for McKinley to have conscientiously set out to work *against* American expansion. But what did he do *for* it and how did businessmen respond?" ("The Question for Empire," in *American-East Asian Relations: A Survey*, ed. Ernest R. May and James C. Thompson, Jr. [Cambridge, Mass., 1972], 136).

39. Field retorted that LaFeber's argument about the McKinley administration's willingness to move so rapidly in the Pacific "is hardly supported by the Philippine reinforcement, an exercise in improvisation if ever there was one." Critical of the use by some historians of "mutually supporting references" and "a usage of assertion and verbal prestidigitation which imposes false geographic unities . . . and confuses words with things," Field concluded that he remained "persuaded that unanticipated events can bring unanticipated results and that the *Maine* and Manila Bay (like Fort Sumter and Pearl Harbor) led to attitudes and consequences that could hardly have been foreseen (James A. Field, Jr., "American Imperialism: The 'Worst Chapter' in Almost Any Book," with additional comments by Walter LaFeber and Robert L. Beisner, and a response by Field, in *American Historical Review* 83 [June 1978]: 644–83).

40. Although Williams's study first appeared in 1959, his comments on McKinley are from an expanded edition published in 1962; see William Appleman Williams,

The Tragedy of American Diplomacy (New York, 1962), 30–41. See also Williams, *The Tragedy of American Diplomacy* (New York, 1959), 24–44; Walter LaFeber, *The New Empire: An Interpretation of American Expansionism* (Ithaca, N.Y., 1963), 326–417; Thomas J. McCormick, Jr., *China Market: America's Quest for Informal Empire, 1893–1901* (Chicago, 1967), 105–25; and William Appleman Williams, *The Roots of the Modern American Empire* (New York, 1969), 408–53.

41. May found "traces of virtue but few of character" in McKinley's career prior to the presidency. May also concluded that McKinley, greatly deficient in boldness and courage, had "led his country unwillingly toward a war that he did not want for a course in which he did not believe." Yet, May also found it "hard not to sympathize with him" as the president "had used all his talent, tact, and charm to prevent war." May also wrote that "there can be little doubt that it was McKinley who made White House decisions." Moreover, May's research revealed that the Spanish government had not capitulated, as earlier historians had assumed, to all of the points in McKinley's ultimatum of late March. Reading between the lines of May's study, it is hard not to conclude that both governments had very limited options in avoiding war (*Imperial Democracy*, 112–15, 153–54, 158–60).

42. This may have reflected a tendency among some diplomatic historians, in view of the increasing complexities and irrationalities of international affairs, to view the past from a more somber and fatalistic perspective. As Charles E. Neu has noted, an emphasis on multinational research may also have heightened a sense of the inevitability of certain historical events ("The Changing Interpretive Structure of American Foreign Policy," in *Twentieth-Century American Foreign Policy*, ed. John Braeman, Robert H. Bremner, and David Brody [Athens, Ohio, 1971], 23–37).

43. Excellent summaries of McKinley historiography for this period can be found in De Santis, "Imperialist Impulse," 69–74; Fry, "William McKinley," 90–93; and Combs, *American Diplomatic History*, 269–71, 275. See also David F. Trask, "Writings on American Foreign Relations: 1957 to the Present," in *Twentieth-Century American Foreign Policy*, ed. Braeman et al., 58–71.

44. De Santis, "Imperialist Impulse," 69; William Reynolds Braisted, *The United States Navy in the Pacific* (Austin, 1958), 21–23; Leech, *Days of McKinley*, 169; Halle, *American Foreign Policy*, 180–81.

45. John A. S. Grenville and George Berkeley Young, *Politics, Strategy, and American Diplomacy: Studies in Foreign Policy, 1873–1917* (New Haven and London, 1966), 267–78. John A. S. Grenville made a briefer statement of this argument in "Diplomacy and War Plans in the United States, 1890–1917," *Transactions of the Royal Historical Society* (London, 1961), 2:1–21.

46. John A. S. Grenville, "American Naval Preparations for War with Spain, 1896–1898," *Journal of American Studies* 2 (Apr. 1968): 33–47; Oscar M. Alfonso, *Theodore Roosevelt and the Philippines, 1897–1909* (Quezon City, 1970), 21–25; Ronald Spector, "Who Planned the Attack on Manila Bay," *Mid-America* 53 (Apr. 1971): 94–102. David F. Trask provides the best detailed analysis of war plans in *War with Spain*, 72–94, 514–20, 108–12, 136–37, 144–46, 383–86.

47. Renato Constantino, *A History of the Philippines: From the Spanish Colonization to the Second World War* (New York and London, 1975), 198–99; G. J. A. O'Toole, *The Spanish-American War: An American Epic—1898* (New York, 1984), 90–104. For a critique of O'Toole's study, see Lewis L. Gould, "Chocolate Eclair or Mandarin Manipulator? William McKinley, the Spanish-American War, and the Philippines: A Review Essay," *Ohio History* 94 (Summer-Autumn 1985), 182–87. Richard H. Collin, *Theodore Roosevelt, Culture, Diplomacy, and Expansion: A New View of American Imperialism* (Baton Rouge and London, 1985), 114, 117–18.

48. Russell A. Alger, *The Spanish-American War* (New York and London, 1901), 326; Timothy G. McDonald, "McKinley and the Coming of the War with Spain," *Midwest Quarterly* 7 (Apr. 1966): 225–39; Robert L. Beisner, *From the Old Diplomacy to the New*, 1st ed., 148. Ronald Spector offers the best account of the events on 24 Apr. in *Admiral of the New Empire* (Baton Rouge, 1974), 1–2.

49. Gould, *Presidency of William McKinley*, 97; May, *Imperial Democracy*, 244; McCormick, "Insular Imperialism," 155–69; LaFeber, *New Empire*, 360–62; Morgan, *America's Road to Empire*, 71, 74, 97.

50. Graham A. Cosmas, *An Army for Empire: The United States Army in the Spanish American War* (Columbia, Mo., 1971), 117–21; Daniel B. Schirmer, *Republic or Empire: American Resistance to the Philippine War* (Cambridge, Mass., 1972), 66–72; Trask, *War with Spain*, 93, 382; Richard E. Welch, Jr., *Response to Imperialism*, 4.

51. Leech, *Days of McKinley*, 282–91, 323–47; May, *Imperial Democracy*, 246–60.

52. Coletta felt that the decision to attack the Spanish squadron rather than blockading the islands, the sending of troops to Manila, and the appointment of a peace commission tilted in favor of expansion were steps along the way to the October speaking tour that either completed McKinley's "conversion or, as friends suspected, solidified his decision" (Paolo E. Coletta, "McKinley, the Peace Negotiations, and the Acquisition of the Philippines," *Pacific Historical Review* 30 [Nov. 1961]: 341–47).

53. Morgan, *America's Road to Empire*, x, 75–83, 85–97.

54. Grenville and Young, *Politics, Strategy, and American Diplomacy*, 285–88; McCormick, "Insular Imperialism," 155–69; McCormick, *China Market*, 105–25.

55. Charles S. Campbell, *The Transformation of American Foreign Relations* (New York, 1976), 282–90, 295–301. Many historians continued to see McKinley as a cautious or indecisive expansionist; see, for example, David Healy, *U.S. Expansionism: The Imperialist Urge in the 1890s* (Madison, 1979), 61–64; John Morgan Gates, *Schoolbooks and Krags: The United States Army in the Philippines, 1898–1902* (Westport, Conn., 1973), 3–8; and Brian Damiani, "Advocates of Empire: William McKinley, the Senate and American Expansion" (Ph.D. diss., University of Delaware, 1978), 6–8. Just as many historians saw a more purposeful McKinley; see Richard H. Miller, *American Imperialism* (New York, 1970), 10–11; Philip Lyman Snyder, "Missions, Empire, or Force of Circumstances? A Study of the American Decision to Annex the Philippine Islands" (Ph.D. diss., Stanford University, 1972), 240; Robert L. Beisner, *From the Old Diplomacy to the New*, 1st ed., 118–20; George

William Duncan, "The Diplomatic Career of William Rufus Day, 1897–1898" (Ph.D. diss., Case Western Reserve University, 1976), 150–53; and John M. Dobson, *America's Ascent: The United States Becomes a Great Power, 1880–1914* (DeKalb, Ill., 1978), 119–20.

56. Trask, *War with Spain*, x, 78, 91–93, 423–31, 435–56. In a letter to the author, Trask argued that the present debate on McKinley is an attempt to move beyond the old debate between the realists and the New Left positions. Most recent scholarship, he argues, recognizes that McKinley was "a departure from the old-style presidents of the nineteenth century." With most historians "playing from the same sheet of music in terms of information," these accounts differ over whether McKinley was a reluctant or scheming expansionist. Influenced by May's analysis of public opinion and the insights of the realists and the New Left, Trask adds that his position is "that the reluctant imperialism of 1898 is consistent with McKinley's prior behavior whereas enthusiastic imperialism isn't." The debate over imperialism, Trask suggests, reflects a larger disagreement over whether McKinley was the first of a transitional group of presidents or the first modern president. McKinley "is no dummy or jellyfish, but neither is he the highly conscious and advanced innovator of the Woodrow Wilson variety." One element in historical interpretation, Trask writes, "is the specific political environment in which the historian works." Suggesting that his own interpretation may reflect a sense of "chastened internationalism and liberalism—a far cry from the early postwar optimism," Trask adds that the "value of strict adherence of time-honored canons of scholarship is that it keeps one's personal peccadilloes on the reservation" (David F. Trask to author, 27 Dec. 1987, reprinted with permission).

57. Miller, *"Benevolent Assimilation,"* 14–16, 24; Welch, *Response to Imperialism*, 6–10.

58. Gould, *Presidency of William McKinley*, vii, 96–101, 115–21, 129–43, 150. In a letter to the author, Gould noted that he had, as a graduate student, found May's interpretations of McKinley persuasive. Research in Wyoming politics and the work of Holbo and Grenville and Young made him more receptive to the revisionism of the mid- and late 1960s. Subsequent work in the primary sources on Republican politics from 1897 to 1913 continued this process. Research in French archives in the mid-1970s left Gould "impressed with McKinley's tenacity, as the French saw it, in pursuing reciprocity negotiations between 1897 and 1901." Gould was particularly struck by a letter from the French ambassador Jules Cambon reporting a conversation in which McKinley discussed his plans to travel during his second administration to Cuba and, possibly, Hawaii. This anticipated, Gould notes, what happened during the presidency of Theodore Roosevelt. McKinley, Gould writes, "was an *important* president who merits evaluation" and "he was a *strong* president, but that does not mean he was always right, always successful, or always purposeful" (Lewis L. Gould to author, 1 Jan. 1988, reprinted with permission).

59. Robert C. Hilderbrand, *Power and the People: Executive Management of Public Opinion on Foreign Affairs* (Chapel Hill, N.C., 1981), 4, 8–42. For Hilderbrand's as-

sessment of McKinley's able management of public opinion during the treaty fight, the insurrection, and election of 1900, see ibid., 42–51.

60. John S. Latcham, "President McKinley's Active-Positive Character: A Comparative Revision with Barber's Typology," *Presidential Studies Quarterly* 12 (Winter 1982): 491–521.

61. Michael H. Hunt, *Ideology and U.S. Foreign Policy* (New Haven, 1987), 17–18, 19–45, 80–91. This issue of race and cultural superiority is also discussed in Glenn Anthony May, *Social Engineering in the Philippines: The Aims, Execution and Impact of American Colonial Policy, 1900–1913* (Westport, Conn., 1980), 3–17.

62. Trask, *War with Spain*, 423–35, 449–64; John Offner, "The United States and France: Ending the Spanish-American War," *Diplomatic History* 7 (Winter 1983), 1–21. Neither Spain, Cuba, nor the United States, Offner argued, desired intervention in what turned out to be an unavoidable war. Negotiations largely failed because of internal domestic constraints. While McKinley had "worked hard for more time to prevent war," his efforts were frustrated by members of his own party who "made war on Spain in order to keep control of Washington." "Although McKinley made mistakes and suffered from errors of judgment," Offner wrote, "his efforts to prevent the war were commendable." John L. Offner, *An Unwanted War: The Diplomacy of the United States and Spain over Cuba, 1895–1898* (Chapel Hill and London, 1992), ix–xii, 225–36.

63. Walter Karp, *The Politics of War: The Story of Two Wars Which Altered Forever the Political Life of the American Republic (1890–1920)* (New York, 1979), 3–5, 69–116.

64. David Haward Bain, *Sitting in Darkness: Americans in the Philippines* (Boston, 1984), 56–62, 70–79, 423; Gould, "Chocolate Eclair," 182–87. For further evidence of McKinley's rehabilitation, see Robert L. Beisner's comments in his new edition that McKinley "needed no cabal to tell him what to do" (*From the Old Diplomacy to the New, 1865–1900*, 2d ed., 121–22).

65. John Dobson, *Reticent Expansionism: The Foreign Policy of William McKinley* (Pittsburgh, 1988), 82–83, 101–15, 207–8; Stanley Karnow, *In Our Image: America's Empire in the Philippines* (New York, 1989), 79–85, 104–5, 125–30.

66. For Lodge's assessment of the president's attitude, see Trask, *War with Spain*, 439; McKinley's comments to Laffin are in William M. Laffin to Lodge, 14 July 1898, as quoted in Grenville and Young, *Politics, Strategy, and American Diplomacy*, 285–86; Frederick Holls to Andrew Dixon White, 10 Sept. 1898, Frederick Holls Papers, Rare Book and Manuscript Library, Columbia University, New York. See also the diary of George B. Cortelyou, 23 Aug. 1898, in the Papers of George B. Cortelyou, Library of Congress, Washington, D.C.

67. Pierre Smith to William McKinley, 15 Sept. 1898, Cortelyou Papers. George McAneny summarized McKinley's comments to the civil service delegation in a letter to Carl Schurz, 17 Sept. 1898, Papers of Carl Schurz, Library of Congress. Lewis L. Gould refers to the above statements and also the president's comments to Laffin and Holls in *Spanish-American War and President McKinley*, 67, 101–2. Whitelaw Reid's assessment of McKinley as timid and the president's comments to the peace

commissioners in mid-September are found in H. Wayne Morgan, ed., *Making Peace with Spain: The Diary of Whitelaw Reid, September–December, 1898* (Austin, Tex., 1965), 25, 30–31.

68. Morgan, ed., *Making Peace with Spain*, 25; Gould, *Spanish-American War and President McKinley*, 63–67, 101–3. Gould, it should be noted, was apparently the first to place the Holls and McAneny (the civil service delegation) letters into the framework of McKinley scholarship.

69. This is not to imply that economic considerations were not part of McKinley's thinking on the Philippines. He did tell Rusling that it would be "bad business" to turn the islands over to rivals, and told an audience at Hastings, Iowa, on 13 Oct. 1898 that "we want new markets, and as trade follows the flag, it looks very much as if we were going to have new markets" ("Interview with President McKinley," 137). McKinley's former postmaster general, Charles Emory Smith, also recalled in 1902 that among the president's advisers were those who believed that "this unforeseen opportunity of extending the American arm to the other side of the Pacific opened up a welcome pathway for enlarging American influence and commerce, and advancing the civilization of the world" ("McKinley in the Cabinet Room," 7). Yet McKinley also stated in his Home Market Speech in Boston on 16 Feb. 1899: "Our concern was not for territory or trade or empire but for the people whose interests and destiny, without our willing it, had been put in our hands" (*Speeches and Addresses of William McKinley: From March 1, 1897, to May 30, 1900* [New York, 1900], 109, 188–189).

70. Olcott, *William McKinley* 2:109–11; Rhodes, *McKinley and Roosevelt Administrations*, 106–9; Millis, *Martial Spirit*, 383–85; Beard and Beard, *Rise of American Civilization*, 375–76; Morgan, *America's Road to Empire*, 96–97; Garel A. Grunder and William E. Livezey, *The Philippines and the United States* (Norman, Okla., 1951), 37; Paolo E. Coletta, "McKinley, the Peace Negotiations, and the Acquisition of the Philippines," 347.

71. Robert Ferrell, *American Diplomacy: A History* (New York, 1975), 367–69. In an interview with the editor of a German American newspaper in late Nov. 1899, Gould noted, McKinley read from his earlier instructions to the American peace delegation and added that "I have been carried further and further by events" and that "Providence had made us guardians of the group of islands" (*Presidency of William McKinley*, 140–42); Miller, "*Benevolent Assimilation*," 24.

72. "Re[:] Bering Seas Arbitration[.] Interview with Pres. McKinley[.] 1898—Spanish [American] War & Phillipines [*sic*]—November 19, 1898," Chandler P. Anderson Papers, Library of Congress, Washington, D.C.; reproduced in Ephraim K. Smith, "'A Question from Which We Could Not Escape': William McKinley and the Decision to Acquire the Philippine Islands," *Diplomatic History* 9 (Fall 1985): 363–75.

73. Gould, *Presidency of William McKinley*, 137.

74. Smith, "A Question," 374–75.

75. Ibid., 372–74.

76. McKinley to Hay, 28 Sept. 1898, *Foreign Relations, 1898*, 915. Greene's report was published in 1899 as "Memorandum Concerning the Situation in the Philippines on 30 August 1898, by F. V. Greene, Major General, Volunteer, and Accompanying Papers," in U.S. Congress, Senate, *A Treaty of Peace Between the United States and Spain*, 55th Cong., Senate doc. no. 62, 1899, 404–40. Greene's handwritten draft of the situation in the Philippines is found in the Cortelyou Papers. A brief reference to this important draft is made in Smith, "A Question," 371–72. The author is preparing this and other materials in the Greene Papers for publication. Greene's visits to the White House are noted in entries in his "Pacific Coast Diary for 1898," Francis Vinton Greene Papers, Rare Books and Manuscripts Division, New York Public Library, Astor, Lenon and Tilden Foundations. Greene's later account of his interviews with McKinley is found in a typescript entitled "At the Republican Club in the City of New York, Saturday, March 20, 1915, Address of Francis V. Greene, Late Major-General, U.S.V.," Greene Papers. The New York Public Library received its first deposit of papers from General Greene shortly before his death in 1921. General Greene's wife made a formal donation of the papers on deposit in 1925. The last donation of items was made in 1972. According to a communication from a manuscripts specialist at the New York Public Library, the collection was probably open to scholars in 1925 (Francesca Pitaro to author, 23 Feb. 1988).

77. Greene, "At the Republican Club," Greene Papers.

Appendix: Theodore Roosevelt's List of Spanish Naval Assets

Vessels in Cuban Waters

Vessel Name	Type	Displacement (tons)	Speed (knots)	Armament	Date of Launch
Marques de la Ensenada	cruiser	1,030	15	4 4."7 R.F.,ᵃ 5 R.F., 4 machine	1890
Alfonso XII	cruiser	3,090	17.5	6 6."2, 2 2."7, 6 6-pr, 4 3-pr, 5 machine	1887
Conde de Venadito	cruiser	1,130	14	4 4."7, 2 2."7, 2 R.F., 5 machine	1888
Infante Isabel	cruiser	1,130	14	4 4."7, 2 2."7, 2 R.F., 5 machine	1885
Isabel II	cruiser	1,130	14	4 4."7, 2 2."7, 2 R.F., 5 machine	1886
Reina Cristina	cruiser	3,520	17.5	6 6."2, 2 2."7, 3 2."2, 2 1."5, 6 3-pr, 2 machine	1886
Reina Mercedes	cruiser	3,090	17.5	6 6."2, 2 2."7, 3 2."2, 2 1."5, 6 3-pr, 2 machine	1887
Filipinas	torpedo vessel	747	20	2 4."7 R.F., 4 3-pr R.F., 4 machine	1892
Jorge Juan	torpedo vessel	935	13	3 6."2 Pallister, 2 2."9 B.L.,ᵇ 2 machine	1876

Vessel Name	Type	Displacement (tons)	Speed (knots)	Armament	Date of Launch
Galacia	torpedo vessel	570	16	2 4."7 B.L., 4 6-pr R.F., 1 machine	1891
Marques de Molins	torpedo vessel	570	16	2 4."7 B.L., 4 6-pr R.F., 1 machine	1891
Nueva Espana	torpedo vessel	570	16	2 4."7 B.L., 4 6-pr R.F., 1 machine	1891
Legaspi	transport	1,020	8	2 4."7 bronzen	1874
Aguilla	gunboat	71	13.7	1 1-pr R.C.[c]	1893
Alvarado	gunboat	300	14.5	2 6-pr R.F., 4 machine	1895
Alsedo	gunboat	216	9	1 4."7 B.L., 1 machine	1882
Caridad	gunboat	23	5	1 3."1 bronze m.	1879
Contramaestre	gunboat	179	7	1 3."9 Parrot	1869
Criolo	gunboat	179	7	1 5."1 Pallister	1869
Cuba Espanola	gunboat	225	9	2 small guns	1870
Diego Velaquez	gunboat	300	14.5	2 6-pr R.F., 4 machine	1895
Pizarro	gunboat	300	14.5	2 6-pr R.F., 4 machine	1895
Ponce de Leon	gunboat	300	14.5	2 6-pr R.F., 4 machine	1895
Sandoval	gunboat	300	14.5	2 6-pr R.F., 4 machine	1895
Vasco Nunez de Balboa	gunboat	300	14.5	2 6-pr R.F., 4 machine	1895
Fernando el Catolico	gunboat	500	10	1 6."2 Pallister m., 2 4."7 bronze m.	1875
REMARKS: Used as torpedo school ship					
General Concha	gunboat	525	11	3 4."7 B.L., 2 R.F., 1 machine	1883
Magallanes	gunboat	525	11	3 4."7 B.L., 3 machine	1885
Delgado Parejo	gunboat				
El Dependiente	gunboat				
Guardien	gunboat				

Vessels Available for Cuban Waters

Vessel Name	Type	Displacement (tons)	Speed (knots)	Armament	Date of Launch
Vitorio	battleship	7,000	11	6 6."3 B.L.R.,[d] 6 5."5 R.F., 6 4."7 R.F.	1865 (rebuilt 1897)
REMARKS: Virtually ready					
Numancia	battleship	7,035	8	4 6."3 B.L.R., 8 5."5 R.F., 3 4."7 R.F.	1863 (rebuilt 1897)
REMARKS: Virtually ready					
Pelayo	battleship	9,900	16	2 12."5, 2 11", 9 5."5, 6 R.F., 12 machine	1887 (remodeled 1897)
REMARKS: Virtually ready					

Vessel Name	Type	Displacement (tons)	Speed (knots)	Armament	Date of Launch
Cristobal Colon	armored cruiser	7,000	20	2 10", 10 6" R.F., 6 4."7, 10 2."2, 10 1."4, 2 machine	1896
Infanta Maria Teresa	armored cruiser	7,000	20.25	2 11", 10 5."5, 8 2."2 R.F., 8 1."4, 2 machine	1890
Viscaya	armored cruiser	7,000	20	2 11", 10 5."5, 2 2."7, 8 12."2, 4 1."4, 2 machine	1890
Oquendo	armored cruiser	7,000	20	2 11", 10 5."5, 8 2."2 R.F., 8 1."4, 2 machine	1891
Carlos V	armored cruiser	9,235	20	2 11", 8 5."5 R.F., 4 3."9, 2 2."7, 4 2."2, 6 machine	1895
REMARKS: Will have 11" guns in March					
Alfonso XIII	protected cruiser	5,000	20	4 7."8, 6 4."7, 6 2."2 R.F., 6 1."4, 3 machine	1891
REMARKS: About ready					
Isla de Cuba	protected cruiser	1,030	16	4 4."7, 4 6-pr R.F., 2 3-pr, 2 machine	1887
Isla de Luzon	protected cruiser	1,030	16	4 4."7, 4 6-pr R.F., 2 3-pr, 2 machine	1887
Navarra	wooden cruiser	3,400	14	4 5."9, 2 4."7, 2 3."4, 4 2."9, 4 machine	1881
Aragon	wooden cruiser	3,400	14	6 6."2, 2 3."3, 4 2."9, 2 machine	1879
Castilla	wooden cruiser	3,400	14	4 5."9, 2 4."7, 2 3."3, 4 2."9, 8 R.F., 2 machine	1881
Don Antonio Ulloa	wooden cruiser	1,130	14	4 4."7, 2 2."7, 2 R.F., 5 machine	1887
Don Juan de Austria	wooden cruiser	1,130	14	4 4."7, 3 2."2 R.F., 2 1."5, 5 machine	1887
Velasco	wooden cruiser	1,152	14.3	3 5."9, 2 2."7, 2 machine	1881
Temerario	torpedo vessel	570	20.5	2 4."7, 4 2."2 R.F., 1 machine	1889
Destructor	torpedo vessel	450	22.56	1 3."5, 4 6-pr, 4 machine	1887
Furor	torpedo boat– destroyer	380	30		1896

Vessel Name	Type	Displacement (tons)	Speed (knots)	Armament	Date of Launch
Terror	torpedo boat–destroyer	380		2 14-pr R.F.	1896
Audaz	torpedo boat–destroyer	400	30	2 6-pr R.F.	1897
Osado	torpedo boat–destroyer	400	30	2 37 M/M R.F.	1897
Pluton	torpedo boat–destroyer	400	30.12		1897
Proserpina	torpedo boat–destroyer	400	30		1897
Dona Maria de Molina	torpedo vessel	825	20	2 4."7 R.F., 4 1."5, 2 machine	1896
REMARKS: Building at La Grana, Ferrol. Will probably be ready within a few months					
Marques Dela Victoria	torpedo vessel	825	20	2 4."7 R.F., 4 1."5, 2 machine	1897
REMARKS: Building at La Grana, Ferrol. Will probably be ready within a few months					
Don Alvaro de Bazan	torpedo vessel	825	20	2 4."7 R.F., 4 1."5, 2 machine	1897
REMARKS: Building at La Grana, Ferrol. Will probably be ready within a few months					
Ariete	torpedo boat	97	26.1		1887
Halcon	torpedo boat	108	24		1887
Azor	torpedo boat	108	24		1887
Rayo	torpedo boat	97	25.5		1887

Source: Theodore Roosevelt to Commander-in-Chief, U.S. Naval Forces, 16 Feb. 1898, RG 45, entry 20, NA.

Notes: Original spelling retained.   [a]four 4.7-inch rapid-firers   [b]breech-loaders [c]one one-pounder rifled cannon   [d]six 6.3-inch breech-loading rifles

Notes on Contributors

JAMES C. BRADFORD, Associate Professor of History at Texas A&M University, received his B.A. and M.A. from Michigan State University and his Ph.D. at the University of Virginia. His work on John Paul Jones includes a comprehensive microfilm edition of *The Papers of John Paul Jones* and an essay on Jones in *Command Under Sail*, the first of three volumes in the series that he edits, *Makers of the American Naval Tradition*. He also contributed the essay on "Henry T. Mayo: Last of the Independent Naval Diplomats" in *Admirals of the New Steel Navy*, the third volume in the series.

DIANE E. COOPER, a Washington state native, earned her undergraduate degree at Brigham Young University and her M.A. at East Carolina University, where she began her work on George Leland Dyer. She is currently working as a contract employee of the National Maritime Museum in San Francisco.

GRAHAM A. COSMAS is Chief of the Contingency Operations and Low Intensity Conflict Branch of the Center of Military History. He was born in New Jersey, earned his B.A. from Oberlin College, and his M.A. and Ph.D. from the University of Wisconsin. After teaching at the University of Texas at Austin and the University of Guam he worked in the History and Museums Division of the U.S. Marine Corps from 1973 to 1979 before joining the U.S. Army Center of Military History. Cosmas is the author of *An Army for Empire: The U.S. Army in the Spanish-American War, 1898–1899*, and the coauthor of *U.S. Marines in Vietnam: Vietnamization and Redeployment, 1970–71*, and *Medical Support of the European Theater of Operations*, a volume in the Army's "Green Book" series on World War II. He is currently working on a volume in the Army's Southeast Asia series.

JOSEPH G. DAWSON III is Associate Professor of History and the Director of the Military Studies Institute at Texas A&M University. An Ohio native, he earned his Ph.D. at Louisiana State University. Dawson is the associate editor of the *Dictionary of American Military Biography*, the author of "William T. Sampson: Progressive Technologist as Naval Commander" in *Admirals of the New Steel Navy: Makers of the American Naval Tradition, 1880–1930*, and the editor of *Commanders in Chief: Presidential Leadership in Modern Wars*.

HAROLD D. LANGLEY is Curator of Naval History, National Museum of American History, Smithsonian Institution and Adjunct Professor of History at The Catholic University of America. A native of upstate New York, he earned his B.A. from The Catholic University of America and his M.A. and Ph.D. from the University of Pennsylvania. He is the author of *Social Reform in the U.S. Navy, 1798–1862*, coeditor of *Roosevelt and Churchill: Their Secret Wartime Correspondence*, and the editor of *So Proudly We Hail: The History of the United States Flag* and *To Utah with the Dragoons*. His numerous articles and essays on naval and diplomatic history include "Winfield Scott Schley: The Confident Commander" in *Admirals of the New Steel Navy: Makers of the American Naval Tradition, 1880–1930*. He is currently working on a history of medicine in the U.S. Navy.

BRIAN M. LINN, Assistant Professor of History at Texas A&M University, earned his B.A. at the University of Hawaii at Manoa and his M.A. and Ph.D. at The Ohio State University. He is the author of *The U.S. Army and Counterinsurgency in the Philippine War, 1899–1902*, and of several articles on American forces in the Philippines. His current research concerns the impact of service in the Pacific on the U.S. Army's institutional and organizational development prior to World War II.

JACK SHULIMSON is head of the History Writing Unit at the Marine Corps Historical Center. He received his M.A. in history from the University of Michigan and his Ph.D. in American Studies from the University of Maryland. He is the author or coauthor of two of the volumes of *U.S. Marines in Vietnam*, as well as being responsible for the entire series. He has also published several articles on the U.S. Marine Corps in the late nineteenth and early twentieth centuries.

EPHRAIM K. SMITH, Professor of History at California State University, Fresno, earned his B.A. at Hillsdale College, his M.A. at the University of Nebraska, and his Ph.D. at The Johns Hopkins University. He has published in the fields of public history and diplomatic history. His current research concerns Maj. Gen. Francis V. Greene, commander of the second expedition to the Philippines.

DAVID F. TRASK, a freelance historian, received his B.A. from Wesleyan University and his A.M. and Ph.D. from Harvard University. He taught at Boston University, Wesleyan University, the University of Nebraska at Lincoln, and the State University of New York at Stony Brook before serving as Director of the Office of the Historian at the U.S. State Department and later the chief historian of the U.S. Army Center of Military History. He served as president of the Society for History in the Federal Government. His nine volumes include five on World War I, among them *The United States in the Supreme War Council: American War Aims and Inter-Allied Strategy, 1917–1918*, and *The War with Spain in 1898*. He is now at work on a comprehensive study of the role of the American Expeditionary Forces in World War I.

VERNON L. WILLIAMS is Associate Professor of History at Abilene Christian University. A native Texan, he earned his Ph.D. at Texas A&M University and is the author of *Lieutenant Patton and the American Army on the Punitive Expedition, 1915–1916* and "George Dewey: Admiral of the Navy" in *Admirals of the New Steel Navy: Makers of the American Naval Tradition, 1880–1930*. He is currently revising his dissertation on the Navy in the Philippines from 1898 to 1906 for publication and conducting research on Littleton W. T. Waller.

Index

The Naval Institute Press is the book-publishing arm of the U.S. Naval Institute, a private, nonprofit society for sea service professionals and others who share an interest in naval and maritime affairs. Established in 1873 at the U.S. Naval Academy in Annapolis, Maryland, where its offices remain, today the Naval Institute has more than 100,000 members worldwide.

Members of the Naval Institute receive the influential monthly magazine *Proceedings* and discounts on fine nautical prints and on ship and aircraft photos. They also have access to the transcripts of the Institute's Oral History Program and get discounted admission to any of the Institute-sponsored seminars offered around the country.

The Naval Institute also publishes *Naval History* magazine. This colorful quarterly is filled with entertaining and thought-provoking articles, first-person reminiscences, and dramatic art and photography. Members receive a discount on *Naval History* subscriptions.

The Naval Institute's book-publishing program, begun in 1898 with basic guides to naval practices, has broadened its scope in recent years to include books of more general interest. Now the Naval Institute Press publishes more than sixty titles each year, ranging from how-to books on boating and navigation to battle histories, biographies, ship and aircraft guides, and novels. Institute members receive discounts on the Press's nearly 400 books in print.

For a free catalog describing Naval Institute Press books currently available, and for further information about subscribing to *Naval History* magazine or about joining the U.S. Naval Institute, please write to:

Membership & Communications Department

U.S. Naval Institute

118 Maryland Avenue

Annapolis, Maryland 21402-5035

Or call, toll-free, (800) 233-USNI.

THE NAVAL INSTITUTE PRESS

CRUCIBLE OF EMPIRE
The Spanish-American War & Its Aftermath

Designed by Martha Farlow

Set in Adobe Caslon, Adobe Caslon Expert, and Adobe Caslon SemiBold
by Brushwood Graphics, Inc.
Baltimore, Maryland

Printed on 50-lb. Penntech antique cream
and bound in Holliston Roxite A
by The Maple-Vail Book Manufacturing Group
York, Pennsylvania